Reading
Comprehension
Research and Testing
in the U.S.

Undercurrents of Race, Class,
and Power in the Struggle for Meaning

Reading Comprehension Research and Testing in the U.S.

Undercurrents of Race, Class, and Power in the Struggle for Meaning

Arlette Ingram Willis
University of Illinois at Urbana-Champaign

Lawrence Erlbaum Associates
Taylor & Francis Group

New York   London

Lawrence Erlbaum Associates
Taylor & Francis Group
270 Madison Avenue
New York, NY 10016

Lawrence Erlbaum Associates
Taylor & Francis Group
2 Park Square
Milton Park, Abingdon
Oxon OX14 4RN

Printed in the United States of America on acid-free paper
10 9 8 7 6 5 4 3 2 1

International Standard Book Number-13: 978-0-8058-5052-9 (Softcover) 978-0-8058-5051-2 (Hardcover)

Library of Congress Cataloging-in-Publication Data

Willis, Arlette Ingram.
    Reading comprehension research and testing in the U.S. : undercurrents of race, class, and power in the struggle for meaning / Arlette I. Willis.
        p. cm.
    Includes bibliographical references and index.
    ISBN-13: 978-0-8058-5052-9 (acid-free paper)
    1. Reading comprehension--Research--Social aspects--United States--History. 2. Reading comprehension--Ability testing--Social aspects--United States--History. 3. Discrimination in education--United States--History. I. Title.

LB1050.45.W53 2008
428.4'3072--dc22

2007018696

Visit the Taylor & Francis Web site at
http://www.taylorandfrancis.com

Contents

Preface   vii

Acknowledgments   xv

Introduction   xvii

1   Western European Philosophical Foundations of Reading Comprehension Research and Testing   1

2   Ideological and Philosophical Foundations of Reading Comprehension Research and Testing   19

3   Reservoir of Themes and Premises: Social Influences of Early Concepts of Reading Comprehension   51

4   Producing Early Reading Comprehension Research and Testing   87

5   World War I and the Development of Reading Comprehension and Research Testing   137

6   Reproducing and Producing Reading Comprehension Research and Testing   179

7   Reading Comprehension Research and Testing Reinvents Itself   223

8   Federal Involvement in Reading Comprehension Research and Testing   261

Postscript   307

References   315

Author Index   363

Subject Index   367

PREFACE

Since the historic signing of the No Child Left Behind Act of 2001 (NCLB) reading comprehension research and testing have become principal research foci in education. The national reading research agenda is informed by a history of reading comprehension research and testing in the United States and other English-speaking countries. Although the illusion of progress is promoted among reading researchers, when viewed historically, concepts, definitions, and theories of reading comprehension—how one understands text (narrowly defined as printed marks on a page) and how to determine (or test) for reading comprehension—has not changed significantly for over a century. Reading comprehension research and testing have been conceptualized, defined, tested, and interpreted in ways that are consistent with dominant ideologies (beliefs, ideas, knowledge, languages, norms, and values) and least informed by the ideologies of subaltern[1] groups. Reading comprehension research and testing are mechanisms of ideological control that privilege dominant ideologies and promote oppressive reading practices and interpretations of test performance. Current reading comprehension research and testing are inadequately conceived to meet the rapidly shifting demographics (class, immigration status, language, and race) of U.S. school children. Collectively, as a group these are the Underserved—children who live in poverty, who are children of Color, whose first language is not English or Standard English, and who have varying immigration status—who have been underserved by our nation's education system. The question becomes: how will reading comprehension researchers and the research they produce respond, adjust, and address the needs of Underserved children?

---

[1] Subaltern groups (dominated, subordinated, and marginalized people).

This book is an analysis of the ideological hegemony that underpins reading comprehension research and testing. I explore how ideological hegemony historically has operated within reading comprehension research and testing: beginning with the philosophical assumptions that underpin reading comprehension research and testing, to their use as mechanisms by power elites to maintain power and control of education, the reproduction of dominant ideologies in reading materials, and the use media and politics to gain legal and social consent to sustain dominant privileged positions and control of education in society.

In this book I articulate how ideological hegemony operates to reproduce dominant ideologies through education research in general and reading comprehension research and testing in particular. In this context, reading comprehension research and testing are under the ideological control of power elites that historically have been used to sustain, support, and promote their ideas as universal and necessary. This is not meant to suggest a grand conspiracy theory, but to point out how ideological hegemony operates in U.S. society and the role that education and reading comprehension research and testing have played in reproducing and reinforcing dominant beliefs, ideas, knowledge, languages, norms, and values. The crafting of a history of reading comprehension research and testing in this manner demystifies how the philosophical assumptions that underpin reading research emerged and are sustained; centers on the reproduction of dominant ideologies within reading comprehension research and testing; and illustrates the interconnectedness among the social and political forces that inform reading research, researchers, institutions, practices, tests, and testing.

Reading comprehension research and testing are in grave need of reconceptualization and definition as it remains largely anchored in the past and remains isolated from and responsive to political and social realities. This book questions, challenges, and critiques the traditional, sanctioned, or official histories of reading comprehension research and testing as it details the hegemonic processes by which reading comprehension research and testing are mechanisms of dominant groups. For example, traditional historical accounts of reading comprehension present sanitized versions of its complex history without accompanying detail or discussion of the ideological and socio-historical foundations that underpin concepts, theories, research, tests, and interpretations. By way of contrast, this book presents a more inclusive, although not exhaustive, study of how ideological hegemony operates through dominant ideologies to narrowly conceptualize, define, theorize, test, and interpret reading comprehension as it seeks to perpetuate and legalize dominant ideas. What becomes clear is that misguided efforts are not "righted" by tradition, declarations, repetitions, tests, laws, or coercion.

This book is written to be accessible to researchers, teacher educators, school administrators, teachers, and politicians. The content includes a healthy discussion of how, in order to retain ideological hegemony, dominant groups manufacture consent and coerce allied and subordinate groups to support dominant ideas as needful for the common good. Ideology is the terrain of struggle for control by power elites and opposing groups. In this context, reading comprehension research and testing are understood as mechanisms used by power elites to sustain ideological control. Tracing the role of reading comprehension research and testing as mechanisms of ideological hegemony necessitates (a) understanding the social and political contexts in which reading comprehension research has evolved and (b) presenting counterhegemonic positions and discourses that challenge dominant ideologies. In this book, counterhegemonic positioning is drawn primarily from the work of African American scholars and activists whose ideologies (beliefs, ideas, knowledge, languages, norms, and values) and research have been available but seldom accessed to inform reading comprehension research and testing. Finally, I include suggestions for re-envisioning reading comprehension research and testing in a more adequate and socially just manner.

Overview of the Book

This book articulates and traces associations and interconnections among multiple sources to reveal how ideological hegemony supports dominant ideologies and influences reading comprehension research and testing. In my thinking, the best way to present my analysis is to begin with an introduction that offers a fundamental understanding of hegemony, dominant ideologies, and their connections to reading comprehension research and testing. Specifically, I note how the ideologies of scientism, racism, and classism flow beneath the surface as undercurrents within educational research in general and reading comprehension research and testing specifically.

Then, I use broad and complex layers, thick with detail, throughout the remainder of the book to document and examine change over time, as history occurs in the everyday moments of our lives not just in storied events. This process also helps to clarify how ideological hegemony remakes itself in order to sustain power by dominant groups. To ensure that you remember the big picture and do not get lost in the details, throughout, I offer a modest summing up of key points that have, and were available to, influence reading comprehension research and testing.

Chapters 1 and 2 offer overviews of philosophical assumptions that underpin dominant ideologies embedded in reading comprehension research and testing. This layer consists of philosophical assumptions from Western Europe and the United States typically cited as influential at the onset of education research: biological and Social Darwinism, pragmatism, and Herbartianism as their legacies continue, albeit in altered forms, to influence reading comprehension research and testing. In addition, biographical information about the founders of each philosophical school of thought is shared to understand their sense of agency within the sociohistoric moment in which they lived. None of these philosophies is reviewed in its entirety, in part because each has been extensively reviewed by others elsewhere, and, in part, because what I find intriguing and expose are connections and relationships among to the ideologies of scientism, classism, and racism as undercurrents within reading comprehension research and testing.

The introduction of African American scholarship is presented as a counter-hegemonic position reflective of the lived experiences of African Americans in the United States and their resistance to dominant ideologies (beliefs, ideas, knowledge, languages, norms, and values) of power elites. Their individual and collective counter-discourses uncover and deconstruct undercurrents of scientism, racism, and classim within educational research used by reading comprehension researchers, educators and politicians.

I believe that examining the unacknowledged philosophical assumptions of reading comprehension research and testing is an important and necessary first step to understanding how ideological hegemony works through the unconscious adoption of dominant ideologies as they recast themselves throughout history; however, to untangle the myths and commonsense notions that surround reading comprehension research and testing, it also is necessary to illustrate how ideological hegemony has shaped our understandings of history through discourse that positions the thinking and actions of the privileged. Chapter 3 begins with a discussion of political, cultural, economic, and social forces throughout the United States that have supported and influenced the evolving role of education as an institution of the government. Then, I review reading comprehension's role in inculcating dominant ideologies through school textbooks, professional materials, and teachers' manuals that illustrate (a) how reading material was used to inculcate dominant ideologies as common sense, (b) how publishers and teachers believed that gaining meaning from reading textbooks was an important skill to acquire, and (c) how books written for African American school children were designed to reproduce dominant ideologies as natural, commonsensical, and universal.

Chapter 4 adds another layer, typically where traditional histories of reading comprehension begin, in the late 1800s. In this chapter, I continue my analysis of how ideological hegemony evolves within institutions with a focus on the academy and early attempts at reading comprehension research and testing. My review takes a genealogical approach to the lives, research, and relationships among three prominent reading comprehension researchers as I unveil their collective support of dominant ideologies within reading comprehension research and testing.

Chapter 5 continues the layering with a discussion of the growing interest in reading comprehension research and testing prior to, and including World War I. I specify how leading reading researchers and educational psychologists, who firmly believed in dominant ideologies, created and interpreted standardized intelligence tests constructed for U.S. Army officer recruitment in concert with their beliefs, values, and practices. With modifications, these tests were redesigned as national intelligence tests for school children. The use of standardized intelligence tests stirred debate among journalists and scholars, especially scholars of color, who called into question the veracity of the notion of general intelligence and the ability to measure it with a test. These scholars, and their allies, alleged that the reading sections of intelligence tests were constructed to reflect ideas, beliefs, values, interests, and experiences of dominant groups. Included in this chapter is an extension of Franklin's (1980) examination of African American scholars' responses to and research of intelligence testing among African American children and excerpts from the 1922 Lippmann and Terman debate.

Chapters 6 and 7 offer deep layers that review reading comprehension research and testing from the 1920s through the 1990s, with a special focus on research among White, middle-class, native English speakers, as researchers sought to normalize, standardize, and promote their reading comprehension performances as ideal. These chapters document how privileged leaders in the field of reading comprehension research and testing, within a span of a few years, sought to manufacture the consent of subaltern groups through federally and philanthropically supported research as well as through federal legislation. In each chapter, I contextualize historical moments by sharing events that should influence reading research and illustrate that there were resistance and counter-discourses that challenged dominant ideologies. These counter discourses envisaged the role of language and culture in reading and comprehension differently, especially for underserved children.

A final layer, Chapter 8, concludes my analysis of reading comprehension research and testing as mechanisms to promote dominant ideologies by chronicling efforts of the federal government to (a) gain consent of the public by fabrication or illusion and (b) coercion of the public's acceptance of dominant ideologies by federal and state law, rules, and esoteric credentialing. I highlight the role of government institutions, agencies, and leaders as they resurrect scientism as the best (and only government supported) form of reading comprehension research and testing. Their actions also inherently legalize racist and classist ideologies embedded in reading comprehension research and testing while simultaneously promoting and advertising the false impression of working in the best interests of the underserved.

Given the context of this discussion, the growing population of Underserved schoolchildren in U.S. public schools, and the shrinking federal funding of education, reading comprehension research and testing are desperately in need of more complex, adequate, and flexible understanding of how ideological hegemony has functioned to delimit research that is inclusive, democratic, and socially just. The postscript aims to revolutionize how reading comprehension is conceived and theorized for all children.

Robert Bernstein (2007) in a news release by the U.S. Census Bureau reports that the U.S. minority population tops 100 million. Census Bureau Director Louis Kincannon claims, "About one in three U.S. residents is a minority. . . there are more minorities in this country today than there were people in the United States in 1910" (http://www.census.gov/Press-Release/www/releases/archives/population/010048.html).

Acknowledgments

There are literally thousands of people to thank, including my loving and supportive family members, the students I have taught in over 30 years of teaching, my former professors, and my current colleagues. Because it is impossible to thank each of you individually, please accept one large THANKS from me.

I especially thank my mother, Angie White Ingram, who has believed in my dreams, and in me. And I thank my sons, who have watched me work on this project for years, served as my inspiration, and waited for me to finish it to cook dinner, wash uniforms, and so on. Most sincerely I thank my husband, Leonard, whose support has been unwavering.

They, however, are not responsible for the content of this book; that is mine alone, the good and the bad, the beautiful and the ugly. I also want to thank Naomi Silverman whose patience and faith in me, and in this project, have been a blessing. Finally, I thank and owe a tremendous debt of gratitude to the reviewers of the manuscript: Allan Luke, University of Queensland; Richard J. Meyer, University of New Mexico; and Rose-Marie Weber, University of Albany.

Introduction

Histories, including this one, are socially constructed narratives that represent an interpretation of primary and secondary sources within a historical moment. As a constructed narrative, this account presents an alternative construction of the history of reading comprehension research and testing. Academic research is constrained by the perspectives of the researcher and her beliefs and values as well as the traditions and practices within the discipline. For instance, I believe that people's lives, the entirety of their lives—what they believe, value, and desire—affect their work, whether scholarly or otherwise. People simply do not live unaffected and vacuous lives that are disconnected to their beliefs, values, and desires. Nor do people's lives become divorced from the political, social, cultural, and economic status within their nation or locale. It is as true today as it was in the 18th century. These beliefs help frame my research.

I like to think of writing history as a process that articulates the complexity of relationships among multiple sources of influence. Herein, I use the notion of articulation similar to that used by critical and cultural studies theorists in an effort to avoid reducing all issues to one cause. I examine the complexity of relationships among multiple sources that have influenced, and some that continue to influence, how reading comprehension research and testing are conceptualized, defined, theorized, tested, interpreted, and promoted. In this way, I unveil notions of personal agency as well as relationships and connections among political and social events and their influence on reading comprehension and testing. Drawing from multiple sources complicates as well as intensifies the discussion, as layer upon layer of documentation requires fine-tuned analyses. However, the layering is important because it helps to establish and trace relationships and connections among disparate sources that have influenced reading comprehension research and testing in the United States.

Typically, histories of reading and related interests, i.e., comprehension, from both groups have adopted a nonthreatening, allegedly neutral, reasoned approach that seldom questions, challenges, or critiques the past. On the one hand, historians write rich and complex histories that encompass broad understandings of ideologies and contexts of reading and its role within U.S. history. On the other hand, reading researchers typically write celebratory and uncomplicated historical accounts that cover esoteric understandings of concepts and methodology in the field. However, as Best (1995) points out, adopting a cultural or neutral position is to write history as myth.

In short, both types of historical writing about reading comprehension research, testing, and progress have presented accounts that begin and end with the experiences of the dominant group. Thus, they have only told part of the story, a much more complex story has been left untold.

Traditional histories of reading comprehension research and testing also have been written from the perspective of a dispassionate observer, an interloper who peers into the work of others. This form of historicizing also is a myth. Seldom have histories of reading comprehension research and testing included biographies or tied individuals to their philosophical beliefs. Significantly, these histories have not explained why leaders espouse philosophical positions and how their beliefs, values, and ideas have influenced their research. Ironically, the history of reading comprehension research and testing, as well as the lives the educational psychologists and reading researchers, were lived with a great deal of passion and gusto. Their passion was not the unbridled lust of film, though a case could be made in the lives of a few; it was more often passion for sustaining the dominant ideologies.

The ideas I examine in this book center on our understanding of the role of reading comprehension in sustaining the ideological hegemony of the dominant group. This examination includes understanding how dominant ideologies are linked to social and political forces and why this all matters now. I argue that it matters because understanding why and how reading comprehension was conceived, defined, and measured is the first step in dismantling its power to control the thinking of U.S. school children. I am not suggesting some grand conspiracy theory or suggesting that reading comprehension research and testing are fulcrums on which the fate of the world rests. But what I am strongly advocating is that in a just and democratic society, we need a revolutionary alternative that embraces issues of difference, especially race, class, and power. A new definition of reading comprehension would welcome, appreciate, value, and support the cultures, knowledge, languages, and understandings that all children bring to the classroom, but most especially the growing number of underserved children who historically have been disserved by the concept and structure of reading comprehension tests.

What Is Reading Comprehension and Can it Be Measured?

The most fundamental question that underscores reading comprehension research and testing is, what is reading comprehension? The answer, yet to be determined, at least a definitive one, has puzzled researchers for hundreds of years. Researchers with varying points of view have used an array of methods of inquiry as they sought to answer the question. What we can say with some certainty, sans neurological brain scanning images, is that reading comprehension is an elusive act, one that is difficult to capture, and one that is even more difficult to test.

My response to this query is twofold. First, I believe that reading comprehension is a fluid, cognitive, linguistic, and social process that defies exactitude. It is at once and simultaneously invisible, individual, and intimate yet it is affected by a host of influences beyond the control of the reader. Attempting to capture it, whether through standardized reading comprehension tests, informal assessments, or oral reading, is synonymous to catching water with your fingers. There will be seepage, there will be missed ideas, and there will be misunderstandings of the process. Despite the rhetoric in reading comprehension for the correct answer or the best answer, Hall (1984) persuasively argues that an "'essential, true, original' meaning is an illusion. No such previously natural moment of true meaning, untouched by the codes of social relations of production and reading exists" (p. 157). I agree and use his declarations as a springboard in this study in which I illustrate how ideological, cultural, social, and political codes shape reading comprehension research and testing. And, given that codes shape reading comprehension research and testing, I seek to understand for what purpose, and for whose purpose, are these codes shaped? Put another way, who (or what groups) is best served by current definitions of reading comprehension and the standardization of the reading comprehension tests?

Second, I believe that reading comprehension research and testing are politically and socially constructed mechanisms used to reproduce dominant ideologies. These ideas were created to describe the invisible, individual, and intimate process of communicating one's understanding of text (narrowly defined as printed words on a page). An individual's personal history (as well as collective or group history), race, class, gender, and native language can also influence how and what a person understands or how he or she makes meaning from text broadly defined.

Reading comprehension should be understood as a natural meaning seeking process. Given that many children learn to read in schools, are exposed to the idea of reading comprehension, and are tested for reading comprehension, it would be fair to say that schools are institutions that can nurture or inhibit how well students comprehend. In addition, the interactions, or lack of interactions, between the reader and the instructor, between the reader and the text, and between the reader and the context in which reading occurs have unfathomable consequences. What occurs in the translation of the idea of reading comprehension and uses of reading comprehension tests also is part of larger ideological and cultural discussions about reading comprehension's role in society and schools. In the context of this book, schools as institutions are important sites used by dominant groups to sustain ideological hegemony. Schools are where dominant groups have the power to use reading comprehension research and testing as mechanisms to inculcate, perpetuate, and sustain dominant ideologies.

The ideas, beliefs, values, and practices of dominant groups, historically, have shaped reading comprehension tests. Since tests were developed, most have consisted of short or long passages followed by several questions. The most popular form of question is the multiple-choice question where there is allegedly one best answer (the lingo that has replaced one right answer). Too often the preselected answers or responses leave little room for real-world responses, for responses that demonstrate "emotions, imagination, vitality, spontaneity, individuality" (Best, 1995, p. 8). In their place, researchers have sought to persuade readers that there is one best answer, one way to understand the text, one way to see the world in a way that, not surprisingly, reflects a very Anglocentric point of view. Best (1995) captured the problem by stating that there is a

> proclivity of the White middle classes of European descent to proclaim themselves the representatives of all humanity and to project their own values and interests onto other cultures … to represent their ideas as the only valid ones, grounded in nature itself. (p. 10)

I believe Best, although I have often wondered if White reading comprehension researchers consider race at all when conducting research. I also wonder whether they realize how their beliefs and attitudes about race influence the very air they breathe and how the moment-to-moment decisions they make affect, usually negatively, underserved children (children of color, children living in poverty, children who are recent immigrants, children whose first language is neither English nor Standard American English). The proclivity that Best mentions may be especially true in the area of reading comprehension research and testing, where the ability to comprehend is understood as demonstrated when students are asked to read text, that is, text most often written by Whites and assumed to be acultural and possessing universal appeal. To be fair, there are occasions in which the text used on standardized reading comprehension tests includes excerpts from literature written by authors of color. However, the questions and responses or answers have been preselected to fit the researchers' understanding of the text. Furthermore, there are few opportunities during reading comprehension testing to construct written responses, and fewer opportunities when the written responses are positively scored and assessed if they represent multicultural, multilingual, imaginative, or unorthodox responses.

I draw from my own life experiences to illustrate my point. First, over 30 years ago, during my pre-service teaching experiences, I volunteered my time at an elementary school in my hometown. One event remains with me today—the reaction of a student in a racially mixed first-grade classroom to reading comprehension questions that followed the story. Here's how it happened. After I had led the "low" reading group through a story in their out-of-date basal readers, I diligently followed the scripted directions for teachers and began asking the group the list of reading comprehension questions following the story. I asked the group what they thought Alice and Jerry were doing in the story. An African American male responded, "I don't

give a shit 'bout no Alice and Jerry." His petulant response caught
me off guard. I do not recall how I responded, to be sure with some
teacher-like gibberish about what is or is not appropriate language for
school. What I did not do then is ask him why he made the comment.
What is clear now, as then, is that the reader did not engage the text.

Second, not so long ago while helping my son prepare for a national
college examination, we used available pretest materials produced by
the company. Among the passages he read was an excerpt by Stephen
McCauley (1987) where a kindergartner is caught in a custody battle
between his wealthy parents. The text explains in detail the wealth of
his parents from references to executive incomes, BMWs, and Volvos,
and international excursions on expensive jumbo jets. In this passage,
the child travels to Paris one weekend. While there, he is taken to the
Louvre to see the Mona Lisa, on a boat ride down the Seine, and to
visit the Eiffel Tower and Notre Dame. The obvious class issues notwithstanding, this is not a particularly engaging piece and I question
its inclusion, even on a sample test (but that's a story for another time).
One multiple-choice question asks the reader to identify a character,
Theodora, from the passage that contains limited dialogue among the
characters. The options given are (a) sister, (b) French babysitter, (c)
mother, and (d) teacher. The scoring key with explanations suggests
that the "best answer" is (c) mother. My son did not select this answer.
When I asked him why he had selected (a) sister, he replied, "What
kindergartner calls his mother by her first name?"

His response, which makes perfect sense given his cultural and
linguistic background, was not the correct or *the best answer* (which
is a slippery choice of wording that suggests there are other possible
answers that receive credit and might be worth considering, but there
is only one best answer, the one selected by the test developers). His
response, which would have been scored incorrect, would have been
interpreted as a reflection of poor comprehension, an inability to
recognize text structure, or a misreading. I argue, as have countless
scholars of color before me, that it is altogether something else. My
son had comprehended the text as well as the question; however, he
elected to answer the query in concert with his frame of reference,
his reality, and his world. The preferred answer (this is a term used
by Stuart Hall and one I will say more about later) was one that he
rejected as nonsensical.

Do this passage, test item, and best answer reflect the proclivity of Whites to order the world, and do they "deny the histori-

cal and subjective constitution of knowledge" as Best (1995, p. 16), suggested? I am not sure; I do not know how White students would answer the question, but I do know that at least one African American child (and I can only guess others) would not have selected the "best answer" because it would be inconceivable to think that a young child would address adults using their first names. My son not only read and understood the text and the options for answering the query, but he read beyond the text, to his world, his reality, and selected a response that was more aligned with his understanding of the world. His response was not made in opposition to the text (as a form of protest), and he had not elected to negotiate his thinking to fit dominant ideas, beliefs, values, and practices. Is this a singular, unique, or special incident on a reading comprehension test? Or do passages like this one befuddle children whose lives are not reflective of dominant groups? Do readers reason and negotiate among possible explanations? Does this type of reasoning go on all the time, where underserved students move back and forth between their worlds, their realities, their frames of reference, and the text? Are some underserved readers being asked to to compromise or negotiate meaning more than dominant group readers? Does the movement between worlds, realities, and frames of reference by underserved readers slow comprehension, alter comprehension, cause confusion? What must a reader relinquish of himself? If he elects to negotiate among the alternatives, must he forsake his own thinking, or must he embrace the worlds, words, realities, and frames of reference used by reading researchers in order to perform well on reading comprehension tests? Is reading comprehension more invisible, individual, and intimate a process than we have considered in the past? Manguel (1996) captured the process:

> It is true that on occasion the world of the page passes into our conscious *imaginaire*—our everyday vocabulary of images—and then we wander aimlessly in those fictional landscapes, lost in wonder ... but most of the time we tread firmly. We know that we are reading even while suspending disbelief; we know why we read even when we don't know how, holding in our mind at the same time, as it were, the illusionary text and the act of reading. We read to find the end, for the story's sake. We read not to reach it, for the sake of the reading itself. We read searchingly, like trackers, oblivious of our surroundings. We read distractedly, skipping pages. We read contemptuously, admiringly, negligently, angrily, passionately, enviously, longingly. We read in gusts of sudden pleasure, without knowing what brought the pleasure along ... we don't know: we read ignorantly. We read in slow, long motions, as if drifting in space, making

excuses for the text, filling gaps, mending faults. And sometimes, when the stars are kind, we read with an intake of breath, with a shudder, as if someone or something had "walked over our grave," as if a memory had suddenly been rescued from a place deep within us—the recognition of something we never knew was there, or of something vaguely felt as a flicker or a shadow, whose ghostly form rises and passes back into us before we can see what it is, leaving us older and wiser. (p. 303)

Reading comprehension, in this sense, requires a reading of the world and the word. Manguel's notion of reading depicts "images, concepts, and premises which provide the frameworks through which we represent, interpret, understand and 'make sense' of some aspect of social existence" (p. 18). To delimit reading comprehension to interactions with select text with preselected interpretations misses or underestimates relationships and associations with, and in, the world in which ideas are formed, acted upon, and silenced. What I find most intriguing is that we continue to encounter underserved students who respond to text in ways that are similar to those expressed by the first-grade reader and my son. Their engagement with text is representative of how many, but certainly not all, underserved children engage and comprehend text that is removed from their ways of knowing, life experiences, and languages. Many of these children have been labeled as ineffective comprehenders, castigated for lowering a district's or school's standardized test performance, without anyone asking why.

Research Perspective

According to Gramsci (1971), history illustrates "how thought has been elaborated over the centuries and what a collective effort has gone into the creation of our present method of thought which has subsumed and absorbed all this past history, including all its follies and mistakes" (p. 327). Obviously, one book cannot cover every possible ideology, philosophy, approach, or personality that has influenced reading comprehension research and testing. Based on my own perspective and patterns that emerged when reading documents, I have constructed a history of reading comprehension research and testing that details and deconstructs how the idea of reading comprehension emerged and evolved.

I liken the idea of reading comprehension and testing to fine threads that are woven through a tapestry. These threads appear, disappear, and reappear throughout the fabric. Some ideas are like brilliant threads that stand in contrast or as complements to the threads that surround them. At other times, these same threads appear camouflaged, nearly inseparable from threads around them. Regardless of their position in the fabric, the fine threads exist as part of a much larger whole that binds the fabric together. In a similar way, Gramsci (1971) stated that we must understand history and the role of an idea in society:

> What must be explained is how it happens that in all periods there coexist many systems and currents of philosophical thought, how these currents are born, how they are diffused and why in the process of diffusion they fracture along certain lines and in certain directions. (p. 327)

Reading comprehension is an idea that belongs in the sea of ideas that historically have constituted our thinking about the reading process. As such, it is an idea that has been considered and reconsidered throughout its history in the field of education, educational psychology, linguistics, and so forth. Some concepts often are associated with reading comprehension, including vocabulary, rate or speed, and text or context. Other concepts seldom are associated with reading comprehension, including hegemony, ideology, and power. The latter group of concepts is essential to a history of reading comprehension research and to this book.

Given my desire to question, challenge, and critique current understandings of reading comprehension research and testing, I draw on these interwoven ideas: hegemony and ideology to represent a history of reading comprehension research and testing in a much more complex and dynamic manner.

Hegemony

There are multiple definitions and shades of meaning attributed to the idea of hegemony. It is an overused and misused term that has its roots in Marxist thought. Gramsci (1971) equated hegemony with leadership (p. 128f) and distinguished leadership among rulers, leaders, and intelligentsia. In addition, he renamed the ruling class, the dominant class or dominant group and all other classes or groups, allies or subalterns. Unlike Marx, he envisaged hegemony as "'cultural, moral, and ideological' leadership over allied and subordinate groups" (Forgacs, 2000, p. 423). He also identified two functions of hegemony, either to encourage spontaneous consent or to use power coercion (legal enforcement) to secure support and the adoption of dominant ideas by subaltern groups.

Other scholars, Hall, Strinati, Williams, and Kellner, have applied the concept to contemporary life. Hall (1982) asserted, "Hegemony is understood as accomplished, not without the due measure of legal and legitimate compulsion, but principally by means of winning the active consent of those classes and groups who were subordinated within it" (p. 85). Strinati (1995) added that within society, dominant groups "maintain their dominance by securing the 'spontaneous consent' of subordinate groups, including the working class, through the negotiated construction of a political and ideological consensus which incorporates both dominant and dominated groups" (p. 165). Williams (1977) described hegemony as part of the social process that includes discussions of power and influence. Defining hegemony along the lines of class and inequalities, he wrote, "To say that 'men' define and shape their whole lives is true only in abstraction. In any actual society there are specific inequalities in means and therefore in capacity to realise this process" (p. 108). Finally, Kellner (1999) believed that hegemony involves "both analysis of current forces of domination and the ways that distinctive political forces achieved hegemonic power" (p. 4). He also pointed out that discussions of hegemony should include "delineation of counterhegemonic forces, groups, and ideas that could contest and overthrow the existing hegemony" (p. 4). Hegemony is therefore used as both process and analysis.

Hegemony, as Gramsci and Hall noted, is never complete; it is always being revised and renegotiated. Williams (1977) put it this way: "Hegemony does not just passively exist as a form of dominance. It has continually to be renewed, recreated, defended, and modified. It is also continually resisted, limited, altered, challenged by pressures not at all its own" (p. 112). In addition, Laclau and Mouffe (1985) in their seminal work, *Hegemony and Socialist Strategy,* appended their support to the notion of hegemonic change. They argued that hegemonic change is not revolutionary but occurs gradually, especially given the diversity of subordinate groups and their struggles in modern industrialized societies. In sum, notions of hegemony convey relationships among leadership, rule, power, domination, and the influence of one group over allied and subordinate groups. These ideas have given rise to various descriptors of hegemony as cultural, ideological, intellectual, racial, social, and political.

How does hegemony work in a society? The ruling or dominant class must convince the allied and subordinate classes to believe in the dominant ideas, values, morals, and practices. To do so, the dominant class encourages allied and subordinate classes to adopt, accept, and internalize dominant ideas, values, morals, and practices as their own, projecting them as natural and commonsensical. The dominant class also attempts to shape the thinking of allied subordinate classes through leadership (cultural, intelligentsia, or political/rulers). To Gramsci (1971), the real struggle in society is over the ideas, or the struggle for meaning. He suggested that those who have the power to name and define which ideas are most worthy is the dominant group and their ideas are the dominant ideas, or dominant ideologies.

Ideology

A key concept to grasp here is that the dominant class or group seeks to legitimize its ideas through ideology. The terrain of struggle is ideology. It is through ideology that the dominant group uses its power and influence to force other groups to believe that the dominant interests are in the best interest of everyone as common sense. Sallach (1974) asserted that this form of power is important to understand because of its "ability to define the parameters of legitimate discussion and debate over alternative beliefs, values, and world views" (p. 68). Gramsci and his followers believed that the dominant group uses institutions, including schools, to inculcate their ideology and to presumptively win the consent of the masses or, in his words, the "fabrication of consent." At other times, the state uses legal coercion to force subaltern groups to adopt dominant ideologies.

Kincheloe and McLaren (2000) also submitted that an ideology is "a highly articulated worldview, master narrative, discursive regime, or organizing scheme for collective symbolic production" (p. 303). Hall (1982) by extension defines ideology as "mental frameworks—the languages, the concepts, categories, imagery of thought, and the systems of representation—which different classes and social groups deploy in order to make sense of, define, figure out and render intelligible the way society works" (p. 26). Later, Hall (1995) lists three key features of ideology:

> (1) ideologies do not consist of isolated and separate concepts, but in the articulation of different elements into a distinctive set or chain of meanings. (p. 18)

> (2) ideological statements are made by individuals: but ideologies are not the product of individual consciousness or intention. Rather we formulate our intentions *within ideology*. (p. 19, italics in the original); and

> (3) ideologies "work" by constructing for their subjects (individual and collective) positions of identification and knowledge which allow them to "utter" ideological truths as if they were their authentic authors. (p. 19)

Drawing on Hall's outline of ideology, I have identified scientism and racism within several philosophical schools of thought that guided reading comprehension research and testing. To understand dominant ideology(ies) and their role in society it is imperative that we deconstruct how they arise and explain why alternative ideologies exist. Therefore, this book includes a judicious mélange of political and social movements that occurred as reading comprehension research and testing evolved.

In the context of this book, schools as institutions are important sites used by dominant groups to sustain ideological and cultural hegemony. Schools are where dominant groups have the power to use reading comprehension research and testing as tools to inculcate, perpetuate, and sustain dominant ideology.

It illustrates how different but related currents of philosophical thought arose, coexist, and continue to influence reading comprehension research and testing.

Advocates of scientism believe that science, as a method of observation and experimentation informed by physical science, can be applied to all activity and results in facts, laws, or theories, as the only true source of knowledge. Common definitions of *scientism* note; (a) it is the belief that the investigative methods of the physical sciences are applicable or justifiable in all fields of inquiry; (b) it is the principle that scientific methods can and should be applied in all fields of investigation; (c) it [science] alone can render truth about the world and reality; (d) it is a single-minded adherence to only the empirical, or testable; and (e) it requires one to do away with most, if not all, metaphysical, philosophical, and religious claims as truths.

In short, scientism holds that only science and the scientific methods used in the physical sciences permit justifiable access to the truth. Advocates maintain that scientific methods be extended to all the sciences, including social science, and prevent or marginalize alternative ideas or challenges to come to light.

The notion of scientism appeals to me because its central ideas draw from positivism, social Darwinism, and biological determinism, all philosophies that are accepted as foundational to educational research in the United States. Although these philosophies are not practiced in their original forms today, their assumptions are deeply embedded in the thinking of many reading comprehension researchers and test developers. More importantly, scientism reflects the history of theories and practices used in reading comprehension research and testing.

Philosophers have offered varying definitions of scientism. Habermas (1974) defined scientism as "science's belief in itself: that is, the conviction that we can no longer understand science as one form of possible knowledge, but rather must identify knowledge with science" (p. 4). In another instance, Federici (1999) argued that scientism is "grounded on the assumption that facts can be distinguished from values. Facts, it is claimed, are derived from the scientific method, whereas values are the products of uncritical human constructions" (p. 16). Furthermore, he articulated that scientism is "predicated on the belief that the scientific method provides a universal standard for the discovery of truth. Scientifically derived truth, then, provides a body of knowledge that forms the foundation of political and social consensus" (p. 16). Scientism rests on the assumption that knowledge is discovered only through the use of scientific methods and will ultimately inform politics and society as well as lead to new knowledge and truth. Historically, in Western European, and subsequently U.S., social thought, there has been an inordinate faith in science. Popkewitz and Tabachnick (1981) observed that since the mid-1800s, U.S. philosophers have maintained, "science seeks to impose rigor by demanding that theoretical concepts be reducible to variables that can be statistically manipulated from which formal, logical statements can be derived" (p. 15). This faith in humankind's ability, through science, to discover new knowledge has had profound effects on educational thought. Harding (1991) argues, "The conventional notion of a value-free, impartial, dispassionate objectivity that is supposed to guide scientific research" (p. 138) does not exist for all scientists, especially feminists. Some of the first dissent-ers of the alleged claims of scientism were African American schol-ars, activists, and educators. Among the varied reasons for their dissent is the inherent racism within scientism (see Lewontin, Rose, and Kamin's book *Not in our Genes*, 1984). Other scholars also have offered comprehensive discussions of the history and philosophy of science (Giere, 1988; Harre, 1972; Koch, 1959–1963; Kourany, 2003; Kuhn, 1996; Suppe, 1974) and the history and philosophy of educa-tion research (Lagemann, 2000; Shepard, 2000).

A note of caution is therefore warranted: as philosophers of edu-cation are quick to point out (R.P. Page, personal communication, September 14, 2003), intellectual developments in Western Europe from 1700 to the 1900s not only gave the world scientism, they also gave rise to liberalism, out of which it is possible to critique scientism. Liberalism yielded individual rights, the power of reason to supplant privilege by birth, and so forth. Collectively, these traditions are somewhat related; faith in science, technology, and reason were cen-tral components of the rationale to extend the rights to individuals. Their symbiotic relationship makes any separate treatment of them tricky, but I believe necessary.

Let me be clear, I am not antiscience. I support the idea of science as promoted by the late paleontologist Stephen J. Gould (1941–2002). His notion of science eloquently embraces the humanness of science and scientific study as well as lends itself to a critical understanding of science as an ideological and cultural force:

> Science, since people must do it, is a socially embedded activity. It pro-gresses by hunch, vision, and intuition. Much of its change through time does not record a closer approach to absolute truth, but the alteration of cultural contexts that influence it so strongly. Facts are not pure and unsullied bits of information; culture also influences what we see and how we see it. Theories, moreover, are not inexorable inductions from facts. The most creative theories are often imaginative visions imposed upon facts; the source of imagination is also strongly cultural. (1981, pp. 21–22)

Few hard scientists would disagree with Gould's notion of science. By contrast, historically in education research, there has been a reso-lute and unchallenged belief in scientism among reading comprehen-sion researchers (most of whom were educational psychologists).

Another important facet of the dominant ideology that, like a fine thread, appears, camouflages, and reappears throughout the history of reading comprehension research and testing is racism. It is an idea that existed before scientism, and its history is difficult, if not impossible, to trace. What I explain in the book is that racism is inherent in the philosophical assumptions on which dominant ideologies are based and the interpretations made by adherents of scientism in reading comprehension research and testing.

Why is a discussion of racism and classism important to a history of reading comprehension research and testing? Too often racism and classism are undercurrents that flow beneath the surface of reading comprehension research and testing where children of color are used as fodder to bolster claims of White children's intellectual superiority. Examples of these undercurrents are most clearly seen in the comparisons made between groups with unequal access to education as an indicator of the superiority/inferiority between groups. Moreover, power is exhibited when dominant groups promote the performance differences—verified by science, scientific methods, or experimental and quasi-experimental research—between unequal groups on reading comprehension tests and tasks as fact. Collectively they anchor, literally and figuratively, reading comprehension research and testing to their ideological terrain, the terrain of struggle for meaning. An ideological terrain is a way of representing the order of things, presenting them as natural or divine, inevitably making them appear universal, natural and coterminous with "reality" itself (Hall, 1982).

Reading comprehension research and testing reflect scientism, racism, and classism in the concepts, definitions, theories, tests, and interpretations that inform practice. It is this terrain in which the struggle for meaning is fought, where consent is manipulated, and where coercion exists.

Questions that arise for me, include: (a) How do reading comprehension research and testing include and sustain dominant ideologies? (b) How have political, social, and educational movements and traditional beliefs and values in educational research helped to shape reading comprehension research and testing? (c) Which individuals and whose collective efforts have helped frame our ideas of reading comprehension research and testing? How long will the reading comprehension research community continue to bastardize the systems of knowledge, culture, and languages that differ, challenge, and resist dominant and oppressive ideologies and reading research traditions? These questions are answered, in part, through the documentation of reading comprehension's power to determine the roles of language, culture, and thought that are transmitted by dominant groups as well as their ability to disempower alternatives presented by opposing groups. Although hegemony as an idea is not perfect, as a means of analysis it is, I believe, superior to previous attempts to account for the layers of complexity and lack of change in reading comprehension research and testing. Where appropriate, I have acknowledged the relationship between culture and language as well as given examples of how groups and individuals have opposed and resisted ideological and cultural hegemony by proposing counterhegemony, sustaining countervailing ideologies, and using counterdiscourse.

It is an optimal time to transform how reading comprehension research is conceived. Reading comprehension research can help to dismantle the reproduction of oppressive and dominant ideologies that hinder the scholastic progress of underserved children by transforming its role within the hegemonic process and by embracing beliefs, cultures, ideas, knowledge, languages, norms, and values of a broader, global, and democratic world.

1

Western European Philosophical Foundations of Reading Comprehension Research and Testing

Reading researchers seldom acknowledge the multiple Western European philosophical assumptions that inform reading comprehension research and testing, including positivism, Social Darwinism, and biological determinism. In the United States these philosophies were present at the onset of educational research in general and reading comprehension research, in particular. Reading comprehension research continues to draw on these philosophical assumptions popularized in the past with some modifications. For example, positivistic theorizing underscores much of the current educational debate on reading and federal funding. It is not my purpose to examine each philosophy in detail, because their influence on research in education is covered extensively by Karier (1986), Lagemann (1997), and Popkewitz (1984), among others.

Herein the connections among these select Western European philosophical assumptions and U.S. education and reading comprehension are disentangled. Along with a brief discussion of the key points of each philosophy and biographical sketches of philosophers (and great thinkers), I illustrate that philosophical assumptions, beliefs, values, and worldviews are human inventions and social enterprises that influence, and are influenced by, the political, social, and economic contexts of the society in which they are conceived. In addition, because these philosophies underpin reading comprehension research and testing, I also review how each philosophy has addressed issues of race, class, and power primarily through the writings of the founders or leaders of each philosophical school of thought. In this way, the undercurrents of race, class, and power, key ideologies are revealed.

1

This chapter includes a basic review of the philosophical assumptions that underpin historic and current forms of reading comprehension research and testing. It also is important to place philosophical opinions that have informed past investigations within their historical and social settings so as to account for the pervasiveness of the opinions beyond academia. At any one time in history, there are multiple philosophies available. In this context, definitions of reading comprehension used today are the sum total of the history of reading comprehension research and testing, the "collective" effort of countless researchers.

Comte, Spencer, and Darwin are the founders and advocates of positivism, Social Darwinism, and biological determinism, respectively. These men lived with passion and were affected by their beliefs, values, and practices while simultaneously affecting and reflecting the worlds in which they lived. International, national, and local events, along with marriages, affairs, divorces, births, and deaths of children and spouses, affected the lives and work of each man, just as these life events affect the lives for people today. These philosophers were not exceptional men, although they were all members of small intellectual groups within their respective locales that believed they could help ameliorate society's woes. The lives and work of these men reflected the intellectual and cultural ethos of their era as well as their individual beliefs, values, and worldviews. Their thinking about society, for example, is made clear in their discussions of race and, to a lesser extent, gender.

There are countless biographies describing the lives of Comte, Spencer, and Darwin that reflect shifts in approaches to science and the scientific study of education. While I find the biographies of each man a fascinating study within itself, for this work what is important are the linkages between and among their work and reading comprehension research and testing. The academic documents from which my comments are drawn reflect only shadows of these men and their lives. Their philosophical assumptions, with some modifications, continue to influence and delimit how reading comprehension is researched and tested.

Positivism, Social Darwinism, and Biological Determinism

To begin, it is important to point out similarities among these philosophers. As Europeans of wealth and privilege, they had access to education and leisure to study and pursue their life's work. Comte's early academic training, for example, differed markedly from Spencer's, yet both are recognized as founders of sociology. Typically, their lives changed once they challenged their fathers' ideas and moved forward with ideas of their own. Each man sought to please his parents, particularly his father, usually around notions of religious devotion. Although each man's religious views ranged from devotion to denominationalism to agnosticism to atheism, during each man's lifetime, the most profound and lasting shift came with his adoption or replacement of religion with scientism. That is, the belief in the ability of science to lead to greater knowledge, and for some, Truth, is what drove each man's passion, but not without cost. Each man suffered physically and emotionally from his beliefs and constant study, often resulting in a nervous breakdown. Finally, Comte, Spencer, and Darwin were completely devoted to their beliefs and life's work. Comte died poverty-stricken, Spencer became famous, and Darwin became both famous and infamous.

The adoption of these Western European philosophies by thinkers in the United States and the publicized support fueled conflicts simmering between those with traditional religious beliefs and those with belief in a new religion: science. These philosophies threatened traditional religious beliefs, namely, the triune Godhead. Traditional beliefs in a supernatural God, religion, and theology were pushed aside as self-proclaimed agnostic researchers embraced Western European philosophies. One of the great appeals of these philosophies was their focus on the future, as opposed to theology that tended to revere the past and promise a future in the hereafter. Scientism suggested that the present was controllable and the future predictable through scientific knowledge.

Positivism

Auguste Comte believed that science and scientific knowledge were all that was needed to perfect society. Living in a time of social and political reconstruction in France, Comte (1848/1971) argued, "The primary object, then, of Positivism is twofold: to generalize our scientific conceptions and to systematize the art of social life" (p. 3). In his thinking, all knowledge existed in the universe in an external order and could be uncovered through the positive, or scientific, method. His ideas grew in popularity in a country reorganizing itself from aristocratic and military elites to economic and political elites. His philosophic views were supported among many of his contemporaries, such as George Eliot and J. S. Mills, in England, and Albion Small and Lester Ward in the United States, among others. Collectively, these thinkers and writers were drawn to Comte's notion of science directing social policies.

Comte promoted his idea of the Law of Order, where he sought to demonstrate that all sciences could benefit from the use of the scientific method—observe, hypothesize, test the hypothesis (predict and experiment), conclude (and evaluate), form a new hypothesis, and repeat the process. He claimed that the scientific method was a logical process and reasoned that it existed outside of the emotions of the scientist. Furthermore, in his notion of sociology, he sought to apply the scientific method used in the physical sciences to discover the natural social laws that he believed governed society. According to his theory, advances in science would lead to laws and truths that, in turn, would lead to greater intellectual development and eventually to the perfection of mankind and society.

With increased human intelligence, Comte reasoned, mankind could control society and the environment. He thought that the discovery of general laws or principles allowed the formation of theories based on verification of the "facts." Comte maintained that the result of positive inquiry could be used to predict human behavior because the methods were objective and should be tested through observation, experimentation, comparison, and verification. Ideas central to Comte's version of positivism remain (in altered form). For example, he claimed (and some researchers continue to claim) that science is: (a) a way to Truth; (b) deterministic; (c) mechanistic; (d) objective, unbiased, and unemotional; (e) able to uncover laws and theories; and (f) able to predict human behavior and society. Positivism captured the thinking of nonscientists, that is, social thinkers and educators, but had very little impact on practicing scientists. Few "hard" scientists supported his ideas.

Comte also proposed an educational system based on his hierarchy of the sciences and using scientific methods, where observations are made, data collected, and predictions made by educators. In concert with his thinking, he envisioned education's role as a means to increase society's role over nature and thereby control society. Comte (1855/1979) predicted a positive scientific society in which "a universal system of positive education would teach men to know and do their duty in such a way as to diminish, if not eliminate, conflict between individuals" (p. 473). He believed that once men were taught to accept their place in the social order and to accept their role in society, the social order would lead to social perfection without conflict. The education of children he divided into two broad time periods, pre- and postpuberty. In addition, his deep respect for the intellect of White men and his belief in the superiority of White men's thinking, over the thinking of other groups, continues to be a vital part of the academy.

His observations of French society led him to assert that all knowledge progresses in a deterministic pattern, which he tried to tie to his hierarchy of the "hard" sciences. Drawing on Lamarckian theories of evolution in human institutions and social progress, he proposed,

> Every sociological analysis supposes three classes of considerations, each more complex than the preceding: viz., the conditions of social existence of the individual, the family, and the society; the last comprehending, in a scientific sense, the whole of the human species, and chiefly, the whole of the WHITE RACE. (Comte, 1842, p. 268, emphasis added)

Comte did not view all humankind as equal, although he was not a proponent of slavery (he explained his views on slavery as part of human history). He believed that some racial groups were worthy of being part of the human race and others should be eliminated. He so revered the intelligence of (White) men that he created a calendar of male intellectual geniuses (from Prometheus to Gall). Not surprisingly, according to Comte, French men were the most intelligent (Comte, 1854). Furthermore, he believed that women, working classes, and people of color were inferior to White men of intelligence (i.e., educated White men).

Comte maintained that each stage of human intellectual development represented a stage of knowledge that paralleled the evolution of the individual mind (Law of Three Stages). His stages included a theological stage (belief in gods and spirits for the occurrence of natural events and governed by priests and military rulers); a metaphysical stage (other unobservable causes that explain natural events and governed by clergymen); and a scientific or positive stage (quantifiable descriptions and explanations for natural events or descriptions, predictions, and control are governed by industrial leaders and the rules of science). He maintained that science should be conducted without religion or theocracy. Ironically, his denial of the role of religion in the life of humankind led him to mysticism and, finally, to the point where he embraced positivism as a religion. In the United States, his ideas about science, the importance of the scientific method, and the use of science as a means to perfect society were more widely accepted than was his theology.

Twenty years after Comte's death, Ribot (1877) wrote a series of articles that expounded the philosophical advances in France and discussed a distinction among Comte's followers. He argued that Comte's work consisted of three main divisions: a philosophy, a polity, and a religion. The followers of Comte were in one of two camps: those who followed the entirety of his work or those who adopted his philosophy but disregarded his polity and religion.

Habermas, a more contemporary critic, wrote "Positivism stands and falls on the principle of scientism" (1971, p. 67). In fact, he argued that positivism "contradicts the intention of an unprejudiced critique of knowledge" (p. 67) because it assumes a priori the answer to the inquiry. In this view of science, what is most important is a strict adherence to methods or procedures. What is most troubling, however, about this approach to science and the study of education is that it is detached from the specific contexts in which learning occurs. Habermas (1973), in a scathing review of the import of positivism, wrote:

> Interest and inclination are banished from the court of knowledge as subjective factors. The spontaneity of hope, the act of taking a position, the experience of relevance or indifference, and above all, the response to suffering and oppression, the desire for adult autonomy, the will to emancipation, and the happiness of discovering one's identity—all these are dismissed for all time from the obligating interest of reason. (pp. 262–263)

In reading comprehension research, the appeal to science (i.e., the use of scientific methods) is an appeal to positivism, an appeal that recently has been resurrected to support and fund reading comprehension test research.

Social Darwinism

Herbert Spencer (1820–1893), who is often paired with Comte as a cofounder of sociology, developed the idea of social Darwinism, which helps to fill in a social gap in positivistic thought. In 1848, he became a subeditor for the *London Economist*, and three years later, published his first book, *Social Statics, or the Conditions Essential to Human Happiness*. The text, informed by Comte's notion of social dynamics, or human progress, outlines Spencer's views on evolution. In addition, it describes his theory of social evolution as a process of "individuation." He believed that individualism (the belief that society exists for the benefit of the individual, who must not be constrained by government interventions or made to subordinate to collective interests) is a means to greater human progress.

Although recognized as a cofounder of sociology, Spencer (1864) explained there were differences between his thinking and Comte's in the article, "Reasons for Dissenting From the Philosophy of M. Comte":

> What is Comte's professed aim? To give a coherent account of the progress of human conceptions. What is my aim? To give a coherent account of the progress of the external world. Comte proposed to describe the necessary, and the actual, filiation of ideas. I propose to describe the necessary, and the actual, filiation of things. Comte professes to interpret the genesis of our knowledge of nature. My aim is to interpret . . . the genesis of the phenomena which constitute nature. The one is subjective. The other is objective. (p. 7)

Despite his lack of scientific training, Spencer strongly upheld the primacy of science and scientific knowledge for the understanding of society and attempted to use natural selection theories to explain societal and racial differences. The most extensive explanation of his thinking is his nine-volume *System of Synthetic Philosophy* (1862–1896), based on his theories of social evolution. He explains that he sought to "reconcile science and religion and to lay the metaphysical underpinnings of evolution" (Spencer, 1862, p. 570). Specifically, he attempted to integrate themes from biology and sociology with the general culture of his time by replacing theological explanations of life with scientific explanations.

Spencer's views on evolution are attributed to his understanding of the theories espoused by Lamarck (1744–1829) and Malthus (1776–1834). From the former, Spencer gathered his ideas about inherited acquired characteristics and from the latter, Spencer imagined that human suffering (i.e., war, famine, disease) were a part of nature. He drew most heavily from the work of Lamarck, who opined that species inherited characteristics, some of which were developed as they adapted to their environment and were passed on to the next generation.

His theory of evolution rested on the notion of the inheritance of acquired characteristics explained in his 1852 article, "The Developmental Hypothesis." He believed that the connection between physical and mental characteristics was hereditary and that all humanity was generated from a common stock. In an 1852 essay, "A Theory of Population," Spencer summarized his ideas about evolution and coined the phrase "survival of the fittest." He held that the more "fit" acquired unique characteristics that advantaged them over others, and, thus, the "fit" survived (this idea is a misappropriation of Darwin's work, but it was catchy and remains a familiar maxim). He added that differences were exhibited due to the ability of preceding generations to assimilate, accommodate, and adapt themselves to circumstances.

Spencer also believed that natural laws were deterministic. Thus, as the lower species evolved into a higher, more complex species, those most able to cope with change would change and adjust, to survive. Applying his theory to society, he argued that the upper classes of society were genetically superior to the lower classes and more deserving of continual survival. Furthermore, he maintained that the evolutionary process was inherent within each race and each child of each specific race. In his view, the weak, the poor, and the unfit would die off. Thus, he coined the phrase "the elimination of the unfit, through struggle" as a corresponding phrase to his "the survival of the fittest" maxim. For Spencer, this meant that the best adapted individuals in society, which he identified in terms of race, class, and gender, should survive. He was a vocal opponent of all reform, any benevolent support that would allow the survival of the unfit (poor, needy, and less intelligent), and any support that would permit the unfit to pass on their (alleged) weaknesses. He believed that those who survived were chosen by nature to do so.

A self-described agnostic, Spencer argued that the process of evolution was determined by the unknowable's selection of which species would survive and the species' adaptations. He argued, "The poor, the weak, the downtrodden, the stupid, and the lazy must be allowed to die off" (Spencer, 1892, p. 79). He argued that the government should not interfere with nature: If some were poor, Black, or uneducated, and could not help themselves, the government should not intervene. Spencer's views on race made clear that racial hatred, sans America's peculiar institution of slavery, was not unique. His ideas of racial superiority and inherited intelligence were part of the "common sense" of Western Europeans. He called for individualism, where one sought his own means of survival and did not look for, or expect, government intervention.

Spencer found a ready body of believers for his social evolutionary theory in both Europe and the United States. In Europe, his theories seemed to fit the existing hierarchy of the social class system. In the United States, where the same social class system did not exist in such exaggerated form, many Euro-Americans accepted his ideas as they struggled to regain the power and prestige that some felt they had lost during and immediately following the Civil War. Spencer's philosophic views became even more popular in the United States and increased after his lecture tour in 1882. He promoted what he believed was the common sense notion of the genetic and racial superiority of Whites over all other groups. Spencer's thinking was widely disseminated in scholarly journals, books, magazines, and newspapers. Social Darwinism also was a welcomed idea to fledgling U.S. psychologists who embraced scientism because it permitted science to be perceived as an authoritative replacement for religion by supplying an unknowable force to science.

Lester Ward (1896), for example, in a series of articles on the purposes of sociology, noted Spencer's popularity in the United States, where "American writers are virtually disciples of Spencer" (p. 447). Not surprisingly, in the aftermath of the Civil War, some White U.S. citizens were willing to anchor themselves to his new philosophy, which seemed to validate, for White Americans, what some had always thought was true: They were genetically superior to others, especially people of color; they were of a genetically superior breed—biologically, physically, morally, and mentally or intellectually; and their superior physical and mental qualities were biologically inheritable. Spencer's ideas seemed to lie at the core of an evolving Americanism that saw inequalities as a "natural" part of social evolution and that was used to support capitalism, imperialism, colonialism, and racial discrimination.

Spencer's philosophic assumptions also influenced American educational thinking in the late 1800s. In his 1861 article (1861/1963) "Education: Intellectual, Moral, and Physical," he queried, "What knowledge is of most worth?" His answer was knowledge from science. His most popular and widely read book in the United States was *Essays on Education* (1911/1949), a collection of four essays in which he expanded his basic theory of evolution and applied it to education. He viewed the education of children in evolutionary terms similar to those he outlined for the human race: "The education of the child must accord both in mode and arrangement with the education of mankind, considered historically ... . The genesis of knowledge in the individual must follow the same course as the genesis of knowledge in the race" (p. 60). Although he appears to speak broadly of the human race, his thinking is understood to mean the "superior" White race. He believed that each race followed a similar pattern, and Whites were more advanced. Spencer placed great importance on the inheritability of characteristics and individual effort to progress, succeed, and survive, with little respect for the contexts in which one lives (or is educated). In his view, the strongest individuals were middle- and upper-class White males, who had inherited intellect, power, and wealth.

His assumptions remain in the thinking of some education researchers who disregard sociohistorical contexts as important considerations and factors that affect reading comprehension research and testing. As powerful as Social Darwinism was in the United States, the publication of Darwin's notion of evolution by natural selection was unparalleled, for it challenged theological views of creation and humankind's dominion over nature, especially after the Second Great Awakening (1790–1840) had moved Protestantism from its Calvinist roots to the local preacher, along came Darwinism with an alternative view about the Divine source of knowledge.

Biological Determinism

Although Charles Robert Darwin (1808–1882) is best known for his ideas on evolution by natural selection, many other scientists espoused similar ideas earlier, including his grandfather Erasmus Darwin. Charles's version also drew on the work of Malthus for his theory of evolution by natural selection, as he indicates in his autobiography:

> I happened to read for amusement Malthus on Population, and being well prepared to appreciate the struggle for existence ... it at once struck me that under these circumstances favourable variations would tend to be preserved, and unfavourable ones to be destroyed. The results of this would be the formation of a new species. (quoted in Barlow, 1958, p. 69)

Darwin was recalling his reading of Malthus' (1798) *Essay on the Principles of Population*, which reflected early observations of political, social, and industrial revolutions in England, France, and the United States. Collectively, these revolutions help to prompt massive changes in the political and social life of the most powerful nations in the world. England began to expand its empire in Australia, Canada, and New Zealand and was aggressively colonizing Africa (Kenya, Rhodesia /Zimbabwe, and South Africa), as well as British Guyana, Ceylon, Cyprus, Hong Kong, Singapore, and the Middle East (Bangladesh, India, and Pakistan). Malthusian theory suggested that as the population increased, food supplies would decrease to such an extent that there would be a struggle for existence. He opined that if left unchecked, increases in population growth would create a minimal existence for most, unless war, famine, poverty, or birth control stymied growth. Darwin's adaptation of Malthusian theories resulted in his idea of artificial selection, later labeled natural selection.

During his 5-year voyage around the world from England, two significant changes occurred in Darwin's life. First, he kept copious notes on his evolving thinking, which were published in 1839 as *Journals of researches into geology and natural history of the various countries visited by J. M. S. Beagle under the command of Captain FitzRoy, R. N. from 1832–1836*. Second, he began to doubt his strict religious upbringing and denounced his faith in the divine explanation of life. He replaced his belief and trust in the Holy Scriptures with doubts and suspicions of their accuracy based on his close observations and classifications. Darwin (1859/1979) wrote, "In nature the species that are better adapted than others to life in particular environments are likely to leave more descendants, while the species that were less well adapted may diminish and become extinct" (p. 37). In response to his observations of variations of species, Darwin developed his theory of evolution. He defined evolution as "a result of the change that species undergo in reaction to their adaptation to their environment ... at the improvement of each organic being in relation to its inorganic conditions of life" (1859/1979, p. 2). He suggested that evolution is the process of change that a species undergoes as it makes adaptations and accommodations to its environment.

Darwin's theory suggested that organisms best suited to survive in their environment are more likely to reproduce and pass their genetic material to the next generation, whereas those with weaker traits are least likely to reproduce and survive. He observed:

> If variations useful to any organic being ever do occur, assuredly individuals then characterized will have the best chance of being preserved in the struggle for life; and from the strong principle of inheritance, these will tend to produce offspring similarly characterized. This principle of preservation, or the survival of the fittest, I have called Natural Selection. (Darwin, 1859/1979, p. 63)

Darwin's theory of evolution consisted of four major points: overpopulation, the struggle for existence, survival of the fittest (inheritability of traits), and natural selection of variations. What is important to understand here is that Darwin's notion rests on the acceptance of the scientific method as a reasonable (and substitute) explanation for truth, equates the evolution of humankind to that of other species, and suggests that human evolution includes biological and cultural processes.

Decades after his return to England, Darwin continued to work on this theory of evolution by writing a series of drafts and two unpublished outlines (1842 and 1844). At the urging of his friends, Darwin submitted a paper to the Linnaean Society in 1858. The paper was read by T. Huxley and contained Darwin's thinking on natural selection (Alfred Wallace's paper on natural selection also was read at the meeting and made similar claims). Darwin's (1859/1979) paper was an abstract on natural selection drawn from a three-volume text he was completing. The abstract was the foundation of his seminal book *On the Origin of the Species by Means of Natural Selection, or the Preservation of Favored Races in the Struggle for Life* (the shortened title is most often used, perhaps to distance it from its obvious racist overtones), first published in 1859. Paradoxically, on the cover page he wrote the following comment: "*If the misery of our poor be caused not by the laws of nature, but by our institutions, great is our sin*" (italics in the original).

Darwin's ideas were not unique—others had written about the idea of evolution—but what separated his thinking, and continues to divide scholars, was that in his thinking there was no place for Divine creation as explicated in the book of Genesis of the Holy Bible. The book is not only a précis on evolution by natural selection but also a journey into the gradual development of Darwin's thinking. A week later, a second edition, with editorial corrections, was published in part to mend his long, beleaguered relationship with his father, to uphold his family's reputation, and in deference to the Christian faith of his father and wife. The modifications acknowledged all living forms as beginning with God, the Creator.

In the United States, a faithful disciple, Hofstadter, opined, "Darwinism seemed to strike from more than one direction at the very heart of traditional theology … at the very least it clearly impaired the authority of the Scripture by discrediting the Genesis version of creation" (1959, p. 25). Over time, however, Darwin's ideas were accepted by some and began to reflect dominant class beliefs, values, and practices. Darwin struggled with religion throughout his life (later he severed all religious ties and claims, preferring agnosticism). Although read widely internationally, the book was highly criticized in Europe for its denial of the role of God in creation as recorded in Genesis (a debate that continues).

While on his 5-year journey, Darwin made lengthy sojourns onto land, where he observed the indigenous human inhabitants as well as animal life. Later, he attempted to understand humans within their own geographical and cultural context, however his natural comparison was to the life he had left in England, whose pattern of living he always found superior. He attempted to apply his ideas of evolution to humankind and believed that man's intellectual and moral development (as species characteristics) evolved just as man's physical features evolved. He believed that Whites were intellectually and morally superior to all other races and that women were inferior to men. And, he claimed that future generations of each race would inherit the improvements of their race in consideration of environmental norms, ideas he made clear in another book published in 1871, *The Descent of Man and the Selection in Relation to Sex*.

Darwin (1871/1972) explicated his theory of a social evolution by natural selection in this two-volume work. In this text, he applied his theory directly to humans and argued that man descended from lower organisms; this was his attempt to uncover the origin of the human race. He also proffered his thinking on human intellectual and moral development. Darwin's observations of indigenous peoples during his voyage informed his opinion that "each race had been produced to its modern state by modifications of their original ancestral type" (Darwin, 1871/1972, p. 99). He argued that the races that controlled power and wealth were the favored races because they were intellectually and morally superior. He believed that it was important to assure that the favored (White) races remained in positions of power for they were more able to make the best informed decisions about society. Furthermore, he reasoned that society would continue on its evolutionary trek toward the perfectibility of the human race, if the (White) favored races continued to evolve according to his hypothesized natural selection theory. Darwin's view drew support for his theory from his observations of Whites in the United States, where he claimed,

> There is apparently much truth in the belief that the wonderful progress of the United States, as well as the character of the people, are the result of natural selection; for the more energetic, restless, and courageous men from all parts of Europe have emigrated during the last ten or twelve generations to that great country, have there succeeded best. (p. 170)

Moreover, throughout this book Darwin argued

> (a) man is more courageous, pugnacious, and energetic than woman, and has more inventive genius; (b) the chief distinction in the intellectual powers of the two sexes is shown by man's attaining to a higher eminence, in whatever he takes up, than can women—whether requiring deep thought, reason, or imagination; and (c) some at least of these mental traits in which women may excel are traits characteristic of the lower races. (1871/1972, pp. 312–316, 596)

In his thinking, there was no room to consider the complicity of the historical and political structures of society as a plausible cause for inequalities.

Jolly and White (1995) claim that the phrase "lower races" unmistakably was a reference to the indigenous people Darwin encountered during his travels. According to them, it is a phrase that was understood in its time to mean "either savages to be shunned and exploited, or unfortunates to be converted and educated; but either way they were not equals of the 'higher' Whites" (p. 16). This idea, strongly supported by Spencer's notion of social Darwinism, cultural evolution, and the like, confounded biology with culture, heredity with environment, and social and economic systems with civilization. For example, Darwin (1896) claimed,

> With savages, the weak in body or mind are soon eliminated; and those that survive commonly exhibit a vigorous state of health. We civilized men, on the other hand, do our utmost to check the process of elimination; we build asylums for the imbecile, the maimed, and the sick. ... Thus the weak members of civilized societies propagate their kind. No one who has attended to the breeding of domestic animals will doubt that this must be highly injurious to the race of men. ... We must therefore bear the undoubtedly bad effects of the weak surviving and propagating their kind. (pp. 133–134)

Darwin's theories reflected, consciously or unconsciously, his observations of changes in the world.

Scientists in several countries supported and endorsed his work. Darwin received many honorary doctoral degrees and other highly coveted honors. In the United States, for example, Ratner (1936) suggested that conflicts that arose over the "ideas of science and religion began to parallel the struggle over slavery and secession" (p. 106). Many leading U.S. intellectual and religious journals (i.e., *American Journal of Science, North American Review*, and the *Theological Review*) weighed in on the debate between the Divine explanation and Darwin's of variation. Some American educational researchers welcomed Darwin's notion that it was imperative to understand "scientifically" how a child developed, as they made recommendations for instruction, inasmuch as they saw children as evolving organisms. Advocates reasoned that knowledge of how a child grew intellectually would lead them to an understanding of the processes whereby a person acquired mental abilities. Additionally, some researchers thought that by teaching a person his or her proper role in society, mankind could control society. It is an excellent example of how ideas, some considered natural or common sense, can seep into society as facts, theories, laws, and truths.

In sum, educational research, including reading comprehension research and testing, in the United States draws first from Comte's positivism, that is, the idea that all facets of life can be explained by empirical science because its goal is to discover rules, laws, theories, and truths. Second, Spencer's idea of Social Darwinism to describe the evolution and development of Western civilization suggests that each person, group, and race evolved much like other forms of life. All human knowledge is evolutionary, moving from simple to complex ideas. He believed that cultural progress also evolves from inferior individuals, groups, or races to more advanced or superior forms, with wealthy White men being at the top of the hierarchy. Third, Darwin's biological determinism offered a process whereby evolution was understood as equal to natural selection. He proposed the evolutionary process begins with one-celled life forms and evolves over time to humankind, but without the influence of God. Advocates claim there are three key elements to evolutionary change: variation, heredity, and the struggle for existence. Darwin, too, held that European men were intellectually and morally superior to all other humans whether identified by race, gender or class. These ideas became part of ideological hegemony that informed education and reading research. A caveat on racism and its role in the process ideology is in order before moving to the next chapter.

Scientific Racism

Historically, critics of these philosophical schools of thought, especially biological determinism, have pointed out the racist and gendered ideas that are embedded in each philosophy. Then, as now, their concerns were/are dismissed as passionate but naïve. Jean Finot (1916), a French journalist and early critic wrote, "The science of inequality is emphatically a science of White people. It is they who have invented it, and set it agoing, who have maintained, cherished, and propagated it, thanks to their observations and their deductions" (quoted in Stepan & Gilman, 1993, p. 187). Among the more contemporary critiques of Darwin's theories has been the exhaustive work of the late paleontologist Gould, especially his landmark text, *The Mismeasure of Man* (1981, reprinted in 1996).

In Gould's (1996) revised and expanded edition, he critiqued biological determinism by arguing, "The need for analysis is timeless because the errors of biological determinism are so deep and insidious and because the argument appeals to the worst manifestations of our nature" (pp. 26–27). Unlike Darwin, he did not support the notion of favored races. He noted that Social Darwinism, as espoused by Spencer, was not based on Darwin's work but on incorrect assumptions about humankind. Gould also argued that educators misappropriated notions of science in favor of scientism.

An equally inspiring critique of biological determinism is found in Lewontin et al. (1984) *Not in Our Genes.* They argued,

> Biological determinists' ideas are part of the attempt to preserve the inequalities of our society and to shape human nature in their own image. The exposure of the fallacies and political content of those ideas are part of the struggle to eliminate those inequalities and to transform our society. In that struggle we transform our own nature. (p. 15)

They continued their argument by pointing out that Darwin's notion of biological determinism

> locates such success and failures of will and character as coded, in large part, in an individual's genes; merit and ability will be passed from gen-

eration to generation within families ... the presence of such biological differences between individuals of necessity leads to the creation of
hierarchal societies because it is part of biologically determined human
nature to form hierarchies of status, wealth, and power. (p. 68)

Furthermore, the authors asserted, biological determinism has
been used to justify and legitimate discrimination by race, class, and
gender. Under the guise of science, biological determinism exists in
politics, society, and education although biological differences are a
myth. That is, human variation is not equal to race. Poignantly, they
conclude, "The convergence of the two meanings of inheritance—the
social and the biological—legitimizes the passage of social power
from generation to generation" (p. 72). Despite the groundbreaking research findings of palentologist Gould, evolutionary geneticist
Lewontin, neurobiologist Rose, and psychologist Kamin, as well as
their efforts to refute the alleged biology of racial differences, many
educational researchers continue to embrace the idea of innate intelligence and use it to justify and retain social inequities.

The American Anthropological Association (1998) has crafted and
posted a strong statement on race, interpreting it as an ideology rooted
in the notion of inequality. The statement says that in the United
States, people are "conditioned to viewing human races as natural and
separate divisions within the human species based on visible physical differences. ... historical research has shown that the idea of 'race'
has always carried more meanings than mere physical differences"
(American Anthropological Association, 1998, ¶ 2). The organization comments further on how ideas about race and notions of racial
superiority are grounded in people's understanding of U.S. history
from "the English and other European settlers, the conquered, Indian
peoples, and those peoples of Africa brought in to provide slave labor.
... "Race" was a mode of classification linked specifically to peoples in
the colonial situation (American Anthropological Association, 1998, ¶
4). The association continues by noting, in particular, how Europeans
constructed theories about race in defense of imperialism and colonization of others. ... The ideology magnified the differences among
Europeans, Africans, and Indians, established a rigid hierarchy of
socially exclusive categories, underscored and bolstered unequal
rank and status differences, and provided the rationalization that the
inequality was natural or God-given. ... Ultimately "race" as an ideology about human differences was subsequently spread to other areas
of the world. (American Anthropological Association, 1998, ¶ 4)

Collectively, this group of scholars acknowledged that a racist ideology persists in the United States among scholars and the general public, in part, because it has been promoted as common sense. This racist ideology is drawn from assumptions nested in positivism, social Darwinism, and biological determinism, and, in part, because this is the ideology that the dominant group has used to support their interests. The organization's conclusion is significant:

> The "racial" worldview was invented to assign some groups to perpetual low status, while others were permitted access to privilege, power, and wealth. The tragedy in the United States has been that the policies and practices stemming from this worldview succeeded all too well in constructing unequal populations among Europeans, Native Americans, and peoples of African descent ... The present-day inequalities between so-called "racial groups" are not consequences of their biological inheritance but products of historical and contemporary social, economic, educational, and political circumstances. (American Anthropological Association, 1998, ¶ 11)

It is important to understand and place philosophical assumptions within their historical and social settings so as to account for the pervasiveness of the opinions beyond academia. At any one time in history, there are multiple philosophies available with some more prevalent than others yet, collectively, they continue to shape how reading comprehension is defined and studied. The history of reading comprehension research and testing is rooted, philosophically, in the assumptions described previously because they are part and parcel of the roots of educational research in the United States. These philosophical assumptions include an undercurrent of race, class, and power. In the next chapter, I discuss how these philosophical assumptions manifest themselves in U.S. politics and society and appear as remnants in U.S. pragmatism as linked to reading comprehension research and testing. Moreover, I introduce counter-hegemonic positions espoused by African American scholars and activists that challenged ideological hegemony, these philosophical assumptions and the dominant ideologies they promoted.

2

Ideological and Philosophical Foundations of Reading Comprehension Research and Testing

By the early 1800s, education embraced the new science of psychology that called for the use of scientific methods, thereby making education research synonymous with scientific study. Western European notions of biological determinism seemed to offer "scientific proof," that explained what appeared, to some, as the "natural laws" of social phenomena (class stratification and privileged gender and race status). Likewise, scientism affected reading comprehension research and testing as researchers and educators used scientific methods and psychological explanations to unravel the mysteries of reading comprehension. The confluence of positivism, Social Darwinism, and biological determinism influenced the creation of a uniquely American philosophy known as pragmatism. Peabody (1866) captured the mood of the country when he wrote for the *New Englander*:

> Science occupies so large a space in the thought, speculation, and literature of our time, and in the conversation of intelligent men and women, that no one can afford to remain unfamiliar with its terms, its theories, its doctrines, its laws. (cited in Joncich, 1968, p. 111)

Lagemann's (1997) observation that, "wide optimism in American society concerning possibilities for progress through science and its application to social problems" (p. 4), reminds us of the pervasiveness of dominant ideologies. According to Hall (2003), this understanding: "helps us to analyze how a particular set of ideas comes to dominate the social thinking" (p. 27). That is, it helps us to take an insider's view of how dominance is maintained.

This chapter continues an overview of the key elements of the philosophical assumptions that underpin reading comprehension research and testing. Here in the United States a philosophy of pragmatism is set within its historical and social settings to help explain it as well as to illustrate how the notion of scientism influenced reading comprehension research and testing. In this context, definitions and theories that inform reading comprehension research and testing are part of the collective efforts of countless philosophers and researchers. Against this backdrop, I discuss pragmatism, noting the key points of the philosophy as espoused by its advocates, Peirce, James, and Dewey. As with the previous discussion of Western European philosophies, the discussion that follows is selective because it traces and identifies pragmatism's associations and connections to scientism as well as education and, where warranted, reading comprehension. I also review how pragmatism did not address issues of race.

Finally, I offer a counter hegmonic point of view that emerged from centuries of oppression that reflect the ideas, values, beliefs, and practices of nondominant groups. For example, throughout history there has been vocal opposition to dominant ideologies that glorify one group over others. Among the more aggressive opposition has been that posed by African American scholars and activists who have resisted the racism that is part of United States history. Their scholarship is reviewed to offer a more complete and balanced account of ideas that have been available to inform reading comprehension research and testing efforts. Therefore, whereas intellectual and cultural hegemony has controlled reading comprehension research and testing, and used it as a mechanism to instantiate dominant ideologies, subaltern groups consistently have questioned, challenged, and critiqued their underlying assumptions. Deconstructing the discourse illustrates how dominant groups have promoted their beliefs, values, and practices as needful for everyone, while colonizing subaltern groups in an effort to sustain political and economic control of the nation.

There is a special emphasis on the discourse used to support political, economic, and social ideas and their influence on the lives of African Americans. The scholarship and activism of Douglass, Cooper, and Du Bois are examined. These courageous African Americans wrote and published their thinking, ideas, and views, that reflected an ideology, sometimes called radical and at other times labeled resistant. Collectively, they presented a different set of ideas that claimed that intelligence and morals were not inheritable, that White males were not superior to all other humans, that science could not lead to Truth, and that U.S. society would not be perfected until racism was dealt with and defeated. However, without the accompanying political, economic, or social power to spread these ideas, these notions were limited to the African American community and like-minded Whites. Before launching into a review of pragmatism, however, it is necessary to briefly discuss how ideological hegemony operated through political and social forces and to help 'set the stage' for understanding pragmatism in the twentieth century.

A Fledgling Nation

The philosophical assumptions of positivism, and biological and social determinism, were also used to convince society of its right and privilege to extend its dominant ideologies over other peoples. For example, the notion of Manifest Destiny underscores the idea that survival of the fittest was used in an imperial and colonizing way to secure all land from indigenous people. The idea of Manifest Destiny extended Darwinian notions under the guise of progress in support of "the belief that this land and its people had a 'manifest destiny' which includes not only such weighty responsibilities as assuming the 'White man's burden' but also the more awesome, messianic challenge of making the world safe for democracy" (Karier, 1975, p. 130). Included in this colonization was the war with Mexico, which ended with the Treaty of Guadalupe Hidalgo in 1848 and the acquisition of what is now California, New Mexico, and Texas as well as parts of Arizona, Colorado, Nevada, Utah, and Wyoming. Moreover, deals were signed with England for Oregon, and deals were signed with Russia for Alaska and the United States assumed occupation of Hawaii and Samoa.

Schools as social institutions supported and perpetuated dominant ideology, however, have been more positively portrayed as representative of the strong-willed individualism, ingenuity, creativity, and adventurousness of White males and their families. This discourse pattern, according to Hall (1995), suggests "the very idea of adventure became synonymous with the demonstration of the moral, social, and physical mastery of the colonizers over the colonized" (p. 21). When retold in schools, then, dominant ideologies interpret the events as part of common sense or the natural course of events in nation building, not as genocide, imperialism or colonization.

It was also during this time that the population of the United States reached 63 million and two new states were added to the growing nation, Wyoming and Utah. Furthermore, during the post-Reconstruction era slavery had been defeated, at least legally, with the passage of the Thirteenth Amendment, the Emancipation Proclamation, and 1875 Civil Rights Act, respectively. In addition, the Fourteenth and Fifteenth Amendments extended the rights of equal protection to all U.S. citizens and the right to vote to men of color. Despite the amendments to the U.S. Constitution, their provisions were not extended to all people in the United States, as American Indians were constantly forced off their land, mostly through acts of Congress (Indian Appropriations Act of 1871 and the Dawes Severalty Act of 1887), battles (i.e., Battle of Wounded Knee in 1890), and massacres (e.g., of the Cheyenne, led by Chiviginton, in 1864). Moreover, American Indian children were forcibly removed from their families, homes, and environments in a move supported by claims of biological and social determinism to "improve" society.

Economically, U.S. society was changing as powerful men emerged in various industries: banking (August Belmont, Jay Gould, Andrew Mellon, J. P. Morgan), steel (Andrew Carnegie, Elbert H. Gary), oil (J. D. Rockefeller), railroads (James Hill, Cornelius Vanderbilt), and newspapers (William R. Hearst, Joseph Pulitzer). These men, among others, helped to promote the rapid urbanization that accompanied the many new jobs their investments spawned. The rise in jobs saw the formation of labor unions to fight for wages, fair treatment, and collective bargaining. The hope of jobs brought immigrants from Eastern and Southern Europe as well as the Middle East. Excluded from this wave of immigration were Chinese people under the Chinese Exclusion Law of 1882.

Women, too, had a voice in the changes taking place in society. Elizabeth Cady Stanton and Lucretia Mott organized the Women's Rights Convention (Seneca Falls, New York). Susan B. Anthony was a tireless fighter for woman's suffrage, as was Carrie Catt, and Jane Adams and Ellen Star created the Hull House in Chicago (1889) to help needy urban families, teach English, and Americanize immigrants. Women continued to expand their reach, as many more were being admitted to colleges (e.g., Oberlin College) and universities and were able to expand their career options.

Culturally, this was a period of great innovation in the U.S.: the first long distance telephone call, motion picture studio, Hershey candy bar, color comic strips, women's skirts above the ankle, books of matches, X-rays, motorcars, movies or flickers rather than peep shows, subways, Buddhist mission, zippers, self-dial telephones, the World's Fair in Chicago featuring the Ferris Wheel, and self-serve cafeterias. Yet, at the turn of the 20th century, the nation faced many of the same concerns we face today: overcrowded, crime-ridden urban neighborhoods; massive waves of immigrants entering the United States and concerns of how to house and teach them; domestic unrest (ethnic and racial tensions and economic insecurities); inequities in school funding; employment discrimination for women and ethnic and racial minorities; embattled political parties vying for control of the government; the expansion of labor unions; strikes by disgruntled workers; the establishment of alternative political parties; a mélange of social theories; and the support of Jim/Jane Crow segregation laws by the U.S. Supreme Court after their ruling in the 1896 *Plessey v. Ferguson* case, resulting in the "separate but equal" dictum.

Educators were determined to use philosophy, science, and scientific research methods to support their worldviews, beliefs, and values. Educational research was synonymous with scientific study. When an educational researcher referred to research, implicitly he or she meant the research conducted was scientific. It appeared that Comte's prediction of a society in which people would know their social role and want to work within that role for the good of society was emerging. His notions of a positive education for the masses, where their social attitudes could be shaped, appeared within reach with the advent of psychology. Furthermore, science and scientific methods of inquiry were considered, along with positivism, a logical explanation of "natural law." Science appealed to educators because it was believed to be objective, neutral, and a means of explaining how and why society was as it appeared. Social and biological Darwinism also seemed to offer "scientific proof" to explain social phenomena: class stratification and privileged gender and race status. Many educators believed that science, and man through science, was all one needed to explain life.

In conjunction with the blossoming progressive education movement (1830–1920), pragmatists sought to explain the schism between science and religion and between the individual and society, based on four basic assumptions: (a) a belief in science and the scientific method, (b) the influence of philosophical empiricism, (c) the acceptance of biological evolution; and (d) the acceptance of American democracy (Morris, 1970).

Darwin believed that individual differences were important because they emphasized evolution by natural selection. His basic principles of biological and social evolution, especially popular ideas among some White American politicians, philosophers, and educational leaders, appeared to offer scientific proof of their superior nature. Large audiences of devotees read his work and heard Spencer's extension of Darwin's theory, that is, that it was important that the favored races (Whites) retain power, for they were best adapted and were the most fit to continue the human race. These assumptions and the racist theories they suggest, such as the inheritability of intelligence and morals, are still popular in some circles.

The unique philosophy of pragmatism, and its leading advocates were influenced by their personal lives and, and it emphasized to varying degrees different dimensions of pragmatism ranging from the belief in science (the scientific/experimental method), to the role of religion, to the roles of the individual and society. The founders and advocates of pragmatism mirrored their European counterparts, hailing from middle- to upper-class backgrounds, with a range of religious beliefs (from Catholicism to mysticism) and with the privilege of an education. Collectively, they supported, held, and sustained the dominant belief that intelligence and morals were inheritable, White men were superior to all other humans, science could lead to truth, and scientific study was needed in order to perfect society. The contributions and influence of each pragmatist collectively are myriad, but what becomes clear in a larger sense is not just their advocacy of pragmatism but their position as intellectuals, which empowered them, or gave them license, to address and enter the broader public debates on issues that included philosophy as well as politics and education.

Pragmatism

Pragmatism was a response by philosophers to the rapidly evolving political, economic, and social systems, although there are significant differences in the application and emphasis of pragmatism among its most ardent advocates, Peirce, James, and Dewey. Each man aligned philosophy with evolutionary science and the scientific method, albeit Dewey worked against the ideology of scientism.

Other pragmatists at home and abroad (i.e., Lewis, Mead, Papini, Royce, and Schiller) also were important figures but are not discussed in this chapter.

Pragmatism/Pragmaticism

Charles Sanders Peirce (1839–1914) is credited as the founder of American pragmatism and the cofounder of semiotics. His philosophy of pragmatism began to appear in the late 1860s, in discussions with members of the "Metaphysical Club" (a play on words because the members did not believe in metaphysics) in Cambridge, Massachusetts. He recalled, "Wright, James, and I were men of science, rather scrutinizing the doctrines of the metaphysicians on their scientific side … Our thought was decidedly British, … and even my ideas were acquiring the British accent" (Peirce, quoted in Hartshorne, Weiss, & Burks, 1934, p. v). Peirce's pragmatism was inspired by the work of Kant and Darwin as well as Berkeley, Herbart, and Spinoza. He believed that philosophy ought to be more like the hard sciences, that it should "proceed nobly from tangible premises which can be subjected to careful scrutiny, and to trust rather to the multitude and variety of its arguments than to the conclusiveness of one" (Peirce, 1868b, p. 141). From these meetings, Peirce was inspired to write, "We individually cannot hope to attain the ultimate philosophy which we pursue; we can only seek it for the community of philosophers" (1868b, p. 40), a position he maintained throughout his career.

Peirce's thoughts were first published in a six-part series titled "Illustrations of the Logic of Science," in *Popular Science Monthly* (1877–1878). In these articles, he drew heavily from his reading of Bacon and Darwin in the explication of his thinking as well as from his experiences as a chemist. His work in laboratories also informed his thinking although he did not admit such until 1905, when he wrote, "Every master in any department of experimental science, has had his mind molded by his life in the laboratory to a degree that is little suspected" (p. 161). From this series of articles, he declared that his purpose was "to describe the method of scientific" (p. 13). He held that the controversy over Darwin's ideas could be explained through logic.

Peirce's (1877) first article, "Fixation of Belief," is the most often cited. Its popularity stems from Peirce's ability to articulate his support of the scientific method as the only means by which to remove doubt and to form beliefs that become a habit of action. He argued, "Our beliefs guide our desires and shape our actions. The feeling of believing is a more or less sure indication of there being established in our nature some habit which will determine our actions" (p. 5). In his thinking, concepts were hypotheses that needed to be tested through experimentation. He maintained that if the scientific method were followed, eventually all inquirers would come to the same conclusion:

> [The fundamental hypothesis of science is] there are Real things, whose characters are entirely independent of our opinions about them; those Reals affect our senses according to regular laws, and, though our sensations are as different as are our relations to the objects, yet, by taking advantage of the laws of perception we can ascertain by reasoning how things really and truly are; and any man, if he have sufficient experience and he reason [sic] about it, will be led to the one True conclusion. (Peirce, 1877, p. 11)

In this way, Peirce drew a connection between what he calls the "fixation of belief" and the scientific method. He believed that the best way (of the four he described) to clarify hypotheses was through the scientific method. Although not a positivist, Peirce admired positivism's strength in the scientific method and acknowledged its weakness in religion. He argued "the scientific spirit requires a man to be at all time ready to dump with whole cart-load of beliefs, the moment experience is against them" (p. 24). He continued his critique of positivism, noting "experience can never result in absolute certainty, exactitude, necessity, or universality" (p. 24). Peirce suggested that tenacity breaks down in practice because of man's social nature, that is, in his struggle to reconcile his belief with a community of scholars. Therefore, in reality, it is the fixation of belief in a community that needs to be assured. The community thus becomes the authority; however, not even the community can fix all beliefs. For Peirce, truth became that which is agreed on (or could eventually be agreed on by a community of inquirers).

In his second article, "How to Make Our Ideas Clear," Peirce (1878b) used the word *pragmatism* for the first time. He described the conduct/rules of scientific engagement this way:

> But the soul and meaning of thought abstracted from the other elements which accompany it, though it may be voluntarily thwarted, can never be made to direct itself toward anything but the production of belief ... To develop its meaning, we have therefore, simply to determine what habits

it produces, for what a thing means is simply what habits it involves. (pp. 286–287)

His ideas are similar to the process of reasoning from a premise to a conclusion. Next, he explained, "The essence of belief is the establishment of a habit, and different beliefs are distinguished by the different modes of action to which they give rise" (p. 287). For Peirce, pragmatism was the clarification of the meanings of ideas (a human intellectual conception) to discover general truths. He maintained that the best way to clarify concerns was to use the scientific method to "consider what effects, that might conceivably have practical bearings, we conceive the object of our conception to have" (p. 290). Meanings are derived from the use of methods in a prescribed way to clarify concepts that might appear at odds because they are perceived differently. Futhermore, Peirce endorsed the scientific method as the only viable way to discover the truth of ideas. As he articulated,

> This great hope is embodied in the conception of truth and reality. The opinion which is fated to be ultimately agreed to by all who investigate, is what we mean by the truth, and the object represented in this opinion is the real. (p. 300, emphasis in the original)

This statement is more commonly known as Peirce's consensual theory of truth. His theory can be interpreted in two ways: (a) "Truth" depends on agreement of the community of inquirers, or (b)"truth" is the effect of the real that produces agreement among inquirers. He claimed that contemporary notions of science envisioned it as "a mode of life; not knowledge, but the devoted, well-considered life pursuit of knowledge" (Peirce, 1901, pp. 694–695). His observations affirmed the influence, strength, and acceptance of science, scientific knowledge, and scientism in the United States.

As innovative as Peirce's philosophic assumptions were, they fell on either an unknowing or uncaring public. It was 20 years later—when William James used them as a springboard for his thoughts on pragmatism in his 1898 lecture at the University of California—that they were widely heralded as groundbreaking. James delivered his thoughts on Peirce's philosophy of pragmatism during a lecture before the Philosophical Union at the University of California on August 26, 1898 (later printed in *The University Chronicle*). Giving full acknowledgment of Peirce's contribution to advancing American philosophical thought, James reviewed Peirce's ideas and discussed his own. It was James' thoughts on pragmatism that were accepted and popularized; his version of pragmatism was more individually, socially, and morally centered.

Peirce's response to the popularization of James' version of pragmatism was a 1905 article titled "What Pragmatism Is," in which he claimed credit for the philosophy. Although James was a close personal friend, Peirce steadfastly maintained that James never understood pragmatism. Therefore, Peirce renamed his version *pragmaticism* to distinguish it from others, chiefly James's. He reasoned that his new name was "a word so ugly that it was safe from kidnappers" (Peirce, 1905, p. 165). He claimed, "If one can define accurately all the conceivable experimental phenomena which affirmation or denial of a concept could imply, one will have therein a complete definition of the concept" (p. 161). Peirce understood pragmatism as a theory of meaning, a theory of truth, and a methodology.

Jamesean Pragmatism

William James (1842–1910) was a member of the Metaphysical Club in Cambridge that included Peirce, Holmes, and Royce, among others. In his autobiography, he recalled not having heard the word *psychology* until he was asked to teach a course on psychology.

James's thoughts on pragmatism were delivered in a series of eight lectures published in the *Journal of Philosophy* and *Psychology and Scientific Methods,* beginning in 1904 with a reprint of his 1898 lecture. In these series, he compared his version of pragmatism to Peirce's and declared, "The ultimate test for us of what a truth means is indeed the conduct it debates or inspires" (James, 1898/1904, p. 674). He argued, "The effective meaning of any philosophic proposition can always be brought down to some particular consequence ... the point lying rather in the act that the experience must be particular, than in the fact that it must be active" (p. 674). James' version of pragmatism included a theory of truth, meaning, and knowledge.

Two key elements anchor his ideas: the pragmatic method and the genetic theory of truth (James, 1907a). To use the pragmatic method, James claimed that one must "try to interpret each notion by tracing its respective practical consequences ... If no practical difference whatever can be traced, then the alternatives mean practically the same thing, and all dispute is idle" (p. 18). He saw the pragmatic method as "less as a solution, ... than as a program of more work, and more particularly as an indication of the ways in which existing realities may be changed" (p. 53). In his 1907 article, "Pragmatism's Conception of Truth," his concept of a genetic theory of truth is revealed:

> The truth of an idea is not a stagnant property inherent in it. Truth *happens* to an idea. It *becomes* true, is *made* true by events. Its verity is *in fact an event, a process: the process namely of its verifying itself, its verification. Its validity is the process of its valid-ation. (James, 1907a, pp. 77–78, italics in the original)

Much like biological determinists, James held that ideas survived and were improved on. Importantly, he argued, "*True ideas are those that we can validate, corroborate, and verify. False ideas are those that we can not*" (James, 1907b, p. 142, italics in the original). In other words, ideas are hypotheses and can be true, in relation to other ideas, only if they work. James also believed, unlike Peirce, in the role of the individual as well as the role of experience and observation in establishing reality. He explained, "Knowledge is made; and made by relations that unroll themselves in time" (p. 29, italics in the original). Although a supporter of science, he realized that philosophy was a human invention and, therefore, susceptible to human mistakes and misleading.

Darwin's influence on his thinking is most apparent, as James (1900) observed that man evolved from nonhuman life forms and adapted to the changing environment to survive. Bredo (2002) expounded on the influence of Darwin on James by suggesting, "James finds a way of including moral and religious phenomena within a scientifically respectable account, as a way of placing science within a broader view of human life" (p. 3).

James' educational training in Europe and his own wealthy and privileged background doubtless influenced his opinion that the aristocracy and wealthy should become the future leaders. In U.S. society, for example, he believed that the college educated were a privileged class, superior to all others, as evinced in comments he made in a 1908 address given at Radcliffe College titled, "The Social Value of the College-Bred." Despite his attempt to create a U.S. aristocracy from the college educated, James became popular in England, where he was invited to give the Gifford Lectures. His presentations were later published as *The Varieties of Religious Experience* (1902) in which he discussed religion and notions of truth as he reflected on his personal struggle with both. He sensed the convergence of science and religion and offered a strong affirmation of scientism: "Our esteem for facts has not neutralized in us all cognition religiousness. It is itself almost religious. Our scientific temper is devout" (James, 1909, pp. 15–16). Although not a positivist, James sounded much like Comte in his hope for an improved society where an individual should be a scientifically educated man who embodied self-control and millions of such individuals would produce a society of order, a society where men would choose to do the good, moral, right thing. Furthermore, James believed that schools had the opportunity to establish correct habits in life, built on the interests of the child, including self-control.

James (1899) published a series of addresses given in the Cambridge, Massachusetts, area titled *Talks to Teachers on Psychology: And to Students on Some of Life's Ideals.* The text was reportedly the most widely read book on psychology of its era. Curti (1935) claimed, "It has been estimated that nine-tenths of the teachers who studied psychology at all in the years between 1890 and 1910 read James" (p. 443). In reference to teaching, James (1899) wrote, "Psychology is a science, and teaching is an art; and sciences never generate arts directly out of themselves. An intermediary inventive mind must make the application by using its originality" (p. 23). Furthermore, he noted,

> A science only lays down the lines in which art must fall, laws which the follower of the art must not transgress … Everywhere, teaching must agree with psychology. … to know psychology … is absolutely no guarantee that we shall be good teachers. (James, 1900, p. 9)

Given his pragmatic stance, James (1899) argued, "Education … cannot be better described than by calling it *the organization of acquired habits of conduct and tendencies to behavior*" (p. 29, italics in the original). In a later edition of a book by the same title, he implored teachers to adopt "the biological conception" (p. 25). James (1900) cautioned teachers not to think that "Psychology, being the science of the mind's laws, is something firm which you can deduce programmes and schemes and methods of instruction for immediate schoolroom use" (pp. 7–8). He believed that teachers must address the needs of the child before them—be perceptive, conscious, and ingenious—characteristics, attitudes, and behaviors that cannot be learned from psychology. James also endorsed habit formation in learning, the biological basis of mental development, fitting the child to his or her environment, and the natural order of social stratification. In general, he supported an association of ideas approach to education:

> Begin with the line of his native interests, and offer him objects that have some immediate connection with these. … Connect with the first objects and experiences the later objects and ideas which you wish to instill. Associate the new with the old in some telling way. (p. 96)

The idea is key to understanding notions associated with concepts about reading comprehension espoused by James.

James (1900) declared that new knowledge gained during laboratory work in psychology was changing how reading was understood. He dedicated an entire chapter to the discussion of apperception, and deconstructs the concept by examples to teachers. Initially, he explained it as "the process by which we acquire new knowledge,— the process of 'Apperception,' as it is called, by which we receive and deal with new experiences, and revise our stock of ideas so as to form new or improved conceptions" (p. 14). Then, oversimplifying the concept, he suggested that apperception is "nothing more than the manner in which we receive a thing into our minds" (p. 156). Finally, he clarified that apperception entailed

> every impression that comes in from without, be it a sentence which we hear, an object of vision, or an effluvium which assails our nose, no sooner enters our consciousness than it is drafted off in some determinate direction or other, making connection with the other materials already there, and finally producing what we call our reaction … It is the fate of every impression thus to fall into a mind preoccupied with memories, ideas, and interests, and by these it is taken in. (pp. 157–158)

As the discussion shifts more to comprehension, he noted, "When we listen to a person speaking or read a page of print, much of what we think we see or hear is supplied from our memory" (p. 159). James includes both supportive and critical comments about apperception shared by other writers. He wrote, for example, that several critics had suggested there are multiple ways to apperceive, resulting in innumerable types of apperception and that people could employ more than one type of apperception for the same event. James also noted that the swiftest readers were also the best at reproducing the text. His understanding of apperception as a psychological process, when applied to reading, resulted in what would later be labeled *reading comprehension.*

Deweyian Pragmatism/Instrumentalism

One of the most important and influential American philosophers of the 20th century was the pragmatist John Dewey (1859–1952). In many ways, his life epitomizes a cultural and social shift in educational research as more researchers, whose lives mirrored his, entered the profession with life experiences that called for a different shade of meaning and application of the dominant ideology. That is, his experiences allowed him closer contact and interaction with people who were experiencing the underlying struggle and resisting dominant ideologies.

Dewey's ideas drew from his academic training; he was thoroughly impressed by the thinking of Comte and Darwin. His thinking was shaped by his graduate work and membership in the National Herbart Society. At the encouragement of his wife, he also began to embrace the social and political issues of the nation that eventually became part of his idea of a "scientific method." His ideas of the scientific method were not scientific in any specific sense; they were aesthetic/moral/political in a general spirit of reformation. According to Karier (1986), Dewey's methods of experimentation in education were "anthropological if not historical" (p. 142). His ideas were, in fact, as political as they were scientific and suggest that he opposed some aspects of scientism. For example, he declared,

> There is something both ridiculous and disconcerting in the way in which men have let themselves be imposed upon; so as to infer that scientific ways of thinking of objects give the inner reality of things, and that they put a mark of spuriousness upon all other ways of thinking them, and of perceiving and enjoying them. It is ludicrous because these scientific conceptions, like other instruments, are hand-made by man in pursuit of realization of a certain interest. (Dewey, 1929a, p. 135)

In 1894, Dewey accepted a position at the University of Chicago and later was named chair of the department of philosophy, psychology, and pedagogy. While at Chicago, his interests in social concerns were reignited as he saw more clearly the effects of racial and social differences in the lives of people. For instance, Dewey was particularly taken by the events surrounding the Pullman porters' strike and President Cleveland's deployment of federal troops. Dewey's sense of social activism also was enhanced by his work with Jane Addam's Hull House and Colonel Francis Parker's (1901) Cook County Normal School. Later, Dewey established the University of Chicago's Laboratory Schools (1896) as a place where he could experiment with the educational curriculum, the social origins of knowledge, and schools as democratic units. After a strong disagreement about the Laboratory School, Dewey left the University of Chicago to join the faculty at Columbia, where he remained for the rest of his academic career.

Dewey's application of pragmatism, known as instrumentalism was far more personal, realistic, and considerate of the individual as well as the freedom of thought an individual might bring to the learning experience. Dewey's understanding of pragmatism led him to his own version, known as instrumentalism. He believed that science was rationalized knowledge, "Scientific subject matter is organized with specific reference to the successful conduct of the enterprise of discovery, to knowing as a specialized undertaking" (1900, p. 190). Continuing, he declared, "All information and systematized scientific subject matter have been worked out under the conditions of social life and have been transmitted by social means" (p. 190). In this way, he illustrated how social circumstances affect, and are affected by, science, as well as his hope that science would lead to social improvements.

This was a position he defended in his famous 1922 essay, "The Development of American Pragmatism," in which he wrote, "Pragmatism ... does not insist upon antecedent phenomena but upon consequent phenomena; not upon the precedents but upon the possibilities of action. And this change in point of view is almost revolutionary in its consequences" (1922, p. 24). For Dewey, ideas were tools or instruments in the solution of problems that were encountered in nature (or the environment), leading to empowerment. On the one hand, Dewey attempted to apply the methods of the science to philosophy while he acknowledged the need to deal with broader contexts. Like Comte, Darwin, and James, Dewey argued that mankind would one day be empowered (control society) through the intelligent use of science. He envisioned science as one of the means to help mankind evolve toward perfection. On the other hand, like Peirce, he cautioned that the ideas (hypotheses) were man-made and should be understood as such.

Like James, Dewey struggled with religious beliefs and their connection to science. In his 1929 text, *The Sources of a Science of Education*, Dewey clarified his thinking about how science, complete with its goal of deriving laws and facts, must not lose sight of the human factors in education: "The final reality of education science is not found in books, nor in experimental laboratories, nor in the classrooms where it is taught, but in the minds of those engaged in directing educational activities" (1929b, p. 32). He noted that by observing the developmental thinking processes of children as they approached problems, scientists could discover how thoughts evolved, heralding the virtues of the scientific method in education because it "attaches more importance, not less, to ideas as ideas than do other methods. ... The fact the ideas employed are hypotheses, not final truths, is the reason why ideas are more jealously guarded and tested in science" (Dewey, 1938a, p. 86). Dewey's thinking called for careful observations throughout experimentation and beyond, followed by documentation of new ideas and reflections on the process. He believed that educators needed "to view teaching and learning as a continuous process of reconstruction of experience" (p. 37). Dewey maintained that the future of society lay in a well-developed educational plan for the nation. He envisioned schools as miniature communities in which children could learn to act in a democratic manner. In his ideal world, tests were not required and students were not categorized based on test performance. Like James, he believed that the "child is the starting point, the center, and the end. His development, his growth, is the ideal. It alone furnishes the standard" (Dewey, 1902, p. 187).

This was a position he defended in his famous essay, "The development of American pragmatism." Dewey's other beliefs about and methods for education were captured in a number of books, most notably, *School and Society* (1899/1900), *The Child and the Curriculum* (1902), *How We Think* (1910), and *Democracy and Education* (1916/1944). He acknowledged that the philosophical foundations of U.S. education were indebted to philosophies from Europe and implied there was a close connection between philosophies used in U.S. education and those in Europe. His thinking is insightful with regards to hegemony and how ideas become part of the dominant ideologies of society.

He held that science was not as much the replication of hard science as it was aesthetic, moral, and political. He understood the interrelationship among philosophy, positivism, and education as follows: "Positive science always implies *practically* the ends which the community is concerned to achieve. … Education is the laboratory in which philosophic distinctions become concrete and tested" (Dewey, 1944, p. 329). Furthermore, Dewey believed that real learning was an active process that occurred when there was a problem to be solved and suggested a five-step process that replicated the scientific method. He envisioned a general spirit of reformation through experience as the essence of science:

> 1) Experience is primarily an active-passive affair; it is not primarily cognitive. But 2) the measure of the value of an experience lies in the perception of relationships or continuities to which it leads up. It includes cognition in the degree to which it is cumulative or amounts to something, or has meaning. (Dewey, 1944, p. 140)

He used similar ideas about the importance of experience in his thoughts on education and curriculum reform.

Dewey's thoughts on instruction, for example, center on the importance of activities and experiences that are of interest to the student and includes continual reflection. The teacher's role is to recognize the potential in the activity or experience where a student encounters a genuine problem, and has been given enough information to solve the problem and an opportunity to do so. In short, he believed that children learned by doing, which he understood as analogous to the scientific method used by scientific experts Moreover, he fervently believed that the nation needed an educated citizenry and public schools were needed to supply such. Living during the Progressive era he claimed, "Under present conditions, all activity, to be successful, has to be directed somewhere and somehow by the scientific expert … the scientific insight thus gained becomes an indispensable instrument of free and active participation in modern social life" (Dewey, 1899/1900, p. 23).

Reading, Dewey believed, was an activity that should be taught successfully from the primary grades onward. Here are his ideas for enhancing reading instruction:

> The child who has a variety of materials and facts wants to talk about them, and his language becomes more refined and full, because it is controlled and informed by realities. Reading and writing, as well as the oral use of language, may be taught on this basis. It can be done in related way, as the outgrowth of the child's social desire to recount his experiences and get in return the experiences of others, directed always through contact with the facts and forces which determine the truth communicated. (1944, p. 56)

Dewey objected to the use of reading lessons that focused on phonics practices and other unconnected drills. He thought that reading should occur more naturally. And, he detested the use of books as lessons in the subject of reading. He argued,

> A method is ethically defective that, while giving the child a glibness in the mechanical facility of reading, leaves him at the mercy of suggestion and chance environment to decide whether he reads the "yellow journal," the trashy novel, or the literature which inspires and makes more valid his whole life. Is it any less certain that this failure on the ethical side is repeated in some lack of adequate growth and connection in the psychical and physiological factors involved? (1944, p. 116)

Furthermore, Dewey believed in the importance of attending to the needs and interests of children as young readers:

> The qualities of seen and touched things have a bearing on what is done, and are alertly perceived; they have a meaning. But when pupils are expected to use their eyes to note the form of words, irrespective of their meaning, in order to reproduce them in spelling or reading, the resulting training is simply of isolated sense organs and muscles. It is such isolation of an act from a purpose which makes it mechanical. It is customary for teachers to urge children to read with expression, so as to bring out the meaning. But if they originally learned the sensory-motor technique of reading—the ability to identify forms and to reproduce the sounds they stand for—by methods which did not call for attention to meaning, a mechanical habit was established which makes it difficult to read subsequently with intelligence. (1944, pp. 142–143)

His thinking about reading demonstrates that pragmatists voiced concern about philosophical as well as practical aspects of education and the need to comprehend what is read.

Scientism, Psychologism, and Racism in U.S. Educational Research

The false prophets of western Europe and their U.S. counterparts espoused certain "truths" or philosophical assumptions: faith in science to replace, or at least supplant, a faith in an all-knowing God; faith in (White) men and their knowledge and intellect to use science to improve humankind; faith in the ability of (White) men to use science to control, predict, perfect, and conquer the environment and society; faith in the process of science and the scientific/experimental method to discover "truths," theories, and laws of nature and society; faith that the scientific method creates "facts" based on nonemotional, nonevaluative, unbiased observations; an application of scientific methods to the study of human behavior and social phenomena; the use of general laws drawn from scientific inquiry to predict human behavior; the inheritability of behaviors, intellect, and morals that are racially determined (with Whites being the superior race); and the use of science to explain social stratification (sans economics, culture, society, gender, race, religion). The last two assumptions—the inheritability of intelligence and morals and an unchangeable world order and social structure—have been used as a very thin, yet translucent, covering to justify inequalities. As Anderson (1988) observed

> The successful campaign to contain and repress literacy among enslaved Americans triumphed just as the crusade for popular education for free people began to flourish. Between 1800 and 1835, most southern states enacted legislation making it a crime to teach enslaved child to read or write. In contrast, a massive campaign to achieve popular schooling for free [White] Americans developed between 1830 and 1860. (p. 2)

By this time, U.S. educational research was embedded in scientism, psychologism, and racism. African American scholars, activists, and authors historically have expressed their ideas as counter discourses to those espoused by Whites. David Walker's (1830) protestations, or Olaudah Equiano's (1899/1995) narrative, or Phillis Wheatley's (1773/1972) to poetry are testaments to a very different view of life in the colonies. Frederick Douglass (1881), for example, depicted the power racism conveyed in the lives of Whites as part of the dominant ideology in the United States:

> Slavery had the power at one time to make and unmake Presidents, to construe the law, dictate the policy, set the fashion in national manners and customs, interpret the Bible, and control the church; and, naturally enough, the old masters set themselves up as much too high as they set the manhood of the negro too low. Out of the depths of slavery has come this prejudice and this color line … . Slavery is indeed gone, but its shadow still lingers over the country and poisons more or less the moral atmosphere of all sections of the republic. The money motive for assailing the negro which slavery represented is indeed absent, but love of power and dominion, strengthened by two centuries of irresponsible power, still remains. (p. 573)

Jorgensen (1995) translates Douglass' understanding of White supremacy into four tenets, noting that "oppressors must always find a way to scientifically and morally justify their oppression" (p. 235). African Americans were not passive receptors of their oppression; their terrain of struggle was as much ideological as it was physical, psychological, and emotional; to resist oppression, they used their activism, scholarship, and literary works.

As a former slave, Douglass understood that Whites envisioned physical violence as well as psychological terror as forms of power over African Americans. He also believed that Whites regarded slaves as sources of economic wealth. But, perhaps more importantly, he understood that to deny slaves the opportunity to learn to read also was a form of power that would keep them from expressing and publishing thoughts that ran contrary to those of their oppressors, for if actual accounts were preserved, their sins would eternally be recorded. Although Douglass was self-taught, he was literate and in a comment often ascribed to him, he reportedly stated, "Once you learn to read you will be forever free." He also was aware and often implied that most slaves were adept at reading their circumstances; that is, they knew and understood how to interpret the signs and symbols of their world. This type of reading of the world was necessary in order to survive being captured and subjugated to slavery in the United States. He implied that scholastic literate abilities were additional skills for those who had already learned to read the world. The lives, work, and activism of Anna Julia (Haywood) Cooper and W. E. B. Du Bois represent scholars who expressed ideas that ran counter to the dominant ideology and who supported a counter hegemony. In general, as members of a subordinate class, they reflect political, social, and economic positions that critique and demystify the ideas, beliefs, values, and practices of the dominant groups.

The Counter Hegemony of African American Scholars and Activists

According to Hall (2003), it is important to offer "practical as well as theoretical knowledges [sic] which enable people to 'figure out' society" (p. 27). His idea is especially relevant to people of color who historically have had their lives and experiences written about by Whites who sought to offer "objective positioning in social relations" (p. 27), but more often reified stereotypes. Because the dominant classes have historicized the foundation of educational thought, understanding the counter hegemony expressed by African Americans requires a review and description of some critical events around the turn of the century. These are thoughts that help to contextualize oppression in the United States and highlights how the philosophical assumptions (mentioned earlier) influenced our place in society. Although not presented as seamlessly as the events occurred, their conclusion helps to explain how U.S. educational thought and research has been shaped by dominant ideologies. The thinking of these scholars and their actions, along with those of unnamed others, passionately challenged philosophical assumptions that supported scientism (as limitless, unbiased, and universal) as they pointed to its racism. Their thoughts and ideas also foreground similar counter discourses in response to the dominant ideology throughout U.S. history and the history of U.S. education.

Historical Overview

The uniqueness of the African Americans, in the eyes of some Euro-Americans, has been their inability to assimilate into the American mainstream. The problem of assimilation was not theirs but society's. Language and customs, the two most frequently cited reasons preventing their attempts to assimilate into American life, were not problems for most African Americans by the 1900s. For instance, African Americans had been forced to forego their native languages and learn the language of their captors (Dutch, English, French, etc.) generally no other language barriers, (except for special cases in some southern locations, e.g., South Carolina, where Gullah is spoken and in Louisiana where French Creole is spoken). The argument for the failure of African Americans to assimilate into the U.S. cultural mainstream is a rhetorical excuse to hide more racist assumptions, mentioned earlier in this chapter, about the humanity of people of African descent. African Americans were not afforded equal access to educational, social, economic, or political opportunities based on race more often than class. A more accurate reason for the lack of assimilation was that laws and customs prevented African Americans from gaining equal access to educational, social, economic, or political opportunities based on race, or the color of their skin.

After the Civil War, the nation was in search of an identity when the Thirteenth Amendment (1865), the Fourteen Amendment (1868), and the Fifteenth Amendment (1870) freed African Americans from legal slavery and guaranteed due process and voting rights, respectively. In addition, the Civil Rights Act of 1875 granted access to all public accommodations, but this act was overturned. Without government enforcement, however, Jim/Jane Crow laws quickly replaced these amendments. Among the reasons given for its defeat was Prudential Insurance statistician Frederick L. Hoffman's (1896) paper "Race Traits and Tendencies of the American Negro." He argued that through indisputable science, he found that African Americans were a weaker people and would eventually become extinct. His paper influenced the U.S. Supreme Court decision in the 1896 *Plessy v. Ferguson* case that legalized segregation and supported Jim/Jane Crow laws (laws that were based on traditions and customs of racial prejudice and discrimination that are still with us).

These actions helped to deny voting rights to African Americans where the right to vote was circumvented by requirements of poll taxes, grandfather clauses, and literacy tests that most African Americans were unable to meet having been denied access to citizenship and literacy for centuries. The attacks on African Americans were most clearly illustrated in 1892, when journalist Ida B. Wells published *Southern Horrors* in which she declared, "More than 70 percent of the lynchings occurred when the victims tried to vote, demanded their rights, purchased land, or owned successful businesses" (cited in Ruffins & Ruffins, 1997, p. 25). (Only recently, on June 13, 2005, did the U.S. Senate apologize for ignoring the government's inaction toward lynching.) Despite centuries of the untold horrors of slavery, by the early 1900s most African Americans were native born and had begun to migrate from rural southern areas to large northern industrial cities: Boston, New York, Cincinnati, Philadelphia, Chicago, and Kansas City. As emigrants, they were the "other" Americans. In addition, Anderson (1988) notes that concerns about race "set the stage for a bitter national debate about the social purposes of black education" (p. 3). As a group, African Americans were most often educated in separate schools.

The power of literacy to liberate one's thinking was recognized early in this country as laws were established and enforced that forbade African Americans from being taught to read. There were numerous brave Blacks and Whites that defied these laws and offered some literacy instruction to slaves and freed Blacks. After the Civil War, many schools for African Americans were established throughout the South where education was synonymous with literacy (Anderson, 1995). Morris (1981) for instance, described one such gallant effort in the Freedman's schools, where literacy was such a key component of the curriculum that specific books were printed for instruction. The history of literacy at Calhoun Colored School 1892–1945 (Willis, 2002) explores one such rural African American community. This school, like thousands of others established for African Americans throughout the rural South, offered the rudiments of an elementary education along with vocational training. The unique 8-year program took 12 years to complete, in part to discourage African Americans from leaving the South, where entire families were sources of labor for wealthy Whites. Some of these schools were privately owned and managed by African Americans in the community, others were supported by philanthropic organizations and still others were public yet received meager state and federal funding. White and African American teachers staffed these schools, most of which were inferior to their White counterparts.

Smith (1972) described this period in his investigation of educational opportunities for native Blacks and foreign Whites from 1880 to 1950. He argued that the wide gap between the school performance of the children of former slaves and the children of the more recent immigrants was deeply rooted in the racial attitudes and prejudices that hampered the education of both groups more than their desire to obtain an education. He found that the differences in performance centered on "the sharply divergent set of rewards which racially prejudiced urban societies provided those who stayed in school" (p. 335). His findings are in opposition to the dominant ideology that focused on the inheritability of intelligence over contexts. In contemporary urban centers, Smith's findings continue to ring true.

The opposition to misrepresentations of historical, political, and social realties is represented in the writing and advocacy of Anna Julia (Haywood) Cooper and W. E. B. Du Bois. Although their position stands in opposition to the racism and scientism of the dominant ideology, there are other aspects of the dominant ideology that are reflective of living in the United States, such as valuing education and upward mobility. What sets their ideas apart is that they were able to remove the veil that hid the privileged status of the dominant groups to argue for equal rights to be extended to all.

African American Scholars

The racially and culturally distinctive thinking and social activism of African American scholars helped supply intellectual leadership to African American people as well as to progressive Whites without parallel. They were consciously aware of rapidly shifting social, political, and economic contexts of their day that held them, and all people of color, in an inferior social status. In addition, they distrusted the "scientific" research that purported their inferior intellectual and moral status. They challenged the use of science as "proof" of racial, intellectual, and moral inferiority by acknowledging broader historical, cultural, and intellectual lineages than those of their White peers. Finally, they resisted the power of White Americans to define the lives, intellect, and morality of African Americans.

Anna Julia Cooper, the mother of Black Feminism, is representative of the thinking among African American women during the post-Reconstruction era and into the early 20th century. Her writing provides contemporaneous commentary to the common sense rhetoric of her White American male counterparts.

A Voice From the South   Anna Julia Cooper (1858–1967) the daughter of a slave, Hannah Stanley Haywood, and the slave master, unlike most African American girls, attended the St. Augustine Normal School and Collegiate Institute. As an African American woman living in the South, Cooper's life experiences and understanding of U.S. intellectual and cultural hegemony propelled her to change the course of events through education. An outspoken critic of both racial and gender discrimination in the United States, Cooper believed that as an African American woman and intellectual, she had a voice that needed to be heard in the cacophony of voices on both issues.

Cooper's thinking was poignantly stated in her famous book *A Voice from the South: By a Black Woman of the South*, published in 1892. *A Voice From the South* is a collection of essays and speeches written by Cooper between 1886 and 1892. Her style, clear and direct, portrays the interconnectedness and complexity of religion, race, gender, and class concerns of African Americans. She draws from her knowledge and understanding of world history, literature, philosophy, sociology, and personal experience to ground her thinking and writing. Throughout her life, she remained fiercely loyal to improving the educational opportunities of African Americans. Yet, she never left her first love, Christ; she valued her religious commitment and her Christian beliefs as is evident throughout her writings that are filled with Biblical allusions.

Cooper (1892) fearlessly fought for the rights of women when she asked, "Why should woman become plaintiff in a suit versus the Indian, or the Negro or any other race or class who have been crushed under the iron heel of Anglo-Saxon power and selfishness?" (p. 88). She possessed an attitude that questioned interpretations of women's ability to bring about results and the usefulness of their voices in society. Aware of discrimination, marginalization, and silencing of the voices of African American women within the women's movement, she also attacked their injustices and hypocrisy and noted the uniqueness of her position as an African American woman who is "confronted by both a woman question and a race question" (p. 51). In addition, she acknowledged differences and complexities between the positions of African American women and men. For instance, she believed that African American men were archaic in their understanding and acknowledgment of the plight of African American women.

Writing years before Du Bois' famous references to second sight and moving beyond the veil, Cooper boldly placed the history of African Americans on the world stage alongside the histories of Europeans and White Americans with an understanding that the African American experience in the United States was in its infancy. Nonetheless, she displayed little patience for the constant assault on racial, intellectual, and moral inferiority in the name of science.

She claimed that "scientific" notions of racial, intellectual, and moral superiority were presented without any evidence or verification. With regard to issues of race and intelligence, Cooper did not find a community of inquirers seeking truth as suggested by Peirce. She found particularly abhorrent a growing national secularism and racist predispositions that attracted some researchers and educators to "scientific" theories. Decisively, she dismissed all theories as she recalled an old proverb, "The devil is always painted *black*—by White painters" (Cooper, 1892, p. 159, emphasis in the original). Furthermore, she understood the hegemonic process that encouraged scientific racism:

> Whatever notions we may indulge on the theory of evolution and the laws of atavism or heredity, all concede that no individual character receives its raw material newly created and independent of the rock from when

it was hewn. ... The materials that go to make the man, the probabilities of his character and activities, at the conditions and the circumstances of his growth, and his quantum resistance and mastery are the resultant of forces which have been accumulation and gathering momentum for generations. (p. 164)

Cooper found particularly repugnant the use of scientific generalizations and the acceptance of opinions as facts that were used by scientists, White women advocates, academics, and politicians to continue the oppression of African Americans. She believed that scientism reflected "the pride, the selfishness, the prejudices, the exclusiveness, the bigotry and intolerance, the conceit of self, of race, or of family superiority" (p. 131) of most Whites. She claimed that people who held these ideas as facts were often those who tried to distinguish themselves based on their race, class, or gender as well as the new science that allowed them to claim dominance by inheritance.

Cooper noticed that science had become, in the minds and lives of some, a god, one that they worshipped, one that they hoped would lead them to all truth, and one that she could not accept. She called into question and rebuked Comte, Spencer, and Darwin for their rebellion against an all-knowing God and against His power of creation. In her commentary, she wrote, "and as for God—science finds him not. ... Man has simply projected his own personality into space and worshipped it as a God—a person—himself" (p. 189). Likewise, she boldly disputed the dominant ideology replete with its philosophical debates:

To me, faith means *treating the truth as true.* Jesus *believed* that in the infinite possibilities of an individual soul. His faith was a triumphant realization of the eternal development of the best in man—an optimistic vision of the human aptitude for endless expansion and perfectibility. (pp. 193–194, italics in the original)

Cooper's voice continues to ring throughout the ages as an African American feminist who challenged the ignorance, sexism, and racism of her day.

Exposing the Soul of Black Folks   William Edward Burghardt Du Bois, sociologist, historian, journalist, and philosopher, articulated a conception of pragmatism that forced discussions on race to the forefront and provided opportunities for the voices of African Americans to be heard. West (1989) observes that Du Bois' unique contribution to pragmatism "illustrates the blindness and silences in American pragmatists' reflections on individuality and democracy, not one viewed racism as contributing greatly to the impediments for both individuality and democracy" (pp. 146–147). Du Bois' academic life spanned over 60 years, not all of which can be reviewed here. Some of his views are included as a contemporaneous, albeit alternative, point of view to the White males discussed earlier in this chapter. Nonetheless, some background information is helpful to situate his life within the period.

During his undergraduate studies at Fisk, Du Bois was introduced to pragmatism as espoused by William James. Excitedly he recalled, "Above all science was becoming religion; psychology was reducing metaphysics to experiment and a sociology of human action was planned" (Du Bois, 1940, p. 26). On completion of his undergraduate degree, Du Bois entered Harvard College in 1888, but was placed in his junior year. Undaunted, he considered it nothing short of miraculous to have an opportunity to study under William James. He also joined the Philosophical Club and communed with Hart, Palmer, Royce, and Santayana. He wrote:

> I hoped to pursue philosophy as my life career, with teaching for support. ... William James guided me out of the sterilities of scholastic philosophy to realist pragmatism. ... It was James with his pragmatism and Albert Busnell Hart with his research method, that turned me back from the lovely but sterile land of philosophic speculation, to the social sciences as the field for gathering and interpreting that body of fact which would apply to my program for the Negro. ... I conceived the idea of applying philosophy to an historical interpretation of race relations. (Du Bois, 1968, p. 148)

Given the temper of the time, his education focused on the use of science and the scientific method. Whereas he understood them as breakthroughs for conducting research, he also was able to see beyond the rhetoric to the uses of science, which he believed evinced an undercurrent of racism:

> I began to face scientific race dogma: first of all, evolution and the "Survival of the Fittest." It was continually stressed in the community and in classes that there was vast difference in the development of the Whites and the "lower" races; that this could be seen in the physical development of the Negro. I remember once in a museum, coming face to face with a demonstration: a series of skeletons arranged from a little monkey to a tall well-developed White man, with a Negro barely outranking a chimpanzee. (Du Bois, 1940, p. 98)

Du Bois (1940) observed that students were encouraged to consider which race was superior and learned that the White race, with a written history, was glorified as superior. Yet, he noted that other races, also with histories but not well recognized, were deemed inferior, especially Africans, who were taught as "without culture and without history" (p. 98). Of course, he knew better, and the history of African Americans was made more poignant as he struggled to reconcile the notions of biological and social determinism with democracy.

Du Bois thought the time was ripe for discussions of race, in contrast to the popularity of Spencer's social Darwinism and Galton's theories of the inheritability of intelligence advocated by dominant groups (beliefs that ignored historical, social, and cultural influences). He believed that what was missing in those theories was a comprehensive and affirmative history of the people of color in the world, especially African slaves and their progeny in the United States.

Du Bois was deeply troubled about the lynchings of African Americans, or what he called a "continuing and recurrent horror during my college days: from 1885 through 1894, seventeen hundred Negroes were lynched in America. Each death was a scar upon our soul, and led me to conceive the plight of other minority groups" (Du Bois, 1940, pp. 29–30). His concern with the plight of the African diaspora is reflected in his doctoral work where he applied the methods of historical and sociological study to his own ideas of race history and economy in his dissertation, *The Suppression of the African Slave Trade to the United States of America, 1638–1870* (published in 1896 as the first volume of the *Harvard Historical Studies Series).*

Afterward, in 1898, Du Bois accepted an assistant instructor position at the University of Pennsylvania. The position was fictional because Du Bois had no teaching duties and was not permitted on campus. He was hired to conduct a 1-year study of the African Americans in Philadelphia, because a certain faction of the White community believed that there was a crisis in the Negro community, known as the Seventh Ward. The result of his work was his 1899 publication *The Philadelphia Negro.* It was the first case study of an African American community and remains a classic in the discipline. Du Bois claimed that the problems of African Americans were not biological. White academicians, who believed otherwise, largely ignored Du Bois' findings. Reflectively, he wrote, "The Negro problem was in my mind a matter of systematic investigation and intel-

ligent understanding. The world was thinking wrong about race. ...
The ultimate evil was stupidity. The cure for it was knowledge based
on scientific investigation" (Du Bois, 1940, p. 58). His perspective
on the use of scientific inquiry was sociological and includes understanding and accounting for culture and contextual (economic,
social, political) forces. His thoughts were in stark contrast to the
scientism that gripped academicians in the late 1890s, and are worth
quoting at length:

> The best available methods of sociological research are at present so lia-
> ble to inaccuracies that the careful student discloses the results of indi-
> vidual research with diffidence; he knows that they are liable to error
> from the seemingly ineradicable faults of the statistical methods; to even
> greater error from the methods of general observation; and, above all,
> he must ever tremble lest some personal bias, some moral conviction or
> some unconscious trend of thought due to previous training, has to a
> degree distorted the picture in his view. Convictions on all great matters
> of human interest one must have a greater or less degree, and they will
> enter to some extent into the most cold-blooded scientific research as a
> disturbing factor. (1940, p. 59)

Du Bois explicated the history of people of African descent with
the reality of their lives in contemporary U.S. society. Later he
accepted a professorship in sociology at Atlanta University, where
he began a program called the "The Negro Problem" and produced
a series of papers, the *Atlanta University Publications*. Throughout
these publications, he applied historical and sociological means to
understand the social conditions of African Americans. In addition,
he extended and refined James' version of pragmatism toward African Americans living in the United States, where the idea of a free
will was limited by historical and societal conditions. Although he
acknowledged that power (political, economic, social, ideological)
was used by Whites to control and affect the lives of African Americans, he maintained that African Americans could reshape their
own, as well as the nation's, future.

Some of his ideas were best captured in his literary pursuits, for
example, *The Souls of Black Folks,* (1903). He began the work with an
appeal to the readers, especially White readers, to consider a different set of ideas:

> Herein lie buried many things which if read with patience may show the
> strange meaning of being black here at the dawning of the Twentieth Cen-
> tury. This meaning is not without interest, Genteel Reader; for the prob-
> lem of the Twentieth century is the problem of the color line. (p. xxxi)

This often-quoted passage suggested, prophetically, that in the 20th century there would be a struggle with race relations. Du Bois' desire to expose the world to a more comprehensive understanding of the African diaspora is also worth quoting at length:

> After the Egyptian and Indian, the Greek and the Roman, the Teuton and Mongolian, the Negro is a sort of seventh son, born with a veil, and gifted with second-sight in this American world—a world which yields him no true self-consciousness, but only lets him see himself through the revelation of the other world. It is a peculiar sensation, this double consciousness, this sense of always looking at one's self though the eyes of others, of measuring one's soul by the tape of a world that looks on in amused contempt and pity. One ever feels his two-ness—an American and a Negro; two souls, two thoughts, two unreconciled strivings; two warring ideals in one dark body, whose dogged strength alone keeps it from being torn asunder. (1987, pp. 2–3)

In this excerpt Du Bois' demonstrates awareness that there are other ways to think about the world.

His reference to the veil and second sightedness marks the African American experience as fundamentally different from the ideas expressed about African Americans by Whites. Du Bois articulated a humanity and cultural identity that challenged the stereotypical images presented by White American politicians, reformers, philosophers, scientists, and educators of the unintelligent, lazy, immoral subhuman. Because of Du Bois' awareness of the dominant ideology and the lack of interactions between most "scientists" and African Americans, he argued against the inhumanness of non-Whites that is bound in positivism, social Darwinism, and biological determinism: "The silently growing assumption of this age is that the probation of races is past, and that the backward races of today are the proven inefficient and not worth the saving" (1903, p. 186). His thinking explained understandings wrought from the oppression of life in the United States:

> He [the Negro] would not Africanize America, for America has too much to teach the world and Africa. He would not bleach his Negro soul in a flood of white Americanism, for he knows that Negro blood has a message for the world. He simply wishes to make it possible for a man to be both a Negro and an American. (p. 17)

Du Bois opined that education for African Americans was limited because of the fear of Whites that once the African Americans' consciousness was raised, their willingness to consent or to be coerced by the worldviews of others would dissipate. In effect, Whites would no longer be able to convince African Americans of their alleged inferior status as humans or of their alleged subservient place in the civilized world.

His desire for open conversations about race, for research on the topic, for social activism, and for political pressure were realized as he helped to establish the National Association for the Advancement of Colored People (NAACP). From the onset, this was an organization that included men and women, as well as Blacks and Whites. As editor and researcher (1910–1934) for the organization's magazine *The Crisis*, Du Bois was in a unique position to use his power and prestige to discuss his own political and social views of race, class, and gender.

What is important to remember here is that these counter discourses offered by Douglass, Cooper, and Du Bois reflect the thoughts of members of a subaltern group. Collectively, their thoughts presented a different set of ideas that claimed intelligence and morals were not inheritable, that White males were not superior to all other humans, and that science could not lead to truth. They argued unapologetically that society could not be perfected until racism was dealt with and defeated. However, without the accompanying political, economic, or social power to spread their ideas, these notions were limited to the African American community and like-minded Whites. The counter discourse of Douglas, Cooper and Du Bois is representative of alternative and oppositional worldviews that help us to make sense of our world. Further, their ideas encourage an alternative way of understanding the world and word; one that challenges dominant ideologies and fuels a tidal wave of oppositional theorizing. The next chapter explicates how social movements operated in concert with ideological hegemony to influence education at the onset of reading comprehension research. In addition, schoolbooks and teachers' manuals are reviewed as they also helped to reproduce and reinforce dominant ideologies as needful for reading comprehension and academic success in a meritocracy.

3

Reservoir of Themes and Premises
*Social Influences of Early Concepts
of Reading Comprehension*

To understand the impact of ideological hegemony is to consider its influence within society. According to Hall (2003), "Ideas only become effective if they do, in the end, connect with a particular constellation of social forces. In that sense, ideological struggle is a part of the general social struggle for mastery and leadership—or in short for hegemony" (p. 43). For example, building on notions of racial, gendered, intellectual, and moral superiority, the dominant group uses language or discourse to shape and name reality. This idea is evinced in the use of the term *Manifest Destiny*, mentioned in an earlier chapter, as the inalienable right of White males to conquer the land now known as the continental United States. The language used to label this idea is interesting and points to how language is used to mold or shape public opinion. Although some historians have used terms like *colonialism*, *imperialism*, and *nationalism* to describe the Manifest Destiny, another term, *terrorism*, also describes the process. It is an equally descriptive, albeit pejorative, term seldom used in reference to the United States or its national policies. In Gramscian terms the concept of Manifest Destiny, and the propaganda that supported it, were both fabricated and coerced. This example illustrates how dominant groups have used their access to institutions, such as the popular press, to promote their values and to reinforce their frames of reality, while disguising undercurrents of racism, classism, and power, it is a modus operandi we see repeated throughout history, including the history of reading comprehension research and testing.

This chapter helps to place reading comprehension research and testing within U.S. sociohistorical contexts in an overview of social movements and their connections between reading comprehension research and testing, and the struggle for meaning as scholars, researchers, and teachers apply their ideas of the process of understanding words to reading texts and reading performances. Included in this discussion are descriptions of readers, teachers, and textbooks written for African Americans. The documentation used in this chapter aligns with the work of Popkewitz and Tabachnick (1992), who argue that most histories of education obfuscate discussions of the "social and political events that provide the background for scientific practices" (p. 17). Thus, adding to acknowledgement of the philosophical foundations of U.S. reading comprehension is an acknowledgement of sociohistorical forces that played an important role in framing the field.

To help readers understand early reading comprehension research and testing I begin with a discussion of literacy rates in the United States, that is, who had access to literacy. I continue the discussion of influences from western European philosophy with a brief discussion of the thinking of Johann Herbart that emphasizes his thinking about apperception that influenced early reading comprehension instruction. Next, I discuss several social movements that influenced reading comprehension research and testing: scientific management, standardization, and measurement. This chapter also describes and reinserts the importance and influence of social movements in a history of reading comprehension research. It is difficult to disentangle the constellation of forces that Hall (2003) mentions, but it is necessary to acknowledge that these social forces influenced reading research and researchers. Ideologies "pre-date individuals, and form part of the determinate social formations and conditions in which individuals are born" (Hall, 1995, p. 19). Although this chapter examines several social movements, it is not an exhaustive study as there are ample sources of information elsewhere. However, social movements are discussed as they parallel the influence of scientism and racism on education and their influence on reading comprehension research and testing.

To illustrate how the ideological struggle is part of the general social struggle, I review several schoolbooks and professional manuals that demonstrate these effects on teaching reading comprehension. As social institutions, schools and the materials they use reflect the dominant ideology because they are sites for "production and reproduction, and transformation of ideologies" (Hall, 1995, p. 19). Ideas that linked reading with comprehension are mentioned as grassroots ideas about the purposes of reading. For instance, the notion of reading comprehension existed in the schoolbooks (readers) and teacher's manuals, albeit not by the label *reading comprehension*. The characteristics of what would later be called *reading comprehension* were important to educators and book publishers prior to experiments to test for reading comprehension. Educators and book publishers, unwittingly or not, promoted the dominant ideologies in their purposes, structure, and materials for reading comprehension.

Of particular import are the schoolbooks created for the newly freed African American slaves who are the special case examined in this book. These books sought to inculcate attitudes of passivism, compared to the public and private schoolbooks for White children that perpetuated White superiority and dominant beliefs and values. Finally, I remember the work of leaders in the field of reading whose beliefs, works, and writings illustrate how dominant ideas affect thinking.

U.S. Literacy Education

It also is important in a pluralistic society to provide a more inclusive history of reading comprehension research and testing, one that acknowledges and addresses the beliefs and values systems that supported denials of access to literacy. As Gramsci (1971) pointed out, the struggle over meaning involves the power "to create a terrain more favourable to the dissemination of certain modes of thought, and certain ways of posing and resolving questions involving the entire subsequent development of national life" (p. 184). Too often, historians ignore or marginalize nonmainstream histories as "aberrations of the larger experience" (Anderson, 1995, p. 19) and not part of the "American" experience. Let's acknowledge that while some groups were granted access to literacy, they also were forced to abandon their own ways of knowing, language, and literacy. And, they were forced to adopt, and assimilate to, conditions calling for gendered, English-only literacy. The forced adoption of another language, whether by consent or coercion, was an attempt to strip a people of not only their language but also their identity, a process that continues today.

Several historians (Apple, 1986, 1996; Graff, 1995; Kaestle, Damon-Moore, Stedman, Tinsley, Trollinger, 1991; Soltow & Stevens, 1981) have observed that literacy served as a conduit to reinforce ideological, intellectual, and cultural hegemony of power elites. Historically, literacy education has

> ... paralleled the larger structure of inequality, the groups most literate were of course those most highly ranked, just as their children were provided with more literacy and schooling. In theoretical terms, the social order was a high ascriptive one, as distribution of both literacy and reward were tied to the facts of birth: ethnicity, social and economic origins, race, sex and age. (Graff, 1995, p. 57)

There is an interconnectedness among ideological and social, sociohistorical contexts, and reading comprehension research and testing. The bulk of histories of reading, reading research, reading instruction, and special topics in reading are replete with celebrations and chronicles of changes and advancements in the field (see, e.g., Chall & Stahl, 1982; Gray 1915–1928; Huey, 1908/1968; Lamport, 1937; Mathews, 1966; Robinson, 1977; Smith, 1934, 1986; Stanovich, 2000; Venezkey, 1984, 1987 1986). With few exceptions (e.g., Monaghan 1991; Shannon, 1989; Weber, 1992; Willis, 1997), historical accounts of reading research explain the influence of sociohistorical contexts and fewer still acknowledge and interrogate the influence of philosophical assumptions that underpin reading research (e.g., Cunningham & Fitzgerald, 1996; Kamil, 1984; Lamport 1937; Willis & Harris, 2000). These missing elements have created significant gaps in what we know about the history of reading and reading comprehension research and testing. Knowing a more complete history may help to ameliorate the present and future.

Literacy Rates and Herbartianism

The research of Lockridge (1974) is helpful in understanding who had access to literacy and what the literacy rates were in the colonies. He examined literacy rates in 17th-century New England by analyzing the signatures of wills (1750–1795) as representative of literacy among White males and females. He argued, "Signatures on wills suggest a portrait of the level, trend, and social structure, attitudinal or qualitative correlates, and causal sources of literacy in colonial New England" (p. 3). Importantly, he also identified several factors that helped to influence literacy during this period: class, population density, geographical location, and occupation. Lockridge claimed that Protestantism and schooling were important factors that significantly influenced the increased rates of literacy during this period. According to Lockridge, Protestantism was defined as conversion and salvation and was the impetus for literacy training. His findings help to illustrate the variance in literacy rates between White males and females, although he notes that the closeness in similarity among literacy rates for males and females through the 17th century declined around the late 18th century. His initial findings have been corroborated by several studies of literacy rates: Auwers' (1980) study of White female literacy in colonial Windsor, Connecticut; Graff's (1979, 1987a, 1995) examination of literacy in select Canadian and U.S. cities; Monaghan's (1991) examination of the diaries and writings of Cotton Mather; and Weber's (1993) review of *Cornell-Reading Course for Farmer's Wives'* bulletins in upstate New York at the turn of the 20th century. Therefore, if access to literacy is limited, so too is the opportunity to use it to express needs and to effect change.

Soltow and Stevens (1981) have conducted the most extensive investigation of U.S. census data documenting literacy rates during the mid-19th century. They examined a variety of written documents including signatures, school enrollment and attendance records, petitions, book ownership, circulation of newspapers, and military enlistment, among other data sources seeking to link religion, school, and literacy. The authors suggest that the common school movement was controlled by a powerful elite group of conservative men who sought to instill common values in an increasingly diverse (ethnic, linguistic, economic, and religious) nation. They maintain that the common school movement was "intimately involved with the transmission of culture and literacy, [and] it became the focal point of major policy making decisions and represented for educational reformers a historical alternative of cultural intervention in the affairs of local communities" (p. 21). Under this system of political and social control, access to schooling limited literacy for non-Whites and some women. Access to literacy instruction was used to instill and maintain the cultural and political worldviews and values of the dominant class. Literacy instruction was purposive; that is, literacy teaching was not solely for education. According to Soltow and Stevens, politicians and educators were worried about the influence of alternative viewpoints. Furthermore, they argue that early reforms envisioned cultural pluralism "as a fact to be reckoned with because it was perceived to threaten the essential homogeneity of the American population" (p. 95). The idea of pluralism (the idea that reality comprises more than one basic substance or principle) was not envisioned positively by power elites. In fact, they fought to retain power and nationalize their view of reality, dominant epistemology, language, and so on as ruggedly individual and American, although other distinctive cultures, ethnic/racial epistemologies, religions, and languages learned to coexist with them. Power elites who held dominant perspectives about intelligence, race, gender, and class used language and literacy as a conduit for social control.

In the late 1800s, literacy rates improved for most people living in the United States. Kaestle et al. (1991) reported that 1879 U.S. census data reveals literacy rates were lower for White women compared with White males, and the literacy rates for People of Color were much lower when compared to those of White males. They documented that "81 percent of black Americans reported themselves utterly illiterate, compared with 11 percent of Whites. Twenty years later, the black rate was down to 57 percent, compared with 8 percent of Whites" (p. 31). The upsurge in literacy rates among African Americans, although regionally bound, was the result of increased educational opportunities and access to literacy, albeit in underfunded and separate public and private schools. In concert with these findings, Graff (1995) reveals that historically the most consistent barriers to literacy have been race/ethnicity and family circumstances. A brief review of which students were enrolled in U.S. public schools and under what conditions is warranted.

Educating White U.S. Children

During the progressive era, innovations in industry and technology helped to spur increased urbanization. Journalists in the United States, often called muckrakers, exposed some of the horrors, crime, and corruption in the early 20th century. For example, Jacob Riis, in *How the Other Half Lives* (1890), wrote about the plight of immigrants in the New York City slums; Frank Norris (1901, 1903) exposed the corruption in the railroad and wheat industries; Charlotte Perkins Gilman wrote *Women and Economics* (1898/1966) as an alternative view of women's economic worth; and Upton Sinclair's *The Jungle* (1906) detailed the unsanitary working conditions in the Chicago stockyards (a work that eventually led to the Meat Inspection Act and the Pure Food Act).

With increased urbanization came the arrival of vast numbers of immigrants to work in the industrial centers of the Eastern and Atlantic states. The swelling population of cities brought increased poverty and crime as people were forced to live in tenement housing, often in racial/ethnic ghettoes. Immigrant children comprised the majority of new enrollees in the public school systems and brought with them beliefs, customs, languages, religions, and values very different from children born in the United States. In an effort to Americanize the new immigrants from Eastern and Southern Europe, progressives sought reforms in education that included classes that focused on Americanism, patriotism, and democracy for children and adults. By way of example, the U.S. Senate Immigration Commission in 1908 reportedly found more than 60 nationalities represented in 37 cities, and an average 58% of all students had foreign-born parents. In many cities, the percentages were higher: New York City 72%; Chicago 67%; Boston 64%; Cleveland 60%; and San Francisco 58% (Tyack, 1974). Immigrant enrollment, however, was only one concern of school administrators, as increasing numbers of students from other regions of the nation also were entering large city school systems.

During this period, educational theories continued to be heavily influenced by European thought, from Pestalozzi's (1746–1827) famous book, *How Gertrude Teaches Her Children* (1894), which spurred object lessons, to Froebel's (1782–1852) emphasis on the importance of children's self-activity, to Rousseau's (1712–1778) attention to a children's interests and experiences. Elementary education became more student centered and the curricula and materials more age appropriate. In addition, the passage of federal child labor laws and state-supported school attendance legislation brought record numbers of children into classrooms. Florence Kelly was the impetus behind the regulation of child labor. She helped to organize boycotts and strikes, and in 1915 the Keating–Owen Act was passed to help curb the labor of children under age 14. The enforcement of child labor and compulsory education laws resulted in greater increases in school populations, although the school-leaving age appears to have been directly associated with economic and social factors prevalent in the area in which a student lived (Rury, 1985, 1988). Despite these variances, teachers were encouraged to draw on individual differences, build on student interests, and structure lessons and activities from which students could learn from their experiences. Although progressives sought reforms, not all groups benefited from the efforts of progressives, especially People of Color. Schooling was generally segregated by race, and in some locales, gender and/or religion. Racial discrimination, however, was most common whether in the rural South where African American children were denied tax supported public education, in the West where American Indian children were forcibly removed and transported to boarding schools, or the far West where Chinese and Japanese children were barred from attending public schools.

Educators were under tremendous pressure, by the court of public opinion and the muckraking popular press, to control and improve public education, especially for the large influx of European immigrants. Criticisms centered on rising enrollments, crowded classrooms, health and sanitation concerns, and the Americanization of European immigrants who were taught English and U.S. customs during the school day, whereas adults were taught in special Americanization night classes.

Children Underserved by U.S. Education

Progressive concerns seldom extended to People of Color. By the early 1900s, most people of African descent living in the United States, although not recognized as U.S. citizens, were native born. Most people of African descent had been denied access to literacy since they were brought to Caribbean islands in the mid 1600s (slave codes). For the next 170 years, the nearly 4 million slaves and their progeny also were denied access to literacy (see Anderson, 1988). At the onset of the 20th century, African Americans primarily were educated in segregated schools that were either privately owned and managed by African Americans, or supported by philanthropic organizations or limited state funding.

The struggle of the Native Americans against the imposing cultural hegemony of the dominant group is a macrocosm of its effects on other groups. Collectively, Indian people were forced off their land, forbidden practice of their beliefs, and restricted from speaking in their native languages. It is not possible in this chapter to recount the various genocidal practices and policies waged against

Native Americans, but if we begin with the Indian Removal Act of 1830 we can find a pattern of corruption. The Indian Removal Act forced the migration of five nations of Indians (Cherokees, Chickasaws, Choctaws, Creeks, and Seminoles) from their fertile farmland in the southeastern section of the country to lands west of the Mississippi. Although the Cherokee had established schools and printed their own newspaper, like other Indian nations they were forced to begin anew in Indian Territory. Furthermore, the Dawes Allotment Act of 1888 and the Curtis Act of 1898 reestablished discriminatory practices to strip Native Americans of their political, cultural, spiritual, and ancestral heritage. This pattern of colonization—stripping people of their language, religion, and human rights and forcing them to adopt the ways of Euro-Americans—was repeated throughout the southwestern United States, and in Guam, Hawaii, and Samoa.

The U.S. government attempted to force Americanization on Native Americans by removing children from their homes and placing them in government-sanctioned boarding schools. There children were forced to learn English and adopt Euro-American ways of knowing and understanding the world. Spring's (1996) documentation of literacy among Native American people reveals that as early as 1819, the Choctaw Nation avowed its interest and commitment to education. Spring writes that despite the forced removal to western reservations, the Choctaw and the Cherokee nations developed and maintained their own schools, teaching students to read and write in their native languages as well as in English. He cited a Congressional report that claimed, "In the 1880s, the Choctaw Indians of Mississippi and Oklahoma [Indian Territory] operated about 200 schools and academies and sent numerous graduates to eastern colleges" (p. 14). The report added, "Using bilingual teachers and Cherokee texts, the Cherokees, during the same period controlled a school system that produced a tribe almost 100% literate" (p. 14). Other Native American nations, however, did not fare as well.

Mexican landowners in the Southwest (what is now Arizona, California, Nevada, New Mexico, Texas, and Utah) faced similar land seizures and racial discrimination following the signing of the Treaty of Guadalupe Hidalgo in 1848. The treaty granted U.S. citizenship, property rights, and the retention of the language and culture of Mexico to Mexicans, but the enforcement was similar to the experiences of African and Native Americans: it was fraught with discrimination and age-old racial, social, and linguistic prejudices. The depressed economy of Mexico led to massive migration from 1877 to 1910, and by 1914, more than 100,000 Mexicans had migrated to the United States. Many Mexican communities in the Southwest established their own schools, which taught children literacy skills in Spanish (Gallegos, 1992; Jiménez, 1990).

The Spanish–American War (May 1898–July 1898) ended with the signing of Treaty of Paris, which helped establish U.S. colonies and territories and gave the United States a worldwide reputation of imperialism. The terms of the treaty called for Spain to abandon Cuba and the United States to gain control over Puerto Rico, Guam, and the Philippines (for $20 million). The reputation for imperialism spread throughout the Pacific islands when Queen Liluokalani was overthrown and Hawaii was annexed. In response to the acquisition of lands, an American Anti-Imperialist League, critical of the government's policies, was formed. Although in 1901, the United States bartered with England to construct the Panama Canal, the 1904 Roosevelt Corollary to the Monroe Doctrine justified U.S. intervention in the affairs of Latin American nations whether sanctioned or not. Further, Roosevelt's Corollary excluded non-European countries from obtaining land in the Western Hemisphere. Central American people from the Caribbean, Cuba, Panama Canal Zone, and Puerto Rico experienced harsh treatment under the U.S. government's educational policy—banning the use of native languages, forcing allegiance to the U.S. government, and encouraging Americanization of behaviors, attitudes, and values.

Other non-White groups also experienced similar problems in attaining educational opportunities. The shared experiences of Chinese, Japanese, and Korean, people in their attempts to access equal educational opportunities in the Southern and Western states of the United States mirrored the experience of other non-White groups. By way of example, people of Asian descent immigrated to the United States through Angel Island and faced harsh race-based discrimination. Their entrance to America was not met with the welcoming poetry of Emma Lazarus (1883) that was placed on Statue of Liberty in 1903:

THE NEW COLOSSUS

Not like the brazen giant of Greek fame,
With conquering limbs astride from land to land;

Here at our sea-washed, sunset gates shall stand
A mighty woman with a torch, whose flame
Is the imprisoned lightning, and her name
Mother of Exiles. From her beacon-hand
Glows world-wide welcome; her mild eyes command
The air-bridged harbor that twin cities frame,
"Keep, ancient lands, your storied pomp!" cries she
With silent lips. "Give me your tired, your poor,
Your huddled masses yearning to breathe free,
The wretched refuse of your teeming shore,
Send these, the homeless, tempest-tost to me,
I lift my lamp beside the golden door!"

No such greeting welcomed Asians. In fact, so intense was the anti-Chinese sentiment that federal legislation, the Chinese Exclusion Act of 1882 was signed (it was renewed in 1890 and did not end until 1943).

Fueled by racism and the fears of White U.S. males' job losses led to the 1907 Gentlemen's Agreement that limited the number of Japanese immigrants allowed into the United States (later, in 1913, the Alien Land Act made it illegal for Japanese people to purchase land, making it impossible to become naturalized citizens—because they were not landowners).

These agreements were strained when, in 1906, the San Francisco School Board ordered all Asian children to attend segregated schools. Spring (1986) quotes the San Francisco Board of Supervisors:

> Guard well the doors of our public schools that they [the Chinese] do not enter. For however stern it might sound, it is but the enforcement of the law of self-preservation, the inculcation of the doctrine of true humanity and an integral part of the iron rule of right. (p. 187)

With strong social Darwinian overtones, the school board kept Asian families at bay until President Theodore Roosevelt interceded on behalf of the children, and the school board reversed its discriminatory stance. Although Chinese people received little support for educating their children and were forced to create schools within their own communities, by 1890 they had established newspapers, periodicals, and literary societies.

What this brief review of literacy rates and historical events reveals is that educational and literacy access and opportunity have always been closely connected to the dominant ideology, including its racist roots. The dominant group's ideas about whom should have access to literacy in this country have politically and economically been structured to benefit the group in power. This snapshot also illustrates the interconnectedness of the dominant ideology and what has historically been portrayed as the common sense goals of U.S. citizens. Education, a commonly voiced goal for U.S. school children as part of the dominant ideology, can now been seen more clearly to mean primarily a classical education for White children and a rudimentary education for non-Whites. Into this fray came the educational theories of Johann Herbart, a European, who proposed a new set of ideas for education. Although Herbartianism was short-lived in the United States, it deserves our attention for its influence on educators and reading comprehension research.

Herbartianism

Johann Friedrich Herbart (1776–1841) is commonly known as the father of the scientific study of pedagogy. His ideas were germinated during the golden age of German philosophy when Kant (1724–1804) was at Konigsburg, Schilling at Wurzburg, Hegel at Jena, and Fichte at Berlin. As chair of the philosophy department at Konigsberg (1809–1833) and under the influence of a cultural epoch theory, Herbart focused on psychology and education. For instance, drawing on his evolving theories of pedagogy, he established a "pedagogical seminary" or practice school, where a small number of children were instructed by student teachers under the apprenticeship of a professor.

Herbart believed that a child's individuality should be the focus of education and that the curriculum should be structured to support each child. He took a broad view of education, noting, "All its major concepts lie within the circle of common talk and likewise in the well-worn rut of what everyone thinks he knows" (quoted in Dunkel, 1970, p. 68). His goal was to meld education to psychology and ethics, although the U.S. interpreters of his work dismissed this aspect. Herbartianism had short-lived success in the United States (1892–1902), although it initially appeared adequate to meet the rapidly changing, "social and educational needs" of the nation (Dunkel, 1970, p. 241). As scientism and progressivism called for educational reforms, Herbartianism seemed a ready answer to concerns over teacher training. What was needed was a "pedagogy that was academically respectable and scientific and yet simple and practical" (Dunkel, 1970, p. 245).

The American version of Herbartianism was instituted through the efforts of a small contingent of students who studied under DeGarmo and McMurry, from Normal, Illinois, and who had recently returned to the United States after studying in Germany. Although they did not adopt Herbart's philosophical and metaphysical positions, these students imported his psychological ideas. One of his most devoted followers was DeGarmo (1896), who characterized Herbart's influence as focused on "instructing the future leaders of thought (p. 13). It was DeGarmo's and McMurray's versions of Herbartianism that filled U.S. books, clubs, and organizations.

Their distinctive U.S. version of Herbartianism, however, excluded Herbart's ideas on metaphysics and morals, as well as his views on the disconnection among science, psychology, and pedagogy. In a series of articles in the *Illinois School Journal* (1886–1887), for example, DeGarmo explains Herbart's thinking about apperception (relating new experiences to older ones) and abstraction (moving from particular to general understandings), while not acknowledging Herbart's contributions (Dunkel, 1970). He characterizes Herbart's ideas as a set of formal stages of instruction: (a) clearness, (b) association, (c) system, and 4(d) method (DeGarmo, 1891, p. 250). Herbart believed that teaching should begin with the child, include the child's interests, and motivate the child to be a moral person. His thinking was summarized into five key steps: preparation, presentation, association, generalization, and application. He suggested that teachers do the following:

1. Prepare the pupils to be ready for the new lesson.
2. Present the new lesson.
3. Associate the new lesson with ideas studied earlier.
4. Use examples to illustrate the lesson's major points.
5. Test pupils to ensure they had learned the new lesson.

Furthermore, Herbart promoted direct observation and experimentation in education for improved classroom instruction and asserted that it was best to present material to children that was related to a previous experience or interest.

Herbartianism was so popular that U.S. Commissioner of Education, W. T. Harris (1894–1895) reported that there were more adherents of Herbartian pedagogy in America than in Germany. There were numerous national Herbartian clubs (the first being at Illinois State Normal School in 1894) as well as the National Herbart Society.

Support for Herbartianism came from numerous educational leaders: Nicholas Butler, John Dewey, William T. Harris, William James, and Colonel Francis Parker. The U.S. Herbart's Society published its version of Herbartianism in several books of proceedings/yearbooks that shared the thinking of its membership. For instance, the *First Yearbook* states that the purpose of the society is "to study and investigate and discuss important problems in education. Some members of this society are strongly tinctured with the education doctrines of Herbart, others are not, and it is right to expect an honest search for truth" (DeGarmo, 1895/1916, p. 204).

As if prophetic, this statement foretold how the U.S. version of Herbartianism gradually took on a life of its own—one that bore little resemblance to Herbart's thinking (Dunkel, 1970), and one that began to reflect more accurately the importance given to scientism and psychology in the United States. In 1901, the Herbart Society was renamed the National Society for the Scientific Study of Education (NSSE). The demise of Herbartianism was caused by the growing influence of scientism, including psychology's scientific (experimental) foci, whereby Herbartianism appeared "nonscientific or even antiscientific" (Dunkel, 1970, p. 282). McMurry, writing a decade after the popularity of Herbartianism waned, continued to advocate its use for teacher training. Ironically, he wanted "to make the foundation of education immovable by resting it upon growth in moral character" (1903, p. 330), an idea U.S. Herbartians had rejected years earlier. Throughout the next century, the Society continued forming committees among its membership and charging them with reviewing the research and reporting back to the Society. Importantly, the bulk of the chapters written in the *NSSE Yearbooks* reflect changes in how education is understood, the use of measurements in education for school subjects, and the standardization of educational tests.

Herbart on Apperception   Among Herbart's contributions to reading research was his concept of apperception. Although Herbart used the term, in the U.S. version of Herbartianism, it was sacrosanct. Herbart (1891/1896) wrote that *apperception* refers to the process of adding new ideas to the ideas already known:

> To explain this idea we contrast *perception* with *apperception*. In *perception* we have an object presented to our senses, but in *apperception* we identify the object or those features of it which were familiar to us before; we recognize it; we explain it; we interpret the new by our previous knowl-

edge, and thus are enabled to proceed from the known to the unknown and make new acquisitions; in recognizing the object we classify it under various general classes; in identifying it with what we have seen before, we note also differences which characterize the new object and lead to the definition of new species or varieties. (p. vi, italics in the original)

In other words, as you read you add new ideas to those already stored in your head. When new ideas are added to existing ideas, they form a system of ideas, or what Herbart called the "apperceptive mass." Teachers were encouraged to select ideas that were of interest to individual students and within their range of understanding and experience so that reading for meaning could be enjoyed. Herbart's approach to reading also encouraged the use of interesting age-appropriate stories from a variety of genres.

It is in his use of literature that Herbart's interest in reading comprehension is most clearly illustrated

> But give to them an interesting story, rich in incidents, relationships, characters, strictly in accordance with psychological truth, and not beyond the feelings and ideas of children; make no effort to depict the worst or the best, only let a faint, half-unconscious moral tact secure that the interest of the action tends away from the bad towards the good, the just, the right; then you will see how the child's attention is fixed upon it, how he seeks to discover the truth and thinks over all sides of the matter, how the many-sided material calls forth a many-sided judgment, how the charm of change ends in preference for the best, so that the boy who perhaps feels himself a step or two higher in moral judgment than the hero or the author, will cling to his view with inner approbation. (Herbart, 1891/1896, p. 73)

To Herbart, it was important that literature (narrative) selections be of interest to children, reflect strong characters, and explain history. McMurry (1899) repeated the call for the use of classic literature, listing Longfellow's *Hiawatha,* Reece's *Aladdin,* Shakespeare's *Julius Caesar,* and Swift's *Gulliver's Travels* among important readings for children.

An application of Herbartianism can be seen in Gertrude Buck's (1898) article, "Another Phase of the New Education," in which she described how she taught several reading lessons in a multiracial school, "a German, Russian, and Polish settlement, with a thin sprinkling of Americans and Africans" (p. 377) outside Detroit. As Herbart had suggested, the elementary reading lessons included excerpts from Longfellow's *Hiawatha,* Dante's *Kablu,* Greek mythology, and King Arthur, while older students read the *Divine Comedy,* Homer's *Odyssey,* and early American poetry. In each instance, the teacher followed Herbart's five-step method by meticulously building on previous lessons and student understandings. Beyond classroom reading, Herbart's U.S. devotees claimed that multiple language experiences helped to foster and promote an increased awareness of language, and increased language awareness improved reading ability. They suggested that teachers use experience trips, collective storytelling, pictures, and written language exercises to foster improved performance in reading.

Efficiency/Scientific Management, Standardization, and Measurement

Progressivism, industrialization, immigration, and urbanization have been presented as antecedents to efficiency, scientific management, standardization, and measurement (of educational outcomes). One of the clearest examples is the work of Frederick Winslow Taylor's (1856–1915) "efficiency studies" in industry. His work resulted in two basic reforms: the development of "rules, laws and formulas" and the "standardization of methods" (Callahan, 1962). He likened his painstaking studies to that of a scientist; thus, his idea of efficiency became synonymous with the term *scientific management*. Drawing on Comte's notion of a set of procedures for observation and experimentation, Taylor argued that the key elements to scientific management were the setting of standards and efficiency, ideas that were used by business and industry as well as popularized by the press. Karier (1975) argues that Taylorism created "an educational system which would classify, standardize, socialize, and Americanize youth on a massive scale … in the interest of national progress" (p. 130). Unfortunately, the detail and close observations of Taylor were not undertaken in education as school administrators quickly attempted to apply Taylor's ideas. In an age of reform, a system that appeared to be scientific and offered "efficiency" found many ready converts. Educational leaders quickly grasped some of the principles espoused by Taylor as schools were envisioned as key centers for cultural assimilation to educate the masses. Taylor's principles mandated that workers be scientifically selected and trained for their particular jobs. His principles were in concert with positivistic notions of predicting an individual's role in society and training the masses to understand and accept their role in society. Furthermore, Taylor's principles complemented Spencerian social views and pragmatic notions of interaction with reality through the efficient and economic use of time, materials, and personnel. Two concepts characterized educators' response to Taylorism: standardization and measurement. In the late 1890s, the leaders of the measurement movement viewed schools as the ideal agency to "build correct social attitudes, select individuals for their place in society, and educate them for those places" (Spring, 1986, p. 242). Using standard procedures and measurement tools afforded efficiency experts, test developers, teachers, and school administrators a voice in determining the future of each student and the individual student's place in society.

Allen (1979) reviewed Taylor's theories for their impact on reading comprehension testing. Her study reveals two specific areas of influence: speed and factual recall. Specifically, she notes that Taylorism helped to replace the use of essay tests with objective tests (alternative/multiple choice) that took less time to complete and were easier to score. Furthermore, she argues that as a result of Taylor's influence, speed and surface, or literal, comprehension became the most highly valued components of a successful reader as measured in early reading comprehension tests. The most important element, in principle, for the reading test authors was the issue of standardization.

School efficiency, however, rested on educational measurement, and school administrators were encouraged to measure the efficiency of classroom instruction by means of standardized tests. Many school administrators believed that quantifying educational products or outcomes from scientifically derived tests would prove efficiency. Many teachers, believed that the use of tests was a means of monitoring their abilities. Nonetheless, teachers were encouraged by educational leaders to look beyond their thoughts and fears about tests to the greater good of educating children as efficiently as possible.

Additionally, the role of scientific measurement has been reported to be a neutral, objective, and defensible means of identifying intelligence, achievement, or aptitude. Once specific variables were identified, they could be measured and used to place individuals in the "correct" educational, occupational, and social environment for which he or she was most suited. Notions surrounding ideas of individual differences, inheritability of intelligence, and racial differences supported the efforts of early test makers to legitimize and justify their scientific findings.

Standardization

The concept of *standardization* in education at this time denoted the establishment of uniform procedures and implied efficiency. Callahan

(1962) argues "in the process of actually attempting to measure efficiency within the schools … most of the attention was devoted to developing and utilizing 'objective' achievement tests in the language arts and arithmetic" (p. 100). He adds that other measures were developed to rate teacher efficiency as well. However, by and large, standardization meant giving directions, overseeing testing, and scoring and interpreting test results. Reading researchers used the same general definition of standardization as they developed early reading comprehension tests. These tests were published, directions were to be given for the administration of the tests, scoring procedures were outlined, and instructions were to be offered on how to interpret the results of the data.

Resnick and Resnick's (1983) research reveals that even in these seemingly simple means of standardization, there was considerable variation in standards. For example, many early tests were individually administered orally, particularly reading comprehension tests. According to von Mayrhauser (1987), "The testing examiner was expected to coach his subject, assist the subject throughout the exam, keep the subject's attention on the task at hand, and, if necessary, postpone the test if the subject was having the proverbial 'bad day'" (p. 431). The standardization of achievement tests allowed administrators and national educational leaders to urge minimum standards in school subjects and classify, sort, group, and track students according to their achievement scores (Spring, 1986; Tyack, 1974). Another important factor in the sorting process was the teacher's judgment of the student's ability, known as *class rank*. Teacher rankings of students were believed to be subjective; nevertheless, teacher rankings were used in several early measures as professional opinions that were valuable, reliable, and a comparative measurement tool. These discursive formations helped to "scientifically" legitimize the need to select and train individuals for a "place" in society's organizational structure. Educators and politicians argued that educational outcomes could be improved through scientifically determining (measuring) the most efficient teaching theories and methods. Mathematical tools, or statistics, were used to measure efficiency.

Measurement

Measurement was an important feature of standardization because it held the promise of certainty, of precise standards, and ultimately of an ordered and predictable society. The measurement of educational products became the primary goal of educational research and educational researchers adopted the scientific method for conducting inquiry. It was commonly believed that once a number was assigned to account for an observation, it became a legitimate "fact," and educational researchers were consumed with a preoccupation of developing measurement tools and discovering new scientific "facts." Measurement became synonymous with the quantification and verification of educational products, methodologies, teacher performance, and student learning. Most early researchers, however, were poorly trained in mathematics. Consequently, much of the research they produced was little more than arithmetic counts, means or averages, frequency distributions, and comparisons. Comparisons were of two distinctive forms: a) comparisons between teacher rankings and performance scores on achievement tests and b) comparisons of test scores among classmates. The second type of comparison was used to discuss individual differences in reading achievement.

Measuring Reading Performance and Race   Measuring reading performance was not a new idea. Three examples give a brief historical overview of measuring reading prior to the onset of early psychological testing. First, in 1845–1846 the Boston School Committee's survey team used printed tests to determine reading achievement among Boston's school children, although most schools administered tests orally to individual students (Caldwell & Courtis, 1924). Older students from selected schools were given tests in geography, vocabulary, astronomy, grammar, and philosophy drawn from their schoolbooks. Achievement in reading was measured by requiring students to write definitions for selected vocabulary words and to write responses to readings. Key features of the Boston school survey deserve mention. Results of the test were used to compare achievement among schools, and, because the committee recognized that testing would be an ongoing part of the school curriculum, they wanted to better understand the differences in test scores. Smith School, a school serving mostly African American and West Indian students, produced very low achievement scores. The school committee questioned the results. They believed the difference should not have occurred, as all schools used the same basic curriculum. The committee interpreted the results as indicative of the school administrator's lack of faith in the ability of his students to learn (Caldwell & Courtis, 1924). The beliefs held by the school's administrator in terms of race and class, however, were not openly discussed. An additional finding by school administrators was that short answers were preferable to long, handwritten responses.

Second, interest in measuring reading achievement is revealed in Fisher's (1864/1961: see Caldenhead & Robinson, 1987) scale book that placed numerical values on answers to questions in his text. The scale book ranged from one (the highest score) to five (the lowest score) in intervals of one fourth. The scale book was used for a wide variety of subjects from navigation to scriptures. With regard to the subject of reading, Reverend Fisher placed descriptive values of "good," "bad," and "indifferent" on oral reading behavior. He stated that the terms used reflected the general consensus of the masters.

Third, Joseph M. Rice (1893), a physician, became interested in the school achievement of U.S. children following a study tour in Europe. Dr. Rice returned to the United States and conducted a survey, focusing on education. In 1892, he began to collect data on the appropriateness of the curriculum, the efficiency of teachers, and the use of instructional time in American schools. Among the tests he administered was an oral reading comprehension test for third graders. Like his contemporaries, he understood reading was an essentially oral process where a "good" reader read with correct pronunciation, inflection, and rhythm (no long pauses or breaks). Rice reasoned that when comprehension broke down, the reader would make reading errors: admissions, substitutions, omissions, repetitions, pauses, or incorrect inflections. He found that many students were able to read intelligently from sight. Much like Herbart, he believed that schools needed to stress clear goals and objectives for student learning. He suggested that subject-matter tests be used to evaluate whether the instructional goals and objectives had been met. And, he called for the adoption of national standards of achievement.

An overview of early schoolbooks illuminates the influence of prevailing philosophical and psychological theories on reading comprehension research and is helpful to consider before reviewing how student performance of reading comprehension was measured (tested).

Ideas About Reading Comprehension in Schoolbooks, Professional Books, and Teachers' Manuals

One means of illustrating that the idea of reading comprehension existed before the term originated and before testing was formalized, is to review the schoolbooks (readers) used by students and the notes to teachers included in these books as well as to review professional books and teachers' manuals (see, e.g., Robinson, Faraone, Hittleman, & Unruh, 1990). Schoolbooks were a means by which dominant ideologies could be easily spread; in fact, they most often shared the same values, beliefs, and practices of the dominant society, as the originators, publishers, and distributors of schoolbooks. Therefore, schoolbooks reflected the beliefs and values of the individual authors as well as the perspectives of the dominant class especially with regard to culture, religion, and morals. Furthermore, schoolbooks not only influenced the students who read them, but also had the potential to influence the thinking of teachers and parents. This is an important addition to understanding the process of hegemony and the role that reading comprehension plays in sustaining the dominant ideologies. Hall (1982) maintains that this is precisely how hegemony works:

> [It] extends and expands its mastery over society in such a way that it can transform and re-fashion its ways of life, its *mores* and conceptualization, its very form and level of culture and civilization into a direction which, while not directly paying immediate profits to the narrow interests of any particular class, favors the development of and expansion of the dominant social and productive system of life as whole. (p. 85)

Schoolbooks, read and remembered by young children, have the potential to structure thinking. This is not to suggest a conspiracy theory but rather to suggest that, by consent, the dominant ideology is perpetuated.

Three examples from readers used during this period are shared below: readers written for African American students, readers written for White public school students, and teaching reading methods' manuals written for normal school students.

Readers for African American Students

The *Freedmen Series* (Morris, 1980) offers an exceptional example of schoolbooks that were written for African Americans following the Civil War specifically to instill dominant ideas. The dominant group crafted these schoolbooks because "a dominant cultural order is constantly preferred, despite its articulation with structures of domination and oppression" (Grossberg, 2003, p. 161). This series was published in concert with the American Freedmen's Union Commission and the American Missionary Association (AMA), an abolitionist and religious organization, and the U.S. government through the Bureau of Refugees, Freedmen, and Abandoned Lands (Freedmen's Bureau). It is Butchart's (1980) position that the goals of these Reconstruction groups arose out of their twisted notions of racial justice and class consciousness; interwoven with the need to appeal to the Southern White's desire to retain a subjugated Black labor force. Morris' (1976/1981) review of these books suggests that they were part of a larger effort to socialize African Americans into the White mainstream, with content that is overly moralistic and didactic. Butchart's (1980) critical analysis of the same series details how White promoters of African American education held "scientific" ideas about the intellectual capacity and morality of African Americans. Specifically, they believed African Americans were intellectually and morally inferior to Whites. He notes the pervasiveness of these beliefs and cultural assumptions are found throughout the curriculum, textbooks, and instructional materials created by the AMA. Also, he claims there are "implicit messages underlying stories, buried in pictures, and interwoven into the very structure of language and institutions" (p. 135). This series also attempted to inculcate the class, religious, and social beliefs and values of White dominant groups in the lives of former slaves (Butchart, 1980; Morris, 1981) while simultaneously, and markedly, describing African Americans as inferior to Whites. These ideas as we have seen are part of the dominant ideology that emerged over centuries.

Other literature written by African Americans that focused on representing the lives of African Americans in more positive and uplifting ways was not used in the *Freedman Series* readers or in any other reader during this period. Some schools, however, did use *The Freedmen's Torchlight*, a newspaper written by African American men with information appropriate for all levels, much like African American newspapers and magazines. However, very few schoolbooks were written with African American children in mind, until the 1920s (e.g., Elizabeth R. Haynes' (1921) *Unsung Heroes* and Helen A. Whiting's (1938a, 1938b) *Negro Folk Tales and Negro Art, Music, and Rhyme*). As Whiting (1938b) notes, "It is hoped that through such reading experiences the children of all races will cultivate a greater appreciation of the Negro race culture" (p. vii).

A similar scenario existed for Native Americans, who had created their own literary works (Zinn, 1980), and Mexican Americans (see Gallegos, 1992), who were a literate society in their own right before being forced to learn and read in English. Alternative values, beliefs, and practices (especially those of non-Whites and non-Western cultures) were defined by the dominant groups in negative terms, if acknowledged, and portrayed in readers as abnormal, deviant, or revolutionary.

Nationally, schools were racially segregated during this period, and children of color were seldom given new books to use. In the South, for example, in some outpost schools in rural areas children were still using *Webster's Blue-back Speller* in the early 1900s. African American children who were fortunate enough to attend schools in more populated areas used readers that were the castoffs of children in White schools. Willis (2002) reports that at Calhoun Colored School, the school administrators went to great lengths to secure new textbooks for each year as well as to hire teachers that were graduates of top White and African American colleges and normal schools. The titles of their schoolbooks were similar to those found in many White Northern schools: Arnold's (1897) *Stepping Stones to Literature*, Cyr's (1899–1901) *Primer, First* and *Second* readers, among others.

Schoolbooks Used in White Public and Private Schools

The traditional wisdom for reading instruction in the early 1800s followed that found in the McGuffey Readers (1836–1920) without explanation. From the primer throughout the graded series of readers, words were introduced and students were expected to be able to identify them on sight before oral class exercises in reading commenced (Hyatt, 1943). Two McGuffey readers published before the 1880s illustrate this point.

In the first, McGuffey's (1849) *Newly Revised Eclectic Fourth Reader*, we learn "The reading exercises are selected from the best compositions of the model writers in our language" (p. 2). The authors of each exercise are presumed to be White because their writing complements the ideas, beliefs, and values of the dominant group. Schoolbooks also included in this text were rules on elocution, spelling words, vocabulary words, and questions to be used for comprehension checking. By way of contrast, McGuffey's (1866) *First Eclectic Reader* introduced the alphabet for several pages, followed by short two-letter words (*is, it, an, ox*). Alongside these words are equally short sentences of unengaging content because it was believed that instruction for young readers should not focus on comprehension. The impact of the McGuffey reading series is hard to judge, but the *Fifth Reader* indicates that the textbook series held the official recommendation of several Midwestern state boards of education and thousands of school boards. Mosier's (1947) exhaustive review of the ideas within the reading series reveals that the series was more than a set of books; they were used to inculcate and acculturate students into White middle-class values and culture, conservative politics, and Judeo-Christian beliefs.

McGuffey's Readers were the most popular readers available, but there were others. For example, May Kirk's (1899) reader, *The Baldwin Primer*, added photographs, colorful drawings, realistic pictures, and cursive text. Importantly, Kirk outlined what she called "key principles" drawn from "well-established principles of mental science and child study" (p. 4). Her steps for beginning reading instruction included the following: "The letters of the alphabet, as set tasks, are deeply impressed on the mind, while at the same time the child learns to read by recognition of words as wholes" (p. 4). Furthermore, she suggested that by so doing, the child "instinctively unites the results of both methods to a complete and detailed understanding of the words" (p. 4). The idea of reading comprehension, magically, arising out of alphabet knowledge, letter–sound correspondence, and word recognition remains intact.

Kirk (1899) drew on Herbartian theories of apperception: "The choice of familiar objects for the material of each reading lesson gives it a basis in the child's personal interest. The use of classical pictures is designed to awaken and develop the instinct for the beautiful" (p. 4). Her book, though not the first, acknowledged the need to present children with simple and colorful objects of interest. While she references "the child," the implication is the White, middle-class, English-speaking child.

Readers for older students were less focused on aesthetics and more focused on elocution. The term *elocution* denotes "the art of using the voice for the proper expression of thought (Barnes, 1884, p. 15). It was believed that to use the voice properly implied that the reader understood (comprehended) the text and how to present it in accord with the author's intent during oral reading. Therefore, the focus in most upper level readers was articulation and inflection, more commonly known as elocution.

Pierpont (1823/1841) compiled a reader in response to the public concerns over reading instruction in Boston public schools. Although the focus of reading was elocution, he also addressed the need to understand the text. He claimed, "Reading, like conversation, is learned from example rather than rule. ... No one is ever made an accomplished reader or speaker by studying rules for elocution" (p. iii). Furthermore, he suggested once a child has learned the alphabet " [reading] is altogether an art;—an art, indeed, which requires a quick perception, a delicate taste, a good understanding, and especially, a faculty of nicely discriminating and accurately expressing shades of an author's meaning;—but, still, an art" (p. iv). His reading lessons were didactic, which Pierpont explained helped students by improving their minds. In his explanation of the content of his readers, Pierpoint claimed by reading the texts, students would find "pleasure and religious reverence, the character of the Great Author of their being, as discovered in his works, his providence, and his word; and thus help them to attain the end of their Christian faith,—salvation of their souls" (p. vi). The need to reach and teach the masses, by the dominant class, appears to have both nationalistic and moralistic goals.

In England, Lindley Murray (1826) published a successful reading series, *The English Reader* that became popular and was widely used in the United States. Part of its success, according to Murray, was his care in creating a compilation of lessons that reflected the developmental stages of young readers and his careful responsiveness to the interests and understanding of children. Teachers were instructed to be mindful to the importance of habit formation and supplied a list of rules "for assisting children to read with propriety" (p. iv). Murray explained that the rules for elocution should be followed, as the reading selections were especially chosen, not just for reading purposes but also "to season the minds of children with purity and virtue, and to improve them in reading, language, and sentiment" (p. ii). Even though concerns for the needs and tastes of children were claimed, the reading selections also were arranged to improve elocution and enhance comprehension.

All readers for older students supplied an introduction for the teacher that explained the authors' ideas about reading and the impor-

Rule 1. Stand erect; hold the book with the left hand; keep a full supply of breath; and read as if you were talking.

Rule 2. To read *well*, you must pronounce every word distinctly and correctly. In order to do this, you must open your mouth, and move your tongue and lips.

Rule 3. Be careful to give the vowels their full, proper sound, and articulate the consonants distinctly, as exhibited on the 10th page.

Rule 4. Pronounce each syllable distinctly; and avoid blending the termination of the one word with the beginning of another.

Rule 5. Avoid reading too fast. By trying to read fast, you will pass over some words, miscall others, and stammer though the sentence so that no one can understand what you are reading. Read no faster than you would speak.

Rule 6. If the subject be animated and lively, you will read it much faster, than you would one which is grave and pathetic.

Rule 7. Be careful to emphasize properly the more important words; otherwise you will fail to convey the true meaning of the subject.

Rule 8. Read as if you were expressing your own thoughts and feelings; and this you should do in such a manner, as to make yourself easily understood.

Rule 9. Pauses are used to show more clearly the sense and relation of words. At every pause, therefore, the voice should be suspended sufficient time to mark sense, and to take breath, so as not to destroy the sense, by being obliged to make pauses where none are required.

Figure 3.1   Rules to be observed in reading. From *The School Reader, Third Book* (p. 25), by C. Sanders, 1867, New York: Iverson, Phinney, Blakeman.

tance of elocution. For example, Sanders' (1867) schoolbook, *The School Reader, Third Book*, lists nine rules for elocution (see Fig. 3.1).

Beyond the rules of elocution, Sanders believed that teachers needed to prepare students to understand the text. He noted that "questions are appended, which may be increased at pleasure, both in number and variety, and which, rightly managed, may be made highly useful in training the reflection and reasoning faculties."

Another reading series, by the President of Illinois State Normal School Richard Edwards, offers insight into the public view of reading instruction, especially reading comprehension. The preface to his reader *Analytical Series* states:

> The feeling is very general that the pupils of our schools ought to be taught to read understandingly and effectively; and this feeling we consider reasonable and just. But it is almost universal conviction that this very desirable result is seldom attained by the methods that have been most commonly employed in the schools. (Edwards, 1867, np)

His perspective on reading also illustrates the role of reading comprehension in support of the dominant ideology. Edwards declared, "Reading is not only the key to all knowledge ... when properly taught, a direct means of the most thorough mental discipline, being the mind, as it comes into contact with the noblest thoughts uttered in the language" (np). Furthermore, he argues, each reading selection should be thoroughly mastered by every student to improve mental discipline and elocution. To obtain the latter, he thought that the questions used should improve student understanding of text (comprehension). He urged "as much of the original thinking as possible should come upon the pupil, and he should, finally, make full and complete analyses for himself" (np).

Although Edwards does not specify what methods were used at the Illinois State Normal School, methods popular during this time period include whole word and phonics approaches. His readers included poetry, expository, and literature selections. Each literature selection was followed by questions such as "Is this prose or poetry? Why? Is it a humorous piece? Is it imaginative? ... What is the author aiming to do in it? What must the author have done in order to write it?" (p. 74). These questions focused on understanding text, vocabulary words, and elocutionary style. Typical of the readers during this period, the book includes directions for the teacher. In fact, he admonishes:

> Let the teacher see to it that, at every step, he is thoroughly master of the lesson in all its bearings,—that he not only knows it for himself, but is prepared to lead his pupils into a clear and complete understanding of it. (Edwards, 1867, p. 12, emphasis in the original)

The directions for teachers were meant to improve instruction and enhance student learning. However, one can easily see how his admonishments that students read and learn the passage by reading the text several times, and that teachers do much the same, suggest that students are not only reading and comprehending the text, but also ingesting the beliefs, values, and practices of the author, the reading passage, and dominant group, as represented by authors.

Although for years a schoolteacher's mantra for reading comprehension had been "elocution, elocution, elocution," in the late 1880s a shift occurred whereby "thought-getting," "reading for meaning," or what we call reading comprehension, was happening, especially for older readers. This shift was brought about, in part, because there was an accompanying shift in emphasis from oral to silent reading. The authors of readers for older children assumed that reading comprehension occurred after the mechanics of reading were mastered. In the introduction to their schoolbook, *Barnes' Fifth Reader,* Parker and Watson (1874, 1884) take issue with this idea because many young students were being asked to read and understand the classics. They also objected that teachers were being held to unrealistic standards as they struggled to help youth understand the classics. Next, they explained and compared their instructional approach with a focus on comprehension to approaches that focused on elocution:

> Before undertaking to put in application any system of rules for delivery, we must thoroughly understand the thoughts to be expressed. ... "Practice makes perfect" is the motto constantly to be borne in mind; yet it must be *intelligent practice,* and not blind imitation, which can result only in making mechanical readers. (Parker & Wilson, 1874, p. 15, emphasis in the original)

Though this statement does not mention the influence of Jamesian pragmatism, it clearly mirrors James' concerns for intelligent practice and the usefulness of directed drills.

By way of contrast, Charles W. Elliot, the President of Harvard University, advocated against the use of schoolbooks (N. Smith, 1986). He believed that schoolbooks were a colossal waste of time and recommended they be replaced with real literature. His concerns were twofold: (a) the amount of time spent reading real text (he suggested 15 minutes a day would add immeasurably) and (b) quality literature for children should be available in schools. Schoolbooks, however, remained the most popular materials used for reading instruction.

Beyond school readers, professional books and teachers' manuals (methods books) described how teachers should approach the teaching of reading and reading comprehension. Collectively, they also supported the dominant ideology.

Professional Books and Teachers' Manuals

Professional books and teachers' manuals illustrate how notions of the dominant ideology overwhelm the text and are distanced from any discussion of the sociohistorical events of the era in which they are published. This stance, of writing for the academy as if in a vacuum, is repeated throughout the history of reading comprehension.

Cole's (1870) *The Institute Reader and Normal Class-book, for the Use of Teachers' Institutes and Normal Schools, and for Self-training in the Art of Reading* was a methods book that encouraged teachers to use the questions supplied by the authors of readers. He believed that the suggested questions should not be used exclusively; instead, teachers should seek to give and receive genuine responses to students. He believed that textbook questions and teachers' responses would help to improve student comprehension. He stated, "Nothing will add more to your own interest, nor more surely awaken the interest of your pupils, than your own earnestness. Earnestness is the charm, the magnetism of the schoolroom" (p. 24). Cole's admonition brings the teacher into the comprehension process. Prior suggestions for the improvement of reading comprehension focused on the questions that followed the reading lesson with little regard for the teacher, the role of the teacher, other than his or her willingness to use the pre- and postreading activities.

Cole supplied a theoretical explanation for instruction in reading comprehension. First, he exposed two popular views that held reading was successful based on either the quantity of what was read or the expression of the reading. Then, he posited, "Pupils should be taught to remember what they read, and to express it in a connected and intelligible manner" (p. 66). Furthermore, he explained that information obtained from answering the questions at the end of a lesson were of limited use. He argued, "The unity of thought and connectedness of ideas are absolutely essential to render knowledge of practical utility" (pp. 66–67). To that end, he offered advice on how to structure lessons to maximize the potential of the text being remembered. To improve reading comprehension, or "inquiry for meaning," Cole encouraged teachers to "teach your pupils to inquire for the sense of the passage ... when once a spirit of inquiry is aroused, it begets interest, awakens thought, and makes bold, manly readers, instead of slavish imitators" (p. 67). He also thought that teachers should set the example of readers who are able to convey their understanding and interpretation of text through an expressive reading.

Similarly, Clark (1898) published a manual for public school teachers titled *How to Teach Reading*. In this manual he wrote, "The reading lesson should be, primarily, a thinking lesson, and every shade of thought should be carefully distinguished no matter how long a time may be consumed" (p. 12). He suggested, "training in thought-getting" should be the primary purpose of reading, followed by elocution. In addition, he encouraged teachers to build "thought-getting" into a habit, reflecting the influence of the writings of Pierce and James and, more importantly, a growing need to improve comprehension. Sarah Arnold's (1899) *Reading: How to Teach It* also details the importance of reading comprehension. She articulates that reading is the ability to understand and convey that understanding (when reading aloud). What she calls "true reading" begins when one understands that "words are the vehicle of thought, a means to an end. Their mastery is indispensable to reading, but the reader must compass, not the single word-speaking, but the meaning of the related words which express the author's thought" (pp. 54–55). For true reading to occur, she suggests teachers use phonics, vocabulary, pictures, and life experiences to help students understand text. She observed that if reading is to be purposeful, it must replace oral reading with silent reading, followed by questions that improve student thinking. Likewise, Laing's (1908) book *Reading: A Manual for Teachers* criticizes the use of oral reading as a means of assessing comprehension. She endorsed the use of silent reading for comprehension as she compared and contrasted the different purposes of reading:

> The teacher who regards reading as a process of thought getting will proceed in one way, while the teacher who thinks of reading as an oral exercise carried on in connection with the book will proceed in quite another way. (quoted in Hyatt, 1943, p. 68)

She makes an important point here: The beliefs held by teachers about the reading process influences their instruction and student performance. It would be decades before this idea resurfaced in reading comprehension research.

Other educators (Colonel F. W. Parker and Edmund H. Burke) also evince signs of early thoughts about reading comprehension instruction, research, and testing. They who were extremely influential in the conceptualization of reading comprehension, methods of teaching reading and reading comprehension, and teacher preparation. Each excelled in very different but overlapping paths in reading comprehension research. The first was an exceptional educator and the latter a celebrated academic.

The Quincy Method Francis Wayland Parker (1837–1902) was born into a family with a long history as educators. His commitment to education inspired him to travel to Europe in 1872 to improve his knowledge of philosophy and pedagogy by studying the thinking of Froebel, Herbart, Pestalozzi, and Rousseau. On his return, he was hired as the new superintendent of schools in Quincy, Massachusetts. Beginning in 1881, Parker held summer institutes on Martha's Vineyard for teachers. His ideas on teaching were captured by Lelia Patridge's notes of Parker's work. She published these notes in her 1883 book under his name (Parker), *Notes of Talks on Teaching*. She observed that the school committee made an intelligent move in hiring Parker to reform public grammar education. Prior to Parker's arrival, students who attended the Quincy schools could not read, write, speak, or spell well after 8 years of schooling (p. xvi). Parker accepted the challenge to improve the education offered in the Quincy School and devised the Quincy Plan (also know as the Quincy Method). The Quincy Plan was not a method as much as a pedagogy that reflected pragmatic notions of truth. Parker summarized the key concepts of the plan as "first, an honest, earnest investigation of the truth as found in the learning mind and the subjects taught; and, second, the courageous application of the truth when found" (p. 21). Under this plan, education was not the acquisition of skills or knowledge; instead, Parker envisioned education as "the harmonious development of the human being, body, mind, and soul" (p. 22). In short, students were treated humanely; activities and cooperation ruled instruction and replaced rote memorization and harsh punishments. Instruction shifted from teacher- and subject-centered to child-centered, and skill and drill lessons were replaced with object lessons. Seasoned educators questioned the concept of the Quincy Plan, but when the Quincy students outperformed all other students in Massachusetts on statewide tests, it was heralded as a breakthrough. Fortuitously, the Quincy Plan aligned with the progressive reforms, and Parker's career skyrocketed. Although offered numerous and prestigious positions, Parker left Quincy for a supervisory position in Boston, which was quickly followed by his work at Cook County Normal School, then the Dewey's Laboratory School, and finally his own school, Francis W. Parker (1901). The Francis W. Parker School eventually became part of the school of education at the University of Chicago. His brief academic trek, however, did not include work in schools or universities in which there were sizable numbers of People of Color, and there is no indication in his writings that their needs were of any concern to him. The lack of direct reference suggests a universalizing of educational pedagogy and reading instruction.

Parker (1883) offered instruction to teachers, from teacher training in voice to subject matter lesson plans, including reading, writing, spelling, and talking. For example, Parker defined *reading* as "getting thought by means of written or printed words arranged in sentences" (p. 26). He compared and contrasted the four most popular methods of teaching reading used in the late 1880s: elocution, phonics, script, and word and sentence methods. Parker reasoned that children, in general, learn to talk and use language with little direct instruction by observing their worlds and connecting ideas to words, especially when shown objects. He advocated teaching children to read by the whole word/sentence method that he believed was superior to all other beginning reading methods. Parker also suggested that the phonics method, if not too strictly bound to pronunciation, could be helpful in moving children quickly from dependent to independent readers. However, he wanted students to focus more on meaning and less on expression of oral reading. As if through a pragmatist's lens, he observed "reading is thinking, and thinking is the mind's mode of action; and all mental development is rightly directed toward action" (p. 29). He encouraged teachers to assist young children in developing correct habits, seeking meaning, or "getting thought" (p. 29) and to avoid undue pressure to pronounce words correctly without understanding what words mean.

Parker (1883) likened reading to the law of association, claiming, "In all the teaching and the study of the art of teaching, little children to read, that which aids directly in acts of association of words with their appropriate ideas, aids the child in learning to read" (p. 31). Importantly, he adds, "Any other method … that does not aid the mind in these acts, hinders the child in leaning to read" (p. 31). Parker described the following steps in his reading program: language, objects, sketches, pictures, conversations, stories, whole words, and whole sentences. He also suggested that learning to read should be as natural as acquiring language, that all children know the sounds used in language, should be able to transfer those sounds to letters, and read with little or no problem. He believed that because children have the ability to comprehend oral language, they also have the power to comprehend written language. Therefore, he cautioned teachers to follow this rule: "*Never allow a child to give a thought until he gets it*" (p. 38, italics in the original). Put another way, allow children to share their understanding of the text in their own words, returning to the notion that comprehension is the key to reading. Parker's insistence on the use of object lessons over skill and drill and whole word and whole sentences over phonics analysis to improve comprehension, kindled a firestorm of opposition.

Early Synthesis of Reading Methods   Another extremely influential reading researcher and the author of a seminal text in the history of reading is Edmund Burke Huey (1870–1913). After completing his dissertation, which focused on the psychology and physiology of reading, he taught in normal schools, studied in Berlin and Paris, and then joined the faculty at the University of Pittsburgh. There he created a new department that joined education and psychology. His interest in reading and reading disabilities led him to study mental deficiencies.

Huey strongly endorsed the ideology of scientism and the use of scientific methods in all of his studies of reading, many of which (1898, 1900, 1901) focused exclusively on comprehension. His landmark text, *The Psychology and Pedagogy of Reading* (1908) was the most influential reading text to appear at the turn of the century. It includes a review of the history of reading, or, at least as he understood it, a review of the "scientific" literature on reading research, and a discussion of popular methods of reading instruction. His writing reveals the influence of the philosophical, social, and cultural contexts that helped to shape his thinking about reading and reading research.

He devotes four chapters to a historical explanation of the origins of reading and writing in which he traces reading and writing from what he believes is their earliest roots (4000 B. C.) to 1907. Using the cultural epoch approach, he places the ability to read and write within biological and social Darwinist thought as he explains the superior nature of the Anglo-Saxon culture and their progress as readers and writers. His evolutionary description of a developing nation's acquisition of literacy, for example, offered a popular explanation of societies, cultures, and individuals that finds Anglo-Saxons superior to all other groups and denigrates or ignores the histories of literacy among People of Color. In addition, his discussion of individual differences were defined racially much like Comte, Spencer, and Darwin, among others.

In a contemporary review of the text, Buchner (1909), wrote that the text contained "[a] central theme of the conditions and processes of reading both as a racial and an individual experience" (p. 147). Buchner's reference to race fit well into a nation still struggling with racial difference. What is important here is how Huey's work set a standard for later histories in the field of reading that unabashedly link reading research with the ideology of scientism and achievement in reading with race irrespective of historical, economic, cultural, linguistic, and societal inequalities.

Although Huey's views on reading are very similar to those expressed by Herbart and Parker, Huey is most often cited for acknowledging the mental processing that is required in reading. For instance, like Parker, Huey (1908) believed that reading should begin with the interpretation of gestures and pictures, followed by learning the alphabet before reading text. Huey had observed that the mind works in concert with the eyes as they view objects or symbols and apply meanings. Huey also held that silent reading is superior to oral reading because oral reading "too often show(s) only mechanical, stumbling, expressionless readers, and poor thought getters" (1908, p. 302). Further, Huey (1908) reasoned "the attention to reading as an exercise in speaking; and it has usually been a rather bad exercise in speaking at that, has been heavily at the expense of reading as the art of thought getting and thought manipulating" (p. 359). To him, the process of reading replicated the processes of thinking, and, more importantly, to understand what is read is superior to being able to read with expression.

Finally, Huey (1908) maintained that the essence of reading is acquiring meaning and producing thought or enhancing thought from the written materials. He discussed the nature of meaning and suggested "silent readers were generally better readers and read faster than oral readers" (p. 359). Continuing, Huey argued that silent reading is used more in later life than is oral reading and, thus, it should be taught in schools. He maintained that silent reading is a useful skill and recommended its use for classroom instruction. Huey described several methods of teaching beginning reading (e.g., Aldine, Ward) and recommended that reading should begin at home, but reading should not be forced too early on children. The progression of reading instruction should begin with oral work at school, include some practice in silent reading, and not be taught as a skill but as an art (1908, pp. 379–381). Students should be encouraged to love reading, which could be accomplished through the wise choice of literature. He also encouraged speech habits to improve oral communication, but he was not an advocate of elocution. He called for reading instruction to begin as reading comprehension instruction. He argued that early on, students should form the habit of reading for meaning and should practice it often: "At the naturally rapid rate at which meanings come from situations in actual life, the rate of reading and of thinking will grow with the pupil's growth and with his power to assimilate what is read" (1908, p. 359). Like others, Huey noted that rapid readers generally were better at thought-getting as well. The ability to measure reading comprehension was influenced by the onset of the standardized movement. Huey's book has been revised twice (1912, 1915), reprinted in 1968, and a centennial edition is being planned for 2009.

Kohler (1968) commented, "Remarkably little empirical information has been added to what Huey knew, although some of the phenomena have now been measured more precisely" (p. xx).

The acceptance of Huey's work and the acceptance of his thinking about cultural, social, and racial differences demonstrate the pervasiveness of dominant ideologyies within U.S. society and within the reading research community. Scientism became an all-encompassing belief in education where there was a belief in the power of scientific knowledge and its techniques to solve educational and societal problems.

The "particular constellation of social forces" Hall (2003) mentions manifested themselves in social, political, and educational movements explained in this chapter. In addition, undercurrents of racism, classism, and power appeared in educational research in general and in reading comprehension research and testing specifically. The ideas held by the dominant class and found in readers, teacher's manuals, and textbooks illustrate they were mechanisms of ideological hegemony. Given this backdrop, we can begin to better understand the role of reading comprehension research and testing in the hegemonic process. The next chapter documents how these ideas were woven into reading comprehension research and testing.

4

Producing Early Reading Comprehension Research and Testing

Reading comprehension research and testing are ideas created to represent the process of understanding how connections and associations are made between words or images and the meanings we assign. In previous chapters, I have discussed how ideological hegemony has shaped our understanding of reading comprehension from practical associations. In reality, theoretical and practical ideas and their associations are generated by people. Therefore, an account of the history of reading comprehension research and testing must be flexible enough to include biographical sketches of leaders in the field. In addition, histories should include statements that people make as part of the individual and collective efforts that have helped shape the field, even when their ideas are not popular or acceptable today. As Williams (1977) observes, "A lived hegemony is always a process. … It is a realised complex of experiences, relationships and activities, with specific and changing pressures and limits" (p. 112). Traditional accounts of the history of reading comprehension research and testing begin at this point and present an uncritical review or a celebratory parade of the accomplishments of reading comprehension research. Although most accounts review similar studies, they do so without having supplied the philosophical and sociohistorical moorings of previous chapters. Unlike traditional accounts, I unveil and deconstruct many of the shortcomings reflected in the same studies as I determine their place within the hegemonic process.

In this chapter, I examine the relationships and reading comprehension research of three prominent educational psychologists in the United States whose work included research of reading comprehension: James McKeen Cattell, William S. Gray, and Edward L. Thorndike. The relationship among these men represents a genealogical line of reading comprehension research: Cattell studied under Wundt and with Galton, Thorndike studied under Cattell and with Judd, and Gray studied under Judd and Thorndike (Gray is actually presented before Thorndike as his early work focused on oral reading comprehension research and testing which preceded Thorndike's research on silent reading comprehension). Their lives and reading research, collectively and individually, offer a window into how dominant ideas framed and informed their reading comprehension research and testing efforts. Given their close relationships, I illustrate how like-minded individuals sustained the dominant ideology through their definitions, theories, and tests of reading comprehension. In this way, they also reproduced and produced dominant ideas as part and parcel of reading comprehension research and testing. In addition, I include the contributions of several other researchers whose insights have added to what we currently know about the history of reading comprehension. The review of all research, however, is undertaken to clarify how "the rules that guide academic evaluation are inseparable from rules of knowledge production and research" (Kincheloe & McLaren, 2000, p. 295). The inseparability comes, in part, from their shared philosophical moorings.

Dominant ideologies have shaped how reading comprehension is defined and the forms of reading comprehension tests by framing "the concepts and languages of practical thought which stabilize a particular form of power and domination; or which reconcile and accommodate ... people to their subordinate place in social formation" (Hall, 2003, p. 27). Recall that members of the dominant group created these ideas and advocated for them while simultaneously securing their own futures and, in some cases, fortunes. One important way to accomplish both goals was to determine the boundaries of what constitutes reading comprehension, reading comprehension research, and reading comprehension testing. As members of dominant groups, these researchers were poised to use their power to maintain the status quo. Reading comprehension research and testing during this period highlights (a) the importance of language in conceptualizing, defining, and testing oral and silent reading comprehension and (b) the alignment of the interests of dominant groups in reading comprehension research and testing (White male educational psychologists) with the concerns of the political and economic mainstream explained in previous chapters.

Gray (1925) estimated that by 1910 there were 34 studies published on reading with more than half conducted in laboratories; naturally all these studies cannot be reviewed in this chapter. Several representative studies are reviewed as well as three distinct tests of reading comprehension: oral, oral and silent, and silent. In education research, including reading comprehension, when participants are not identified by race/ethnicity or linguistic preference, it usually indicates that the subjects are White, English speakers, or English dominant. By way of contrast, when Students of Color are research subjects, they always are identified by race/ethnicity or, where appropriate, language preference. However, the pattern of identifying participants of color is seldom to glorify their accomplishments, most often they are used as fodder to more positively reflect the accomplishments of White students by pointing to the shortcomings of non-whites. The scientism and racism driving this pattern have already been discussed, but it is important to point to the onset and pervasiveness of the pattern as it illustrates the racist history of educational research and is reflective of the philosophical assumptions that formed its foundations—the intellectual superiority of Whites and the intellectual inferiority of non-Whites.

A Genealogy of Reading Comprehension Research

The genealogy of reading comprehension research reads like a "who's who" in educational psychology. The work in reading comprehension by Romanes, Cattell, Thorndike, and W. S. Gray is discussed in this section, although it is a small portion of their more extensive studies in education and intelligence testing. Their ideas about reading comprehension research and testing are, to varying degrees, interrelated, and their power to shape reading comprehension research, due in large part to their tremendous prestige and productivity, is unfathomable.

George J. Romanes (1848-1894), a Canadian biologist and intimate friend of Charles Darwin, was among the early researchers who considered reading comprehension. He served as Darwin's research associate at Cambridge from 1874 to 1882 and was totally immersed in Darwinian literature and a zealous defender of Darwinism. He was interested in areas of intelligence, especially individual differences in intelligence and considered his work an extension of Darwin's thinking (Robinson, 1977). In his most famous book, *Animal Intelligence*

(1878/1884), he attempted to place human and animal intelligence and psychological development on an evolutionary scale. Romanes also questioned how organisms made adjustments to their environments. Although he believed that only those of superior breeding, wealth, and class, were intelligent, in his work he discovered to his amazement that ordinary people were also intelligent, much like Peirce. He argued that all statements by researchers, famous or not, should be corroborated by similar or analogous observations and independent observers. Among his many experiments were some conducted on the silent reading rate of adults.

Romanes' discussion of his experiment on reading rate and reading comprehension during silent reading by adults leaves out many details, some that were typical of the era: no descriptive information of subjects' educational level, reading ability, or demographics, especially race, class, gender, or native language. Nonetheless, he concluded that there was a wide range of reading rates as well as the ability to gather meaning from text. He held that rapid reading yielded better comprehension than slower reading and silent reading was more efficient, in terms of comprehension, than oral reading. His conclusions were used to support theories in reading research that coupled reading rate with comprehension.

Cattell's Influence on Reading Research

Among the earliest researchers to study reading was James McKeen Cattell (1860–1944). His interest in physical and behavioral concerns, however, began with his work under G. Stanley Hall, George Morris, and Charles Peirce, at Johns Hopkins. It was there that he became interested in individual differences (inherited mental and physical characteristics) in reading as early as 1883. Later in Europe he studied under the "father of psychology," Wilhelm Wundt (1832–1920), who used systematic methods to understand mental operations. Building on Wundt's idea of cognition as active and nonemotive, Cattell experimented with a tachistoscope in a laboratory setting to determine the time it took to read a single letter compared to the time it took to read a single word. He surmised that people read whole words, not letters.

Cattell published his work on reading research after extensive study at Wundt's laboratory (see Sokal, 1971, for a discussion of Cattell's unpublished autobiography). His earliest publications appeared in the journal *Mind* in 1885, making him among the first U.S. researchers to publish a study on reading. He stated that his study was important because "It measured individual differences, it used paper-and-pencil tests, such as are now applied to determine 'intelligence' in the use of words and numbers; and the methods and results were entirely independent of introspection" (Cattell, 1885, pp. 630–631).

Cattell's commitment to scientism and its effect on reading research should not be taken lightly. The excitement over the new field, psychology, peaked the interest of reading researchers who envisioned their work as scientific. Cattell (1896a) argued,

> I venture to maintain that the introduction of experiments and measures into psychology has added directly and indirectly new subject-matter and methods, has set a higher standard of accuracy and objectivity, [and] has made some part of the subject an applied science with useful applications. (pp. 13–14)

Further, Cattell's understanding of the use of scientific methods to ascertain differences among individuals in mental processing also reflected the work of Darwin and Galton. Cattell had become associated with Francis Galton, describing him as "the greatest man I have ever known" (quoted in Woodworth, 1944, p. 203). Like Galton, Cattell was interested in the inheritability of traits, individual differences, and eugenics. As Cattell recalled, it was Galton's interest in individual differences that shaped his thinking about standardizing measures. As a devotee of Galton, Cattell pointed to his own Scotch–Irish heritage as supplying him with "a germplasm" that accounted for his superior intellect.

Sokal (1987b) articulates, "Galton provided him with a scientific goal—the measurement of the psychological differences between people—that made use of the experimental procedures he had developed at Leipzig" (p. 27). Sokal adds, "Cattell devoted himself to an extension of Galton's anthropometric program into what he called mental testing" (p. 29). Not surprisingly, Cattell reveals, "The best way to obtain the knowledge we need is to make the tests, and determine from the results what value they have" (Cattell, quoted in Sokal, 1971, p. 32). By way of example, Cattell conducted experiments on individual differences among freshmen at Columbia that led to the publication of his first book, *Mental Development in the Child and the Race,* published in 1895. Then, writing with Farrand, they suggested that measurements be used to "to study the development of the individual and of the race (white race), to disentangle the complex factors of heredity and environment" (Cattell & Farrand, 1896, p. 648).

Although Cattell's goals appear focused on improving the value of psychology as a science by the use of quantitative measures with some interest in general intelligence, he did not waiver far from Galton's interest in eugenics. In fact, he was an ardent supporter. Cattell's work was not the straightforward indictments of racial superiority of Galton, but the message is clear that Cattell also supported racial and ethnic notions of superiority. His mental tests, however, proved unreliable. Cattell realized that these experiments were flawed, but suggested that the experiments were "measurements of the body and of the senses" more than "higher mental processes" (Cattell & Farrand, 1896, pp. 622–623). He abandoned his experiments after coming under additional criticism by colleagues and the publication of a dissertation by Emily Sharp that compared his work on mental testing to that of Alfred Binet (Sokal, 1981) and found it wanting.

Woodworth (1944) recalled that Cattell's interest "from the very outset of his career was in introducing quantification methods into psychology and especially in using such methods for the measurements of individual differences" (p. 203). What is important here is that, perhaps unknowingly, Cattell's work set precedents in reading: (a) the importance of the use of the scientific method and (b) the use of quantifiable measures to determine individual differences (later more clearly identified as racial, economic, and gender differences). Here's how Cattell, in a 1904 address at the International Congress of Arts and Sciences in St. Louis, Missouri, characterized his work:

> I claim for psychology the freedom of the universe in its subject matter, so I believe that every method of science can be used by the psychologist. The two great achievements of science have been the elaboration of the quantitative method on the one hand and of the genetic on the other ... It would be an irreparable limitation if either of the these methods did not apply in psychology. (quoted in Woodworth, 1914, pp. 60–61)

Cattell's interests also reflect the undercurrent of racism as evinced in support of eugenics. It is important to point out this connection because of Cattell's pivotal role in psychological research in the United States and his influence on early reading research. The close relationship he formed with his students helped to create a network of "reading experts" (Walter Dearborn, Arthur I. Gates,

Fredrick Kelly, Edward L. Thorndike, Margaret Washburn, John B. Watson, and Robert S. Woodworth) who had successful careers in psychology and helped to shape the course of reading comprehension research and testing in the United States.

Cattell's role in intelligence and early reading research and testing was influential and continues to shape reading research. His life and work mirror the complex history within the history of educational psychology and reading research that are anchored in positivism, scientism, and racism. His most important contributions to reading research are (a) his belief that responses to stimuli reflect nervous system (brain) functioning and indicate intelligence, (b) his demonstration that the time it takes for an adult reader to read a single letter is similar to the time it takes to read a short familiar word, and (c) readers read more words in less time when words from sentences. His crusade to legitimize psychology as a science, one useful to the field of education, helped to normalize the performance of English-dominant, European American males from upper- to middle-class environments as the standard group by which reading performance is measured.

Cattell's reading research drew on his understanding of the mental and physical processes that produced varying reaction times which, he believed, were connected to intelligence and attributable to race/ethnicity. In addition, he sought to measure and identify differences between genders and races, while surreptitiously seeking to confirm his beliefs about the intellectual and moral superiority of White males. Cattell's experimental psychology and professional clout, in relation to reading research, center on his insistence on conflating individual and racial differences that have traditionally been used to support deficit notions about non-Whites popular among some psychologists and reading researchers since the early 1900s. What is imperative to understand today is that Cattell set a precedent in reading research whereby positivism continues to underpin many research projects, especially those that seek to identify differences among students and to quantify them without consideration of historical, social, and political contexts.

The early reading tests of comprehension were conducted orally. To many researchers and teachers, oral reading appeared useful and appropriate in primary reading instruction and in the testing of comprehension. Proponents of oral reading declared that oral reading was the traditional means of assessing reading comprehension, particularly in the elementary grades. Many teachers believed that early phonetics drills and word recognition were necessary to develop a sufficient vocabulary in order to read fluently. Word-attack skills and phonetic analysis were taught when students began to note differences and similarities in words. Oral reading performance tended to increase steadily and rapidly in the lower grades and less rapidly in the upper grades. Likewise, pronunciation and accuracy also increased steadily in the lower grades. In terms of oral reading ability, the mechanics acquired were easily accounted for, that is, when words were pronounced during oral reading correctly it was assumed that students understood the text. Oral reading tests, however, were not considered efficient measures of reading comprehension because they were individually administered and scoring was very time consuming and tended to be subjective.

Oral and Silent Reading Comprehension Tests

The debate over oral and silent reading comprehension centered on issues of efficiency, that is, which type of comprehension was more efficient, which could most easily be tested, and which cost the least to administer. Efficiency concerns, however, were not the only reasons a debate over oral and silent reading comprehension emerged. Other concerns were raised by reading researchers who conducted laboratory studies of reading, school administrators who monitored student progress in large school systems, and classroom teachers who taught children daily. Their concerns sought to 1) replace oral reading with silent reading and 2) elocution with an emphasis on thought-getting, or reading comprehension. The oral reading tradition, however, was hard to break. Several reading researchers diligently sought to illustrate the effectiveness of oral reading as a means of comprehending text well into the 20th century because it was viewed as a habit that could be understood through scientific study.

Although the National Education Association voted in 1912 against the use of measurement techniques in education and national standards, a deluge of experimental studies spurred a call for national standards—a trend that continues. The call for national standards was allegedly to improve and reform the educational opportunities of students who attended public schools. The teaching of reading comprehension—from the normal school classrooms to elementary schools—was shaped, in some part, by the philosophical assumptions of the educational leaders who supported the scientific study of reading. The Herbartian Society (aka the National Society for the Scientific Study of Education) in 1914 appointed the Committee on the Economy of Time in Education. This committee was charged with analyzing the learning environment during instruction, identifying instructional methods, measuring the effects of various methods with specifically designed tests, and adopting the methods that produced the highest results (1915–1919). In addition, in a report written by William S. Gray, Jr., members of the Committee added their endorsements to those of university professors who supported Joseph Rice's ideas (mentioned earlier) regarding testing as a means of assessment of school achievement.

Early Reading Comprehension Tests

Among the first U.S. tests of oral and silent reading were those by Quantz (1897) and Pinter (1913b). Francis (1894) emphasized the use of the story technique in which students read a story silently, then responded to questions asked orally. Quantz's (1897) research focused on reading rate in oral and silent reading. He found that (a) retention of material was superior in silent reading than oral reading, and (b) lip movement tended to hinder speed of oral reading.

Pinter (1913b) tested the oral and silent reading comprehension ability of fourth-grade students by giving students eight tests of oral reading and eight tests of silent reading. Materials for his tests were taken from the students' schoolbooks. Each test was timed for two minutes, although speed was not an integral part of his investigation. The oral reading tests were conducted individually and the silent reading tests were conducted in a whole class setting. After each test, the students were asked to write down as much as they could remember from the text. This measure for evaluating comprehension was commonly referred as a written reproduction—the amount and accuracy of a verbatim reproduction. Tests were scored by an analysis of the reproductions, called "thoughts" by Pinter. Student-generated reproductions of "thoughts" contained in paragraphs were compared to the "thoughts" that the researcher believed was present in each paragraph. The researcher's interpretation was the only correct one. This is perhaps the beginning of the "one right answer" syndrome. Pinter concluded that students comprehended more when reading silently than when reading orally. As a progressive, he also supported the use of silent reading because it was more economical. Pinter's interest in testing reading led to his interests in intelligence testing, including investigations of racial differences of intelligence (see his 1917 publication).

Adelaide Abell (1894), one of the first women to publish an article on reading comprehension, was unique in an age when most women shared authorship of articles with males. Her research sought to determine the relationship of reading comprehension and rate among college coeds in a Wellesley psychology class. She required 41 students to read a short passage before class, asked them to time themselves, but did not indicate what she hoped to accomplish in the experiment. Once in class, students were asked to write a verbatim account of their reading as a way to determine their level of comprehension. Based on the self-reports of the students Abell claimed, *People differ widely in the rapidity of reading* [and] *people differ greatly also in the amount comprehended* (p. 283, italics in the original). She likened slow reading to oral reading and argued that it was a poor habit to form because it often interfered with comprehension. Rapid silent reading, however, appeared to aid comprehension, indicating the reader's ability to make multiple complex "apprehensions and associations" (p. 286). Abell also argued that "*comprehension may be independent of the absolute rate of reading*" (p. 284, italics in the original). Her study seemed to confirm not only Herbart's idea that the available knowledge from which a person has to draw is important for comprehension but also Romanes' notion that individual differences varied significantly among adults.

Other women who conducted reading research during this period include Roxanna Anderson (1912), Josephine Bowden (1911), Francis Hamilton (1907), Maude Merrill (1918), Jean Rankin (1911). Barbara Roethlein (1912), Myrtle Shotly (1912), Bessie Stillman (1912), and Clara Vostrosvky (1899). Generally, their studies were small in nature, usually confined to schools or school districts, or conducted in collaboration with male colleagues or spouses. Considering the barriers faced by women in their pursuit of equal access to a university education as well as the general attitude toward women and their low social and intellectual status, their publications are an impressive feat. Because it is not possible to review each study, only one example is given.

Boggs was a university professor and former classroom teacher. She brought a different point of view to reading comprehension to the field as she drew on her experiences in the classroom and her close observations of children in the daily task of learning to read. Boggs insisted that the alphabetic and phonetic methods were passé. In her study (Boggs, 1905), each of the four preschool boys who participated were shown syllables and given ample time to respond. She claimed that what was needed were methods that helped students learn to get meaning from print. She suggested that reading material should be interesting to children and spelling and pronunciation drills be rapid and short (2–3 minutes). Although she does supply information about the boys' reading ability, race, class, or native language, she attributed variance among the boys to individual differences. Boggs surmised that with proper training each child could be taught to comprehend.

Standardizing Reading Comprehension Tests

In 1913 Charles Judd, a member of the Committee of Standards of the National Council on Education, argued, quite persuasively, that standardized tests could provide a means whereby "the individual teacher could obtain objective evidence of what a pupil accomplished" (1913, p. 2). As editor of the 1913–1914 issue of the *Elementary School Teacher* (later renamed the *Elementary School Journal*), Judd promoted the use of standardized tests to improve school and teacher efficiency. In a 1913 editorial, Frank Freeman, an editorial assistant offered a preview of a series of English tests that were being developed in Detroit, Michigan, by Stuart A. Courtis. Judd mentioned Courtis' work in arithmetic and praised Courtis for his "great ingenuity in devising tests that were convenient and could be used by large groups of people" (Freeman, 1913, p. 146). Judd encouraged school superintendents to give the new tests a try, suggesting that by doing so they would gain experience, support their supervisory duties, and help to standardize the tests. He outlined four functions of the standard educational test:

> (a) to secure information that will enable school authorities to formulate in objective terms the ends to be attained in any educational process;
> (b) to measure the efficiency of methods designed to produce desired results; (c) to determine the factors and laws which condition learning

and teaching; (d) to furnish data that will enable comparison of school with school, and teacher with teacher for purposes of supervisory control to be made upon scientific, impersonal, and *objective* data. (p. 375, italics in the original)

Judd's ideas supported positivistic assumptions about the source of discovery and knowledge. His call for standardized testing use in education and as a means to obtain data that was "impersonal and objective" foreshadows future research in education in general and reading comprehension specifically.

Judd (1913) also outlined his thoughts on reading research in the article "A Reading Test," where he suggested that teachers made judgments of a child's performance subjectively and standardized testing would improve judgments by supplying an objective measure by which to judge a child's performance. He proposed that by judging large-group performances with standardized tests, usable standards for schoolwork could be obtained. Furthermore, he provided specific criteria for the selection of materials and specific directions for the administration of reading tests. He maintained that teaching efficiency also should be judged by the results of student performance. His argument was tempered to appeal to the teacher's sense of reason about testing because many teachers had been openly vocal about their dislike of supervisory judgments regarding their teaching, based on the results of test scores (Travers, 1983). Nevertheless, Judd stated that teachers should not fear testing and used reprints of the article as a vehicle to convince teachers that the real importance of standardized testing was to improve social standards.

As editor of the *Elementary School Journal,* Judd was in a pivotal position to sway professional opinions about reading and reading research in the educational community. In 1914, he wrote a series of articles and editorial commentaries about reading testing in which he sought cooperation from school officials for the testing of reading processes and skills. He argued that oral and silent reading comprehension should be measured separately, for they represented different skills. He reasoned that oral reading was a childhood activity and silent reading was an adult activity.

Like Pinter, Judd envisioned reading comprehension as a thought-gathering act, one in which a "group-of-ideas" could be produced and tested against the "group-of-ideas" suggested in a paragraph. The number of idea groups were to be determined by the test developer through a pretesting phase in which the majority of students' interpretations of the paragraphs' "group-of-ideas" were used as the standard. Correct scores were obtained when a student's reproductions used two or more "groups-of-ideas" in the right relation. Judd's most important contribution was his clear outline of the proper procedures (standardization) to follow in the administration of reading tests.

One of the most overlooked contributors to early oral reading comprehension is Clara Schmitt, the Assistant Director of Child Study for the Board of Education for Chicago Public Schools. Schmitt examined the number of school children in large urban schools that had "unfavorable reactions to the school situation" (Schmitt, 1914, p. 150). In her position, Schmitt examined and categorized several hundred children. According to her,

> Since it is the child's reaction to the school situation which is at fault, it is well to test him along the line of the special abilities which he is expected to develop under the conditions of the school's situation. (p. 150)

Schmitt's (1914) article explained the directions she gave to teachers for the selection of children to participate in her study. She requested that teachers from five public schools located in immigrant sections of the city "select children who are average good readers for the grade, do not select the very best readers you have" (p. 155). Schmitt implied that the immigrant's educational experience differed from that of others. She focused on not only reading comprehension but also linguistic differences that may have interrupted comprehension.

She tested 85 children in Grades 1 to 6 from homes where English was spoken by the mother (38) and from homes in which the mother did not speak English (47). She assumed that students whose mothers spoke English at home were more proficient in English than those whose mothers did not speak English at home. The latter group she labeled defective. She reportedly "pre-tested the defective children ... to assure that all had a mental age of at least seven and could complete first grade work regardless of their chronological age" (p. 152). The reading tests she used consisted of the time taken to read the story, errors in pronunciation, verbatim reproductions of the stories, and the correctness or falseness of the interpretation of the motive of one of the major characters in the stories. Additionally, she used a series of questions to probe for fuller interpretations.

Young children were given a story from their schoolbooks (read-ers) that she believed was familiar to them, "The Fox and the Grapes." Schmitt (1914) reasoned that all the children were familiar with the story in some way, either having read it themselves or having heard others read it in their classroom. A second selection, for older students, was selected from the fifth-grade *Jones's Reader* because it was believed to be unfamiliar to most students. According to Schmitt, there were two components of reading: quantity and quality. She hypothesized that quantity was the amount of text a child was able to read (ranging from a total lack of word recognition to the use of word-attack skills with unfamiliar words), whereas quality referred to oral reading from mechanical (word calling) to voluntary reading by the child. Her quality-of-reading scale included *apperceptive ability*, or what she defined as "the relation of what is read to a larger complex of knowledge or experience in addition to the reproducing of content" (p. 154). Unfortunately, her notion of "larger complex of knowledge and experience" gets lost in her interpretation of the student's oral and written reproductions, yet her thinking predates notions of prior knowledge of the 1980s.

Schmitt measured reproductions in three large categories: scant, adequate, or full. Scores were tabulated and comparisons were made of the types of errors committed by normal and "defective" students. She noted that the errors made by the normal students centered on language errors. She listed the following errors: mis-placed accent, the omission of an obscure syllable in long words, giving a different phonetic value than is the right one for the work in which the letter is found. The types of errors made by the "defec-tive" students varied to the extent that Schmitt did not offer any characteristic descriptors.

With the assistance of a school principal, Schmitt interpreted the errors of the immigrant children as indicative of their backwardness and slow ability in learning to read, supporting claims of the domi-nant class that "native born" Whites in the United States were intel-lectually superior to immigrants from all countries. She observed that the oral reading errors of this group of children generally "con-sisted of some unerring recognition of words and more or less filling-in to supply a remembered context" (p. 161). By today's standards, her tests obviously lack sophistication, but it is important to note that, unlike her male counterparts, she made important contribu-tions to the field by acknowledging linguistic differences as well as the economic, social, and psychological trauma that were often part of the immigrant school experience.

Pelosi (1977) suggested that Schmitt's work was an important change in the understanding of reading, and he lists several innovations in her research. First, she was among the first reading comprehension researchers to account for language differences in pronunciation and interpretation of text. Second, her comments regarding language usage centered on her investigations into the language spoken in the homes of the students tested. Third, she believed that much of the variance in her study was due to issues of language. Finally, her suggestions regarding the language spoken in the home and whether or not the English language was spoken well, illustrate her sophistication in discerning and reporting differences of language as they affected reading achievement. Subsequent articles that cited Schmitt's work made reference to her discussion of immigrant populations and her theory regarding immigrant children's apparent low-level performance on oral reading tests.

Early Silent Reading Comprehension Tests

One of the first examples of standardized testing in reading was Stuart Courtis' (1914) "Standard Tests in English," which combined tests of reading and writing (penmanship, dictation, original story, normal reading, careful reading, and reproduction). He maintained that his experimental studies in arithmetic had revealed a connection between the reasoning needed in arithmetic and the reasoning needed in reading and reading comprehension. He offered a philosophical explanation for educational testing as he envisioned his work, and that of others, as illustrative of how "the tests of the psychologist are 'pure science' tests. The test itself often deals with a single elemental phase of mental action" (Courtis, 1914, p. 374). This type of thinking promoted scientism whereby experiments were believed to represent "pure science," and to operate outside of the broader contexts in which experiments were generated and interpreted. Courtis captured these ideas when he argued that the work of psychologists was linked to greater social goals:

> Day by day, however, the school is attempting to make certain well-defined changes in the minds and habits of the children in its care. The character and amount of these changes is not determined by chance,

but in accordance with laws, which, in their operation, are as constant as those which determine other phenomena of the natural world. Until these laws are known, scientific control of the efficiency of the educational process will be impossible. (p. 374)

Furthermore, he claimed that standard tests of school achievement fell somewhere between informal and formal experimental examinations.

Courtis (1914) also believed that testing should be practical, which meant that the function of testing in schooling should be twofold: a measure of the abilities of students to complete the work in a subject area and a tool for improving the efficiency of teaching. His ideas echoed the contemporary views of efficiency, consideration of the individual needs of the child, and the need for standardization of educational tests that were scientific and quantifiable. He outlined the following procedures to standardize tests:

The test sheets are printed on paper of a uniform size and bound with appropriate record and sheets in pamphlet form. Exactly the same tests are given to all grades from the fourth through high school and university, and that conditions may be kept uniform, instructions for giving, scoring, and tabulating the tests have been printed in convenient form together with necessary record sheets, answer cards, and graph sheets. The tests themselves contain many devices tending to make scoring easy and to reduce the time required to a minimum. They will be supplied at cost to those who will return their results for tabulation with those of other schools. (p. 376)

Like other researchers, Courtis found that the range of individual differences was as great in reading as it was in arithmetic and that the general causes of success, efficiency, and teaching method were similar in arithmetic and reading. He did not offer demographic information relative to race, class, gender, or language of the students tested. It is not clear whether the lack of information was an oversight or an assumption of homogeneity.

Courtis's powerful position within the Detroit, Michigan, school district and his publication of the test results helped to define, frame, and shape how reading was understood and how to create tests. He also benefited financially, as he charged districts for each test. He reviewed his study (Courtis, 1915) as did others (Gray, 1917b, 1917c; Monroe, 1918a) and found important limitations: The inordinate amount of time involved, the difficulty of scoring the reproductions, and the standardization of the tests with adults made them unattractive tests for school children.

Bessie's Adventures.
Part C.

Once out of the yard, Bessie ran straight down the street as far as her two little legs could carry her. From the corner around which the dog and cat had disappeared, she could see, half way up the block of the cross street, a dog barking furiously at the foot of a tree. So Bessie ran in that direction, getting quite out of sight of her own home. When she drew near, however, she stopped running and stood gazing at the dog in dismay. Her cute little playfellow was nowhere to be seen. This dog was larger and darker, and his voice loud and savage. What big teeth he had! How viciously he growled and snapped at the cat up the tree!

Suddenly a sense of loneliness oppressed the little girl. The world seemed big and strange; she must get back to her home and her mother. She turned and started to run again, making for the corner. A great auto-truck thundered by, blowing its horn loudly. A group of children jeered at her, and a small boy tried to block her way. Bessie reached the corner at last, but, confused and bewildered, she turned in the wrong direction.

On and on she ran, finding nothing but strange houses and unfamiliar scenes. A suspicion that she was lost flashed across her mind and filled it with terror. The suspicion grew to a certainty. She was lost! She would never see her mother any more! In a dumb agony of terror the little girl sank helplessly upon the nearest horseblock, then gave way to a storm of sobs she could no longer restrain.

Figure 4.1   Courtis (1915) English Test No. 5: Careful reading.

Cyrus Mead (1914) is another researcher who sought to determine whether oral or silent reading produced greater correct responses. In Cincinnati, Ohio, he administered six 2-minute tests to 112 sixth-grade students (there was no information relative to race, class, gender, or language of the students tested) using material from a passage in *Alice in Wonderland*. Unquestionably, he found that the written reading reproductions after silent reading were more correct than the oral reading reproductions. Mead repeated his study annually for 2 years and increased the number of students and grade levels involved while reducing the time allotted to 1 minute. He observed that even when less reading time was given, silent reading reproductions were superior to oral reading reproductions. He concluded from these studies that silent reading was a better measure of reading comprehension than oral reading.

Interest in reading comprehension research and testing was not limited to academics. In 1914, Harry A. Brown, who was assistant commissioner of education and Director of Educational Research for the New Hampshire State Education Department (and thereafter until 1930, he was president of the Wisconsin State Teachers College in Oshkosh), published the results of an elaborate study of silent reading comprehension. From 1913 to 1917, he reported on a reading comprehension investigation he had conducted "as part of his regular duties" (p. 477), although the research project also was supported by the General Education Board of the Rockefeller Foundation. Brown published his study in the *Elementary School Teacher* as a description of a "scientifically" devised reading test designed to measure reading achievement of the children of New Hampshire. He maintained that through the use of scientific methods, researchers could use the outcomes of children's ability to evaluate methods of teaching reading. Brown's article is a testament of the proliferation of the rhetoric of scientism.

Brown was interested in the reading ability of school children in New Hampshire, the reading methods used by teachers, the type and amount of reading instruction used in classrooms, and teacher efficiency in teaching reading. He selected seven schools in the Alberta, New Hampshire, school system. His tests were administered to a relatively small population of third and sixth graders, slightly over 400 students in total (there was no information about the race, class, gender, or language reported). His goal was to "see what could be done in the way of measuring reading ability, and for the purpose of finding out how it might be conducted" (Brown, 1914, p. 478). Brown argued that once an effective means of measuring reading ability was discovered, then methods of teaching reading could be evaluated to discover which reading method was the most effective.

Brown (1917) saw three aims of research in reading. First, he considered the role of reading in a person's life:

> Reading is the greatest tool for thought-getting which an individual may have at his disposal. A comprehensive survey of the needs of the individual as a member of the social group must be made and those specific reading abilities which will function in the most serviceable way as a tool in the life of the individual must be determined. When the social needs of the individual in terms of reading power are set forth clearly in the form of certain specific reading abilities, we shall have a statement of the need to be attained by the educative process as far as this subject is concerned. (p. 477)

His thinking reflects similar ideas expressed by Herbart and Parker years earlier. Second, Brown believed that reading research should

be based on scientific investigations, further reflecting his positivistic stance:

> We must have, however, working hypotheses based upon the known laws
> of learning and on the nature of mental processes in children, and the
> most fruitful source of such hypotheses, and about the only one of great
> scientific value is a study of child nature in all its aspects, for it is uni-
> versally recognized that knowledge regarding the laws pregnant in the
> physical organism and predominant in the mental life of the child can
> furnish the only valid foundation for methods of teaching. (p. 478)

Third, Brown emphasized the need for a formulation of a valid scientific
pedagogy of reading. He envisioned the process as evolutionary and one
in which "the former are selected and retained and the latter eliminated,
until in due time a new pedagogy of reading will be evolved which will
be in harmony with the laws of the most economical learning" (p. 479).
His thinking on this point mimics Peirce's idea of the need for some
level of consensus among a community of inquirers.

He also identified three factors in reading efficiency that could
be evaluated: reading rate, quantity of reproduction, and quality of
reproduction. His tests were among the first to use a long connected
passage, drawn from grade-level materials, that included an answer
key for scoring the written reproductions. Below is an example of a
passage, "The Long Slide," used by Brown (1914).

During the administration of the tests, students were directed to
read as much as they could and to "get the thought" from reading.
All reading tests were timed for one minute. After the timed reading,
each child was to mark the word last read. The students were then
asked to reproduce, in written form, as much as they could remember. In defense of this method Brown (1914) writes, "It cannot be
pointed out too often that reading is more than mere word-pronun-
ciation" (p. 490). Then, he suggests there are flaws in the ways that
reading is typically taught:

> Undue emphasis is placed on too rapid and too complete mastery of the
> difficulties of word-pronunciation in the earliest stages of reading at the
> expense of apperceptive and assimilative activities and that this type of
> reading produces a pronounced word-consciousness and a confirmed
> habit of reading words instead of thoughts from the printed page which
> the pupil never completely outgrows and which proves a real hindrance
> to real thought-getting in later stages of his reading. (pp. 489–490)

Brown's commentary is a restatement of similar ideas held by Herbart and Parker although he used descriptive statistics to interpret

The boys and girls who live in a certain part of a small town in a country several miles from any village attend school in a little red schoolhouse know as the Long Hill school.

It has this name because it is situated on the top of a very long, steep hill. Ever since anyone can remember, the scholars of the Long Hill school have always had time to slide down the hill just once at recess in winter and get back to the schoolhouse before the bell rings to call them back again into school. They can go down very rapidly, but it takes a long time to walk back.

Last Monday morning Frank Lane appeared at school with a fine, new sled. It was a double-runner which his uncle, who owns a carriage factory in the city, had given him. He named his new sled the Simon and almost had to fight with Tom Smith, who said it was foolish to put such a name on a sled, but he kept on calling it the Simon.

At recess that day Frank invited the whole school to go for a coast and the twelve boys and girls got onto the sled and away they went down the steep hill. When recess was over, Miss Black, the teacher, rang the bell but not a scholar appeared. Thinking that the children had stopped to play on the way back from the slide, Miss Black went to door and looked down the hill and rang the bell again. But not a scholar was in sight. Then she was greatly astonished and began to be very angry, for nothing like this had ever happened in all of her twenty-eight years as a teacher. She waited and waited, but still no scholars appeared. She stopped every team that came up the hill, but no one had seen anything of them.

She stayed at the schoolhouse and wondered what had become of her children until it was time to let out school and then she went over to John Reed's who lives nearest the schoolhouse and whose son and daughter were among the missing scholars. Mr.Reed was greatly frightened at what Miss Black told him about the disappearance of her school children and immediately hitched up his horse to go in search of the lost children. Just as he was driving out of the door-yard, the scholars appeared far down the hill. It was almost dark before they got back to the schoolhouse.

Frank Lane, who was the largest boy in the school and the owner of the Simon, had to explain to Miss Black the cause of their absence. At the foot of the hill there was a road broken through the field to a logging road which ran down through a swamp to a stream. When they reached the foot of the hill, Frank steered the Simon into the road which led through the field. The Simon ran so easily over the frozen snow that it took the children clear through to the logging road. This had been before sprinkled with water and had frozen hard the night before and ran down the hill. When the Simon struck this road it kept on going faster and faster and Frank was unable to stop it. When it reached the stream, which was covered with smooth ice, it went clear down to Rand's mill, which was three miles from the schoolhouse. Frank told Miss Black about their long slide and said that he did not intend to run away with the whole school, but he could not stop the sled. He explained that they came back as quickly as they could, but the road was so slippery that they had to haul the girls and some of the smaller boys and that for this reason it took a long time to get back. He said that he hoped the teacher would consider it an accident.

Frank does not know yet what is going to happen to him, but he can bear up under quite a severe punishment, for Edward Post has been telling for the last ten years about the long slide he made once on Long Hill. But Frank's slide was a mile and a half longer than Edwards. Ever since that day no has dared to take even a short coast at recess.

Figure 4.2   (Brown, 1916) The Long Slide.

the data between classrooms and among schools (this information was not part of his original report but appeared later). Brown found wide variations in the reading scores produced by the different reading methods in the seven participating schools. He expressed his hope to isolate those factors that seemed to hinder or support learning to read.

By 1916, Brown's book describing his initial and follow-up studies, *The Measurement of the Ability to Read* was in its second printing. The publication was intended to give simple directions for the measurement of silent reading ability in children and included a description of his reading comprehension test, one sample reading selection, a sample of his "thoughts" (or interpretation) for evaluating quality of reproductions, directions for administering and scoring the test, charts for recording and tabulating data, and charts of oral reading and school reports. In addition, the 1916 monograph contains Brown's definition of reading: "The ability to interpret and remember the thought conveyed by the symbols of the printed page" (p. 7). Sounding like Herbart, he added that real reading involved comprehension:

> … carrying the thread of the story or argument or description, grasping the essentials or gist of it, sensing the significance of the whole, retaining it in mind in a well recognized form, with ideas in a rational sequence, after reading. (p. 7)

He believed that reading comprehension was produced in the use of connected passages—a short story, a description, or an exposition. Brown commented that these forms "would allow students to better respond to the entire amount of text read during the timed testing period" (p. 7). And, he saw the value of testing in the comparisons it afforded school administrators to make by comparing the results of one school with others in terms of reading rates, quantities, qualities, and units of reading efficiency by grade level. He argued that comparisons would help to show which methods of teaching reading, which teachers, which schools, and which school districts were more or less efficient. Despite Brown's claims, his tests were criticized for being insufficient measures of reading ability. Three specific reasons for their insufficiency were given: (a) The same reading passage was used for Grades 3 through 8. (b) The lack of alternative passages hindered any significant comparable measure. (c) The method of scoring was too time consuming (Gray 1917b, 1917).

Daniel Starch, a professor of psychology and education at the University of Wisconsin, in his 1914 book *The Measurement of Efficiency in Reading, Writing, Spelling and English*, described tests and presented standard scores for the four school subjects. In progressive rhetoric, he claimed that the measurement of efficiency of school subjects were in objective tests. Starch reasoned that in all subject areas, directions should be clear and should tell students what was expected of them. Thus, in his book he shared the results of reading tests given to approximately 10,000 students in 42 schools in 12 cities in 4 states: Minnesota, New York, West Virginia, and Wisconsin. And, he made available to school administrators and teachers the test directions, tests, and results so that they could compare the performance of their students with his published results (answer keys and scoring tables were available on written request).

His silent reading comprehension tests required students to read rapidly and be prepared to write a reproduction of the text, not necessarily a verbatim response using the same words but containing the same thought. Students were given the text, timed for 30 seconds of reading, asked to mark the word on which they stopped reading, and write what they remember from the text on the reverse side of the test sheet. In his test, reading comprehension was determined by "counting the number of words written which correctly reproduced the thought" (p. 3). All other words or ideas, not expressed, or repeated, were omitted. An average score for each student from the two readings was the final score. An example from one of his tests is given in Figure 4.3.

Increased testing of reading comprehension was not welcomed by some reading researchers or by some classroom teachers. The reading comprehension tests that were created consisted largely of a timed reading of text (orally with a test administrator or whole class silently reading with a teacher or graduate student proxy). Three basic types of test data emerged: verbatim reproductions, thought-getting responses, and written answers to questions. Both groups warned that an overreliance on standardized tests of reading presented an artificial and incomplete understanding of a student's ability to comprehend. In other words, standardized reading comprehension tests were not good indicators of "real reading." Nonetheless, reading comprehension research and testing continued.

No. 1

Once there was a little girl who lived with her mother.

They were very poor.

Sometimes they had no supper.

Then they went to bed hungry.

One day the little girl went to the woods.

She wanted sticks for the fire.

She was so hungry and sad!

"Oh, I wish I had some sweet porridge!" she said.

"I wish I had a pot full for mother and me. We could eat it all up!"

Just then she saw an old woman with a little black pot.

She said, "Little girl, why are you so sad?"

"I am hungry," said the little girl.

Figure 4.3   Efficiency in reading from typical first grade reader (Starch, 1915, p. 3).

The Reading Comprehension Research of William S. Gray, Jr.

One of the most accomplished reading researchers was William S. Gray, Jr., who began his studies of reading by testing the effect of oral and silent reading comprehension, although his work with oral reading tests is most often cited.

In a biography of Gray, Mavrogenes (1985) presents his life as a reflection of the "pragmatic and empirical orientation to thought, individualism, faith in the work ethic, a desire to improve their social status, and intellectualism" (pp. 24–25), typical of his Midwestern upbringing. At the age of 19 he began teaching in a rural one-room school, where he taught all subjects but felt least prepared to teach reading. His feelings of insufficiency led to a career in reading research. According to Mavrogenes, Gray wanted his students to acquire the mechanics of reading, to read well orally, and to appreciate literature.

When W. Gray attended Illinois State Normal University, under the leadership of its President David Felmley, a member of the Herbartian Society, he insisted that Herbartianism become a major influence in education for all students. He was devoted to scientism and also insisted that all students learn the laws of mental development and learning. Furthermore, he was adamant that the new science of psychology be included in the curriculum for teacher educators. Consequently, one of the most profound influences during Gray's undergraduate days was his acquired devotion to Herbart's thoughts on education. In 1908, Gray enrolled in graduate courses at the University of Chicago, although he participated in a special exchange program with Columbia Teachers College. While at Teachers College, he completed his degree requirements under Edward L. Thorndike. In his brief autobiography, Gray recalled,

> I went to Columbia University during 1913 and 1914 and there came in contact with men such as Thorndike, Kilpatrick, Murrary, Stayer, and others. The opportunity to sit as a student under the leaders in both the School of Education and Columbia University was an unusual one. It gave me an opportunity to compare points of view and to realize the great need for scientific study of numerous educational problems. (W.S. Gray, personal communication, July 15, 1988)

One of W. Gray's goals in his graduate program was to establish a scientific measure for oral and silent reading comprehension. As a former classroom teacher, his other goal was "to place in the hands of teachers the means of determining with something approaching the precision of objective measurement the amount of each school ability possessed by a pupil or groups" (Gray, quoted in Mavrogenes, 1985, p. 111). To accomplish the latter goal, Gray used Thorndike's statistical procedures to develop the steps of difficulty used in his timed oral reading paragraphs by drawing on the principles outlined in Thorndike's *The Equality of Equally Often Noted Differences* (1913a) and *Introduction to the Theory of Mental and Social Measurements* (1913b).

In his initial oral reading study, conducted in partial completion of his Masters degree, W. Gray (1917c) reported that his test was given to 565 students in Grades 3 through 8 from three large New York City schools and one small city school in Illinois. On his tests, he required students to list their nationality because he believed that there were ethnic and economic differences represented in the populations tested. He used this information to describe the schools in his study: "two foreign districts" and one 'truly' American population, economically independent" (p. 68). Furthermore, he stated that the Illinois school "represents an American population of average economic rank" (1917c, p. 68). As we noted in Schmitt's study mentioned earlier in this chapter, the xenophobia that has existed between U.S.-born Whites and others was apparent in descriptions of research subjects. Ironically, the same researchers who were careful in their analysis to attribute differences in test performance between U.S.-born Whites and international-born students to the customs, folkways, and languages, ignored the influence of students' customs, folkways, and languages. This study culminated in 1914 when he completed his unpublished thesis "A Tentative Scale for the Measurement of Oral Reading Achievements."

Thorndike's opinion of W. Gray's work was not as optimistic as he had hoped, although he earned a passing mark. Thorndike commented on the inadequacy of W. Gray's scale for measuring oral and silent reading. Although W. Gray agreed with Thorndike's assessment, he spent the better part of the rest of his life rethinking, revising, and rewriting his oral and silent reading comprehension tests. Nonetheless, W. Gray's thesis (1914) contained a discussion that was heralded as one of the clearest representations of the method recorded and illustrates how reading researchers began (and continue) to characterize their work as exemplary when there is a strict adherence to methodology. This thinking thus supports notions of scientism that regards empirical research as superior to other methods of inquiry.

In a monograph published several years later, W. Gray (1917c) summarized the research in the field on oral and silent reading comprehension and reviewed all of his research. Also, he described the lengthy procedure he followed for the selection of oral reading materials in 1914 and subsequent revisions (Cleveland, Ohio; Grand Rapids, Michigan; and various cities throughout northern Illinois). In addition, he explained changes that he had made to the selection and scaling of the oral paragraphs. He began by selecting 60 paragraphs from schoolbooks (readers) that met three criteria: approximately 50 words, of interest to children, and an expression of a somewhat complete thought unit. From the 60 paragraphs, he selected 16 paragraphs to pretest. He solicited help from 20 graduate students to order the paragraphs in difficulty for oral reading with "emphasis particularly on pronunciation" (W. Gray, 1917c, p. 61). The opinions of the graduate students on the selections of paragraphs of increasing difficulty served as a guide. W. Gray suggested, however, that the most accurate rankings of paragraphs would be obtained from elementary school students.

During his tests, students were required to read each paragraph orally until they had committed seven or more errors in two paragraphs. Oral reading errors were classified as: (a) gross errors (overall mispronunciations), (b) minor errors (slight mispronunciations), (c) omissions, (d) substitutions, and (e) insertions. His scoring was based on reading rate (the time required to read the passages orally) and errors (the number of mistakes committed during a timed reading). According to W. Gray, his findings revealed that in the elementary grades the mechanics of reading were stressed. Other findings he drew from these data included that the results of oral reading tests were highly correlated with teacher rankings, there were marked differences between oral and silent reading instruction, and there was a need for efficient curricular materials to reflect changes in reading development.

Most importantly, W. Gray acknowledged that he had not directly considered the effect of foreign language on oral expression during oral reading testing. Interestingly, he had tested for pronunciation and types of errors, although he did not discuss the students' errors in terms of their familiarity with the English language. However, he required each examiner to carefully distinguish whether the error was due to a slight accent and record the exact nature of each error. Unlike most reading researchers, then and now, he admitted that his tests failed to consider the interpretative and emotional elements involved in oral reading, the limited number of students tested, the lack of a more representative sample, the use of only one form of the test, and the individual testing format.

He returned to the University of Chicago to pursue a doctoral degree, and in subsequent investigations (1915–1917) he attempted to correct the limitations he acknowledged in his initial study, a process that he details in his 1917 dissertation. Collectively these studies reveal (a) evolution of his oral and silent reading test development; (b) statements regarding linguistic differences among students and his interpretation of comparisons between English speakers and others; (c) statements regarding race/ethnicity (what he called nationality) among students as well as his interpretation of the differences between Whites (which he called native-born U.S. students) and others; (d) statements regarding social economic class differences and his interpretation of the effects of poverty; and (e) high regard for classroom teachers' participation, comments, and interpretation about reading comprehension and testing. His discussion of each describes not only his thinking but the acceptance and pattern each point set for future descriptions of reading comprehension research in each area. Several examples illustrate this point.

The settings for W. Gray's studies represented a variety of schools: city, country, village, "ward," "homes for friendless children," university laboratory. He described schools based on their location and student population. He used the term *native-American* to distinguish foreign- and domestic-born European Americans from one another. Unfortunately, his idea of what constitutes a "truly" American student, one who is a native-born White and one who is economically independent, was translated into the White middle class as the standard population for many years to come in reading comprehension research. For instance, schools for native-born Whites of middle-to-upper class were described as being in the best or most desirable areas, schools for immigrant students were described as being in industrial or foreign areas, and schools for African Americans were described as being in areas for "negroes." His purposeful selection of schools illustrates that historically reading comprehension research has been complicated by researchers who have hand-selected schools for specific purposes. Although W. Gray did not present social economic data, given the time period, it can easily be assumed that the students from the best neighborhoods were middle-to-upper class native English speakers; the students from the foreign neighborhoods were low-to-middle class recent immigrants who may have had limited or no English proficiency; and the students from the "Negro" neighborhoods were low class, receiving an education that was inferior to that of either of the other groups. The school experiences of the students, the education of the teachers, and the materials used were unexamined. Like many others, W. Gray compared and contrasted the performance of students on his reading comprehension tests and found that students from the foreign and "Negro" schools lagged behind their White peers from the desirable neighborhoods. He was under the impression that the students, not the education they received, were inferior.

When Gray was asked to join the Cleveland, Ohio, public school survey by Judd and Ayers, he trained classroom teachers and normal school seniors to administer his tests. W. Gray (personal communication, July 15, 1988) recalled the experience noting, "My contact with this survey was one of the most interesting and inspiring experiences of my early professional career." He found that the teachers in Cleveland were effectively and efficiently teaching the "mechanics of reading in the primary grades to a population containing large concentrations of children who spoke languages other than English and have various national and ethnic origins" (W. Gray, 1917c, p. 129). Some teachers also made recommendations regarding the measurement of comprehension, suggesting that students be given a few extra seconds at the onset of testing to familiarize themselves with the subject matter before beginning the tests. Interestingly, many teachers felt that relying on questions as a method of determining comprehension was too narrow a means of assessment. They proposed other methods be used in combination with standardized tests to determine a student's silent reading comprehension ability.

His silent reading tests sought to determine reading ability as measured through the use of reading selections/paragraphs of increasing difficulty (he and Thorndike used some of the same paragraphs). He stated, "The aspect of reading ability measured by the test were rate of silent reading, ability to reproduce the subject-matter read, and the ability to answer specific questions concerning what was read" (W. Gray 1917c, p. 47). As in his selection of oral reading paragraphs, Gray considered the developmental stages and interests of children in the selection of silent reading paragraphs. His reading selections included one paragraph for Grades 2 and 3, one paragraph for Grades 4 through 6, and one paragraph for Grades 7 and 8. (Actually, some of his silent reading paragraphs were shorter versions of passages used by Brown, 1916, and Starch, 1915). The selections were graded as easy, hard, and hardest, respectively. The reading selections for Grades 2 and 3 also were evaluated according to the "group-of-idea" method promoted by Judd.

W. Gray reported that for validating his silent reading comprehension tests, he had solicited an analysis of "group-of-ideas" from students and compared the most frequently suggested ideas to a set of ideas he had identified as the substantive content of each passage. In areas of difference, he claimed that he always yielded to the students' suggestions. He allowed half credits for partial reproductions, an uncommon practice among his contemporaries. Gray also devised a list of questions "so difficult that very few pupils of a class would be able to answer all of the questions and at the same time easy enough so that no pupil would fail entirely" (W. Gray 1925, p. 111). In each set of 10 questions, the first six tested literal comprehension and the remainder tested interpretive, analytical, or inferential comprehension. Generally, the more difficult paragraphs focused on issues of

---

16

George Washington was in every sense of the word a wise, good, and great man. But his temper was naturally irritable and high-toned. Through reflection and resolution he had obtained a firm and habitual ascendancy over it. If, however, it brook loose its bonds, he was most tremendous in his wrath.

17

He was six feet tall, and his body was well-proportioned. His complexion inclined to the florid; his eyes were blue and remarkably far apart. A profusion of hair covered his forehead. He was scrupulously neat in his appearance, and, although he habitually left his tent at an early hour, he was well dressed.

Figure 4.4   (Gray, 1917c, Standardized oral reading paragraphs, p. 67.)

moral character, helpfulness, neatness, industry, self-control, and perseverance. Of particular note were two paragraphs, numbers 16 and 17, that were part of his original 1914 paragraphs for oral reading. The content and discourse used in these passages support and encourage a dominant set of beliefs that portrays the former president in folk-hero respect and that reinstates, not too subtly, thoughts of the racial, moral, and aesthetic superiority of "truly" American White men. These paragraphs describe George Washington, the nation's first president, as wise, temperate, good, great, neat, and attractive. The selections appear to be in concert with notions of the superiority of White males, intellectually, physically, and morally (see Figure 4.4).

W. Gray (1925) revealed, "Whenever questions arose, ease of giving the tests was usually sacrificed for increased accuracy in results" (p. 103). For instance, he adopted the teachers' suggestions to eliminate written answers to questions for second and third graders, and allowed younger students to dictate their reproductions of the selection and answers to questions. He believed that a combination of oral and written responses would create the ideal test of reading comprehension. He also frankly admitted that there were limitations to his test of silent reading comprehension: (a) The steps of difficulty between paragraphs were not exactly equal. (b) There was only one form of each test. (c) Scoring differed in the beginning and ending levels. (d) The quality (comprehension) of reading was not directly measured by his test (W. Gray, 1917c, pp. 96–97). Later, other reading researchers—C. Gray (1917), Gates (1921c), and Monroe (1924)—also noted similar limitations.

W. Gray's findings suggested that girls read better orally than boys in all grades, children of American-born parents read better than children of other nationalities in primary grades, and the Aldine (phonetic) and Ward (eclectic) methods of teaching beginning reading produced similar achievements in reading. In addition he made several important claims:

> 1. The written reproduction "differs greatly in different children, and is affected by the kind of ideas presented in the reading matter."

> 2. "Measurements of speed (rate) and power of interpretation (comprehension) will be worth collecting only when such measurements bring out the normal facts which are always present, but are for the most part unrecorded in reading exercises."

> 3. "The measurement of silent reading will "be preceded and followed in every case by some real instruction and questioning . . . until the pupils come to realize what a silent-reading exercise really is." (W. Gray, 1917c, pp. 112–114).

His analysis and interpretation of data over these studies was the most extensive synthesis to date as he attributed some variation to gender and race. Furthermore, he wrote, "More emphasis should be laid on interpretation and relatively less on drill in formal reading" (W. Gray, 1917c, p. 141). His call for more interpretation should not be read as the freedom to interpret text within one's frame of reference but as a freedom to select the answer most expected by the researcher.

Judd, W. Gray's doctoral advisor, however, interpreted the results of W. Gray's Cleveland survey differently. Specifically, he focused on the relationship between speed and quality of silent reading and identified differences between the passages adopted from district schoolbooks (readers) and the passages constructed for standardized reading comprehension tests. Judd argued that with a little supervision, the classroom teacher could conduct studies with the reading materials from schoolbooks (readers) that were used in ordinary classrooms.

He also concluded that reading instruction for the upper grades was severely lacking as evaluated by the results of oral and silent reading tests, and that both types of tests needed to be improved particularly the quality of selections for the upper grades. Generally, he saw the need to improve general reading instruction, especially silent reading to foster and improve reading rates. Prophetically, Judd warned that the public administrators and teachers might become too dependent on school achievement test results as indicators of learning and progress.

W. Gray received his doctorate in 1916 from the University of Chicago, magna cum laude, on the recommendation of Judd (Mavrogenes, 1985). His dissertation, *Studies of Elementary School Reading Through Standardized Tests*, served as a model for future research studies and dissertations in reading because it was among the first to include a statement of the problem, a review of the literature with accompanying annotated bibliography, a description of earlier oral and silent reading tests and their revisions, a description of the procedures used in the standardization and validity, and a chapter on special problems in reading. The review of literature compared and contrasted his studies as well as those of others interested in oral and silent reading tests. For example, he suggested that children of different nationalities (home language was used to determine student nationality) performed at varying levels and that there was variance within groups as well. He also surmised that other factors affected student performance: chronological age, sex, intelligence, methods of teaching, economic conditions, and the amount and quality of reading material. In addition he included charts, diagrams, and curves used in discussion of the descriptive statistical procedures he followed. It was widely acclaimed as one of the finest dissertations and later was published in the University of Chicago's *Supplementary Monograph* series.

W. Gray's early prominence in the field began with his acceptance to the exchange program with Teachers College and his work with Thorndike, followed by his work with Judd and Ayers; it continued with Judd as his advisor and culminated when he joined the faculty of the University of Chicago as an assistant professor in 1917–1918. He was promoted to full professor by 1921 and retired emeritus in 1950. His myriad contributions to the field of reading include serving as the reading director for the Scott Foreman publishing house and as senior author of the famous "Dick and Jane" basal reading series. This series portrayed Gray's notion of an idyllic "truly" American family living in the suburbs and living out what can only be called the "American Dream." Little conscious thought was given to the use of this reading series with underserved students. The marginalization of their lived realities and languages suggests that the "truly

American" way to live centered on the dominant class beliefs and values. In this way, reading content used for reading comprehension instruction and on reading comprehension tests perpetuated dominant beliefs, ideas, and values.

Another notable contribution to the field was W. Gray's compilations of reading research in the *Annual Summaries of Investigations in Reading*. Gray's chronicling of research related to reading began with his initial annotated list of research in Thorndike's 1914 issue of *Teachers College Record*. In 1925, along with the aid of Laura Zirbes, he published the *Summary of Investigations Relating to Reading Supplementary Educational Monographs, Number 28*. It was a compilation of his previous bibliographies and was published in conjunction with the *School Review* and the *Elementary School Journal*. The publication project, financed by the Commonwealth Fund of the Rockefeller Organization's Research Committee, included a general overview of reading research conducted in the United States and England beginning in 1824. Over the next 40 years, W. Gray edited, or coedited, the *Annual Summaries of Investigations in Reading*, which was published annually until 1997. For years his reviews were limited to research conducted in the United States and the United Kingdom, thus projecting an equally narrow view of what research is of value to the field. Later publications did expand their international reach and review of publications but generally only to other countries where English is the official language, that is, Australia, Canada, and New Zealand.

Many, but not all, of the studies of reading and reading comprehension reviewed were conducted in select public schools; schools that were chosen for the allegedly "superior status" of their "native-born" American students. These students were overwhelmingly Euro-American, middle-to-upper class, native English speakers, and their performance became the standard of measure for all other students. This normalization of the Euro American middle-to-upper classes as the standard helped to strengthen and promote notions of an intellectually superior White race. A result was reading comprehension testing served to strengthen the idea that science could verify White superiority when the test results were compared to subaltern groups. Test performance was interpreted collectively and used to support racist notions of inferior hereditary genes (all non-Anglo Saxons), lack of individual effort, deviant moral character, and parental ignorance.

Most reading researchers expressed little concern for the socio-historic and cultural barriers to literacy access and educational opportunities experienced by underserved students. Their standardized test results were of marginal concern; that is, they were merely used as fodder to highlight the differences between the Underserved and Whites. This pattern continues within the field as Underserved children are revictimized in educational research as the reason for their low performance on reading comprehension tests.

Finally, reading researchers, under the guise of scientism, promoted the idea that high performance on reading comprehension tests was an indicator of superior intelligence. Claims for the consideration of individual differences were left unspecified by most researchers, although it was common to interpret individual differences by race/ethnicity, gender, and class. In reading comprehension test research whereby demographic differences were marginalized and individual differences were assumed, this started a pattern that continues. Most importantly, it was during this period that reading comprehension research and testing drew on empirical methods to validate the educational psychologist's claims of measuring reading comprehension. This period also is noteworthy, as the role of reading comprehension research and testing becomes central to the hegemonic process of control in the struggle for meaning as measured by test performance

Reading Comprehension Research Expands

The review of early reading comprehension research and oral and silent reading tests mentioned in the previous section reveals that although grounded in the philosophical assumptions positivism, Social Darwinism, and biological determinism, these tests also reflected how reading comprehension is a mechanism in the reproduction and production of the dominant ideologies. Hall (1982) asserts, "The world has been *made to mean*. Language and symbolization is the means by which meaning is produced" (p. 67, italics in the original). However, as we have seen, the manufacturing of consent is also produced when educational experts declare what it means to comprehend text and images. The ideas surrounding and associated with reading comprehension research and testing have been shaped by the dominant group, whose specific and particular ideas, values, and beliefs in reading comprehension materials and on reading comprehension tests have been promoted as universal.

The philosophical assumptions and the social and political forces that contributed to the institutionalization of reading comprehension research and testing also helped to produce what appears to be a consensus among researchers. Under these conditions, theories, definitions, and tests of reading comprehension assumed a greater role in the nation by empowering the dominant group to define reading comprehension while simultaneously validating their ideas, beliefs, and practices. In this way, the dominant group socially reproduced and inculcated their beliefs, values, and practices in the lives of generations of school children.

The Reading Comprehension Research of Edward L. Thorndike

Edward L. Thorndike, known as the father of educational psychology influenced educational psychology and reading research, perhaps more than any other researcher in the early 20th century. His stature in the field, his position as teacher of required graduate courses at Teachers College, and his extensive publications in professional and popular presses helped shape the thinking of a vast number of educators and individuals. In fact, Thorndike's influence spawned a reading of like-minded folks who supported the same ideas as represented by Thorndike's former students, his true disciples. Collectively, they produced, reproduced, and advocated for a form of reading comprehension research and testing that shaped its future. Their collective and individual statuses within the field of education and educational psychology point to a growing use of reading comprehension tests as a part of the "apparatus of the ruling group" (Gramsci, 1971, p. 170f). That is, performance on standardized reading comprehension tests became a "legitimate" way to determine who would have access to increased educational opportunities and services and whose access and educational opportunities would be curtailed or eliminated.

(The following biosketch illustrates how the beliefs, values, and practices of one person have influenced reading comprehension research and testing. From his concepts, definitions, examples, tests, interpretations, and recommendations, Thorndike's word was golden.)

The life and work of Edward L. Thorndike serve as exemplar of researchers whose ideological and cultural beliefs are demonstrated in their application of the scientific approach to reading comprehension research and testing. Arguably, Edward L. Thorndike of Columbia Teachers College was the most dominant educator and researcher in educational psychology of his era. Thorndike's scientific orientation began when he studied under James at Harvard (1895–1896) and continued under Cattell at Columbia (1896–1898). Thorndike was exposed to the experimental laboratory and to statistical methods that he applied to the study of school subjects, including reading comprehension. His publications of silent reading comprehension tests helped to shift professional and public opinion and encouraged the use of silent reading instruction and comprehension as the most efficient use of time and resources (for a more complete biography, see Joncich, 1968). Moreover, throughout his career he received generous support from numerous funding agencies, many headed by his personal friends or colleagues. This support granted him tremendous latitude by allowing him to conduct investigations of his choosing and interest.

Edward Lee Thorndike (1874–1949) was raised under the watchful eyes of his Methodist father, mother, and maternal grandmother. In a 1932 single-page and self-effacing autobiographic sketch, Thorndike characterized himself as a healthy, intelligent, industrious, and committed worker. Introspectively, Thorndike made two observations about his career and work habits. First, he believed that there were three methods that could be used to advance the knowledge of human nature: observation and thought, observation or experimentation of facts, and a question and the pursuit of its answer. Second, he discussed the conditions he believed were needed for productive scholarly work: freedom from interruption, freedom from personal conflict, and freedom from financial worries. Admittedly, he wrote this short autobiography at the request of the editor of the autobiographical series, C. Murchison—and took a decidedly modest and even humble stance toward his personal history.

Joncich (1968) offers a more rounded portrait of the man and his life. She argues, in part, that he was not modest and was known to advocate for and adamantly endorse science, the scientific method, and his own research, hence the moniker she used to title her biography of his life, the sane positivist. Karier (1986) also has written extensively about Thorndike's life, research, and influence. He claims Thorndike assumed "a positive correlation between intellect, character, and wealth, and usually assumed that each was determined primarily by heredity" (p. 96). Furthermore, Karier argues that Thorndike believed that the more intelligent were also wiser and wealthier than others, which made them more fit to be leaders.

While attending Methodist Wesleyan University, Thorndike was introduced to James' *Principles* (1890). His response to the text in an essay contest won him an opportunity to study at Harvard under James' tutelage. The two became great friends and devoted scientists, with James housing Thorndike's experiments with animals in the basement of his home. Following his graduate degree, good friend, Robert Woodworth, convinced Thorndike to apply for a fellowship at Columbia. There too, Thorndike impressed his reviewers and was assigned to study under Cattell. His scholarship also afforded him unusual student privileges as he was permitted to complete the experiments that he had begun at Harvard. The result was his dissertation, *Animal Intelligence: An Experimental Study of Associative Processes in Animals* (1898/1911), later published as a book by the same title.

The text, regarded as a classic in the field, also is an explication of Thorndike's devotion to positivism. He postulated that in the psychological explanation of learning, neural connections were made between situations and responses. Taking a decidedly evolutionary stance similar to those held by Darwin and Spencer, he argued that over time the more intelligent animals would learn to respond to situations, which, if left unchecked, would lead to their continued existence and the extinction of the less intelligent animals or the extinction of those that failed to adapt to the environment. He extended his theories of intelligent and learning from animals to humans, which he viewed as a higher animal form.

In reference to humans, his theories were informed by Galton's ideas of the inheritability of intelligence, morals, and values, or what he called mental evolution. Thorndike held that adaptations to the environment were made by those with superior inherited mental qualities and were passed on to their offspring.

During Thorndike's tenure, Columbia Teachers College was the center for the training of teachers, school administrators, and researchers. Significantly, his graduate educational psychology course was required for all students. This requirement extended Thorndike's influence beyond his own graduate students to the entire college (Joncich, 1968). As an instructor, Thorndike followed the style of his mentors, James and Cattell, strongly urging students to read books and pursue investigations of their own interests. As early as 1901, Thorndike and his graduate students were in public schools collecting data for his scientific investigations of child study and school hygiene. He published his lecture notes in his book *Notes on Child Study* in 1901. His influence is captured in a 1908 letter from one of his students Leta Hollingworth. She declared,

> Sometimes I almost shake with the joy of thinking that I lived in this day of the world, and that before I die, I shall see the coming of a new religion which is to touch the heart of all the hungering people through Science and Scientists. (quoted in Joncich, 1968, p. 585)

Likewise, Thorndike shared his respect for scientific study in his 1903 book, *Educational Psychology.* In this text he observed,

> It is the vice or the misfortune of thinkers about education to have to choose the methods of philosophy or of popular thought instead of science. … We conquer the facts of nature when we observe and experiment on them. When we measure them we have made them our servants. A little statistical insight trains them for valuable work. (p. 164)

In his introduction to *Heredity, Correlation and Sex Differences in School Abilities* he claimed, "Our educational endeavor is conditioned by the original natures of the individuals whose mental traits we attempt to change for the better" (Thorndike, 1904c, p. 5). Clearly, he grounded much of his thinking in the philosophical assumptions of positivism, social Darwinism, and biological determinism as well as Galton's notions about individual differences or hereditarianism.

Thorndike also published two landmark texts on descriptive statistics, *An Introduction to the Theory of Mental and Social Measurements* (1904a) and *Theory of Mental and Social Measurements* (1904b) which remain classics in the field today and from which he earned the title, "father of the modern movement in educational measurement." The texts were the most popular books on elementary statistics used in the early 20th century. In the texts, he explained descriptive statistics (units, scales, frequency distributions, probability, measures) and differences in measures of reliability and correlation. The text made available for educational researchers tools of statistical measurement needed to construct tests and interpret results. For example, Thorndike and his students developed scales for measuring achievement in arithmetic (1908), handwriting (1910), English composition (1912–1913) and reading (1914). Thorndike (1912) saw a connection between scaling for physical measures and education, arguing that they were equal: "If we get scale points defined, and their distances defined, and establish an absolute zero, there is no further difficulty in constructing a scale for achievements in human nature" (p. 298). In December 1909, he presented his scale for handwriting to the American Association for the Study of Science in Boston. Later, Thorndike (1918) captured the heart of the use of measurement in education when he proclaimed,

> Whatever exists exists in some amount. ... This is obviously the same general creed as that of physicist or chemist or physiologist engaged in quantitative thinking. ... And, in general, the nature of educational measurement is the same as that of all scientific measurements. (pp. 16–17)

His desire was to make education a field of inquiry that used the scientific method as a means of discovering how the mind works and how humans learn.

Thorndike (1906) also published several books especially for teachers. One such book, *Principles of Teaching Based on Psychology,* included his laws of learning and their application to classroom instruction. He claimed that the aims of education should be "good will to men, useful and happy lives, and noble enjoyment" (Thorndike, 1906, p. 82). In keeping with his positivistic views, he believed that each individual "had a job to do" in the proper working order of society. The task of education and schooling, according to Thorndike, was to help each child find the proper fit, after acknowledging the capacities of the child. He stated that the capabilities of each student could be discovered only through objective measurement. Furthermore, he declared that science was the only way to discover, measure, and perfect mankind and society accurately. He also believed that lasting social changes would occur only when scientific principles were utilized in decision making:

> The judgments of science are distinguished from other judgments by being more impartial, more objective, more precise, and more subject to verification by any competent observer and being made by those who by their nature and training should be better judges. Science knows or should know no favorites and cares for nothing in its conclusion but truth. (Thorndike, 1906, p. 265)

One of his most significant texts, the massive three-volume *Educational Psychology* (1903), was the first text to succinctly bring together the science of psychology and the science of education, a refinement of his learning theory begun in *Animal Intelligence*. The volumes extended his laws of learning, the inheritability of mental traits, and individual differences.

Thorndike the Eugenicist

Thorndike's study of intellectual ability and individual differences included investigations with twins, women, and racial groups. He maintained that there was less intellectual variability among women, concluding, therefore, that more brilliant men existed. He suggested that on the average, due to females' more limited capabilities, they should restrict themselves to high school work. On racial issues, he claimed to have found, in his experiments with African American and White American high school students, differences on intelligence tests that pointed to the superior intelligence of Whites and that also supported his theory of racial differences in intellectual functioning. His beliefs about African Americans and their alleged inferior intellect, character, and morals were extended to include immigrants from Southern and Eastern Europe, and people of Asian and Mexican descent (Thorndike, 1920a).

When Thorndike's former mentor, Cattell, became the president of the American Eugenics Research Association, Thorndike also joined the organization. An active member, he served as chair of the Committee on Inheritance of Mental Traits. Not coincidentally, his interpretation of the theories of evolution and hereditarianism appeared in *Popular Science Monthly*, edited by Cattell. In the article "Eugenics: With Special Reference to Intellect and Character," Thorndike (1920c) articulated, "Men's original nature has selective powers over his environment; man will choose and reject, exploit or be exploited by elements in that environment according to his capacity" (p. 128). Furthermore, he endorsed eugenics as the only way of perfecting mankind (he restricted progress to males) and believed that eugenics was a way to control the evolutionary process. In another article that appeared in *Harper's Magazine*, Thorndike (1920b) clarified his point: "To him that hath a superior intellect is given also on the average a superior character" (p. 235). His ideas about the perfectibility of human life and his elitism led him to conclude, "What is true in science and government seems to hold good in general for manufacturing, art, law, education, and religion" (p. 235). Thorndike believed that men who were White, Protestant, and middle- to upper-class—that is, men like him—were morally and intellectually superior to all other races.

Thorndike and Reading Comprehension Research and Testing

Thorndike's interest in reading reflected his general interest in intelligence, learning, and mental processing that were involved in reading comprehension. He expressed his ideas about children and reading comprehension this way: "A child cannot be assumed to know the meanings of words which he uses or responds to; moreover, children may be ignorant of their ignorance" (cited in Joncich, 1968, p. 394). In this way, he was among the first researchers to equate the ability to read with general thinking abilities by postulating that errors in reading were errors in thinking. Furthermore, Thorndike developed a theory regarding thinking errors that was linked to his theory of mental evolution. Specifically, he asserted that thinking errors, and therefore reading errors, were of essentially three types: under potency, over potency, and dislocation or disrelation. The three types of errors were described in his 1912 text, *Education: A First Book*. In the discussion of the three types of errors, he continually referenced his earlier theories in *Animal Intelligence*.

Thorndike's investigations into reading comprehension consumed the field. For example, the entire 1914 September issue of *Teachers College Record* was devoted to Thorndike's early work in reading comprehension, or what he termed his "working paper." He extended this working paper into subsequent issues of the journal (*Teachers College Record* 1915A, 1915b, 1916a, 1976, 1917, 1934a, 1934b, 1934c). Renowned for his work in educational measurement by this time, he apologized for the rough measurement found in his initial article; however, he thought it was important to offer some insight on measuring school achievement in reading. Here's his explanation:

> It is obvious that educational science and educational practice alike need more objective, more accurate and more convenient measures of (1) a pupil's ability to pronounce words seen; (2) a pupil's ability to understand the meaning of words and sentences seen; (3) a pupil's ability to appreciate and enjoy what we roughly call "good literature;" and (4) a pupil's ability to read orally, clearly, and effectively. (Thorndike, 1914a, p. 207)

Like Cattell, Thorndike compared the ability to read with the physical abilities of sight, strength, and height. He believed that the ability to read could be reduced to simple components. He reasoned:

> Any progress toward measuring how well a child can read with something of the objectivity, precision, commensurability, and convenience which characterize our measurements of how tall he is, how much he can lift with his back, squeeze with his hand, or how acute his vision, would be a great help in grading, promoting, and testing the value of methods of teaching and in every other case where we need to know ourselves and to inform others how well an individual or a class or a school population can read. (Thorndike, 1914a, pp. 207–208)

Thorndike also claimed that up to 50 students could be given his test at once. He encouraged reading tests be administered at regular intervals, preferably at the beginning and end of the school year.

In his first test, "Scale A for Visual Vocabulary," he sought to measure students' understanding of single words (see Figure 4.5). The test was designed for Grades 4 through 8; however, Thorndike suggested the test "may be used in grade 3, and is useful in the high-school" (1914a, p. 13). The directions stated.

> Look at each word and write the letter F under every word that means a flower … Then look at each word again and write the word GOOD under every word that means something good to be or do.

The test consisted of 13 separate exercises that directed students to perform 4 separate tasks on groups of isolated words. Given the nature of the tasks, each line of the test was scored separately. The teacher was directed to record the time the students were handed the test and to note the highest line on which one error or omission occurred. The error or omission ended the test for the student.

Thorndike believed that certain words might be easier for some children than for other children. He suggested that differences might, in fact, be due to teacher use, local use, or the gender of the child. Nonetheless, he declared that his method of scoring was objective, definitive, convenient, and more or less equally scaled. Thorndike suggested that teachers use his latest invention, a stencil, to assure accuracy in scoring. He provided an answer key with an extensive list of possible responses, noting that although the key was more subjective than his stencil, it allowed students and the test examiner some room for interpretive response, especially for the more diffi-

Look at each word and write the letter F under every word that means a flower.

Then look at each word again and write the letter A under every word that means an animal.

Then look at each word again and write the letter N under every word that means a boy's name.

Then look at each word again and write the letter G under every word that means a game.

Then look at each word again and write the letter B under every word that means a book.

Then look at each word again and write the letter T under every word like now or then that means something to do with time.

Then look at each word again and write the word GOOD under every word that means something good to be or do.

Then look at each word again and write BAD under every word that means something bad to be or do.

4.   camel, samuel, kind, lily, cruel

5.   cowardly, dominoes, kangaroo, pansy, tennis

6.   during, generous, later, modest, rhinoceros

7.   claude, courteous, isaiah, merciful, reasonable

8.   chrysanthemum, considerate, lynx, prevaricate, reuben

9.   ezra, ichabod, ledger, parchesi, preceding

10.   crocus, dahlia, jonquil, opossum, poltroon

10.5 begonia, equitable, pretentious, renegade, reprobate

11.   armadillo, iguana, philanthropic

Figure 4.5   Scale A, Visual vocabulary. Thorndike (1914a).

cult paragraphs. However, he cautioned users of his test, "What are called 'standards' here are simply achieving a little above those actually made in schools under the possible disturbing conditions of testing by an outsider" (1915b, p. 458). Teachers also were encouraged to tabulate results alphabetically and derive averages for their class (a table of means accompanied the test).

In his second test, Scale A, Thorndike developed a measure for understanding paragraphs that was very similar to his first test because the paragraphs were lists of words (see Figure 4.6). He acknowledged limitations in the choice of the words used to form categories per line. Thorndike also noted that the directions required

Write the letter c under every word that means a color. Write the letter m under every word that means a thing that makes music. Write the letter w under every word that means some thing that boys or girls wear. Write the letter d under every word that means some thing that a boy can do.

(p. 22, boldface in the original)

red, green, guitar, hat, coat, run, work, play, shoe, jump, hide, piano, ink, cuff, shout, study, organ, reach, yellow, grasp, scream, collar, request, shiver, crawl, shirt, violin, violet, disagree, purple, inquire, scarlet, harp, flute, trumpet, practice, ramble, crimson, cornet, apron, mandolin, trespass, prevaricate, sweater, confess, ribbons.

Figure 4.6   The derivation of Scale A. Thorndike (1914a), p. 228.

students to be well read and experienced in order to complete the task correctly. Finally, he admitted that the scale did not measure the ability to understand words in context:

> The scale does not measure ability to understand the meaning of these printed words in general, or as they come in ordinary texts or completely, but only to understand them well enough to classify them as required by the test. (Thorndike, 1914a, p. 20, italics in the original)

These two reading tests required the reader to make thought connections or to discern similarities. To Thorndike, these tests were examples of a type of reasoning instrument. For example, on this test the words listed represented several different classes of words and concepts, but together they became an amalgam. He held that the reader needed to decide how the words were analogous as indicated in the directions. He claimed that the exercises helped readers acquire habits of response to elements and ideas that they may have never truly experienced. Echoing Herbart and his notion of apperception, Thorndike claimed that as a reader read, he tried to make connections among situations expressed in the text with those he had experienced. Thorndike believed that people worked at making connections in reading to "make sense" of what they read from the experiences they had either in the text or life. In this way, Thorndike argued, new combinations of experiences or connections were made as readers used reasoning capacities to make the connections.

In his third test, Thorndike attempted to separate the ability to understand text from the ability to produce written reproductions in a clear, simple, and economical manner. In his words, "the ability to understand a paragraph and certain questions asked is measured by the correctness of verbal responses, in much the same way as done in the daily reading in school" (Thorndike, 1914a, p. 248). This test comprised was a printed text followed by 1 to 10 (literal) questions. Students were directed to read the text as often as they needed and then to answer the questions, most of which required short answers. An example is shown in Figure 4.8.

Thorndike alleged that this test measured a reader's understanding of sentences and paragraphs:

> Mere word knowledge is much less important than the ability to get the message carried by a continuous passage ... Probably no other one scale for educational measurements is so important as a scale for measuring the understanding of sentences and paragraphs ... The special difficulties in this case are to measure ability to understand unmixed with ability to express and to do so without ambiguity and at small time-cost. (1914a, p. 238)

In his final test, students read a declarative sentence that directed them to "do" something, or act on what they read. The responses of the students were scored as either correct or incorrect. A key was provided for teachers (see Figure 4.7).

Thorndike acknowledged that with more complex reading tasks, answers to questions could be interpreted differently than those supplied in the key, but for ease in scoring only, the answers listed on the key were considered correct. He also stated that reading comprehension should be a goal of elementary school reading programs, a goal that continues to this day.

Thorndike continued to publish improvements to his initial tests. The most important improvement that he made in subsequent revisions was scaling—the grading of the difficulty in his series of paragraphs (although the paragraphs did not change). As with the original Scale A tests, students were permitted to re-read paragraphs if they desired because there was no time limit. Thorndike revised his tests and expanded the questions immediately following each paragraph. In Fig. 4.8, a sample paragraph from his test demonstrates how Thorndike placed his own thinking and beliefs within the test items he created and how his ideas validated the dominant ideology through reading comprehension testing. Further, the content of reading comprehension tests can be interpreted as, consciously or unconsciously, legitimizing White middle-class standards and racial prejudices in education.

Do what it says to do

1. Write the letter n three times.
2. Draw a line under the word that begins with w. big dog sick well had
3. Make the shorter line longer.
4. How many are two and one?
5. How many ears has a cat?
6. Put a dot over the i in pig. Pig.
7. Put two dots in the square.
8. Put one dot in the middle of the circle.
9. Draw a line below the square.
10. Draw a line around the circle.
11. Write your name.
12. Copy the second of these words. big bat beg
13. Copy each of these words. rose nose goes
14. Cross out the smallest dot.
15. Cross out the largest d.
16. Cross out each a in these words. Advantage derivation.
17. Which is the coldest—spring, summer, autumn, or winter?_____
18. Which is the longest—an inch, a mile, a foot, or a yard?_____
19. When is it warmest—in spring, summer, autumn, or winter?_____
20. Which moves most rapidly—a snail, an automobile, a horse, or a chicken?_____

Figure 4.7   Derivation of Scale A, IV (Thorndike, 1914a, p. 230).

Difficulty Number 9 (Figure 4.9), is interpreted as an expression of Thorndike's (1917b) personal disillusionment with Judeo-Christian beliefs and his resolute faith in science. It seems reasonable to assume that the correct answers to the questions that followed the passage affirmed Thorndike's ideological and racist theories.

Thorndike's use of testing as an avenue to support his views was not unique; as Karier (1975) noted, most successful test developers endorsed and supported middle-class standards. Cooper (1892) argued more poignantly that such men represented "the self-congratulation of 'dominant' races, as if 'dominant' meant 'righteous'

> Read this and then write the answers to 1, 2, 3, 4, 5, 6, 7, and 8. Read it again as often as you need to.
>
> Tom gave a gray cat to Mary. She gave him a black dog.
>
> 1. What did Tom give the girl?
> 2. What did the girl give Tom?
> 3. What was the girl's name?
> 4. What color was the dog?
> 5. What color was the cat?
> 6. Was the dog the same color as the cat?
> 7. Did Mary give Tom anything?
> 8. Who gave the cat to Mary?

Figure 4.8   Scale for measuring the understanding of sentences and paragraphs (Thorndike, 1914a, p. 250).

and carried with it a title to inherit the earth?" (p. 73). Thorndike's research in educational psychology as well as reading comprehension monopolized the field and influenced other researchers for decades. Part of Thorndike's success came from his grantsmanship, the ability to raise funds to support his research.

Foundations tended to be supportive of selective institutions; for example, the General Education Board of the Rockefeller Foundation subsidized many research efforts in education at the University of Chicago and Teachers College (Monroe, 1918b). The Carnegie Institution subsidized many research efforts at Teachers College under the directorship of Keppel, a close friend of Thorndike's. Another friend of Thorndike's, Leonard Ayres, was the director the Russell Sage Foundation Division of Education and an active supporter of numerous research efforts, including those several by Thorndike. Ayres also was a member of several school survey teams. For example, he joined members of the faculty and staff from the University of Chicago when they conducted the famous Cleveland Survey. (The Cleveland Survey, however, was financed through a local fund, the Cleveland Foundation.) Foundation support of faculty and research also made it possible to accommodate growing enrollments, expand graduate programs, offer endowed chairs, and offer a more extensive curriculum.

Collectively, Cattell's, W. Gray's, and Thorndike's legacy illustrates how a "network" or community of like-minded researchers, men-

DIFFICULTY 9

Read this paragraph and then write the answers to questions 1, 2 and, 3. Read it again if you need to.

Science is so new a thing and so far from final, it seems to the layman so hopelessly accurate and extensive, that a moralist may well feel some diffidence in trying to estimate its achievements and promises at their human worth. The morrow may bring some great revolution in science, and is sure to bring many a correction and many a surprise. Religion and art have had their day; indeed, a part of the faith they usually inspire is to believed that they have long ago revealed their secret. A critic may safely fore judgment concerning them; for even if he dissents from the orthodox opinion and ventures to hope that religion and art may assume in the future forms far nobler and more rational than any they have hitherto worn, still he must confess that art and religion have had several turns at the wheel; they have run their course through in various ages and climes with results which anybody is free to estimate if he has an open mind and sufficient interest in the subject. Science, on the contrary, which apparently cannot exist where intellectual freedom is denied, has flourished only twice in recorded times—once for some three hundred years in ancient Greece, and again for about the same period in modern Christendom. Its fruits have scarcely begun to appear; the lands it is discovering have not yet been circumnavigated, and there is no telling what its ultimate influence will be on human practice and feeling.

1. What condition is stated in the paragraph as making it impossible for science to exist?
2. What, according to the paragraph, gives any interested and impartial student a right to draw conclusions concerning the influence of art?

What sentence in the paragraph states that the devotee of religion often thinks that religious truth will not be increase?

Figure 4.9.   Scale Alpha 2 Extension (Thorndike, 1916a, p. 60).

tioned by Peirce, develops. This group of educational psychologists who were interested in reading comprehension research and testing and held similar values, beliefs, and worldviews grew incestuously over the next few generations as their followers emphasized the rules of formal logic, procedures of data collection, and application of statistics. Graduates of Teachers College, for example, influenced the course of education throughout the nation as they secured positions of prominence as professors, university presidents (Iowa, Minnesota, Purdue, and Washington), government officials, faculty at normal schools and colleges, and public school administrators (Joncich, 1968).

Members of the network and many former students of Thorndike included E. P. Cubberly, Walter Dearborn, Arthur I. Gates, William S. Gray, Jr., and G. P. Strayer, to name a few. Strayer unmistakably captures this idea when he observed, "All our investigations with respect to the classification and progress of children in elementary schools, high schools, and in higher education are based upon Professor Thorndike's contribution to the psychology of individual differences" (quoted in Curti, 1964, p. 483). Other commentators questioned Thorndike's free mixing of science and personal opinion, noting that Thorndike's "social opinions are truly related, scientifically, to his experimental work, and to what extent they are determined by his own unconscious participation in the prejudices of our own time" (Curti, 1964, p. 498). Thorndike, along with others, "created tests which reflected that social order (with Whites as superior) and the values implicit in that order" (Karier, 1975, p. 162). In so doing, under the guise of science they justified the dominant ideology.

The previous chapters unravel how the hegemonic process fuels the dominant ideologies imbedded in reading comprehension research and testing, beginning with the philosophical assumptions that underpin reading comprehension research and testing in the United States and disentangling the roots of scientism, racism, and classism that are entrenched in its history. There are complex and intricate relationships within the social and political forces as well as among power elites that keep it afloat and help dominant ideologies retain their buoyancy.

There was strong support within the academy for Cattell's research on the inheritability of intelligence and for Thorndike's and W. Gray's use of descriptive statistics to measure educational outcomes. Their work supported popular notions of intellectual differences between the more privileged White, middle-class, English-dominant males and other groups that included non-Whites, people who lived in poverty, people whose first language was not English or Standard English, and women. In addition, their personal memberships and affiliations with other like-minded White males outside of the academy led to opportunities that helped to shape intelligence testing in this country. The next chapter discusses how early research in reading comprehension continued and was gradually transformed from the academic research agendas of researchers to center stage in the intelligence testing of recruits for the Unites States Army. The results of the tests were advertised and unapologetically promoted as evidence confirming the intellectual superiority of White males. Alternatively, a tide of oppositional voices arose from African American scholars and strong-minded White advocates who recognized the undercurrents of race, class, and power.

5

World War I and the Development of Reading Comprehension and Research Testing

Between 1914 and 1916, two thirds of the educational tests published in the United States focused on the standardization and measurement of reading comprehension. Although a great deal of research has occurred since then, very little has changed in reading comprehension research and in the structure of reading comprehension tests, other than increased sophistication and the use of statistics (Farr & Tone, 1986; Readence & Moore, 1983). In this chapter I examine how reading comprehension research and testing supported dominant ideologies.

First, this chapter continues the review of reading comprehension research just prior to World War I. Then, it examines the foundation of intelligence testing and reading comprehension research and testing it spawned during and immediately following the war. Intelligence and reading comprehension test developers worked with the U.S. government to create the Army Alpha and Beta tests and later pushed for national intelligence tests. Additionally, this chapter details how ideological hegemony functioned within intelligence and reading comprehension research and testing movements.

Reading comprehension research and testing continued to evolve as the United States galvanized for participation in World War I and as dominant groups struggled to win the consent of educators, the general public, and the federal government. The need to scientifically verify U.S. genius, or White male superiority, was unending. In this young nation on the brink of war, reading comprehension and intelligence test researchers indicated there was a national crisis—the lack of intellectual acuity among U.S. males—as determined in U.S. Army testing. Left out of this discussion was a thorough description of the test items, many of which discriminated against groups that lacked educational access and opportunity. As Forgacs (2000) explains, "Many elements in popular common sense contribute to people's subordination by making situations of inequality and oppression appear to them as natural and unchangeable" (p. 421). Historically, U.S. intelligence and reading comprehension testing are inextricably linked. Finally, African American scholarship in response to World War I, officer recruitment testing, and national intelligence tests offer a counterhegemonic position in resistance to dominant ideologies of power elites, challenging the scientism and racist ideologies. In addition, counterhegemonic positions by like-minded Whites on the nature of intelligence and standardized testing are presented.

Insights and Improvements in Reading Comprehension Research and Testing

Prior to World War I, there were several improvements to reading comprehension research and testing that are worth reviewing briefly. The research by Starch and Gray provides a better understanding of the process undertaken in reading comprehension test development, while the experiments conducted by three former students of Thorndike, Kelly, King, and Zeilder also depicted improvements to reading comprehension tests.

Starch and Gray's Improvements of Reading Comprehension Research

In 1915, Starch described his investigations into the measurement of reading comprehension and standardization procedures used in the *Starch Silent Reading Tests*. He stated that his tests "will furnish the tools for evaluating quantitatively the results of methods and factors in teaching and learning, and for examining various aspects of efficiency of instruction and administration of school systems" (p. 1). Drawing from the published research of Courtis and Thorndike among others, Starch argued that the primary values of tests were scientific and practical in nature, thus appealing to both progressives and pragmatists.

Like many of his contemporaries, Starch viewed reading as a complex mental process, and he believed that the best way to measure reading was to identify the major components of reading comprehension. He identified three means of gaining information during reading: comprehension of materials read, speed of reading, and accurate pronunciation. In his pragmatic view, the two most important elements of reading were speed and comprehension because together, they represented a "fixation of belief," borrowing liberally from Peirce. Starch (1915) used the term *reading comprehension* and offered the following words of caution: "A very important matter to take into account is the extent of their [students'] vocabulary and the range of their ideas" (p. 2). His regard for student interests is similar to the ideas expressed by Herbart's apperception notion. He also believed that vocabulary was a factor that contributed in scoring written reproductions but not one that was accounted for in reading comprehension tests. By way of contrast, he measured reading comprehension as the number of words written which correctly reproduced the thought of the passage, usually written immediately after reading a passage.

Starch claimed to have administered his reading tests, at the close of the school year, to 3,511 third-grade students in 15 different schools in 7 cities in Minnesota, New York, and Wisconsin. His tests did not differ significantly from Brown's, and like Brown he selected passages from graded readers. The published results of Starch's tests focused on the testing process. He recalled that on the first day of testing, the test was given to students at grade level, and on the second day, tests were given one grade above and below a student's grade level. He suggested that this procedure permitted a comparison of difficulty among the passages. In an attempt to standardize the testing procedures, Starch (1915) gave the following directions to teachers and examiners:

> Explain to the pupils that they are to read silently as rapidly as they can and at the same time to grasp as much as they can, and that they will be asked to write down, not necessarily in the same words, as much as they will remember of what they read. They should also be told not to read anything over again, but to read on continuously as rapidly as is consistent with grasping what they read. (p. 6)

Based on test results, Starch reported tentative standards of reading efficiency in a series of tables and charts with accompanying narrative explanations. Openly, he admitted that the numbers represented on the tables and charts were not actual arithmetic averages but estimated values. Nevertheless, he claimed that his investigation confirmed earlier findings that suggested that there was a wide range of individual differences among students in the same class and grade level.

Impressively, Starch identified four limitations of the design of his test. First, he acknowledged his sensitivity to the need to ensure uniformity of difficulty and content of passages. However, he declared that by supplying briefer, unconnected passages, he had built in a check for difficulty and content. Admittedly, he recognized that some passages of fables or literature may have been more familiar to individual readers. However, he protested that scores on reading comprehension tests indicated that familiar passages were not better comprehended than unfamiliar ones. Second, Starch suggested that there existed different means to assess reading comprehension achievement. Appearing to resurrect elocution, he stated that the most valid tests for reading comprehension should be orally ascertained. Yet, he believed that the fairest reading comprehension tests would require reproduction of thought after a long time span (albeit, he had rejected both methods in the design of his tests because they required more time and labor to accomplish, thus making them uneconomical). He declared that his method of measuring reading comprehension was "simple and objective" (p. 13). Starch also believed that by comparing the scores received on his tests with the teacher's marks in reading for each student, an accurate measure of a student's comprehension was possible. Third, Starch maintained that a higher correlation between teacher assessment and his tests could be obtained if the tests were given four times a year instead of twice. He mentioned the possibility of changing the reproduction portion of the test to a short answer format. Finally, he argued that written thought reproductions were easier to score than trying to account for the number of ideas in a sentence or passage. He believed that the number-of-ideas theory of measuring reading comprehension was too subjective.

Two years later, W. Gray's most influential articles on reading comprehension testing, "The Relation of Silent Reading to Economy in Education," appeared in the *Sixteenth Yearbook of the National Society for the Study of Education, Part One.* In the first part of the two-part article on the methods of testing reading, he sought to describe "in some detail certain rough general tests which may be readily administered under normal school room conditions, and, in addition, to describe standard tests in reading which are organized for the purpose of securing more exact results" (Gray, 1917b, p. 23). He described three different methods of testing reading that were available: preliminary tests, uniform tests, and standardized tests. Although he did not reflect on the philosophical orientations of the researchers, W. Gray suggested that the "facts" of reading included information about rates of reading, reproduction, and interpretation of reading materials. The "facts" to which he referred were the results, or the interpretation of the results drawn from "scientific" experiments. For instance, with regard to rate, he declared that all reading progressed at some rate and that rate should be considered an element of reading ability, noting that students varied in their rate of reading ability as they advanced through schooling. He argued, "Rate is one of the symptoms by which we can readily measure the stage of development of the pupils" and that "rate and ability to understand are interdependent" (W. Gray, 1916c, p. 232). Though W. Gray acknowledged that reproduction and interpretation were the aims of reading, he further commented, that "differences in students' abilities in these areas were affected by the kinds of ideas presented in the reading matter and the quality of the teaching" (p. 232). Seemingly drawing on Herbartian philosophy and Parker's idea of choice, he believed that students should be interested in the subject matter and that quality teaching needed to occur if text were to be comprehended. W. Gray's disclosure—that it was difficult to measure how much a student understood and how well he or she could reproduce with the measures available—suggested that he believed the measures were imperfect, but nonetheless important, indicators of both student reading comprehension and quality of instruction

Wholly Right or Wholly Wrong

Another researcher interested in reading comprehension research and testing, and a former student of Thorndike's, was Frederick J. Kelly. His research, in many ways, is an extension of the work by Thorndike discussed in the previous chapter. In 1915, Kelly was the director of the Bureau of Educational Measurement at the State Normal School in Emporia, Kansas, when he published *The Kansas Silent Reading Tests*. His goal in undertaking this research was to produce an efficient objective test of reading and which could be easily administered and scored. Kelly outlined four criteria for measuring educational products: (a) something worth measuring, (b) simplicity, (c) measure of progress, and (d) efficiency and economic use of time. More importantly, Kelly defined the most important aspect of reading as "the ability to get meaning from the printed page" (p. 63). These are criteria that continue to influence the structure of reading comprehension testing.

In his letter to the Kansas school superintendents (considered educational experts), Kelly explained that he desired to "standardize the work in reading in Kansas" (1915, p. 27). He critiqued Thorndike's (1914a) theories of testing silent reading comprehension by arguing that although vocabulary was helpful in comprehension, it was not the same as comprehension. By way of contrast, he believed that the efforts in Kansas were best served if they concentrated on developing a test to assess children's ability to get meaning from the printed page. He claimed that the "ability to interpret the meaning of sentences and paragraphs was more important than vocabulary" (p. 27). Kelly pointed out that children were asked to perform this complex task daily in subjects like geography, history, and arithmetic. He reasoned, therefore that reading was an ability used throughout life:

> While it was realized that it would be advantageous to test separately for the several elements which compose this complex ability to interpret the printed page, it seemed worthwhile to propose a measure with which to determine how children compare in this complex ability, learning for further study the determination of what constitutes the causes of the differences found. (p. 27)

Kelly suggested that most teachers wanted to know if their instruction was supportive of students' ability to "get meaning from the printed page" (p. 63). Without acknowledging any specific research, but appealing generally to notions of individual difference, he claimed that there are great individual differences within any class, school, or school district. Interestingly, he does not contribute the individual differences among student performance to students but instead he claimed that the differences are due to the conceptions of reading held by various school superintendents and teachers. Kelly believed that reading was a complex task that consisted of two main factors, speed and accuracy of comprehension, the latter being the most important in his estimation. Kelly opined that a shortcoming of Starch's (1914) tests was the separation of measures of speed and accuracy. By way of contrast, Kelly's tests were devised to best measure the ability to read quickly and accurately comprehend short exercises. Nonetheless, he cautioned that the ability to read quickly and answer correctly the exercises did not measure the written reproductions of meaning, which he saw as separate from the ability to gather meaning from print.

In an effort to make clear the role of school administrators, who were asked to write the test exercises, Kelly explained that each superintendent should produce simple reading exercises (one to two sentences in length), each of which had *only one interpretation and only one correct answer*. The guidelines for each exercise were as follows: Each exercise must be on separate slips of paper; vary exercises in difficulty level from those appropriate for grade 2 to those appropriate for Grade 12; use no fewer than 15 words and no more than 60 words in each exercise; each exercise must have only one interpretation; each exercise must call for only one response; and the exercise should concentrate on the ability to get thought from the printed page—no other knowledge should be called on. The superintendents responded by supplying numerous exercises of which 192 met the criteria and several others were modified to meet the criteria. These exercises were used in his silent reading comprehension tests.

Kelly also explained how he divided the selections into three sets of 12 questions each and formed a series of passages for Grades 3 through 12: Level One for Grades 3 through 5; Level Two for Grades 6 through 8; and Level Three for Grades 9 through 12. All of the passages either required the student to make decisions among alternatives or "do" something directed in the passage. The choice among alternatives has become known as the *multiple choice*, the first of such tests. The content of the passages consisted of simple reasoning exercises. The correct answer to each passage depended on the student's ability to follow the directions correctly. (This test was similar to a second series of tests by Thorndike, known as Scale Alpha). Important to note, however, is that in Kelly's test an answer was either "wholly" right or "wholly" wrong. He reasoned that in this manner, he was testing only the ability to gather meaning from the paragraph and not knowledge already possessed by the reader, which is not really accurate as Fig. 5.1 indicates. Nevertheless, to standardize the test, Kelly used the exact same directions and sample test question on each level. He wrote, "The simplicity of these directions served to secure uniformity, even though the tests were

This little five-minute game is given to see how quickly and accurately pupils can read silently. To show what sort of game it is, let us read this:

Below are given the names of four animals. Draw a line around the name of each animal that is useful on the farm.

cow   tiger   rat   wolf

This exercise tells us to draw a line around the word *cow*. No other answer is right. Even if a line is drawn under the word *cow*, the exercise is wrong, and counts nothing. The game consists of a lot of such exercises, so it is wise to study each exercise carefully enough to be sure that you know exactly what you are asked to do (p. 65).

Figure 5.1   Test I Grades 3, 4 and 5 (Kelly, 1916, p. 65).

given by teachers and not by persons especially prepared for giving tests" (Kelly, 1915, p. 19). The directions for the sample test question are shown in Fig. 5.1.

Following the sample test item, the teacher was instructed to time the testing episode for exactly five minutes. To score the tests, teachers were directed to count answers as either right or wrong, add the values of the correct answers, and place the score in a box. For the more difficult questions, some answers were provided for the teacher because Kelly felt that some teachers may not know the correct answers. He stated that answers were provided for difficult questions so teachers' scoring would be uniform and comparisons could be made. He also suggested that by following the directions, teachers would vary little in their administration or scoring of the tests. Additional directions were given for teachers on how to make a distribution of students' scores and for finding the median score of their classes.

Kelly defended his tests as an efficient means of evaluating reading comprehension ability, for it had been administered to 9,252 children in 19 cities in Kansas. Although he claimed the tests were representative of children in three different grade levels (3–5, 6–8, and 9–12), no other demographic information was supplied. Kelly suggested that the total time commitment for a teacher to administer and grade the test for a class of 35 students would be approximately 40 minutes in the lower grades and approximately 55 minutes in the upper grades. The economical use of time and the production of efficient scientific test measures were also important. He desired to test reading comprehension through measurement by producing a scientifically based instrument and justifying its existence and veracity through quantification.

He found that a wide variation of ability existed within each grade and noted that some students in each grade were being promoted when they could not read well, as judged by their poor performance on his tests. In addition, Kelly observed the year-to-year differentiation in reading ability was insignificant. However, he stated that there seemed to be a real break in this pattern between fifth and sixth grades, and a similar break between eighth and ninth grades. Kelly reasoned that the breaks were due primarily to different tests being administered at the grade-level breaks. He perceived that there was a marked difference between the silent reading abilities of students in various cities which he attributed to differences in conceptions of reading and in reading instruction.

Kelly (1915) identified two attributes that most aided the ability to comprehend: speed and accuracy of reproductions. His investigations had devised a combined score for speed/rate and accuracy of reproductions as a single score so that he could "measure the child's ability to read by the number of reading exercises which he could comprehend accurately within a given period of time" (p. 64). He argued that his tests differed from other measures of comprehension because his did not use the reproduction method to measure comprehension. His tests were designed to measure the comprehension of each paragraph a child read in a 5-minute timed test. Kelly claimed that since a child had to indicate his understanding of each paragraph before proceeding to the next item, he had an accurate measure of the ability to comprehend a paragraph or series of paragraphs in a given time period.

In subsequent publications in 1916, Kelly restated what he understood to be the aims of measurement and testing in public schools. He suggested that tests should meet four criteria: They should measure a school product (subject area), provide simple directions for administration and scoring; measure ability and achievement in a subject area; and be structured to minimize the time spent in scoring.

Samelson's (1987) review of Kelly's work acknowledges that Kelly had been successful in his attempt to reduce time and effort required in the administration of reading comprehension tests. He acknowledges that Kelly's "invention had spread as quickly as any other technological breakthrough, legitimized by major social values, and supported by a rapidly developing establishment of experts and producers" (p. 124). Samuelson concludes that Kelly's multiple choice tests were "efficient, quantitative, objective, capable of sampling wide areas of subject matter, and easily generating data for complicated statistical analyses—had [has] become the symbol or synonym of American education" (p. 122). The acceptance of "one right answer" in Kelly's test clearly reflected the social and cultural understandings of the school administrators, at least those who were in agreement with Kelly.

In this analysis, however, I want to point to an even greater fundamental problem with Kelly's contribution of the multiple choice answer form of "wholly" right or "wholly" wrong answers. Then, as now, the form is limited and inadequate in its perspective. Answers reflect the dominant groups' ideas and are thus socially and culturally bound and incapable of addressing the complexity of reading comprehension for all students. The most damaged by this universalization of ideas are the underserved. Hall (2003) writes that "the search for an 'essential, true original' meaning is an illusion. No such previously natural moment of true meaning, untouched by the coeds and social relations of production and reading, exists" (p. 157). The entire field of reading comprehension has evolved based on Kelly's notion of one "wholly right or wholly wrong" answer for decades; even today's "best answer" is only a slight variation of the same. Underserved students who have been required to participate in reading comprehension testing, using this inadequate format, whose culture and languages are not reflected in the content or context of the tests, undoubtedly have suffered.

King and Zeidler Extend Reading Comprehension Research

In the world of reading comprehension testing, where student participants are considered to be functioning normally, that is, making steady progress as readers, King (1916), a pragmatist, criticized commonly voiced assumptions that slow readers were not good readers and that fast readers were not poor readers. He questioned whether the rate of reading, as used to measure silent reading comprehension, accurately measured comprehension. He suggested that the measurement of reading efficiency referred to "what is understood and remembered of that which is read" (p. 830). King maintained that reading efficiency, so defined, could be interpreted in two distinct ways: either as "immediate or deferred memory," or as a "general grasp of the meaning as distinct from the memory of the specific details" (p. 830). King believed that the two distinctive definitions of reading efficiency called for two particular manners of reading, and both affected reading rate. Specifically, he differentiated between whether or not the reading of a passage required the reader to read for general comprehension of the material and whether the reading of a passage required the reader to remember distinct details. Furthermore, King linked reading comprehension to memory and suggested that reading comprehension should be separated into three types: immediate nature (short-term memory), deferred nature (long-term memory), or a general grasp of the meaning distinct from memory (comprehension).

He also challenged what was really meant by slow and fast reading rate by questioning the use of rate as a variable in measuring comprehension. He observed that individuals could vary in the rates they used when reading and that reading rate could depend on a number of factors not previously considered (innate or acquired factors, and reaction time). King determined that a general statement of the effect of reading rate on reading comprehension was unreliable as measured. He was among early reading researchers who began to question the inclusion of rate in silent reading comprehension testing, but more importantly he called for clarity of the definition of reading comprehension. He also likened this dilemma in reading comprehension research to a similar one he noticed in pragmatism: "The strong point of pragmatism is, however, that it does assert a connection between thought and action. Its greatest weakness is that it does not give an adequate account of just what this relationship is" (King, 1916, p. 518). In sum, King suggested that philosophically, pragmatism could help researchers by "defining mental contents through their place in a process of reconstruction of experience, by making the question regarding reality one as to the functions of its elements rather than as to its structure" (p. 521). His discussion of the usefulness of memory and of pragmatism in reading comprehension research and testing was unheeded.

Finally, Zeilder's (1916) interest in reading comprehension testing moved testing beyond urban centers as he examined the reading performance of students taught in rural areas. He used the *Starch Silent Reading Tests* in his study of roughly 200 students in 26 schools, with slight variations in test administration. For instance, Zeilder over-lapped the reading passages to serve as a check of single test valid-ity and he asked university faculty to evaluate the students' written reproductions. He found that results of the written reproductions by the rural students were significantly lower than the standards suggested by Starch and somewhat below the local town standards. Zeilder interpreted the low reproduction scores as indicative of stu-dents who were taught in either one- or two-teacher rural schools. He attributed the higher local town scores on written reproductions as evidence of the school's better organizational patterns. Zeilder interpreted the gap in scores as a reflection of the instruction offered to the rural children but did not also factor in the possible effect of their impoverished economic conditions. Nonetheless, he voiced the commonly held belief, during this era, that most large school districts were better organized, teachers better trained, and student achievement higher, than found in rural settings.

Monroe's Influence on Reading Comprehension Research

Walter S. Monroe published his research in the *Journal of Educa-tional Psychology* (1917). He reportedly analyzed 100,000 *Kansas Silent Reading Tests* results. Although his study was an extension of Kelly's testing, Monroe insightfully observed that "a score repre-sents only a pupil's performance at a given time under given con-ditions" (p. 601). He noted that a change in conditions (physical, emotional, personal) could result in a change in a student's score. To compensate for this possibility, he suggested that the test exam-iners needed to control the conditions under which the tests were administered. He asserted that the ability to comprehend could "be inferred accurately from the performance only when we know of the conditions attending the performance" (p. 602). Monroe's thinking represents important social insights about classrooms and children not mentioned by other researchers. Later (in 1920) he suggested that it is best to complete all testing in one setting, as children may become fatigued.

His influence, however, was not limited to academicians and school administrators. Along with De Voss and Kelly, Monroe (1917) edited a normal school reader, *A Teacher's Handbook on Educational Measurements, Reading, Writing and Arithmetic*. In this text, the latest educational research in the select elementary subjects was reviewed and explained, and an entire chapter was devoted to silent reading. In their chapter, Monroe, De Voss, and Kelly (1917 acknowledged an important distinction between "the ability to get meaning for oneself from the printed page" and "the ability to express the meaning of the printed page to others" (p. 53). Of course, what they really meant is the ability to get the meaning that the authors or test developers believe is the correct meaning from the page ... They also declared that even if oral reading in elementary classrooms continued to occupy an unusual amount of the school day, a teacher's time was better spent on training students in silent reading. Not surprisingly, they concluded that by using Kelly's (1915) *Kansas Silent Reading Tests,* educators could answer their questions regarding student reading comprehension ability, as the new tests reflected student understanding of text. They posited that silent reading was a skill that students would use throughout their adult life and to ignore its importance was a mistake. Moreover, the editors admitted that school administrators, principals, and teachers were hampered by the intangibles of silent reading in their attempts to use it more effectively. Two key questions surfaced: "How could the ability to read silently be measured accurately?" and "How much meaning of a paragraph could be said to be a standard at a given grade level?" They dismissed the traditions of oral reading and written reproductions as indicators of reading ability. Surprisingly, they argued that written reproductions used to measure reading comprehension were a better measure of written composition.

Thorndike's Second Series of Articles on Reading Comprehension

In the spring of 1917, Thorndike resumed publication of his work on reading comprehension in the article "The Psychology of Thinking and the Case of Reading" (1917a). His revision described what he considered to be the "facts and laws of thinking" that people used to respond to questions asked following the reading of a paragraph. Using test items from earlier studies, he attempted to analyze students' written responses to questions. He claimed to have discovered a general law of thinking used during reading. Specifically, he observed that reading was an active process that required hierarchical connections that were somehow kept balanced. These shared connections were the result of a relationship that evoked the responses. In his analysis, he drew on theories espoused by James (habit formation) and Cattell (reductionism) as well as his own theory of connectionism.

Thorndike (1917a) believed that knowledge gained from experiences helped a person to choose among elements "by increasing or reducing the potency of certain of its elements" (p. 233). The importance of this article cannot be understated. Thorndike proposed a psychological explanation of the mental processing used during reading comprehension. He was among the first researchers to attempt to explain what cognitively occurred during the act of reading comprehension and how it affected responses to questions.

In a follow-up article, he described reading as "a very elaborate procedure" (1917b, p. 323), and, much like Kelly, he likened reading to the task of reasoning required in mathematics. Thorndike arrived at this conclusion also by analyzing written responses by students to several questions. From this analysis, he identified three types of errors: failure to understand the author's intended word associations, incorrect emphasis on words (over-potency or under-potency), and failure to understand the text. He concluded, "The mind is assailed, as it were, by every word in the paragraph. It must select, repress, soften, emphasize, correlate, and organize, all under the influence of the right mental set or purposes or demand" (p. 329). Although he did not call for "one" right answer, as he supplied alternatives in his answer keys, there were clearly answers that he expected and accepted over others. Significantly, as if in response to elocutionists and oral reading comprehension advocates, he observed that fluent reading did not indicate fluent understanding.

In the final article of the series, Thorndike reviewed his previous articles and offered directions for administering his tests in the final article of the series. His analyses of previous research indicated that some of the errors made by students may be attributed to the complexity of the paragraphs, poorly written questions, lack of critical reading, or students "fishing around in the text" for an answer. He called the understanding of ideas needed for comprehension "thinking things together" (1917c, p. 114) and suggested that for comprehension to occur, all elements had to be organized and balanced during reading. Thorndike concluded that readers, during reading comprehension, should "think, evaluate, invent, demonstrate, and verify" (p. 114).

Dawn of World War I: Intelligence and Reading Comprehension Research and Testing

World War I began in Europe in August 1914 without U.S. involvement, in part because President Wilson preferred a program of neutrality; however, three years later in April 1917, growing fears led the United States to enter the War. Wilson claimed to have entered the war to "make the world safe for democracy" and to spread democracy to the world. One concern during the massive recruitment was which men were best suited for officer's training. Early intelligence and reading comprehension test developers drew from the dominant ideology that guided their research, to create an intelligence test for the U.S. Army, and, later, tests for schools. Reading researchers drew from the dominant ideologies and their work on reading comprehension in the development of intelligence tests.

Standardized Intelligence Testing

U.S. versions of intelligence tests were adaptations of the work of Alfred Binet and Theodore Simon. Binet's (1857–1911) interest in psychology began after he completed his law degree and began working in a Paris hospital for the insane. In 1891 he was named the director of the Laboratory of Experimental Psychology at the Sorbonne and, along with Henri Beaunis, established the *L'Année Psychologique,* the leading French journal on psychology, in 1894. Like his contemporaries Cattell and Galton, Binet experimented with different physical ways to assess intelligence: head size, reaction time, vision, and so forth; however none proved reliable. In 1904, Binet, along with three other psychologists was chosen by the French government's Ministry of Public Instruction to serve on a Commission on the Education of Retarded Children. The charge of the commission was to determine which children would most benefit from a regular public education and which would benefit from an alternative educational program. Binet and Simon devised tests in 1905 and revised them in 1908 and again in 1911. The test guidelines are shown in Fig. 5.2.

Three Cardinal Principles

1) the scores are a practical device; they do not buttress any theory of intellect. They do not define anything innate or permanent. We may not designate what they measure as "intelligence" or any other reified entity; 2) the scale is a rough, empirical guide for identifying mildly retarded and learning-disabled children who need special help. It is not a device for ranking normal children; 3) whatever the cause of difficulty in children identified for help, emphasis shall be placed upon improvements through special training. Low scores shall not be used to mark children as innately incapable. (p. 185)

Figure 5.2   The dismantling of Binet's intentions in America (Gould, 1996, p. 185).

The tests were diagnostic and designed to improve the education of slower functioning children. Trained testers individually administered each test, consisting of 30 cognitive tasks constructed to correspond with what was believed children could do at certain ages (mental age). Binet (Binet & Simon, 1905) insisted on using only trained testers because others, he feared, could inadvertently skew the results. In 1911, German psychologist William Stern added the idea of dividing children's mental age by their chronological age, or a mental quotient. The ideas that underpin Binet's tests were quite different from the ideas that had guided early standardized testing in the United States where (a) it was assumed that intelligence was inherited, (b) tests were given to normal functioning children, and (c) low scores were used to label children as morons (a popular term used during this period).

The development of U.S. Army tests was led by Goddard and Terman and included support from Thorndike and his team of researchers. Goddard, Terman, and Thorndike—much like their predecessors Galton and Cattell—believed that intelligence was biologically inherited and that class and social factors had little effect on measures of intelligence. Henry Goddard translated the tests and introduced the Binet–Simon intelligence scales in the United States. Like most U.S. academicians, he believed that intelligence tests measured biologically inherited mental ability of individuals, groups, and races. Faith in the dominant ideologies and its attendant racism led him to assume that Whites were of superior intelligence to all people of color and that women and people living in poverty were also inferior intellectually. In 1906, Stanford University education and psychology professor, Lewis Terman, adapted the Binet test and created the *Stanford Revision of the Binet–Simon Scale (Stanford–Binet)*. Later, in 1916, building on Stern's idea, Terman introduced the notion of an intelligence quotient (IQ). A child's IQ was found when his or her mental age (MA) was divided by his or her chronological age (CA) and multiplied by 100. The 1916 version of the Stanford-Binet was dominated by verbal items, as were the 1937, 1960, and 1973 versions. Like Galton and Goddard's, Terman's version of the test reflected his belief in the inheritability of intelligence (the superiority of the Nordic race) and the ability of his test to measure innate ability. A positivist, Terman adopted biological and social Darwinian views as well as Galton's eugenics in his belief that feeble-mindedness needed to be eliminated and genius should be privileged for future leadership. and Terman also equated intelligence with race, and expressed racist and class-based concerns about intelligence testing.

Goddard began to administer the Stanford–Binet version as early as 1912 as a form of intelligence testing given to immigrants entering the country through Ellis Island and to the feeble-minded hospitalized in Vineland, New Jersey (1912–1913). His own beliefs about positivism, social Darwinism, and biological determinism informed his understanding of the inheritability of intelligence and eugenics. For instance, he believed in the need to sort and classify people for their roles in society and he feared that the germplasm of the poor and less intelligent might overpopulate the nation. In his book *Intelligence Classification of Immigrants of Different Nationalities* (1917), Goddard claimed that most of the Ellis Island immigrants were mentally defective. His beliefs about the inheritability of intelligence and his fear of germplasm among the poor and less intelligent, led him to create the mythical Kallikak family. (Research by Gould in 1996 reveals that Goddard found a group of destitute people living in the woods of New Jersey near Vineland on which he based his fictional story of the Kallikak family.) The Kallikak surname was derived from the Greek words for beauty *(kallos)* and bad *(kakos)* and suggested the theme of Goddard's fictive tale of the effects of defective germplasm. In his story, Martin Kallikak had an intimate relationship with a feeble-minded tavern girl that produced a son, "Old Horror," who fathered 10 children. The children of "Old Horror," in turn, reproduced in the hundreds many more "of the lowest types of human beings" (p. 65). Later,

Martin Kallikak married a worthy Quakeress and during their marriage they produced seven "upright worthy children" who produced "hundreds of the highest sort of human beings" (p. 65). This fictive tale was reported, published, and believed to represent what could happen with defective germplasm (it replicates an earlier tale from New York in the 1870s by Richard Dugadale). Goddard also made claims regarding the inheritance of criminal tendencies about the Jukes family based on very suspect information. Years later, he recanted many of his erroneous claims (see Zenderland, 1998). What is important here is Goddard's tendency to create scenarios to replace theoretical shortcomings, reflect a narrow understanding of the world, support the interests of dominant groups, and reinforce stereotypes and racial prejudice.

Terman (1916a) also offered his thoughts on intelligence and individual difference in his book *The Measurement of Intelligence*. He agreed with Goddard's general assessment of the feeble-minded, stating that "all feeble-minded are at least potential criminals. ... Moral judgments, like business judgment, social judgment or any other kind of higher thought process, is a function of intelligence" (p. 11). He added, "As far as intelligence is concerned, the tests have told the truth. ... No amount of school instruction will ever make them intelligent voters or capable voters in the true sense of the word" (p. 91). He argued that students should be segregated into homogeneous groups in schools to make them better workers and recommended that school administrators segregate the feeble-minded and children of color into special education classes. He believed that these children should be offered a rudimentary, or practical, education to prepare them to be good workers. Moreover, he strongly encouraged the sterilization of the less intelligent.

Terman held very strong opinions about the intersection of intelligence and race. For example, in his doctoral dissertation Terman (1916a) measured the intelligence of seven "bright" and seven "stupid boys." He claimed, "We have only to compare the negro with the Eskimo or Indian, and the Australian native with the Anglo-Saxon, to be struck by the apparent kinship between general intellectual and inventive ability" (p. 20). In another example, Terman (1916a) made the following claims about low-level intelligence:

> [It] is very, very common among Spanish-Indian and Mexican families of the Southwest and also among negroes. That dullness seems to be racial, or at least inherent in the family stocks from which they come. ...

> The writer predicts that... there will be discovered enormously significant racial differences in general intelligence, differences which cannot be wiped out by any scheme of mental culture. (pp. 91–92)

Terman's racist views are even more apparent in the conclusions he drew from his study. He observed, "The fact that one meets this type with such frequency among Indians, Mexicans, and negroes suggest quite forcibly that the whole question of racial differences in mental traits will have to be taken up anew and by experimental methods" (pp. 91–92). Clearly, his statements reflect remnants of the Western European philosophical assumptions that underpin much of educational research. What is most important to recall, however, is that Goddard and Terman were in very powerful positions to foist on an unsuspecting but largely supportive public their thoughts about intelligence, race, and the ability of standardized tests to measure intelligence.

Thorndike also was a member of the test development team whose thinking mirrored the thinking of Goddard and Terman. He believed that intelligence was inherited and that high moral character was associated with greater intelligence. These researchers also used the results of early intelligence tests to support their racist views of the superiority of Whites over all other racial groups in the United States. Lewontin et al. (1984) have summarized the six propositions of the mental testing movement, many of which can be evinced in the work of Goddard and Terman (see Fig. 5.3).

Eugenics

Like the philosophical assumptions reviewed earlier, Galton's notion of eugenics and its power to shape society (Gould, 1981; Karier, 1975; Stoskopf, 2000) was imported from Western Europe, although the United States had its own racism without the alleged scientific support of Galton's research. It is important to realize, however, that all of U.S. testing is closely tied to Galton's assumptions and measures. In 1904, Galton defined *eugenics* as "the science which deals with all influences that improve the inborn qualities of a race; also with those that develop them to the utmost advantage" (p. 1). The eugenics movement was based on the Greek word *eugenes,* meaning "well born." The term was used by Galton, who reasoned that the success of families like his was due to the biological inheritance of

1. There are differences in status, wealth, and power.
2. These differences are consequences of different intrinsic ability, especially "intelligence."
3. IQ tests are instruments that measure this intrinsic ability.
4. Differences in intelligence are largely the result of genetic differences between individuals.
5. Because they are the result of genetic differences, differences in ability are fixed and unchangeable.
6. Because most of the differences between individuals in ability are genetic, the differences between races and classes are also genetic and unchangeable. (p. 84)

Figure 5.3   Generate basis of intelligence testing (Lewontin, Rose, & Kamin, 1984).

the traits of talent and genius and that superior heredity was the root of superior offspring. In addition, he believed that environment had only a marginal effect on the success of wealthy families although he maintained that progress was dependent on natural environment. His theories pleased people who considered themselves in the superior class like many academicians and the wealthy, both in Europe and in the United States. Those who endorsed eugenics argued that they had discovered a unique science, one that combined biology, psychology, sociology, and statistics and that would lead to scientifically superior humans.

Galton (1904) suggested that the practice of eugenics would raise "the general tone of domestic, social, and political life" (p. 3). His zeal for eugenics pushed forward his racist and class-based ideas. He strongly petitioned supporters to acknowledge the following stages that were needed for eugenics to become of national importance:

> 1) It must be made familiar as an academic question, until its exact importance has been understood and accepted as fact. 2) It must be recognized as a subject whose practical development deserves serious consideration. 3) It must be introduced into the national conscience, like a new religion. (p. 5)

Under this perspective, White males of middle- to upper-class backgrounds were deemed the most fit to rule and lead nations. Galton founded the Eugenics Laboratory, later renamed the Eugenic Education Society, and remnants continue today.

The racial attitudes of White U.S. researchers in the early 20th century suggested that selective breeding, among wealthy and middle-class Euro-Americans, caused their superior race to hold power and wealth due to their superior intellectual and moral abilities. Intolerant racial attitudes grew with the increasing popularity of social Darwinism and eugenics. Likewise, advocates for immigration restrictions believed that by restricting the number of inferior immigrants from Southern and Eastern Europe, America could be assured of a superior race of intelligent people in a generation or two, as the race's superiority was found among those from Northern and Western European ancestry. More importantly, the concept of eugenics and the companion notion of hereditarism were championed by many political leaders, educational researchers, school administrators, and classroom teachers. Politically, as African Americans and women sought greater equity in labor and in the social world as their numbers grew, the fears of an economic and social decline propelled White males to support eugenics—not through military force but through scientific claims of racial, gender, and moral superiority. In education, several very influential educational researchers embraced the eugenics movement.

The "science of eugenics" found many supporters in a racially biased, reform-minded, socially stratified U.S. society, especially among the Euro-American wealthy and middle-class professional and professorate groups who lent their time, money, and influence to the support of the movement in this country after 1900. Karier (1975) notes that in the United States, national pride and racial attitudes easily mixed with the science of eugenics. U.S. citizens who adopted the eugenicists' assumptions of racially defined intelligence believed that the Nordic race had evolved intellectually to an advanced state by noting that U.S. society was socially, politically, economically, and culturally structured to reflect the advanced status of Nordic intelligence. They also maintained that the more intelligent were also the more attractive and virtuous. Advocates of eugenics also found financial support in the Carnegie Foundation and the Rockefeller Fund as well as President Woodrow Wilson and the *Journal of the American Medical Association*. They believed that the germplasm of inferior people was spread more rapidly because such people reproduced more quickly. In evolutionary terms, then, the natural selection process of the "fittest" appeared to be reversed. Those who possessed the inferior germplasm were reproducing at a much faster rate than those who possessed the superior germplasm. Many U.S. citizens also believed that if the evolutionary course were to continue unchecked, it would create a society where greater numbers of less capable people would exist. Therefore, to prevent the inferior germplasm from spreading and inferior people from reproducing, controls were needed. Sterilization was suggested as a quick and efficient means of curbing the spread of the germplasm of inferiors. Reports on the spread of germplasm were issued, and groups were identified as alleged carriers of inferior germplasm. Some historians (Black, 2004; Carlson, 2001) have called this movement the forerunner of Hilter's idea of an Aryan superior race, or Nazism.

Supporters of eugenics believed that intelligence, good moral character (industrious, creative, good, and kind), physical size, physical strength, emotional stability, and beauty) were traits exhibited by those of superior germplasm (Karier, 1975). In the United States, advocates of eugenic controls expanded the notion of the eugenics and established governing agencies and political laws, especially laws that prohibited intermarriage among racial groups. Laws also were enacted to sterilize the mentally ill and moral "defectives," over 60,000 people, many of whom were poor and of color. (Two recent publications, Carlson's 2001 text, *The Unfit: A History of a Bad Idea*, and Black's 2003 book, *War Against the Weak*, describe in greater detail the eugenics movement.) The movement secured financial support from the Rockefeller Foundation, the Carnegie Institution, and Cold Spring Harbor (NY) Laboratory. Advocates published their work in *Eugenics News* (now known as *Social Biology*) or the *Journal of American Medical Association* (*JAMA*), which also included critiques of the movement. Moreover, many prominent researchers of reading comprehension and test creators in the 19th and 20th centuries were central players in the eugenics movement and proponents of its tenets.

Several leading U.S. educational psychologists and reading researchers were members of the U.S. Eugenics Record Office (among whom were Cattell and Thorndike). Karier (1975) notes that the committees of the Eugenics Record Office "took the lead in identifying those who carried defective germplasm and in dissemination of the propaganda which became necessary to pass sterilization laws" (p. 131). As we have seen, these attitudes were part of the ideological and cultural hegemony that supported social class stratification, a biological inheritance of intelligence and morals, and the racial superiority of the White race. People of color, in general, were considered less evolved on the intellectual, cultural, and moral evolutionary ladder toward the perfection of humankind. Some of the leading educational researchers, including those whose work focused on reading comprehension research and testing, were key players in these efforts. Members of the dominant class embrace eugenics and envisioned its use beyond U.S. Army testing to include national intelligence testing and a system of meritocracy based on test results.

Reading Comprehension Research Influences
U.S. Army Intelligence Testing

In 1916, Arthur S. Otis, Terman's graduate student, working with Dr. Percy E. Davidson, published "Considerations Concerning the Making of a Scale for the Measurement of Reading Ability" in *Pedagogical Seminary,* in which they critiqued the available silent reading comprehension tests and reviewed the definitions for reading tests as posited by Thorndike (1914–1916), Starch (1915), and Kelly (1915). Specifically, they noted that Thorndike defined reading ability as "the ability to understand words and sentences seen" (p. 530); Starch defined reading ability as "the ability to read a certain amount of a passage in a certain time and reproduce a certain amount of it" (p. 531); and Kelly defined reading ability as "the ability to read a certain number of short paragraphs in a certain time and comprehend them to a degree at least sufficient to correctly answer certain specific questions [or execute certain commissions contingent upon certain comprehension, etc.]" (p. 531). They surmised the definitions were an inaccurate characterization of reading ability and none of the tests created by these three researchers adequately measured reading ability. The authors noticed that each test defined reading ability for the purposes of measurement differently and tested accordingly. Furthermore, they realized that each test measured some element of the ability to read or that each test measured an ability, of which reading was a component. To end this confusion, they proposed that a standard definition of reading comprehension was needed:

> To make a careful psychological analysis both of the reading act and of the present tests, to settle upon a working definition of reading ability which is in accordance with customary usage, and to determine the degree of correspondence between that variable which we shall call read-

ing ability and the variables which the present scales measure. (Otis, 1916, p. 529)

To clarify these issues, the authors proposed a definition of reading ability as well as a means to measure and score it. By way of example they acknowledged that the act of reading, known as reading ability, was measured as the efficient combination of rate and comprehension. However, they redefined reading ability as "embodying in essence only those mental processes which are concerned directly with the specific visual symbols as such. Other mental activities involved in the total reading complex may be spoken of as 'supra-reading' or the accompaniments of reading" (p. 534). Drawing from Thorndike's research, *supra-reading* meant understanding gained from inferences. Inferences could emerge from grammatical relations, logical relations, or content relations. The heart of their idea was the differentiation between a person who could read and a person who was unable to read (literate vs. illiterate). They argued that the degree to which comprehension occurs is a matter of life experience and for purposes of measurement, this opposition was a logical, yet overlooked, principle.

Otis (1916) further explained that their concept of reading ability went beyond the physical act of reading and acknowledged the social and psychological influences of comprehension. They believed these influences were important:

> Whether a reader can "get the point" of a passage or comprehend it to the extent of the ability to make some generalization or abstraction, or draw some conclusion, or execute some commission, or build some composite image, or think of the thickness of the peelings of apples and oranges, may be a matter of life experience, with no essential connection at all with reading ability. (p. 534)

Additionally, they believed that nonreaders could do all these things, if read to, because they had life experiences. They saw reading as essentially two separate acts. The first was the translation of "visual symbols into language, in order to dispense with the former so far as the comprehension of the passage is concerned" (pp. 534–535), and the second suggested that people who were competent readers "may associate meanings quite directly with printed symbols" (p. 535). This was not an original idea, as several other early reading comprehension test authors had expressed the same notion, albeit not as eloquently.

Otis (1916) recognized that there was a marked difference between individuals struggling with the mechanics of reading and those who had surpassed the mechanical stage. Recalling Herbart's notion of apperception, the authors wrote, "The degree of comprehension or apperception which is considered as constituting the essence of reading ... if [a word] is apperceived to any degree capable of ordinary use, it is at least known to be an attribute" (p. 537). They also held that it was important to measure the rate of apperception once it had been determined that the reader had full grasp of the symbol system and understood that comprehension was necessary. Specifically, they wrote,

> The rate of apperception of printed symbols is a manifestation of the degree of automatization of apperception—the degree of habit formation—the effect of practice in apperceiving the specific symbols in question, whether these be printed words, shorthand symbols, dots and dashes or the peculiar handwriting of some individual. (p. 537)

They surmised that practice with visual symbols and groups of symbols would help readers to increase their speed or rate of reading. Their ideas exceed common sense notions of reading comprehension as understanding print.

In conclusive fashion, Otis and Davidson (1916) outlined several steps they believed should be considered when developing tests of reading ability. For example, they suggested that it was impossible to exactly measure reading ability, but a close approximation could be made using their formula. Their "ideal" test used elements from Thorndike's Visual Scale, a resemblance they freely admitted, and required readers to categorize words (nouns) according to test directions. However, they suggested that the Thorndike test (1914) lacked one important element, reading rate, which they supplied. They claimed that there were degrees of comprehension and that Thorndike's categorization of single words was a good example of broad categories that allowed a range of life experiences to help a reader respond to specific tasks. Otis maintained the fact that the influence of grammar or content was eliminated by the use of single words and pronunciation was not important. In addition, they listed advantages that their proposed scale would have over earlier silent reading comprehension tests: (a) It allowed for the measurement of the degree of apperception, and (b) it could be used with students who were not able to write because it only required students to read words.

Most importantly, Otis and Davidson (1916) encouraged the administration of their test "en masse" (p. 544) to large numbers of students. They suggested that the test be given a number of times, but not in too close succession, in order to gain a more accurate picture of ability. The authors also declared that their test could be scored with "unskilled labor" because a template was used to mark correct answers. By using such procedures, they claimed that their test would be a logical, psychological means of fulfilling Thorndike's requirements of "objectivity, precision, commensurability and convenience" (p. 544). Otis, the first author, did not complete his plans to conduct an investigation based on his descriptive model but offered his conclusions to those conducting studies in the measurement of reading ability. His own plans to study reading ability were interrupted by his involvement in the mass intelligence testing of U.S. Army recruits.

Calling a Few Good Men

Under the Selective Service Act (1917), the U.S. government needed additional troops to bolster the military. Therefore, the government required men ages 21 to 30 to register for military service. In an overwhelming response, 24 million men registered; 3 million were actually drafted. Although initially men of color were barred from military service, the great need for additional troops permitted them to defend the nation; however, they were segregated by race within the military. In the spring of 1917 educational psychologists, working on behalf of the U.S. government, moved with missionary zeal to categorize men for military service. Their mission was to determine which men were fit for officer training. Members of the American Psychological Association's Committee on Methods of Psychological Examining of Recruits who developed tests for the U.S. Army included Goddard, Terman, Thorndike, and Yerkes (Yerkes and Thorndike were members of the Eugenics Record Office and served on the Committee on Inheritance of Mental Traits, and Goddard served on the Committee on the Heredity of the Feeble-minded). The beliefs, values, and practices of these men left little room for objective test development as their allegiance to eugenics and racism overshadowed their thinking. Reading researcher Otis also helped to shape these intelligence tests.

Colonel Robert Yerkes, a leading Harvard psychologist and eugenicist, led the efforts to devise a test for the 1.7 million army recruits. He passionately recapitulates the essence of the dominant ideology at this point in history: "Most of us are wholly convinced that the future of mankind depends in no small measure on the development of the various biological and social sciences" (Yerkes, quoted in Gould, 1966, p. 223). Yerkes did not think that the current methods of measurement were infallible; in fact, he thought that improvements were needed. Given the expertise of each man, together they devised three different tests for the army in less than two weeks: Army Alpha, a written test; Army Beta, a pictorial test; and an individual test. The link between general intelligence and reading in general and reading comprehension in particular surfaced during this testing and continues to this day.

Thorndike was chair of the Statistical Unit, and with assistance from Otis he developed the Army Alpha Test for literate recruits. The tests were based in part on (a) Otis and Davidson's work of 1916 that focused on the measurement of reading comprehension, (b) Thorndike's (1914–1916) categorization of words and his stencil for ease in scoring, and (c) Kelly's (1915) fixed alternatives and true/false questions. Otis proposed the use of paper-and-pencil tests and recommended en masse testing using formats similar to those suggested by Kelly (1915) and extended by others. Thorndike, ever interested in human learning, intelligence, and individual difference, suggested that a similar test be prepared for the illiterate recruits to determine their literacy level. He also determined which test was most appropriate for draftees.

Thorndike proposed using his early reading comprehension tests, but Terman suggested time-saving modifications that included shortening the tests, eliminating the preliminary testing period, dividing the categories in half, and placing a three-minute limit on the tests. Terman's modifications were not acceptable, and the tests were scrapped. However, the idea of a separate test for the illiterate recruits eventually became a reality as the Army Beta tests were developed by one of Thorndike's student assistants, J. L. Stenquist (Joncich, 1968). The directions for this test were pantomimed to the soldiers.

Recruit test results were labeled as "superior," "average," or "inferior." Researchers believed that results indicated that "native" Whites were the most intelligent, with an average mental age of 13, and other groups lagged behind them, intellectually. The test results for recruits were rank ordered as follows: immigrants from Northern and Western Europe, immigrants from Southern and Eastern Europe, and African Americans. The superior recruits—most of them native Whites—were to be given officer's training; others were placed in the general corps or discharged (reviews and recalculations point to the flaws in statistical procedures and the interpretation of the data; see Montagu, 1945; Rury, 1988; Spring, 1972; Travers, 1983). Given these results, educational psychologists joined politicians who encouraged immigration quotas and eugenic means for "race betterment," making race, ethnicity, and class silent partners of intelligence testing and use. In addition, numerous studies followed that focused on racial differences in intelligence, including Arlitt (1921), Ferguson (1919), and Fukuda (1923). The army testing of male recruits, the results of the tests and the interpretation of the tests, were published in newspapers throughout the nation. As one might expect after the publication of the Army's test results, there was a public outcry of a crisis in education (i.e., the education of Whites) and the need for improvement and reform.

Following World War I, there was increased pressure to develop and support a national intelligence test, which consisted of a large reading comprehension section, much like the one used in by the U.S. Army, and a nonverbal section. When the federal government discontinued the use of the Army Alpha and Beta tests, the extra tests were sold to governmental agencies, businesses, and educational institutions. Educators adopted the army's definition of intelligence to classify and to sort individuals for their alleged role in society. The educational testing movement exploded and testing became profitable, especially for Haggerty, Hipple, Otis, Terman, Thorndike, and Yerkes. Although Terman's Stanford–Binet test became the most widely used intelligence test, Haggerty, Terman, Thorndike, Whipple, and Yerkes received funding from the Rockefeller Foundation and extended the reading comprehension test formats used in the army recruiting tests. They constructed the *National Intelligence Tests* for students in Grades 3 through 8.

Under the auspices of the National Research Council, council members also created two booklets with five subtests for each examination. The first test extended Thorndike's early work in reading comprehension. The test, Scale A, consisted of (a) arithmetical problems, (b) sentence completion, (c) checking attributes possessed by a given word, (d) synonym–antonym, and (e) copying numbers corresponding to given symbols from a key. The second test consisted of (a) computation, (b) general information, (c) logical judgment, (d) analogies, and (e) discrimination of similarity and difference as applied to numbers and forms. In addition, Terman's (1916) *Stanford Achievement Test* was used to determine individual differences and promote more efficient use of school instructional time by grouping students according to their ability (also known as tracking). He believed that students from higher social classes inherited intellect from their parents and thus preformed better than their peers from lower social classes who likewise inherited less intelligence from their parents. They sold over 400,000 copies to schools in 6 months.

Resnick et al. (1982) pointed out that educational psychologists quickly saw how schools could use intelligence tests for grouping students for instruction:

> The legitimacy that educational testing has enjoyed is the result of the deep rooting of this technology in American social and institutional development. Standardized testing enjoys the support not only of the organized groups which have fostered its development—psychologists, school administrators, and publishers alike—but of public agencies, state and federal, and of taxpayers, whose contributions help support our localized schools. (pp. 173–174)

Furthermore, other researchers developed reading achievement tests that bore their names and lined their pockets. These tests were advertised in professional education journals as well as mass-market publications.

Not all researchers, however, were convinced of the veracity of the army's tests or of the new intelligence tests. For instance, Margaret Mead (1926), Joseph Peterson (1934), and Terence C. Pihlblad (1926), among others, raised serious questions of methodology, race, social class, and language. Opponents stood against the ideas swirling around the results of the army's intelligence tests and the propaganda that supported their interpretation. Of particular concern to them were issues regarding how the tests, or similar tests, were going to be used to discriminate against those who performed poorly. These opponents and countless others who resisted the intelligence testing movement were waging a battle against the dominant ideology that made the test possible and that supported the promotion of intelligence testing to sort and categorize individuals. They were not only objecting to the faulty assumptions and psychometrics of the test researchers but also questioning and challenging the government, military, and educational leaders who supported testing. These opponents, to paraphrase Hall (1982), were challenging the "partial explanations" (p. 86) given for racial differences in intelligence, in part because they realized the explanations were not comprehensive or adequate. These opponents also realized supporters of intelligence testing needed to offer a more complete and complex explanation of intelligence. Thus, supporters of the explanations of racial differences in intelligence suggested that intelligence was inherited but that education could offer some minimal help. Consent to the use of standardized tests to assess intelligence was secured by articulations that pointed to the need to perfect society and bolster U.S. efforts to remain one of the most powerful nations in the world.

African Americans' Counter Discourse of Standardized Intelligence Testing

Foremost among those with dissenting views were African American scholars who had long fought against racist implications used to interpret intelligence. As early as 1897, T. H. Kelly, a professor at Ohio State University, argued that racial differences in scores on intelligence tests were better understood to reflect differences in social and economic conditions between Blacks and Whites. African American scholars argued that the poor test performance of African Americans and other ethnic groups was due to historical, social, cultural, and linguistic differences as well as to educational access and opportunities. Du Bois (1940) recalled that after World War I, psychological testing became popular, especially testing that supported racist theories and placed African Americans on the lowest ranks:

> I see absolutely no proof that the average ability of the White man's brain to think clearly is any greater than that of the yellow man or of the black man. If we take even that doubtful but widely heralded test, the frequency of individual creative genius (when a real racial test should be the frequency of ordinary common sense)—if we take the Genius as the savior of mankind, it is only possible for the White race to prove its own incontestable superiority by appointing both judge and jury and summoning its own witnesses. (p. 141)

African American scholars also resisted notions of the "mulatto hypothesis" whereby African Americans with a trace of White blood were believed to be intellectually superior to "pure African Americans." (For an in-depth review of this era and the response of African American scholars and educators, see Franklin, 1991.) Other mixed races were investigated as well (Garth, 1927), however, most psychological research focused on comparisons between African American and White children, as in Schwegler and Winn (1920).

To combat the constant maligning of African American intelligence, Du Bois, as publisher of the *Crisis*, and Charles Johnson, as publisher of *Opportunity*, used their magazines as outlets for discussions of race and intelligence testing (1923–1935). In the article "Mental Tests of Negro Groups," Johnson (1923) cited the U.S. Army's official "Report of the Psychological Division's use of Negro testing." The report claims that Negroes were tested for the "practical needs" (p. 25) of the army and not for officer training. He noted the cultural bias in several of the test questions which required knowledge of a White Hollywood actress, types of automobiles, brands of tobacco and coffee, and bowling and golfing terms. The cultural experiences of most of the African American recruits did not include the latter, and, if they included the former, their very lives could be lost. (It is important to note that the use of questions based on a White middle-class lifestyle remains the norm in intelligence testing.)

Likewise, Long (1923) opposed interpretations of the army intelligence tests, arguing that environment was a stronger indicator of performance than "native intelligence" between racial groups. Long (1925) offered several conclusions for his research on intelligence. "We need to question very seriously the tests applied to groups having quite different experiences and the incentives from those on whom tests have been standardized" (p. 138). Long (1934, 1935a, 1935b, 1957) continued to refute the results of the claims of intellectual inferiority as determined by race by conducting his own experiments of intelligence among African American children.

While a graduate student at the University of Chicago, Horace Mann Bond, another African American researcher, called for action on the part of intellectuals in fighting the growing tide of racism allegedly justified by "scientific facts" gleaned from the misinterpretation of army test data. Writing in the *Crisis*, Bond (1924a) declared, "But so long as any group of men attempts to use these tests as funds of information for the approximation of crude and inaccurate generalizations, so long we must continue to cry 'Hold'" (p. 64). He was quick to point out the economic differences between the African Americans and Whites that the tests could not measure. Bond's argument rested on two complementary ideas: (a) "to claim that the results of the test given to such diverse groups, drawn from such varying parts of the social complex, are in any wise accurate," and (b) "to expose a fatuous sense of unfairness and lack of appreciation of the great environmental factors of urban life" (1924a, p. 64). In another article, he noted that the test results "assumed that the groups which they compared had a common background of experience, while a careful analysis of the fact would have shown that variation among social classes will explain the phenomena they ascribe to inherent intelligence" (Bond, 1924b, p. 202). Later, in 1927, Bond reported the results of his own intelligence testing of African American children in Chicago where he found that they outperformed White children. As the Director of the School of Education at Langston University, Bond continued to refute the notion of racial factors in intelligence tests. Specifically, he questioned whether the tests reflected "native intelligence," suggesting instead that tests were more a reflection of social and educational environments.

Besides these men, other African American scholars of this period challenged the validity of the testing instrument, including Martin Jenkins (1936a, 1939, 1950), Joseph St. Clair Price (1934), Ira Reid (1940), and Charles Thompson (1934). Their work was published in the *Journal of Negro Education*, an important outlet for the research of African American scholars. The work of Jenkins and Price is illustrative of their position. Jenkins (1936b, 1939) took special interest in African American children who scored well on the Stanford–Binet tests. His first study focused on gifted African American children, who he believed did not represent the "two brightest Negro children in America" (Jenkins, 1936b, p. 159), a remark commonly made by White researchers. His case study consisted of 14 African American children with IQs of 160 and higher. He found a larger incidence of such children but noted that social and geographical issues (none were identified in Southern states) often hampered his efforts. His second study extended his previous research, but his subjects were drawn from seven Chicago public schools. Jenkins pointed out that few researchers found these children because "most of the studies concerned with the mental test performance of Negro children have been conducted in localities which proved meager opportunities for educational and cultural development" (Jenkins, 1936c, pp. 189–190). And, unlike many White researchers, Jenkins found no "mulatto effect." In his research, the incidence of high IQs appear to be evenly distributed among African American children.

Price (1934) reviewed the research on intelligence and race as well and reported on the racial and class demographic composition of participants in several well-known standardized tests: Stanford–Binet, National Intelligence test, Otis Primary and Advanced Examinations, Terman Group Test of Mental Ability, among others. He concluded:

> The tests used have been standardized upon Northern Whites, largely, whose schooling has been different in amount and kind from the great bulk of Negroes who, of course, are in the South. And, on the other hand, the sampling has neither been random or representative, for the groups compared have either (or both) been too small and/or they have been unlike in socio-economic status, school training, and cultural background. (p. 452)

White researchers and historians have long ignored Price's research, yet he addressed the effects of institutionalized racism, school enrollment, and employment. Since his publication, other researchers—Montagu (1945), Rury (1988), and Galloway (1994)— have extended his premise by examining school enrollment figures of African Americans in the early 1900s and by using more sophisticated statistical procedures.

In another approach to addressing the issue of alleged racial inferiority, during the 1920s Du Bois published a magazine for African American children as part of the *Crisis*, known affectionately as *The Brownie's Book*. Jessie Redmon Fauset (1882–1961), a literary editor of the *Crisis*, was a frequent contributor, along with Langston Hughes and other Harlem Renaissance noteworthy authors and poets. *The Brownie's Book* sought to uplift the race by featuring stories, poetry, art, advice, and biographies about famous African Americans. A poem by Madeline G. Allison serves as an excellent example of this point:

CHILDREN OF THE SUN

Dear little girl of tender years,
Born of a race with haunting fears—
Cry not nor sigh for wrongs done you,
Your cloud has sliv'ry lining, too
Dear little son, be not in gloom,
For fears this world has no more room;

God in his Wisdom gave you hue
Of which He's proud—yes, proud of
    you! (Allison, 1996, p. 50)

The purpose of the *Brownie's Book* was to instill self and racial pride and to limit the deleterious effect of the negative and stereotypical portrayal of African Americans in popular press for children and in the mass media.

Although there were numerous opponents to the published results of the army tests, African American scholars, collectively, did not accept the ideas of educational leaders with regard to the connection between intelligence and race. They found particularly abhorrent the use of the claims of "science" as factual proof that African Americans were intellectually inferior, especially given the philosophical assumptions on which the "science" was based. This group of scholars also acknowledged how ideological hegemony as a means of racial control, and as "scientists" advanced claims of African Americans' racial, intellectual, and moral inferiority as affirmed by standardized testing. Moreover, they were aware of the discourse used in the popular press and academic journals that also supported and promoted the notion of racial and class inferiority.

Besides the outcry of African American scholars there were sympathetic Whites, who not only challenged the science and the interpretation and use of testing by educational researchers but also had power enough to use journalism to convey their criticism. Paramount among this latter group of oppositional thinkers was Walter Lippmann. A very brief overview of his debate with Louis Terman is presented next to illustrate that his views ran counter to the dominant ideology.

Lippman and Terman Debate

Among the more celebrated critiques of the intelligence testing movement was a series of articles between Lippmann and Terman, published in *The New Republic* in 1922. The Terman–Lippmann debate, as the exchange came to be known, offers a revealing glimpse into opposing views of intelligence testing and illustrates the tenor of the debate over the use of standardized testing in general. This review also helps to establish a framework for understanding the influence of dominant groups to shape public perception.

The debate began when Lippmann (in seven articles) raised questions about defining intelligence, the inheritability of intelligence, and whether tests actually measured intelligence. He observed that the developers of intelligence tests narrowly defined intelligence based on their preset standards, notions of heredity of intelligence, and tradition. In his article "The Mystery of the 'A' Men," Lippman (1922b) articulated, "The intelligence tester starts with no clear idea of what intelligence means. He then proceeds by drawing upon his common sense and experience to imagine the different kinds of problems men face" (p. 246). Furthermore, he observed that intelligence testing

> does not weigh or measure intelligence by any objective standard. It simply arranges a group of people in a series from best to worst by balancing their capacity to do certain arbitrarily selected puzzles, against the capacity of all the others. The intelligence test, in other words, is fundamentally an instrument for classifying a group of people. (p. 247)

Lippmann was so outraged by the biases in the test that he dubbed them "tests of hereditary intelligence," knowingly challenging the research of Goddard and Terman as well as the tests they created and promoted as indicators of intelligence.

In a follow-up article, "The Reliability of Intelligence Tests," Lippmann (1922c) called for a closer examination of the new industry of intelligence testing, the interpretation of the data, and the uses made of the testing results. Lippmann suggested that performance-based testing would be a more accurate predictor of school success, although he did not equate school success with intelligence or a successful life: "If a child fails in school and then fails in life, the school cannot sit back and say: you see how accurately I predicted this" (p. 276). Furthermore, he continually questioned the power of test developers to set standards for the nation's children. He was most concerned about how the intelligence tests would be used in schools. Prophetically, Lippmann warned,

> If, for example, the impression takes root that these tests really measure intelligence, that they constitute a sort of last judgment on a child's capacity, that they reveal "scientifically" his predestined ability, then it would be a thousand times better if all the intelligence tests and all of their questionnaires were sunk without warning in the Sargasso Sea. (1922d, p. 297)

In one of his last articles in the series, "A Future for Tests," Lippmann (1922f) tried to emphasize the connections he observed between the thinking of eugenicists and intelligence testing: "The scoring of the test itself favors an uncritical belief that intelligence is a fixed quantity in the germ-plasm and that, no matter what the environment, only a predetermined increment of intelligence can develop from year to year" (p. 9). He cautioned the public to consider the impact of testing:

> If it were true, the emotional and worldly satisfactions in store for the intelligence tester would be very great. If he were really measuring intelligence, and if intelligence were a fixed hereditary quantity it would be for him to say not only where to place each child in school, but also which children should go to high school, which to college, which into the professions, which into the manual trades and common laborer. (1922f, pp. 9–10)

Lippmann realized the power that designers of intelligence tests would have in determining the futures of school children. He also cogently wrote that the tests tested "an unanalyzed mixture of native capacity, acquired habits and stored-up knowledge, and no tester knows at any moment which factors he is testing" (p. 10). Importantly, he noted that it was wishful thinking to believe the tests reflected notions of "native intelligence." In fact, he warned that no such test existed, and those that did are "designed to lead to social injustice and to grave injury to those who are arbitrarily classified as predestined inferiors or superiors" (p. 11). Finally, Lippmann criticized the importance that educational psychologists and school administrators placed on test results:

> The danger of intelligence tests is that in a wholesale system of education, the less sophisticated or the more prejudiced will stop when they have classified and forget that their duty is to educate. They will grade the retard child instead of fighting the causes of his backwardness. For the whole drift of the propaganda based on intelligence testing is to treat people with low intelligence quotients as congenitally and hopelessly inferior. (1922d, p. 297)

Lippmann's articles ignited more public debate about how intelligence testing was used by schools, but they did not change the opinions of most educators and educational researchers.

Lewis Terman (1922a) responded with a sarcastic rebuttal to Lippmann's charges in his article "The Great Conspiracy," claiming that Lippmann did not understand science well enough to articulate a reasoned or logical response to the testing movement. Terman, however, did not limit his attack of naysayers to Lippmann. He withstood anyone who challenged the "scientific" findings of intelligence testing, including educators at the National Education Association in 1923. Moreover, he unashamedly promoted the importance of heredity in determining intelligence and racial betterment. He argued, "The racial stocks most prolific of gifted children are those from northern and western Europe, and the Jewish. The least prolific are the Mediterranean races, the Mexicans and the Negroes" (Terman, quoted in Gould, 1981). Terman was not alone in his interpretation of the army test results along racial, ethnic, and class lines. The president of Harvard University, Lawrence Lowell, who also was a eugenicist and supporter of Terman's thinking, was moved to action. He curbed the number of Jewish enrollees and barred an African American student from living in the dorms. Takaki (1993) notes that Harvard's policies changed under Lowell to include a photo of incoming students and requirements of well-roundedness as well as regional representativeness. Harvard eventually voted on a nondiscrimination policy of racial and ethnic separation.

What is captivating about the Lippmann–Terman debate on intelligence testing is that it moved the conversation beyond the halls of the academy and into the popular press. It also offered the general public an alternative and oppositional point of view seldom presented in the press. This debate illustrates how ideological and cultural hegemony moves from abstraction to concrete day-to-day events. It also clarifies the relationship among intelligence testing, the U.S. Army's use of standardized intelligence tests, and subsequent use of national standardized tests of intelligence. To be clear, reading comprehension researchers, whether educational psychologists or educational leaders, exercised extensive power/authority to conceptualize, define, test, interpret, and justify their view of reading comprehension research and testing as scientific.

Standardized Intelligence and Reading Comprehension Testing

The previous discussion articulates the connection among reading comprehension research and testing, intelligence testing, and the U.S. Army's use of intelligence tests as well as foreshadows a national testing movement in public education. Spring (1986) observes that tests were used to "reinforce ethnic and social class differences by claiming they reflected differences in intelligence" (p. 242). The involvement in the construction of the U.S. Army officer recruitment tests by leading educational researchers also helped to redirect reading comprehension testing in three significant ways. First, reading comprehension test developers were less concerned with reading rate, and rapid reading was less often equated with greater reading comprehension. Second, there was a demand for improved reading instruction in the public schools and improved standardized tests of reading comprehension. Third, there was an increased interest in reading research in general and reading comprehension testing in particular.

A residual effect found several reading researchers revising old tests or creating new reading comprehension tests that included the use of the multiple choice format. Unfortunately, this practice stripped students of the opportunity to respond to text in a thoughtful manner. All interpretive and creative responses were disallowed (there was only one right answer and that was the one selected by the test developers). It also meant that the reader had to have experienced and understood the passage in concert with the developers' intended purposes for questioning. By allowing only one correct interpretation, the tests required the reader to acknowledge that only the test developers' interpretation was the correct one for the test item. As we have seen, the developers of the tests brought influences from their lives into the test content, questions, and interpretations. Thus, the more like the lives of the test developers (White, Protestant, middle-class, male) the test takers (students) were, the more likely their answers would be correct. As Gramsci (1971) avows, this is part of the hegemonic process:

> The old intellectual and moral leaders of society feel the ground slipping from under their feet; they perceive that their "sermons" have become precisely mere "sermons," i.e. external to reality, pure form without any content, shades without a spirit. This is the reason for their reactionary and conservative tendencies; for their particular form of civilization, culture and morality which they represented is decomposing ...

Given the nation's response to the interpretation of the U.S. Army recruit testing data, it appeared to be an optimal time to re-inscribe dominant ideas. Whenever members of the dominant class believe they are losing ground, as Gramsci (1971) notes, they concoct reasons to reinvent their ideology and push for consent of the masses.

During this period, there was a proliferation of studies focusing on reading comprehension and reading comprehension testing. In fact, according to W. Gray (1925), reading comprehension became one of the most often-tested school subjects. Prominent educational psychologists such as Courtis, W. Gray, Kelly, Monroe, and Thorndike improved their early tests, and others such as Burgess, Gates, Haggerty, and Ogelsby developed new reading comprehension tests. Interest in reading comprehension testing was twofold: The tests were seen as indicative of intelligence, and there was a tremendous amount of profit to be made publishing tests. As more researchers worked within the field, it became evident that reading comprehension tests were not evaluating the same skills, causing researchers to look more closely at the purpose and skills of reading during testing.

Several other researchers published chapters in the 1919 *National Society for the Study of Education Yearbook*. The report by the Committee on the Economy of Time in Education, "The nature, purposes, and general methods of measurements of educational products" was written by Thorndike. He wrote that the goal for education was "to change human nature for the better in respect to knowledge and taste and power" (Thorndike, 1919, p. 1). In addition, he called for the use of exact measurements and quantifiable educational products and wrote his now-famous quotation, "Whatever exists at all exists in some amount. To know it thoroughly involves knowing its quantity as well as its quality" (p. 11). Further, he admitted that educational measurement was not as exact as general scientific measurement, due to its complexity. However, he offered the following definition of the purpose of educational measurement: "to provide somebody with the knowledge that he needs of the amount of some thing, difference or relative. The 'somebody' may be a scientific worker, a superintendent of schools, a teacher, a parent, or a pupil" (p. 19).

In another chapter, W. Gray (1919a) declared that no one method of teaching reading was more effective than another. In fact, he suggested that the effectiveness of any method depended in large part on the materials available, the teacher's use of the materials, and the students. In accordance with his Herbartian training and his editorship of a basal series, he reiterated the importance of using "interesting text for young readers for improved comprehension, retention, and rate" (p. 41). This idea continues to be resurrected by reading researchers and classroom teachers in the interest of improving and expanding our understanding of the power of text and its communicative ability to help readers comprehend. Gray (1919a) also listed reasons for student success or failure in primary reading that, according to him, were drawn from his research and reflected popular opinion. These reasons include the classroom teacher, students' social economic status, students' race/ethnicity, and reading supplemental materials. Troubling then, as now, is the opinion of reading researchers and teachers that a student's success or failure in learning to read is linked to his or her race/ethnicity.

Reading Comprehension Research and Testing's Role in the Process

The field of reading comprehension research and testing, although in its infancy, played a critical role in maintaining dominant ideologies, from its philosophical underpinnings, to the content and interpretation of tests, to the promotion of test results as scientific facts. The case of the U.S. Army tests, and subsequent national intelligence tests that drew on reading comprehension research, illustrates this point. As these tests sought to validate a common set of assumptions as "scientific facts," they more accurately reflected the beliefs, values, and practices of the dominant class. Some reading comprehension researchers became national leaders of the testing movement, their careers buoyed by the "success" of U.S. Army testing and subsequent sale of national intelligence tests. Powerful reading comprehension test researchers sought to explain variance in test performance from a racial perspective that, in the minds of many White academics, supported their views of the inheritability of intelligence. Despite opposition by Scholars of Color and some Whites, the process and tradition of comparing the performance of underserved students with their White counterparts, only to find the former lacking and claiming the latter superior, continued.

The ideological hegemony that supported the conception, thinking, and publication of the results of the U.S. Army recruits' test scores and the dawn of massive intelligence and achievement testing began, in part, as an outgrowth of reading comprehension research and testing. Ideological bias, social and political forces, and the individual and collective efforts of researchers and educational leaders coalesced and appeared to justify the use of tests in general and reading comprehension tests in particular. The media's role in support of these ideologies heightened during the World War I era, as it appeared to manufacture the consent of the U.S. public in support of the idea of the inferiority to non-Whites, especially as it appeared validated by educational tests. As these ideas began to permeate society more broadly, faith was placed on the expertise of reading researchers and the results of testing in general and reading comprehension testing in particular. Scholars of Color, however, recognized that racial and class differences are inherently part of the tests, especially as evinced in the content of the test questions. In fact, they pointed out that these differences accounted for greater variance in test performance than notions of intelligence. The next chapter considers how reading comprehension research and testing continue to evolve in response to changes in educational theorizing about learning. However, the rapidly shifting political and social landscapes spawned movements from localized grassroots efforts for social justice to media events and that culminated in rulings by the U.S. Supreme Court. They were clarion calls for change in how issues of race and class were understood and addressed by Scholars of Color who opposed the use of tests as a measure of intelligence and to the marginalization of cultural and linguistic differences as well.

6

Reproducing and Producing Reading Comprehension Research and Testing

Foundational to understanding the role of reading comprehension within the process of ideological hegemony is understanding it within the contexts in which it developed, and acknowledging that the approaches to reading comprehension always have been inadequate to explain how reading comprehension takes place. The inadequacy arises because the theories proposed are not complex enough to capture the process for all. Hall (2003) avows:

> One-sided explanations are always a distortion. Not in the sense that they are a lie about the system, but in the sense that a "half truth" cannot be the whole truth about anything. With those ideas, you will always represent a part of the whole. You will thereby produce an explanation which is only *partially* adequate—and in that sense, "false." (p. 37, italics in the original)

It is a form of ideological and cultural imperialism to suggest that the explanations proposed by the dominant class are adequate or universal and can explain the process for all learners. The one-sidedness that Hall observed continued among reading comprehension researchers throughout early 20th century. Most egregious were reading researchers who were seemingly unaffected by the shortsightedness of their explanations of reading comprehension research and testing.

This chapter continues to review the influence of dominant ideologies that influenced reading comprehension research and testing. What becomes readily apparent is the resiliency of scientism, psychologism, racism, and classism, despite political and social changes in the nation. Researchers continued to reproduce the same research on comprehension and testing, in part because it was part of dominant ideologies and in part because it was convenient. There were some changes in reading

179

comprehension, most notably from disciplines outside of educational psychology. In addition, this chapter continues its pattern of discussing political, social, and cultural historical moments and the role that racism plays in the explanations offered for test performance differences between Underserved students and their White counterparts in intelligence and reading comprehension testing. Finally, in consideration of reading comprehension as mechanisms used on the terrain of struggle, I illustrate the counter discourses that accompanied protest movements as indicative of resistance to dominant ideologies.

Reproducing Reading Comprehension Research

During this post war period, several studies by W. Gray (1927), Starch (1927), and Thorndike (1921) again sought to correlate reading rate, comprehension, and intelligence. Gates (1921a), for example, compared the results of several reading comprehension and vocabulary tests by Burgess, Courtis, Gray, Monroe, and Thorndike with the reading ability results of students in Scarborough, New York, on the Stanford–Binet. Although demographics of the students involved in his study were not presented, historically, the community has been predominantly White and upper class. Gates (1921d) argued that reading comprehension represented numerous complex abilities, and "intelligence, as measured by Stanford–Binet shows itself only when the mechanics of reading are fairly well mastered" (p. 459). He found that reading rate and comprehension were correlated although most tests do not differentiate the two. He also suggested that the reading comprehension tests he used in his study were not perfect.

Another example comes from the research of Starch (1927), who characterized the relationship among intelligence, reading rate, and reading comprehension this way:

> The rapidity with which ideas arise in the mind in response to printed word stimuli is apparently dependent upon the reader's general intelligence and upon the amount of experience which he has had with the realities symbolized by the words. ... Meanings in reading are the associates which through direct and indirect experience become connected with words. Comprehension in reading arises from the number, relevancy, and orderly grouping of these meanings. (p. 314)

According to C.T. Gray (1922), there were a number of different types of reading comprehension tests formats available including "oral and written questions, oral and written reproductions, out-lining, drawing, dramatizing, emotional reactions, and direction tests as seen in assignments" (pp. 40–41). The most enduring format because of its link to educational psychology's standardized testing emphasis, has been the multiple choice question because of its link to the army testing results that implied a link between intelligence and reading ability.

Teacher Education and Reading Comprehension

As the importance of educational psychology began to grow, so did its influence in reading research. A careful look at a normal school method's book makes clear this connection. Brooks (1926), in his book *The Applied Psychology of Reading With Exercises and Direc-tions for Improving Silent and Oral Reading,* described the field as composed of Judd's laboratory experiments at the University of Chi-cago and Thorndike's experiments regarding the nature and mea-surement of reading at Columbia University's Teachers College. The host of reasons that he listed for the lack of reading achievement in school children included undue emphasis on oral reading, unsuitable teaching methods, unsuitable and insufficient reading materials, lack of teacher interest and preparation, the intellectual ability of students (equating low intelligence with poor reading achievement), and influ-ences beyond the school. In a separate list, he mentioned several other factors that contributed to poor reading: chronological age for the onset of reading instruction, nationality, attendance, time devoted to reading, kindergarten training, phonics and the phonics system used, motor habits, gender, and supervision. Interestingly, he argued,

> Reading is often popularly defined as the process of getting the thought from the printed (or written) page. Strictly speaking, this is not correct; we do not *get thought* from the printed page or from any source outside of the individual. Thought comes or develops from within the individual. (p. 26, italics in the original)

Brooks (1926) also claimed, "The stimuli may come . . . from with-out, but the thinking arises within" (p. 26). Then, he added,

> It is better to define reading as a series of more or less habitual responses, known as thought, feeling, attitude, etc., which are stimulated by the printed page. It is a form of behavior involving complex motor habits

and associative processes. ... The symbols on the printed page, however, are merely the stimuli which evoke the responses which are so largely conditioned by habit (previous experience, or training). (p. 26)

His discussion aligns with the ideas about reading comprehension not surprisingly expressed earlier by Thorndike. That is, Brooks divides meaning into two distinct phases: comprehension of words (vocabulary) and comprehension of sentences and paragraphs. And, like Thorndike, he understood the latter to be akin to thinking or reasoning.

Germane and Germane (1922) also conducted a comprehensive review of reading comprehension (including their own work) in their book *Silent Reading: A Handbook for Teachers*. They reported a common, but unfounded, complaint among teachers: "A single reading to measure children's ability to comprehend is unfair and impractical. ... If pupils had been given an opportunity to read the lessons at least three times, the scores would have shown they have much thought-getting ability" (p. 56). The authors rejected the idea that single readings of silent reading comprehension were an invalid measure of reading comprehension. They alleged, "The responsibility for promoting improvement in the ability to comprehend, rests almost entirely with the teacher" (p. 61). Then, they declared, "Nothing aids reading like reading" (p. 65). In other words, increasing the amount of time spent reading also improves reading comprehension. Finally, in a review of the many available tests of reading comprehension, Hillard (1924) found that the difficulties surrounding the study of reading comprehension involved factors such as low general intelligence, limited vocabulary, poor environment, poor school attendance, lack of motivation, and inability to reason, among others. Not surprisingly, his list was strikingly similar to the list of reasons given for inferior intelligence test performance during army testing.

At the University of Iowa, Yoakam (1924) and a team of reading researchers published the results of a series of studies they conducted on the effects of a single reading and reading comprehension. Their findings indicated that the ability to comprehend what is read differed depending on the type of material offered and that using expository material was as valid as using other types. They also observed that students differed in their ability to read and comprehend materials given once, as in a single reading event. In both studies the researchers reverted to the earlier practice of using school materials as test content as opposed to creating new or novel reading comprehension test materials.

Most classroom teachers had disregarded the tradition of measuring reading comprehension by oral fluency and written reproductions. Most used one of the many standardized reading comprehension tests available, prompting a renewed debate over a definition of reading comprehension. Among those concerned were Pressey (1922), who believed that the term "silent reading" was unfortunate. He held that what was really important during reading was what he called "thought getting." He noted that the modern tests of reading comprehension offered a short paragraph followed by several questions to which the student was to write a response, circle a word or letter, or write true or false.

This is not meant to imply that reading comprehension research and testing moved forward unchallenged, especially during attempts to translate research into practice. Sounding like positivists and pragmatists, Judd and Buswell (1922) voiced their concerns about the nexus of research and practice. They argued, "wherever the mental processes of pupils show fundamental differences, practical school procedure will have to fit its methods to these differences. ... The duty of the scientist is to devise methods of discovering and describing fundamental differences" (p. 2). Unfortunately the concerns of these researchers were not heeded.

Challenged by the charges, test developers attempted to more accurately measure specific abilities used during reading comprehension. Drawing on the work of Thorndike, Woody (1923) for instance created a scale that he claimed was in keeping with "a slowly maturing conviction that the best way to guarantee the teaching of a particular aspect of a subject is to construct a test which purports to measure that aspect of the subject" (p. 315). Like Kelly, he used short paragraphs, followed by fixed-alternative sentences, to help students "pick out the central thoughts" (p. 315). He claimed his reading comprehension tests measured higher order reading ability based on classroom trials.

The importance of reading research and testing emerged as *Twenty-fourth Yearbook of the National Society for the Study of Education* (1925) that devoted an entire volume to research on reading. Chapter 9 focused exclusively on reading tests, specifically informal and standardized tests including silent reading comprehension. The author, Gray (1925), proposed that standardized reading comprehension tests be given periodically throughout the school year, along with informal tests, as part of normal instruction. School districts as social institutions of the State, were complicit in fueling ideological hegemony and supporting dominant ideologies.

Reading Comprehension, Race, and Language

In 1928, Livia Youngquist and Carleton Washburne, of Winnetka, a White middle-class suburb north of Chicago, Illinois, published their reading materials, *Winnetka Primary Reading Materials*. Three years later, Mabel Morphett and Carleton Washburne published results of a 10-year longitudinal study of the effects of the Winnetka Plan (1931). Building on the ideas of the Progressive era and drawing on Dewey's notion of schools as social communities, the Winnetka Plan separated the curriculum into subjects and encouraged cooperative learning. In Winnetka, the *Detroit First-Grade Intelligence Test* and *Stanford-Binet Test* were administered to all children in an effort to determine their general intelligence and to determine how closely they were tied to reading progress. Next, the children were taught to read by the Winnetka technique before being tested on the *Gray Oral Reading Check Test*. Their results indicated that for successful reading, children should be taught to read at age 6. The Winneketa Plan, called for diagnostic tests, self pacing, and workbooks. The authors, however, are most often cited for their research regarding beginning reading instruction. Their research sought the optimal time to teach beginning reading instruction for the students in the White middle-class suburb north of Chicago. Their findings became the benchmark for beginning reading instruction nationwide. The promotion and widespread acceptance of their findings is indicative of how reading research is normalized to support racist ideologies; in this case, White middle-class suburban students are used as representative of all U.S. school children. The children in their study were hardly representative of all U.S. school children, as they were predominantly White, middle-to-upper class, native English speakers.

In another experiment, among a similar population of students, Parkhurst (1887–1973) instituted the Dalton Plan in Dalton, Massachusetts (Parkhurst, 1922). Under her plan, built on Dewey's principles, instruction was individually guided and paced according to a child's interests, talents, and abilities. The Dalton Plan called for increased responsibility on the part of the learner, including writing a contract for learning. Further, students could work at their own pace, fulfilling their contractual obligations; then they could create a new contract.

Tireman's (1929) study, "Reading in the elementary schools of New Mexico," offers another example of how a reading researcher used racial and linguistic misunderstandings in his interpretation of reading test data. He administered the *Monroe Standardized Silent Reading Test (Revised)* to children in New Mexico and found "a grave situation" in that the Mexican American children "all fell below the median on reading rate and comprehension" (p. 623). Then, he reviewed the scores, looking specifically at the students' first languages (English, Spanish, and other foreign languages). The English-speaking children scored the highest and the Spanish-speaking children the lowest. When Tireman reinterpreted the data, it revealed that the Spanish-speaking children, like so many U.S. Army recruits, had failed to learn to read in English. He argued, "It is a matter of common belief, and there is some statistical evidence to show, that the amount and character of the material read are significant factors in producing individual differences in reading accomplishment" (p. 624). He also attributed the students' poor performance on his reading comprehension test "to a lack of interest, effort, and practice in reading" (p. 625). Although his findings were in error, they were greatly supported by similar research throughout the country when the test performance of Whites was compared to that of Underserved children.

A sterling example is documented in The Lemon Grove (California) Incident in 1930, when the San Diego school board sought to segregate schools, brings the issue of the importance of language into full relief. Briefly, the San Diego School Board identified two major problems: (a) overcrowding which led to unsanitary conditions, and (b) language concerns as many of the Mexican American students did not speak English (albeit the school board sought to categorize the children as Native American/Indian). The brave parents of the Mexican American students fought, despite possible deportation and loss of jobs, to have their children attend the same schools as other students. The State of California ruled it was illegal to segregate Mexican children. Issues of educational access and language of instruction would continue to resurface throughout the century.

Tireman's subsequent work at the University of New Mexico included the *Mesaland Series* (1949), which focused on bilingual education, curriculum, reform, and community education. In a 1951 text titled *Teaching Spanish-Speaking Children*, he illustrates his empathy toward the racial prejudice experienced by students of Mexican descent, the intolerant attitudes and low expectations by teachers of Spanish speakers, and the perception of Spanish speakers as problematic. Tireman's description of racial discrimination is indicative of how oppression is made to appear normal by the dominant class, without a discussion of the political and social forces that accompanied Mexican removal from the land now known as Texas:

> This fact has resulted in the development of certain attitudes and prejudices, on the part of English-speaking people, which are most unfortunate, but perhaps natural. The only class of Spanish-speaking person that many English-speaking people have seen is the lowest economic and social class from Mexico. They do not know and appreciate the qualities of Mexicans who are in the upper levels of Mexican society. Many of the English-speaking people of Texas, therefore, are accustomed to consider all Mexicans as though they belonged to the low income type of workers that live in their midst. This is obviously unfair to the Mexicans. ... Pigmentation may help explain Anglo intolerance, since many Mexican-Americans are dark. Texas is a Southern state and, as such, has many of the traditional Southern attitudes toward the dark skin. (pp. 12–13)

His comments reveal how racial discrimination is linked to skin color, how social economic class is often an underlying concern, and how little value is placed on languages other than English.

Woodson's concerns about the state of education for African Americans in the United States were expressed by Carter G. Woodson (the father of Black history and founder of the *Journal of Negro Education*). Woodson, like Du Bois, held a doctorate from Harvard University, and, like Cooper, had studied at the Sorbonne in Paris. He was an educator, and social activist. Woodson (1933) observed how the consciousness of African Americans was shaped by the contexts of their lives,

> When you control a man's thinking you do not have to worry about his actions. You do not have to tell him to stand here or go yonder. He will find his 'proper place' and will stay in it. ... His education makes it necessary. (p. xiii)

Woodson's thinking reflects Cooper's and Du Bois' earlier statements with regard to double consciousness and the importance of raising the consciousness of African Americans. These dominant ideologies spurred misguided assumptions that African Americans were unconscious of the ideological and cultural hegemony that structured their lives and were unwitting participants; that is, they offered their consent or were easily coerced in supporting dominant ideologies. Woodson argued that not only were some African Americans conscious of the efforts to coerce them into ways of thinking but they were also eager to fight against the coercion that questioned their intelligence, morals, and humanity. He proffered that what appeared to be an African American consensual response to the lack of education and educational opportunities was not consent, but rather the illusion of a coerced response of an oppressed people in the context in which they lived.

Woodson (1933) understood race as central to understanding African American consciousness and life experiences in the United States.

> The same educational process which inspires and stimulates the oppressor with the thought that he is everything and has accomplished everything worthwhile, depresses and crushes at the same time the spark of genius in the Negro by making him feel that his race does not amount to much and never will measure up to the standards of others. (p. xiii)

He spoke out against the ideological and cultural hegemony that structured society and underlay education. For instance, the hegemonic and relational forces that made possible and acceptable chattel slavery, discrimination and segregation, and physical violence (lynching, murders, mutilations, rape) within U.S. society also simultaneously kept these events out of U.S. history books. He felt strongly that the U.S. system of education was as much ideological and cultural as it was pedagogical, such that it was structured to coerce readers to see African Americans as inferior to Whites whether based on "science," history, or morality. He understood that public education needed to play an ever-increasing role in dismantling racist ideologies. Woodson (1933) argued that the history and accomplishments of people of African descent were missing in the American story, and he believed "the education of any people should begin with the people themselves" (p. 32). To that end he created avenues for the publication of Negro history and books that celebrated the accomplishments of African Americans. Woodson, though often overlooked, was not alone as a researcher who was reconceptualizing learning.

Behaviorist Approach to Reading Comprehension Research

Behaviorism was a popular theoretical approach to learning used by social scientists in the U.S. There are three distinctive types of behaviorism: methodological, psychological, and analytic. Methodological behaviorism emerged in educational psychology from the research of John B. Watson, who built on classical British empiricism and the findings of Russian physiologist Ivan Pavlov. Watson (1913) claimed, "Psychology as the behaviorist views it is a purely objective experimental branch of natural science. Its theoretical goal is the prediction and control of behavior" (p. 158). In his book *Behaviorism,* Watson (1930) claimed that behaviorism should focus on observable and measurable behavior, measurable in the sense that mental representations could be mathematically computed. His idea drew on positivism and called for experiment, control, objectivity, careful record keeping, concise definitions of behavior, and statistical analysis. He argued that behavior could be understood and predicted: "To predict, given the stimulus, what reaction will take place; or, given the reaction, state what the situation or stimulus is that has caused the reaction" (Watson, 1930, p. 11). Watson believed that meaning was an abstraction that "never arises in the scientific observation of behavior. We watch what the animal or human being is doing. He 'means' what he does. … His action shows his meaning" (p. 354). This form of behaviorism does not acknowledge human thinking, internal processes, emotions, or consciousness.

Psychological behaviorism is best illustrated in the work of B. F. Skinner (1974), although his form of behaviorism is more correctly known as *radical behavorism*. It focuses on external observable and measurable behavior and gives little credence to unobservable mental functions, internal processes, emotions, consciousness, or the context in which thoughts evolve. Skinner's version, a blend of all three forms of behaviorism, promotes positive reinforcement over punishment for an ordered social world, thoughts which he outlined in his 1948 publication *Walden II.* He grounded his positivistic ideas of the perfect society in accordance with behaviorist principles.

Critics of Skinner's ideas, including Chomsky (1971), argued that his work ignored human thinking and prowess in their environments.

Applications to Reading Comprehension Research and Testing

Harold Rugg (1934) reviewed the evolution of behaviorism in *Teachers College Record* and summarized the behaviorists assumptions as follows:

> Human nature is mechanism and not organism; that human personality is indeed the sum of all its traits; 2) whatever exists, exists in some amount, and can be measured; that is, that we know a thing only as we can measure and describe it quantitatively; 3) human traits which are quantitative-qualitative fusions can be reduced to quantitative measures; and 4) certain traits of an organism can be held constant, and changes which are produced in others can be measured by the use of the statistical method of correlation. (p. 116)

He acknowledged that the use of the scientific method in education had been a search for "facts," by looking to models from physical science and working toward reliability and validity. Rugg also believed that the gains found in scientism needed to be tempered, by understanding that the theories held by the researcher determined, in large part, how the experiment was framed and how the data were interpreted. He noted that most of the investigations of education were of the "rank-order method," that is, comparisons of norms. This caused him concern:

> The measure of the product or the growth of one individual was assumed to be those of other individuals, rather than his own capacity for production and growth. I am confident that the widespread use of this external norm of measurement has contributed to the setting of false standards within the school. (pp. 120–121)

In addition, he observed that attention to philosophy, theory, and values were missing from the endeavors of educational researchers. Rugg referred to earlier efforts as mechanical in their search for improved methods of observation. Finally, he concluded by praising the gains made by the use of the scientific method in education and warned it should be held in check and not allowed to overwhelm other means of understanding.

When behaviorist assumptions were applied to reading compre-hension research and testing, the results were theories and research based on attempts to determine the process of comprehension from observable behaviors, or test results. Although some researchers theorized about how to measure author intention, purpose, and the like, the tests of reading comprehension altered little. For example, Thorndike (1931) elaborated on the importance of science in educa-tional research when he wrote, "The methods of science are impar-tial, paying no heed to the immediate satisfyingness of any idea to any individual. They require verification and test of prophecy" (p. 192). He also continued to publish articles in *Teachers College Record* on reading. His 1934 (1934a, 1934b, 1934c) series "Improv-ing the Ability to Read," focused on vocabulary and the use of read-ers (basals) for instruction in reading. One of his findings was that children needed numerous reading materials and that the greatest improvements in reading came from reading books, not basals, a thought that continues to be voiced.

Other reading researchers also attempted to use behaviorism in its varied forms to shape reading comprehension research, instruction, and testing. Reading comprehension researchers, then and now, have sought to observe, manipulate, and measure reading comprehension, largely through written and oral reading tests.

Raguse's (1930) article "Qualitative and Quantitative achievements in First Grade Reading" offers a view into how reading comprehen-sion research applied behavioral objectives in research. She reported on a classroom study where her objectives for teaching reading were "word comprehension, phrase comprehension, sentence comprehen-sion, paragraph comprehension, and large unit comprehension" (p. 426). Raguse reported the following findings:

> 1. Children are able to read many books with a high degree of accuracy in first grade.

> 2. The number of books read depends to a large degree upon the train-ing that a child has received in reaction to words and reading materials, which require the five types of comprehension.

> 3. A low I. Q. does not always necessitate poor qualitative and quantita-tive achievements in reading.

> 4. Only a few children in first grade were too immature to learn to read widely.

5. The mechanical arrangement of materials in reading is an essential factor in developing various word-perception skills.

6. The careful reading of many books improves the quality of reading if correct reading skills, habits, and attitudes are used and maintained by procedures which constantly stimulate and provide for the systematic development of those essential factors in reading. (p. 434)

Likewise, Gates (1931) in his book *Interests and Ability in Reading* claimed that "what the classroom teacher needs to know is in what particular skills or abilities a class or a child is relatively strong in the light of his capacity" (p. 223). He believed that his tests would help teachers to know where a child was experiencing difficulties. In 1937, Gates listed other techniques that teachers used to guide and measure reading comprehension: drawing a picture, choosing the best illustration, selecting items on an illustration, giving illustrations a title, following directions, and answering questions (multiple choice, true/false, and completion).

New work in the field continued to be selectively recorded and reported by Gray in the *National Society for the Study of Education* throughout the 1930s and in his "Annual Summaries of Investigations in Reading," published in the *Journal of Educational Research*, thereafter. Gray reviewed more than 100 studies of reading research ranging from purposes of reading to silent reading comprehension, to word recognition, to reading during summer vacations in his 1931 *Summary of Reading Investigations*. His publications shaped the framework for reporting reading research. Two examples illustrate this point. First, despite the political, economic, and social unrest in the country in the midst of the Great Depression, W. Gray made only veiled references to the "situation" in his reports on reading research, effectively ignoring the impact of larger contexts on the field. Second, Gray's scant discussions of what he called improvements in the field lacked description and detail. Insightfully, W. Gray (1934) observed a more important shortfall in reading comprehension research and testing: "Improvements in the tests themselves important though it be, is less important than the development of a rational philosophy in using them" (p. 59). He shared this thought initially in presentation at the National Education Association meeting and later it was published in the *Review of Educational Research*.

In a more current review of the era, Sheppard (2000) lists several key assumptions held by behaviorists that remain a part of educational research and testing:

- Learning occurs by accumulating atomized bits of knowledge;
- Learning is tightly sequenced and hierarchical;
- Transfer is limited, so each objective must be explicitly taught;
- Tests should be used frequently to ensure mastery before proceeding to the next objective;
- Tests are isomorphic with learning (tests plus learning); and
- Motivation is external and based on positive reinforcement of many small tests. (p.5)

The staying power or survival of these ideas is part and parcel of the ideological hegemony that delimits change, growth, and progress in reading comprehension research and testing.

Associated Ideas That Influenced Reading Comprehension Research

Reading researchers of this era seldom focused exclusively on one aspect of reading, preferring to investigate a wide range of interests. Meanwhile, two projects in psychology were emerging that pointed to the connections among memory (Bartlett, 1932) and intelligence and cognition (Piaget, 1936). Sir Frederic S. Bartlett, a British psychologist conducted research in the area of memory for 23 years before his seminal work *Remembering: A Study in Experimental and Social Psychology* was published. He tested the memory of subjects at various intervals by asking them to recall and write verbatim reproductions of the folktale, "The War of the Ghosts." The story is alleged to be a Native American folktale considered unfamiliar to his subjects. Readers were asked to recall the passage twice, once 15 minutes after reading it and again, 2 weeks later. He found that the reproductions differed significantly over time. Bartlett interpreted the results as indicative of the subjects' desire to make sense of the material within their existing frames of reference; thus they made adjustments to content of the actual passage that were more in line with their experiences. Specifically, Bartlett (1932) wrote, "Remembering is not a completely independent function, entirely distinct from perceiving, imagining, or even from constructive thinking, but it has intimate relations with them all" (p. 13). He used the word schema to define how we build our memories on prior experiences.

Venezky (1984) reported that Bartlett borrowed Sir Henry Head's term 'schema' in his discussion of "an active organization of past reactions, or of past experiences, which must always be supposed to be operating in any well-adapted organic response" (p. 15). What is important here is that Bartlett was concerned with how thinking and remembering were socially constructed and how prior knowledge influenced what was remembered. The notion of cultural schema also was introduced but was short lived. As we have often seen, when issues of culture, ethnicity, race, class, and non-English language usage are illustrated as informative for comprehension, they are either quickly dismissed, ignored, or marginalized.

Piaget (1936) also suggested that individuals construct knowledge through two complementary processes: assimilation and adaptation. Like Bartlett, he believed that children formed "schemes" to organize this information for themselves. Bartlett's research was resurrected in the 1970s when schema theory was used to explain how reading and writing were constructive processes. Here is how Strang (1938) expressed her understanding of reading comprehension:

> In reading to obtain proof on any point the student will first formulate the assumptions, which are to be studied. Then he will select, as he reads, the ideas significantly related to the assumptions. He will search for evidence in support of or opposed to the assumptions and weigh each bit of evidence as he reads. If evidence accumulates against one of his original assumptions, he will change it. Finally, he will act upon the assumptions for which he has obtained proof. ... [This requires] scientific thinking which includes elements of observation, analysis, synthesis, selective recall, and imagination as well as ability to recognize the problem, judge the adequacy of the data, discover the essential relationships and suspend judgment until enough reliable evidence is available on which to draw conclusions. (pp. 47–48)

Her thinking aligned with the assumptions of behaviorism and Piaget's notion of development.

Researchers continued to discuss and critique reading comprehension research and testing during this period. For instance, in a review of reading research, Gates (1930) outlined considerations needed for appraisal of reading ability and listed general levels of comprehension (understanding sentences, paragraphs, and longer selections), rate of reading, accuracy of comprehension, recall and use of material read. He frankly admitted that standardized reading tests were often used in unintended ways: "One of the most common misuses is to employ norms as if they were ideals of attainment instead of statistical statements of average achievements" (p.369). He went further, arguing, "No single test, however long or complicated, can provide a measurement of the totality of abilities involved in reading; each test measures only one aspect or type" (p. 369).

Gates concluded by listing several different reading comprehension tests, describing their particular foci and what they purported to measure, and recognizing that most measured levels of comprehension, rate and accuracy.

Dolch (1933), writing in the *Elementary School Journal*, also articulated that one of the great fallacies behind the testing movement was that "many tests of school subjects are designed to suit the needs of the supervising officer... other tests are designed to suit the purposes of the psychologist...somehow these tests have not revolutionized school work" (p.36). Another example of discontent was Bigelow's (1934) review of student performance on standardized reading comprehension tests. She concluded, "Those with the lowest scores were from foreign-speaking homes, the majority were Italians, but there were also some Poles, Armenians, Negroes, Irish, and [White] Americans" (p.261).Furthermore, she questioned the principals of the schools in which she conducted her study asking, "What are some of the common mistakes in the teaching of reading?" Bigelow listed some of their responses and noted,

> "The tendency to work with groups, rather than individuals, failure to appreciate the differences in background among children in the same group, failure [inability] to appreciate the limited vocabulary of children" (p. 262). It would be decades before their observations were taken seriously as impediments to comprehension among non-mainstream children.

J.C. Dewey (1935), in a review of reading comprehension tests, also observed that most actually measured literal comprehension. Dewey (1938a) continued his critiques of reading comprehension tests in his book, claiming, "The majority of test items deal with directly stated facts while others operate as vocabulary tests...This does not seem to test the pupil's ability to make inferences from the material read" (p.1112).

Surprisingly, W. Gray (1938) also joined the critics when he declared, "The varied nature of comprehension has been emphasized by the variety of objective tests that have been used in measuring it; in fact, there is ample evidence now that the term is too loosely used"

(p. 104). As many other reading researchers mentioned, the lack of definition of reading comprehension resulted in tests that differed widely in what was measured as reading comprehension, ranging from results that measured vocabulary, word attack skills, memory, problems solving, and gaining meaning from print, all under the moniker of reading comprehension.

As educational psychologists and reading researchers wrangled over the definition of reading comprehension and how it could best be measured by a standardized reading comprehension test, scholars in literary criticism, including Harris (1948), Richards (1929, 1938), and Rosenblatt (1938/1995) posited theories on the complex process of reading and of reading comprehension. In her seminal work, *Literature as Exploration*, she argued for a wider view of reading that included a more active role of the reader. Her text was not a treatise on reading comprehension research or testing; in fact, she claims that the themes of her book were democracy and literature (Rosenblatt, 1938/1995, p. xv). She felt that democracy was threatened for U.S. citizens and sought a place for democracy within the classroom. Although she does not discuss her work in terms of reading comprehension, she does discuss the importance of gaining meaning from print. This is how she puts it:

> I have used the terms *transaction* and *transactional* to emphasize the essentiality of both reader and text, in contrast to other theories that make one or the other determinate. ... *Transaction* .... permits emphasis on the to-and-fro, spiraling, nonlinear, continuously reciprocal influence of reader and text in making meaning. The meaning—the poem—"happens" during the transaction between the reader and the signs on the page. (p. xvi, italics in the original)

Her reasoned, nonscientific approach to understanding and articulating the process of gaining meaning from text was the forerunner to similar concepts that took decades to be accepted as a way to understand reading comprehension. Unlike the behaviorist models, Rosenblatt envisioned the reader as an active, decision-making participant whose cognitive processing did not necessarily proceed in a linear fashion. She also acknowledged that various affective, experiential, and social influences could influence a reader's response to text. Importantly, she points out that each reader is unique and brings the entirety of oneself and world to the reading process. This approach tacitly assumes that comprehension is beyond the management and control of test developers. Rosenblatt also emphasized that reading occurred on a continuum; that is, there were multiple possible readings/transactions that could occur with a text, depending on one's purpose for reading (a 1978 publication, *The Reader, the Text, the Poem: The Transactional Theory of the Literary Work*, continues her argument).

World War II: U.S. Policies, Reading Research, and Learning

While the United States exercised its right to isolationism, ethnic and racial hatred had reared its head and taken control in Europe under the leadership of Adolph Hitler. The Nazi party declared a dictatorship in 1933 and began a program of genocide against the Jews, although Hitler is known to have hated all non-White Christians (before his killing of the Jews, he had experimented with similar methods in Africa). The United States was drawn into World War II when the Japanese attacked Pearl Harbor, Dec 7, 1941, and it soon joined the Allied powers (part of an earlier North American Alliance Organization agreement). World War II was fought on two fronts by the United States: a) in Europe against Axis Powers and b) in the Pacific Ring. The war affected every American and, as during World War I, women entered the workforce to replace the men who were fighting overseas. Women also participated in the war as members of the Women's Army Corps (WAC) and Women Accepted for Voluntary Emergency Service in the Navy (WAVES). Although the military remained racially segregated, African Americans and American Indians joined with other Americans to fight for the safety of our country. Despite the fact that People of Color were vigorously fighting and dying for the United States, they were being denied basic human and citizenship rights in the United States. Racial discrimination and prejudice continued unchanged in the lives of People of Color as the United States entered the war. A group of African American protesters in 1942 established the Congress of Racial Equality (CORE) in opposition to racial discrimination.

In a telling portrayal of how ideological and cultural hegemony structure society, Asian Americans of Japanese ancestry were treated with suspicion, that is, they represented the journalistic idea of "Yellow Peril." Japanese American men of draft age were asked to take a loyalty oath to serve in the armed forces, and others were relocated to concentration camps for fear they were spies. Furthermore, the U.S.

government's internment of almost 120,000 Japanese Americans, most of whom were U.S. citizens, forced them to leave their businesses, homes, schools, and lives and be corralled into living quarters in internment or concentration/detention camps. Hall (1982) writes, "One of the means by which the powerful can continue to rule with consent and legitimacy is, therefore, if the interests of a particular class … can be aligned with or made equivalent to the general interests of the majority" (p. 86). Internment was sanctioned through Executive Order 9066 issued by President Franklin Roosevelt on February 19, 1942. In 1981, hearings were held throughout the nation in which interned Japanese Americans testified about their lives before, during, and after internment. President Ronald Reagan signed H. R. 442 in 1988, which provided individual reparations of roughly $20,000 dollars to each internee and set aside over $1 million for educational funding.

Pak (2002) documents the experiences of seventh- and eighth-grade Japanese American students who were forced to leave Seattle, their homes, neighborhoods, friends, schools, and childhood for a relocation center in Puyallup, Washington. Her provocative book *Wherever I Go, I Will Always Be a Loyal American: Seattle's Japanese American Schoolchildren During World War II* centers on letters that students wrote to the their teacher, Ella Evanson. In the letters, many students, although they were U.S. citizens, felt compelled to describe their loyalty to the United States.

In an assumed sign of loyalty, the students worked to distinguish themselves from their Japanese roots and culture by aligning their mannerism and speech with U.S. Whites (Pak, 2002 p. 17). The students' letters reveal their understanding of their place in the U.S. war effort and, for some, their willingness to be incarcerated for the "good of the nation." Pak explains how the school administrators and teachers in Seattle, who ironically were participating in an intercultural education program aimed at improving racial and religious tolerance in public schools, "acted as moral agents … in the context of injustice" (p. 146). Unfortunately, school administrators and teachers "knew that the political forces of the Second World War and the incarceration could not be stopped" (p. 146). Many of the students continued to write to Ms. Evanson for many years after they returned to Seattle.

Similarly, although often depicted in literature and film as intellectually inferior to Whites, or as noble savages, Native Americans aided the war effort by speaking in their own language, a language that only decades before was banned by the U.S. government. Much like the World War I Choctaw Codetalkers (Albert Billy, Mitchell Bobb, Victor Brown, Ben Caterby, James Edwards, Tobias Frazer, Ben Hampton, Solomon Louis, Pete Maytubby, Jeff Nelson, Joseph Oklahombi, Robert Taylor, Calvin Wilson, and Walter Veach) during World War II, the U.S. Marine Corps employed Navajo Indians as radiomen (i.e., codetalkers or wind talkers) to communicate around Japanese intelligence. The Navajo language, or as used here, code, was never deciphered (in 2001 many of the surviving codetalkers throughout the country received a Medal of Honor). Ironically, these nations of Native peoples are representative of the many indigenous people that the U.S. government, under their earlier colonialist/imperialist/terrorist acts, had tried to force into submission by stripping them of their culture, language, and identity. Their ability to communicate in their native languages helped win the war.

Reading Comprehension Research and Testing Continues

The most groundbreaking research of the 1940s to affect reading comprehension research and testing came in the unpublished dissertation of Frederick Davis (1942). Davis attempted to identify and measure through the use of psychometrics (factor analysis) what he considered to be the most basic skills needed in comprehension. He listed nine skills of reading comprehension drawn from his review of the literature: word meanings, word meanings in context, follow passage organization, main thought, answer specific text-based questions, text-based questions with paraphrase, draw inferences about content, literary devices, and author's purpose. In addition, he used factor analysis to separate and measure each skill. His findings also indicated that all the following are important considerations for measuring comprehension: word knowledge, reasoning in reading, author's intent or purpose, author's ideas, organization of the paragraph, and knowledge of literacy devices or techniques. However, he noted that only word knowledge and reasoning in reading were reliable. In a separate study, Harris (1948) used factor analysis to identify major elements of comprehension used in understanding literature: translating; summarizing; inferring tone, mood, and intent; and relating technique and meaning.

Reading comprehension testing flourished and several new tests were published: *American School Reading Readiness Tests* (Pratt, Young, & Witmer 1941), *Cooperative English Tests: Reading Comprehension* (Davis et al. 1940), to name a few. Each test, with some variance, tested reading rate, vocabulary, story comprehension, word meaning, sentence meaning, and paragraph meaning and inferential knowledge. Scientism continued to reign unashamedly as the way in which educational research should continue to pursue knowledge. The underlying assumptions about the importance of the individual in the process of reading comprehension, an individualism much like that of Spencer, continued to overshadow the influence of cultural and societal views of educational psychology, reading comprehension, and reading comprehension testing.

Approaches to Learning

Five major works helped to reshape and produce innovations in reading comprehension research at mid-century. First, Skinner's (1938) behaviorism and its notion of reinforcement helped to generate interest in programmed instruction. This form of instruction required clearly stated objectives, small frames of instruction, self-pacing, active learner response to inserted questions, and immediate feedback. Second, Glaser's (1962) focus on mastery learning and his criterion-referenced measures changed how researchers looked at subskills. Criterion-reference referred to measures of how each student performed against a standard (criterion). Criterion referenced tests could be used to show mastery of multiple skills as well as show growth and development. Not surprisingly, much of reading comprehension during this period focused on subskill testing.

Third, Bloom, Engelhart, Furst, Hill, and Krathwohl's (1956) *Taxonomy of Educational Objectives: The Classification of Educational Goals. Handbook I: Cognitive Domain* described the work of teachers and researchers who sought to classify the goals of education, and was followed by Bloom's (1965) text. Three domains were identified in the taxonomy: cognitive, affective, and psychomotor. The cognitive domain includes "the recall and recognition of knowledge and the development of intellectual abilities and skills"; the affective domain includes "changes in interest, attitudes, and values, and the development of appreciations and adequate adjustment"; and the psychomotor domain includes "the manipulative or motor-skill area" (Bloom et al. 1956 pp. 7–8). Most educational objectives, however, are drawn from the cognitive domain that includes knowledge, comprehension, application, analysis, synthesis, and evaluation. The actual taxonomy of educational objectives for curriculum and testing development reflects the collective effort of psychologists and helped to spawn another wave of reading and reading comprehension tests: *California Reading Test* (Tiegs & Clark 1957), *Davis Reading Test* (Davis & Davis 1956), *Developmental Reading Tests* (Bond, Clymer, & Hoyt 1955), to name a few.

Fourth, Bruner's (1960) landmark text *The Process of Education* revolutionized educational policy in the United States. His work emerged at a time when behaviorism was the frame of reference in education research, as it called on researchers to observe and measure behavior. Bruner's cognitive approach focused on learning as an active process in which learners construct new ideas based on their current knowledge. Much like John Dewey, he argued that instruction should reflect the developmental stage of the learner and be carefully sequenced to allow the learner to both build on what he or she already knows and go beyond the information to discover principles. Bruner helped to issue in the era of cognitivism, which posited that learners constructed mental models that they used to categorize information and build on existing information. His work also was instrumental in the establishment of Head Start. In the 1970s and 1980s, Bruner became critical of the cognitive model that he believed was overly focused on measurement and did not address societal issues. During the 1990s, Bruner became an outspoken proponent for the need to address historical and cultural issues.

Finally, Thomas Kuhn's (1962/1996) *The Structure of Scientific Revolutions* transformed the philosophy of science and caused quite a reaction within the scientific community. Kuhn's historical and philosophical treatise of science rocked the foundation of the scientific community. He believed that science should be understood historically and socially, leading to what some have termed *social constructivism* (the belief that all factors that influence scientific ideas should be explored). Kuhn introduced the idea of paradigms, paradigm shifts, and revolutions in scientific thinking. He also opposed the idea that science was an objective enterprise.

He argued that science was conducted by humans and, thus, was influenced by the world in which humans lived. Furthermore, he declared that humans, on a very emotional level, bring their points of view about the world and culture into their scientific work, a point that caused his critics to call him a relativist. Kuhn held his ground, maintaining that theories are manmade, fallible, and exist until replaced by other theories. He did not see progress in science as necessarily cumulative, but rather as a process of filling in gaps of knowledge in existing theories. Moreover, he insisted (much like Peirce) that paradigms and methods exist as agreed on by a community of scientists, who instruct the next generation of scientists; thus, a traditional way of understanding, producing, and interpreting science emerges.

Despite the revolutionary thinking of Bruner and Khun which illuminated cultural, economic, historical, and social differences as influences on how people make sense of their world, most educational psychologists; reading comprehension researchers continued to embrace scientism. That is, they continued to characterize reading comprehension in attempts to find observable and measurable data. However, when this invisible behavior could not be explained, they created scenarios to explain differences in student performance. Among their more popular scenarios were those that focused on differences between White and Black students, where White students were portrayed as well-prepared children from two-parent, supportive, middle-class homes, and children of color were portrayed as ill-prepared children from single-parent (maternal), unsupported, dysfunctional, poverty-ridden homes. The stereotyping and overgeneralizations about African Americans caused Du Bois (1940) to comment:

> Not only do white men but also colored men forget the facts of the Negro's double environment. The Negro American has for his environment not only the white surrounding world, but also, and touching him usually much more nearly and compelling is the environment furnished by his own colored group. (p. 173)

The notion promoted among educational researchers, including reading comprehension researchers that African American children lacked cultural knowledge and led to the use of the phrase culturally deprived and similar terms emerged that depicted all African American children as deficient learners.

Reading Comprehension Research's Emphasis on Vocabulary and Linguistics

Historically, reading comprehension research has been paired with research about the influence of vocabulary on the comprehension process. Werner and Kaplan (1952) added to this line of research by noting that not just vocabulary but also the context of words as well as their relationship to one another affects comprehension. They found that the ability to understand the relationships between and among words improved with experience and age but only if the reader "grasps the nature of the sentence as a stable and articulate structure" (p. 55). Within this idea is the sense that students not only attach the correct word meaning in context but also understand something about the structure of language. In a similar way, Taylor's (1953) cloze procedure drew on students' ability to understand relationships among word meanings, context clues, and text and language structure. Taylor believed that the cloze procedure mimicked the Gestalt notion of closure; that is, readers would want to fill in the blanks to understand the text. He crafted the procedure to determine readability and not to assess reading comprehension; however, it was later co-opted as a means of measuring reading comprehension (Bormuth, 1963, 1965; Ruddell, 1964).

The cloze procedure begins with a sentence or two of text followed by the deletion of every fifth word. Like multiple choice test items, only the *exact* word was considered a correct response. The rationale given by reading researchers for using the cloze procedure for reading comprehension stems from the high frequency in the language patterns (of native speakers) that correspond favorably with oral and silent reading comprehension. Since its inception, there have been variations that allow students to choose from among alternative words. The procedure has been criticized for lexical and structural reasons. For example, higher scores are obtained by readers who are more similar to the writer linguistically (style, vocabulary, written sentence structure and patterns), readers who are familiar with the content, and readers who are more proficient.

Interestingly, Bormuth (1967) in "Comparable Cloze and Multiple-Choice Comprehension Test Scores," couches educational concerns in terms of social fears and financial waste. His common sense appeal and the taken-for-grantedness of his discourse is a reduplication of Taylorism and the rhetoric that accompanied earlier calls for educational reforms as well as a forecast to the revision of similar rhetoric that combined the economic and human cost of poor instruction with the need for more testing. Bormuth thought, "the waste may run into the millions of dollars" and "the contributions to the dropout rate with consequences of unemployment and poverty result in a staggering drain on the nation's resources" (p. 291). In his study, 100 elementary school children (Grades 4 and 5) were asked to read nine passages and respond to an untimed, 50-item cloze test, and a 1-item multiple choice test. In the cloze test, there was only one correct answer and it had to be an exact match to the deleted word. His interpretation of the results indicated that the cloze procedure was a measure of comprehension.

Piekarz (1956) used a qualitatively different approach to reading comprehension research when she interviewed good and poor readers to better understand what they learned from reading. She found that poor readers focused on a literal interpretation of text whereas good readers varied their level of attention by relying on both literal and more sophisticated interpretations. Her work, among others, represents a departure from the heavily experimental approach that drew on cognitive science and quantification of "facts."

In a similar way Chomsky's work in linguistics, particularly his *Syntactic Structures (1957)*, which was the forerunner to *Aspects of the Theory of Syntax* (1965) and the research of Charles Fries (1963) in *Linguistics and Reading* were significant additions to understanding reading comprehension. Chomsky distinguished between different levels of meaning in language—surface structure and deep structure—and he emphasized the generative properties of language. He argued that knowledge of phonology was not needed by teachers or children in teaching or learning to read.

> The dominant factor in successful teaching is and will always remain the teacher's skill in nourishing, and sometimes arousing, the child's curiosity and interest and in providing a rich and challenging intellectual environment in which the child can find his own unique way toward understanding, knowledge, and skill. (1970, p. 5)

Furthermore, he doubted the effectiveness of phonemics (phoneme–grapheme correspondence) as a support in beginning reading and comprehension. In fact, he argued that phonemics were a "methodological artifact" of linguists, not something that should be learned or taught by teachers to children. Chomsky (1970) remarked, "The conventional orthography corresponds closely to a level of representation that seems to be optimal for the sound system of a fairly rich version of standard spoken English" (p. 16), phonological system that he doubted a 6-year-old could master and one fraught with irregularities. Moreover, he suggested that perhaps the best way to teach reading was "to enrich a child's vocabulary, so that he constructs for himself the deeper representations of sound that correspond closely to the orthographic forms" (p. 18). Later, he added, "I do not see what concrete conclusions can be drawn, for the teaching of reading, from the study of sound structure" (p. 18). Reading, to Chomsky, occurred at a much deeper linguistic level.

Political, Social, and Cultural Shifts

Political, social, and cultural issues consumed U.S. life by mid-century as shadows of historic injustices were challenged, questioned, and critiqued. The 1950s through 1970s were watershed years for addressing the history of racial discrimination in this country. A second wave of the Great Migration occurred, as thousands of African Americans migrated to Northern cities and waves of Mexicans and Puerto Ricans joined the trek North. Native Americans, however, were forced to move to ever more isolated spaces as the government seized reservation lands under the Relocation Act of 1956, allegedly in an attempt to assimilate Native peoples into mainstream society. While People of Color flocked to the cities for work, middle-class Whites migrated to the suburbs. Life in the suburbs was portrayed in the media as ideal, in television shows such as *I Love Lucy (Oppenheimer, 1951), Leave It to Beaver (Ackerman, 1957), Dennis the Menace (Fonda, 1959),* and *The Adventures of Ozzie and Harriet (Nelson, 1952).* Collectively, these images were used to promote White, middle-class family values and beliefs as representative of the "common culture" of all law-abiding U.S. citizens, while images of subaltern groups were used to reinforce racial and ethnic stereotypes of people as dependent, irresponsible, and unintelligent. Each supports Hall's (1982) notion that ideology shapes "mental frameworks—the languages, the concepts, categories, imagery of thought, and the systems of representation" (p. 27). Hall (2003) argues, persuasively, "Culture is the struggle over meaning, a struggle that takes place over and with the sign. Culture is the particular pattern of relations established through social use and of things and techniques" (pp. 157–158).

Given this idea, I have elected to depart from typical accounts of this period that focus on the launching of Sputnik as the catalyst for educational change or what Samelson (2005) calls the Sputnik Syndrome that "transforms a few selective economic happenings—a satellite here, a Toyota there, poor test scores everywhere—into a full-blown theory of economic inferiority, or superiority" (p. 43). I do, however, retain the link between notions of educational reform and national security. The next section reiterates the importance of understanding the process, role, and influence of ideological hegemony in society and its influence on reading comprehension research. As Grossberg (2003) draws from Hall's work, he articulates "If we are to understand ideology as a contested terrain, we must not only recognize the struggle but also learn to 'read the cultural sign-posts and traces which history has left behind without an inventory'" (p. 160). Below I trace how the past and associated ideas continued to haunt and frustrate efforts for social justice and revolutionary change and how despite these efforts, there was very little impact on the ideological structure of the dominant groups, which is borne out in the production and reproduction of reading comprehension research or testing.

Seeds of Change

Politically, the passage of the *National Defense Education Act* (NDEA), which provided millions of dollars in loans for higher education to train teachers, was a turning point in the country's commitment to funding public education. Under President Lyndon B. Johnson's administration, known as the Great Society, countless other social programs began; including the Office of Economic Opportunity Headstart, Follow Through, Job Corps, Peace Corps, and Volunteers in Service to America (VISTA). His idea of a Great Society also included the passage of Medicare (1965), the *Voting Rights Act* (1965), and the *Immigration and Nationality Services Act* (1965). As part of his War on Poverty, Johnson signed legislation that expanded Social Security, abolished immigration quotas, and established the Department of Housing and Urban Development. For instance, Johnson's War on Poverty sought to end racial injustice and poverty, improve medical care, and bring renewal for cities. Johnson, in a powerful, emotional speech to Congress in 1965, recalled:

> My first job after college was as a teacher in Cotulla, Texas, a small Mexi-
> can American school. ... Somehow you never forget what poverty and
> hatred can do when you see its scars on the hopeful face of a young child.
> ... It never even occurred to me in my fondest dreams that I might have
> the chance to help the sons and daughters of those students and to help
> people like them all over this country. But now I do have the chance —
> and I'll let you in on a secret: *I mean to take it.* (italics in the original)

His speech moved Congress to pass the *1965* Elementary *and
Secondary School Act,* giving federal financial support to public and
parochial schools. It created $1.3 billion to aid in the improvement
of underprivileged schools, funded research and development labs,
and mandated the evaluation of educational projects. Although
Johnson's idea of a Great Society has yet to be realized, his ideas and
laws governing education, science, and health and welfare remain.
Of special interest to reading researchers is Title I:

> In recognition of the special educational needs of low-income families
> and the impact that concentrations of low-income families have on the
> ability of local educational agencies to support adequate educational pro-
> grams, the Congress hereby declares it to be the policy of the United
> States to provide financial assistance ... [to] local educational agencies
> serving areas with concentrations of children from low-income families
> to expand and improve their educational programs by various means
> (including preschool programs) which contribute to meeting the special
> educational needs of educationally deprived children. (*Elementary and
> Secondary School Act*, Section 201, 1965)

Although notions of poverty cut across race, in the United States poverty is often equated with people of color and recent immigrants.

As we have seen in previous chapters, literature during this period
also offered a venue to express the effects of dominant ideologies and
the influence of lived realities of society's Underserved. Of import
are Ellison's (1952) *Invisible Man*, Fanon's (1967) *Black Skin, White
Masks*, Harrington's (1962) *The Other America*, Friedan's (1963) *The
Feminine Mystique*, and Loretta Lynn's (1976) *Coldminer's Daughter*,
among others.

Resistance to Dominant Ideologies by People of African Descent

Fanon (psychiatrist, political thinker, revolutionary, and social activist) expressed his ideas of the effects of colonialism before the onset
of the well-documented events of the civil rights movement. His

publications capture the period of unrest among people of African descent worldwide. In his writings and presentations, he drew on his early experiences with racism in his homeland of Martinique and later experiences in France. His writings focus on colonial domination as when he declared in *Black Skin, White Masks,*

> My life should not be devoted to drawing up the balance sheet of Negro values. There is no White world, there is no White ethic, any more than there is a White intelligence. There are in every part of the world men who search. .... In the world through which I travel, I am endlessly creating myself. (1967, p. 229)

Challenging dominant ideologies of the United States, he points to the fictional notion of universalism that is not reflective of the lives of most People of Color who face racial oppression, often at the hands of Whites. Appreciably, much like Du Bois and Woodson before him, Fanon describes a sense of consciousness about his and his peoples' understanding of their place in the world and the importance of acknowledging how dominant ideologies works. He humanizes people of African descent who have, heretofore, been maligned as unconsciously giving consent to their oppressor. Although his writing focused on colonialism, the popularity of his book is often cited as a key work of the black liberation movement worldwide, including by those in the U.S. civil rights movement. In his oft-quoted essay, "Racism and Culture" (delivered in Paris to the Congress of Negro Writers and Artists), he spoke out against colonialism and the values of dominant groups:

> The apparition of racism is not fundamentally determining. Racism is not the whole but the most visible, the most day-to-day and, not to mince matters, the crudest element of a given structure. ... The project of racism is no longer the individual man but a certain form of existing. ... Racism, as we have seen, is only one element of a vaster whole: that of the systematized oppression of a people. (Fanon, 1956, p. 11)

In his observation of U.S. culture, Fanon noted that many African Americans appeared to have internalized their subordinate status, believing that they were inferior to Whites, and were politically alienated from government. He admonished us to understand the invasiveness of racism within every facet of life in the United States and fight against it, in all its manifestations. In addition, he encouraged African Americans not to be tricked by verbiage or so-called scientific arguments. Racism, he claimed, is exploitation. In a second book, *Wretched of the Earth*, Fanon (1963) describes the effects of internalized self-hate and racism in ways very similar to those used by Cooper and Du Bois:

> Every effort is made to bring the colonized person to admit the inferiority of his culture which has been transformed into instinctive patterns of behavior, to recognize the unreality of his "nation," and, in the last extreme, the confused and imperfect character of his own biological structure. (p. 236)

The mental frameworks from which he drew inspiration and the language he used to express his ideas differed significantly from those used by White researchers and educators.

In the United States, African American scholars and authors also decried the racism that they faced daily. Ralph Ellison (1952) captured the phenomenon in his novel *The Invisible Man:*

> I am invisible, understand, simply because people refuse to see me. Like the bodiless heads you see sometimes in circus sideshows, it as though I have been surrounded by mirrors of hard, distorting glass. When they approach me they see only my surroundings, themselves, or figments of their imagination — indeed, everything and anything except me. (p. 3)

For decades there had been discontent among African Americans about the discriminatory policies stemming from the U.S. Supreme Court's ruling in the 1890 *Plessy v. Ferguson* case that declared separate facilities were equal. Their discontent call to a legal point during the civil rights movement.

Politics and Civil Rights

The civil rights movement had become a powerful force and one that was propelled to the international and national attention by media coverage of the *Brown v The Board of Education of Topeka, Kansas (1951),* the murders of four little girls (Addie Mae Collins, Denise McNair, Carole Robertson, and Cynthia Wesley) in Montgomery, Alabama while attending Sunday school, and the Montgomery bus boycott. The U.S. Supreme Court decision in the *Brown v. Board of Education of Topeka, Kansas* should have improved every aspect of education for African Americans. The mental frames from which African American children drew their ideas of the world appeared in Clark's studies where African American children ages 6 through 9 preferred White dolls to Black dolls. When asked what they thought about the dolls, the children stated the Black doll was bad, but the White doll was nice; depicting distorted "concepts, categories, imagery of thought, and the systems of representation" (cited in Hall, 2003, p. 27) of themselves produced by their experiences in a racist society. In fact, Chief Justice Earl Warren opined,

> A feeling of inferiority ... that may affect [children's] hearts and minds in a way unlikely ever to be undone. ... In the field of education the doctrine of "separate but equal" has no place. Separate educational facilities are inherently unequal.

Although Marshall and the NAACP won the case for school desegregation, enforcement of the law was stalled by the fears of some Whites, especially as other racially charged cases took center stage: (a) NAACP's boycott of bus transportation in Montgomery, Alabama in December 1955 and the U.S. Supreme Court ruling that segregated public transportation was unconstitutional; (b) nine African American teenagers' attempt to enter Central High School in 1957 in Little Rock, Arkansas; (c) President Eisenhower's signing of the Civil Rights Act of 1957 and 1960 meant to outlaw racist policies (grandfather clauses, literacy tests, poll tax, and White primaries) which were later brushed aside (see Lucas Johnson's 2003 book, *Finding the Good*).

One such racist policy was the so-called literacy tests, required of African Americans, many of whom had not had access to education or literacy training, as a condition to voting. Myles Horton (1905–1990), founder of the Highlander Folk School (later renamed the Highlander Research and Education Center) in New Market, Tennessee and long-time worker with labor unions, began his involvement with the civil rights movement to improve literacy in the 1950s and 1960s (Horton, 1998). His literacy programs were designed to teach African Americans to read in order to pass the literacy tests and thereby gain the right to vote. Horton organized the literacy program, but he firmly believed that it would be more effective if run by African Americans. He enlisted the help of Septima Clark, a local South Carolina schoolteacher and freedom fighter, who called on her niece, Bernice Robison (not a teacher), to lead the program. Robinson taught African American adults by asking them to tell her a story, a story that she wrote down and asked them to read. She used their interests to teach the adults to read, a method which as we have seen is much more than word recognition. Their understanding of the world and her ability to draw upon that knowledge is what, amazingly, helped many adults learn to read and pass voter registration literacy tests.

Two unforeseen outcomes of the civil rights movement deserve mention as they foreshadow the fate of countless African American children. First, the enforcement of school bussing to achieve racial desegregation resulted in the displacement of countless African American teachers (Foster, 1998). African American teachers, who knew and appreciated these children, whose life experiences mirrored their own, and whose cultural understandings and language were similar were replaced with White teachers, many who held low academic expectations of the children. Second, many African American children were identified as mentally retarded or slow learners based on their performance on standardized intelligence tests. The experiences of Mexican Americans and American Indians were similar to those experienced by African Americans; hence, Brown and Red Power groups were formed, respectively.

Pendergast's (2002) review of the intersection of literacy, race, and federal law uses a legal timeline to consider these issues and uses primary source documents to illustrate sociohistorical contexts and legal arguments. Her research demonstrates that several pivotal U.S. Supreme Court cases—*Brown v. Board of Education, Washington v. Davis*, and *Regents of the University of California v. Bakke*—that underpin educational equity for African Americans view property and literacy as the property of Whites. For example she writes, "The ideologies of literacy supporting the *Brown* decision may have propelled the Court to condemn segregation, but the goal of ensuring equality of education remained elusive and the true character of racial discrimination remained unrecognized" (p. 216). In addition, she observes that the outcome "served to confirm the equation of literacy and Whiteness already established and entrenched in the minds of the White majority to rationalize the exclusion of African Americans from authority positions" (p. 221). Likewise, in the Bakke case, she notes that what was really at stake was "the standards used to judge literacy attainment as racially and culturally neutral—standards whose arbitrary nature had not been examined even in the face of a racially disparate impact" (p. 223). Pendergast concludes that in each case, Whites viewed education and literacy as property and worked to ensure that these ideas were legally maintained by positioning arguments where literacy was neutral, where literacy was acultural, and where racial discrimination was individual.

The culture, beliefs, knowledges, and values of African Americans remained ignored by reading researchers in general and reading comprehension researchers in particular, inspite of these legal rulings.

Freedom of Thought

Hall's (2003) ideological and cultural hegemony supports the dominant notion of reality as natural and universal. However, as he reminds us,

> Reality could no longer be viewed as simply a given set of facts: it was the result of a particular way of constructing reality. ... Definitions of reality were sustained and produced through those linguistic practices (in the broad sense) by means of which selective definitions of "the real" were represented. But representation is a very different notion from that of reflection. It implies that active work of selecting and presenting—of structuring and shaping: not merely transmitting an already existing meaning, but the more labor of making things mean. (p. 64)

Reflecting on their lives under oppression, many African Americans banned together under Black nationalism, or the national struggle of civil rights for Black people. The experiences and life of Malcolm Little (Malcolm X, later known as el-Haii Malik el-Shabazz), following the death of his father at the hands of the KKK, and his conversion to the Nation of Islam, illustrates this point. First, he replaced his slave surname (Little) with the letter "X" to force others to acknowledge, as he did, his unknown African roots and culture. A gifted orator, Malcolm X gave an impassioned speech in Washington Heights, New York, that outlined the philosophy of Black Nationalism:

> We are Africans, and we happen to be in America. We are not Americans. We are a people who formerly were Africans who were kidnapped and brought to America. Our forefathers weren't the Pilgrims. We didn't land on Plymouth Rock; the rock landed on us. We were brought here against our will; we were not brought here to be made citizens. We were not brought here to enjoy the constitutional gifts. ... The first step for those of us who believe in the philosophy of Black Nationalism is to realize that the problem begins right here. (March 29, 1964)

Although Malcolm X was slain in 1965, his life and work live in his book *The Autobiography of Malcolm X* (with Alex Haley

1965), published posthumously. Other outspoken African Americans would follow his lead, especially young people who sought to redefine themselves on their own terms. Hall (1995) notes that on the ideological terrain of struggle are "the images, concepts, and premises which provide frameworks through which we represent, interpret, understand, and 'make sense' of some aspect of social existence" (Hall, 1995, p. 18). African Americans were recasting their images on their own terms, changing how they were represented, collectively. Once referred to as "negroes," "coloreds," and "darkies," by Whites, young people renamed themselves and their reality by adopting the term Black, followed by Afro-American, African American, and people of African descent/diaspora. Nonetheless, our knowledges, languages, and culture continued to be viewed in a deficit manner by reading and reading comprehension researchers.

Race, Intelligence, and Standardized Testing

The national commitment to testing remained strong even when faced with disconfirming evidence and expanded understandings of science. Standardized intelligence tests also continued to be an enslaving yoke as notions of meritocracy were used to regulate admissions to colleges and universities and other educational opportunities for non-White, non-English-speaking, non-middle-class children. The ethnic bias within intelligence tests is evident in the third edition of the Stanford–Binet (1960/1973), standardized with a representative sample of only 2,100 White children. Six-year-olds were asked to look at pictures of a White American and Mexican American and determine, "Which is prettier?" The only correct answer — was the White American. The 1972 standardization group for the 1973 version included non-White children as have subsequent versions of the test in 1986 and 2003 (the latter claims to reflect the 2000 U.S. Census).

Arthur Jensen's (1969) article in the *Harvard Educational Review,* "How Far Can We Boost IQ and Scholastic Achievement?" re-energized the debate over the inheritability of intelligence. Jensen, an educational psychologist at the University of California, Berkeley, argued that the answer was "very little." He claimed that 80% of intellectual abilities were genetically determined. His theses were (a) "intelligence" can be defined by Spearman's g and can be measured by IQ tests; (b) intelligence is the key factor in determining academic, occupational, and social success; (c) intelligence is inherited, stable, and permanent; and (d) intelligence differences between Whites and non-White groups are genetic, with minorities being inferior to Whites on intelligence. Moreover, he argued that the differences in IQ scores between Blacks and Whites were genetically determined and that social programs would not be a wise use of public funds. His ideas resonated strongly with conservative politicians who were fighting against federal spending programs to improve the educational environment of the poor.

Throughout this era, there was considerable lip service given to ameliorate educational opportunities "for all." This notion of universalism denies the reality of the lives of the People of Color, who as oppressed people are keenly aware that it is part of the discourse of the dominant class but not part of their actions. As Du Bois (1940) noted, "There has been an understandable determination in the United States ... to minimize and deny the realities of racial difference" (p.135). This denial and minimalism is especially true in the history of reading comprehension research and testing. Although the idea of "success for all" had great appeal and was a handy slogan, it created a conundrum for reading comprehension researchers and test developers whose ideological assumptions (universality of knowledge and faith in scientific methods) were inadequate and in opposition to democratizing reading comprehension research. How then, does reading comprehension research and reading comprehension testing become more equitable when it is built on a narrow and inadequate foundation?

Recently, Brookfield (2003) has argued that theorizing in the field of education has sustained an "unproblematic Eurocentrism .... [that] reflects the racial membership of 'official' knowledge producers in the field" (p. 497). He also observes "concepts are identified mostly with scholarship conducted by White Euro-Americans, Europeans, and Commonwealth males" (p. 499). Further, he notes that in society as well as the academy, race is generally invoked for people of color, but not for Whites. Central to his theorizing is an understanding of Whiteness as an ideology (p. 516). Although the focus on racial injustice brought special attention to the importance of improving the U.S. educational system for all students, the actual improvements for underserved students were limited.

Reviews of Reading Comprehension Research and Testing

Given the political and social unrest in the nation, one would think that reading comprehension research would reflect the issues of race, class, gender, language, and power that permeated lives of U.S. citizens; however, there was scant research then, as now, that focused on how the Underserved read and comprehended text. Incredulously, the aforementioned political, social, and cultural events during this period were not referenced in most publications that were written to offer historical insight and analysis of the field of reading in general and reading comprehension research and testing specifically. No linkages were made to whose history was not included or whose discourse was not represented silencing the experiences of People of Color. Yet, works by Mathews (1966) and Miller and Smith (1966) remain important to the field, if for no other reason than to highlight these limitations.

Compilations of educational thinking were published in new encyclopedias on education (forerunners to today's handbooks). Included in these works were entries by W. Gray (1957) and Harris (1969) that summarized recent research in reading. W. Gray, for example, continued his chronicling of reading research from the United Kingdom and the United States, as well as his affinity to Herbart's idea of apperception. Sounding much like an ambassador for positivism, he declared, "Research in reading must continue on a broad scale if reading is to serve ultimately its broadest function as an aide to personal development, scholastic progress, and social betterment" (W. Gray, 1957, p. 1087). He also indicated that despite the proliferation of reading research, there were severe limitations. Specifically, he cited the fragmentary nature of much of research, the need to improve research procedures, and the need to coordinate research efforts among the various disciplines interested in reading. Importantly, he seemed to grasp the narrowness that infuses the field:

> Interpretations have often been based on traditional concepts of learning and as a result are not sound or widely applicable today. Nevertheless, much of the evidence available is so significant that it serves as a value guide to reorganizing and improving instruction in reading at all levels and in defining with increasing clarity the role of reading in contemporary life. (p. 1088)

Much like Tireman (1951), W. Gray was unwilling or unable to hold accountable research efforts that added little significant improvement and thereby he helped to maintain the status quo, that is, a predisposition toward scientism, racism, and classism and a dis-regard for sociohistorical contexts.

In a similar explanatory discourse, Harris (1969) described the limits of reading research despite its proliferation. Like W. Gray, he argued that much of the research lacked methodological rigor and was overly descriptive and disjointed. Harris observed that there is a tendency in reading research to shift its focus with changes in the educational landscape and thereby miss the opportunity to conduct longitudinal studies of serious reading concerns. Adopting a behav-iorist stance, he declared, "Reading is a learned act" (p. 1070). Fur-thermore, he urged reading researchers to consider "environmental" influences such as "race, socioeconomic status, social mobility, home and parental influences, bilingualism, and mass media other than the printed word" (p. 1071) a call that remains inadequately addressed. His review of reading research included Deutsch's (1965) idea of a "cumulative deficit hypothesis" to explain a host of "dis-advantages" that sustains the gap in performance on standardized tests between Students of Color and their White peers. Yet, given the historic social and cultural "disadvantages" outlined by the researchers, it seems nonsensical to compare their performance with that of their more privileged White peers. Nonetheless, and some-what ironically, this is just what happened and what continues to be a central part of interpreting reading research. The performances of differently advantaged children are compared to one another as if similarly advantaged and where Children of Color are primarily referenced as minority, disadvantaged, culturally deprived, and cul-turally disadvantaged, and held accountable for historic and mod-ern systemic inequalities. The message was clear to and not lost only on African American scholars. The loaded terms have been decon-structed by R. Jones (1991), who points to their deleterious effects on young learners. Reading the research from this era, seldom does one get the sense that it was conducted to benefit these children or improve their performance on such tests but, rather as a means by which to compare them to their White counterparts and maintain the idea of White intellectual and cultural superiority. In terms of reading comprehension testing the focus continued to be on concep-tions of reading comprehension based among White, middle-class, Standard English speakers, and comparisons were made to under-served students, while highlighting the failure of the latter to reach the achievement levels of the former.

Importantly, Harris (1964) comments on how researchers continued to explain a positive relationship between intelligence and reading: "Intelligence, reflecting as it does to a large measure the capacity to engage in symbolic language activity, is itself a major correlate of reading" (p. 1070). He concedes that although the positive relationship exists, it appeared that factors other than intelligence affected reading achievement on standardized tests. Many of these factors had been previously addressed decades earlier by Scholars of Color. Buros' (1965) *Sixth Mental Measurements Yearbook,* also noted that standardized reading tests proved to have wide variability. These chronicles of reading research, as Farr and Carey (1986) would later observe, were devoid of an analysis of the philosophical underpinnings of the research, theory(ies), and methods.

Ruddell (1965) renewed interest in oral language use in reading comprehension when he examined whether there is a correlation between student oral language use and reading comprehension. He argues, "Reading comprehension scores on materials that utilize high frequency patterns of oral language structure are significantly greater than reading comprehension scores on materials that utilize low frequency oral language structure" (p. 273).

Farr (1969), in his review, also noted that students tended to perform better on reading comprehension tests when their oral language mimicked the language structure of the tests. Although the term oral language is used, the implication is oral Standard English. Later, Farr and Tuinman (1972) recognized a number of measurement concerns in the field of reading comprehension: validity, reliability, scores for analysis, and description of tests (some researchers were using tests that were 50 years old, and others were using unpublished tests). They mentioned that reviews in leading professional journals lacked a full or complete description of the reading tests used. They found that the reviews also failed to adequately name the tests as part of the background information; unpublished tests or researcher-developed tests were not available for (peer) review; there were poor descriptions of the test and the process used to select and develop the tests; and many studies failed to report the testing conditions, that is, number of students tested, when, where, and by whom the test was administered. Reading comprehension testing, especially subskill testing, continued unabated as if a neat little package of skills that needed to be taught in an undisclosed hierarchical sequence magically leads to improved reading comprehension.

Carroll (1977) argued that there were three basic components of reading comprehension: language, cognition, and decoding. Others, including Davis (1968), Lohnes (1968), Samuels (1976), Spearritt (1972), and Thorndike (1977), took a factor-analytic approach to understanding the components of reading comprehension tests. It was Lohnes (1968) who most accurately captured the state of reading comprehension testing. He alleged that reading tests measured a complex set of reading skills and that there was no evidence to support a claim for five major reading comprehension skills as was often reported. In fact, Lohnes argued that that the five skills were really components of reading ability: "All we know is that a committee of authorities agreed on this breakdown of reading into competent skills" (p. 327). Prophetically, he described the trend of research in reading comprehension and testing that would consume researchers for the next 30 years. Reanalyzing Davis' (1968) research, Thorndyke (1977) pointed to verbal reasoning as the most distinguishing factor, whereas Spearritt (1972) found word meaning, inferences, author's purpose, and passage structure to be the most important.

Throughout this era, there was considerable lip service given to ameliorate educational opportunities "for all." This notion of universalism denies the reality of the lives of the people of color, who as oppressed people are keenly aware that it is part of the discourse of the dominant class but not part of their actions. As Du Bois (1940) noted, "There has been an understandable determination in the United States ... to minimize and deny the realities of racial difference" (p. 135). This denial and minimalism is especially true in the history of reading comprehension research and testing. Although the idea had great appeal and was a handy slogan, it created a conundrum for reading comprehension researchers and test developers whose ideological assumptions (universality of knowledge and faith in scientific methods) were inadequate and in opposition to democraticizing reading comprehension research. How then, does reading comprehension research and reading comprehension testing become more equitable when it is built on a narrow and inadequate foundation?

Another review by Lennon (1962) focused on 12 research studies of reading comprehension with a special focus on the skills (multiple choice, fill-in the blank, matching, definitions, review and lack of review of passages). He concluded that there were four factors of reading ability that were measured: a general verbal factor, comprehension of explicitly stated material, comprehension of implicit or latent meaning, and appreciation. His findings appear to have led to a call for a more thorough study.

The International Reading Association (IRA) in cooperation with ERIC Clearinghouse on Reading, for example, commissioned a review of literature on reading tests and measurement that resulted in Roger Farr's (1969) book *Reading: What Can Be Measured?* The book is a resource for study on the history of reading comprehension, especially reading comprehension testing. It includes a comprehensive list of tests, glossary, and bibliography. In this text, Farr attempts to offer a balanced discussion of reading comprehension testing without self-identifying his ideological and philosophical position. He appears knowledgeable about the political and social barriers faced by the Underserved. Specifically, he implies that there are no tests that are unbiased or culturally free and that tests which report high correlations between social economic status and low test performance should be used to improve educational opportunities. He emphatically states, "The fault does not lie with the tests or with the student; it lies with society and the educational system which produced the test performance" (p. 14). In addition, he does not appear to embrace a behavioristic point of view as he lists multiple factors that affect reading comprehension, including environmental factors, mental and emotional states, and interests of the reader along with cognitive abilities. Despite these insights, the text evinces a traditional discussion of theories and methods of reading comprehension research and testing. Farr concludes, "There have been few new procedures for measuring reading comprehension in over forty years. If these 'old' methods have been shown not to be valid, new ones should be tried" (p. 65). Farr makes two important observations about the shortcomings of reading comprehension tests. First, reading comprehension tests remain deterministic, or in Farr's own words, "Usually standardized reading tests have been developed to compare one student's reading performance with that of another rather than with some specific goal" (p. 65). Second, he notes that standardized reading tests "rarely account for why the student performs as he does ... because tests merely describe reading behavior rather than explain it" (p. 80). Unfortunately, as he concludes in the updated edition of this book 25 years later, little has changed.

Farr's text was published during a rash of social and political upheaval in the nation, namely protests against the Vietnam War and protests against discrimination based on race, age, and gender.

The U.S. involvement in the Vietnam War (1964–1975) that began, in part, to halt the spread of communism grew increasingly unpopular, especially among college students—many of whom were exempted from service. Although 2.6 million Americans served in Vietnam, the troops were overrepresented by men and women who were poor, less educated (than their peers), and/or African Americans and Latinos. College students, many of whom were supporters of the civil rights legislation, and others, who fought for the rights of the underclass, protested the Vietnam War. Several people, students and nonstudents were killed at Kent State and Jackson State as they protested U.S. involvement in the war. With the fall of Saigon, on April 30, 1975, President Nixon skillfully led the United States out of the Vietnam War by relinquishing the affairs of Vietnam to the South Vietnamese.

Counter Discourse

One of the most fascinating phenomena of these protests, was the discourse used by protestors. Their discourse offered an alternative worldview, one that was not part of the mainstream. Whether in text (broadsides, posters, bumper stickers, pamphlets, books, poetry, educational curricula), in film (documentaries, movies, and home movies), or in song, protestors voiced strong opposition to the traditional views propagated in U.S. media, classrooms, and textbooks. Media outlets, for example, made possible a public airing of alternative points of view; live television coverage and radio broadcast, in particular, helped to clarify differences between dominant and alternative worldviews. No longer did the public need to depend on political and military leaders, educators, journalists, or social activists (conservative or radical) to form an opinion; they could inform themselves. These actions personified Gramsci's (1971) notion of ideological struggle:

> What matters is the criticism to which such an ideological complex is subjected by the first representatives of the new historical phase. This criticism makes possible a process of differentiation and change in the relative weight that the elements of the old ideologies used to possess. What was previously secondary and subordinate, or even incidental is now taken to be primary—becomes the nucleus of a new ideological and theoretical complex. (p. 195)

Gitlin (1980) argues that media coverage of the protest movement by the dominant class was structured to minimize its import. He lists media devices that lessened the impact of the discourse surrounding the protest movement: trivialization, polarization, marginalization, disparagement, emphasis on violence, and delegitimizing protestors' claims, among others. These devices were also used earlier to dispel the protests for civil rights as well as Black Nationalism.

The African American community was experiencing a phenomenon that offered not only a counter discourse to the rhetoric of the dominant class but also a new art form of resistance as an outlet for radical ideology. The Last Poets (Suleiman El Hadi, Umar Bin Hassan, Gylan Kain, Felipe Luciano, David Nelson, Jalal Nurridin, Abinodun Oyewole) were a group of young men who used poetry as a vehicle for social and political commentary about their lives in vivid and graphic language not customarily used in public. What is important here is that their use of language and unorthodox spelling of words were informed by ways of knowing and a reality that was offered by the mass media or centuries of negative and destructive research. Their work resonated with other Black young people, who also wanted to speak in a powerful oppositional voice and tell of political and social injustice. Other groups aligned with the Marxist, Maoist, and socialist teachings included the Black Panther Party and the Student Non-Violent Coordinating Committee (SNCC), which sought to improve the economic, educational, social, and political interests of African Americans. No group emerged completely formed or representing a new systemized way of thinking or acting. Their ideas, formed in response to the world in which they lived, included ideas that had been expressed by other African American activists of the past. The dominant class, however, also made use of these forms of mass media to push forth a conservative agenda, one that supported its viewpoints, values, and beliefs as normal, moral, and peaceable. The dominant class also had the privilege of naming the beliefs, actions, and concerns of the oppositional view, and did so, using provocative discourse: deviant, militant, reactionary, and violent.

Connecting and Redefining Reading Comprehension

What is the connection between these historical events and reading comprehension? An articulation of ideological and cultural hegemony permeates the abstract and practical. It is at the point where and when we understand the power of language to define and shape meaning to determine categories, create and interpret images, and frame representations that we understand Hall's notion that meaning is not fixed; rather it is multireferential. In the examples in this chapter I illustrated how discourse was used to describe the U.S. imperialistic stance and involvement in international wars as the "spread of democracy," while similar domestic struggles were defined as "social unrest or riots," under the notion of democracy. Another example mentioned in this chapter is that the media's discourse characterized the civil rights movement, Black Nationalism, and the Black Power/aesthetic movements as social unrest, whereas the anti-war movement, freedom of speech movements, and the women's movement are characterized as antiestablishment. In this way, language is used to shape opinions and notions of reality.

A final example is seen in the way discourse was used to portray non-Whites. During this era, some journalists redirected the anger of African Americans back on them by referencing people of African descent as "Blacks" as a collective noun without further description of gender or age. In the media, it became acceptable to note that "a Black" did this or that, or that someone was "the first Black" to accomplish a feat. What is missing in these statements is any reference to personhood or humanity. The writer or speaker whose focus is skin color or Blackness rapes the person in one word: Black. Yet, when some read the words, "the first Black," the reader comprehends, knows, or infers, that the reference is to a Black person.

Behaviorism, mastery learning, and universal developmental stages of cognition are inadequate models to explain comprehension. It cannot account for all the possible dimensions of human thinking, for the mind and how it operates is far more dynamic and unbounded than first perceived; it is also influenced, in unfathomable ways, by the context of people's lives and the power/authority relations in which they live. Moreover, the consent they offer, or are coerced to offer, to fulfill the dominant's groups' notion of reality may not be an accurate representation of their ability to comprehend but rather a representation of their ability to comprehend in the manner expected and accepted by the dominant class.

When talking about reading comprehension, it is clear that words convey much more than black marks on white paper. The terrain of struggle, ideology, helps us understand that there is a connection between and among words that exceeds linguistic and structural boundaries of print. The concept of reading comprehension is much more complex when you consider that the connection between and among words is shaped by the beliefs, values, and "systems of knowing" (Ladson-Billings, 2000, p. 257) of the sender and receiver or the writer and the reader. The psychological theories and approaches of the early- to mid-20th century conveniently ignored or marginalized the influence of cultural, linguistic, and social forces on the reader and within the field, as scholars of color noted in the 1920s. In the following chapter, several reading researchers move beyond purely cognitive explanations of reading comprehension. Collectively, this group of researchers acknowledges psychosocial influences, cultural and linguistic differences, and the role of power in understanding the role that reading comprehension testing plays in controlling opportunities. In addition, there is some minor movement in reading comprehension testing that suggests alternatives to how reading comprehension is assessed, as opposed to measured. Nonetheless, the basic format of reading comprehension tests did not change, although there is greater pressure for test developers to include literature written by or about people of color, Unfortunately, possible connections, between critical and cultural theories and reading comprehension theorizing have been overlooked in traditional histories of reading comprehension research and in reviews. Although there were some researchers that adopted and adapted those theoretical positions to better understand the influence of culture, language, and power of reading comprehension, their efforts were short-lived.

7

Reading Comprehension Research and Testing Reinvents Itself

Interest in reading comprehension research and testing reached its zenith in the late 20th century. Given the historical, social, and political changes in the nation, as well as the international and national involvement in military campaigns, it is striking that researchers ignored the impact of these changes and failed to account for them in reviews and definitions of reading comprehension. Their actions remind us how ideological and cultural hegemony reacts and recasts itself as "a shifting set of ideas by means of which dominant groups strive to secure the consent of subordinate groups to their leadership" (Strinati, 1995, p. 170). The discourse used by dominant groups in the past also continued to inform reading comprehension research and testing during this period. For instance, the philosophical assumptions that underpin reading comprehension research rest on the ability to isolate, or give the illusion of isolating it from the contexts in which it develops.

The focus of this chapter is on how ideas about reading comprehension research and testing consistently serve best groups that reflect the dominant groups and fail to serve, or, adequately address, the needs of Underserved groups, in the midst of theoretical, political, and social change.

The Impact of Psycholinguistics on Reading Comprehension

Sociolinguists (e.g., Halliday, Labov, Meeks, Rickford) challenged the field to envision reading as a part of the complex set of language processes. They maintained that language was acquired naturally and, as a natural part of language development in a literate society, reading also could develop naturally. Miller's (1965) classic paper "Some Pre-liminaries to Psycholinguistics" began this wave of investigation. He argued that the behaviorist understanding of language use in terms of conditioning was too narrow and restrictive for use in the reading process. He observed that the ability to decode the letters/words on a page was an insufficient explanation because it could not describe how words mean; meaning was dependent on context and purpose. Here are a few of his memorable examples that highlight how similar phonetic and orthographic words convey very different meanings: a Venetian blind is not the same as a blind Venetian, and the pen in fountain pen is very different from the pen in playpen.

Each example, he makes cultural assumptions about the knowl-edge the reader brings to the text. The first example assumes the reader understands what venetian blinds are and where they might be used or where Venice is geographically located in the world as well as what it means to be blind. The second example assumes the reader understands what a fountain pen is and why one might use it, as well as what a playpen is and why and where it is used. In both cases, there are some cultural assumptions made on the part of the author about what constitutes common knowledge on the part of the reader; whether or not the reader possesses this knowledge will determine whether or not, or to what degree, he or she is said to comprehend the text.

Miller listed seven implications for research, but the most ger-mane to reading comprehension declared,

> The meaning of an utterance should not be confused with its reference; the meaning of an utterance is not a linear sum of the meaning of the words that comprise it; the syntactic structure of a sentence imposes groups that govern the interactions between the meanings of the words in that sentence; and there is no limit to the number of sentences or the number of meanings that can be expressed. (quoted in F. Smith, 1973, pp. 15–16)

According to psycholinguistics, language learning is rule gov-erned. That is, children do not merely imitate the language of adults; rather, they are constantly inventing and discovering language anew. Orasanu and Penny (1986) also point out in their summary of Miller's early work that "behavior theory cannot account for the creativity of language or for the comprehension of novel utterances" (p. 4). Miller's research, nonetheless, helped to reshape reading com-prehension research.

The connection among psycholinguistics, reading, and reading comprehension gained considerable clarity from the extended doctoral work and research of Kenneth Goodman and Yetta Goodman (1979). Their research of oral reading errors is, in many ways, reminiscent of Schmitt's and W. Gray's studies discussed earlier in this book. Kenneth Goodman published two groundbreaking articles, "A Linguistic Study of Cues and Miscues" (1965) and "Reading a Psycholinguistic Guessing Game" (1967), in which he applied and extended the research of linguistics to reading. He observed that reading was a process that "involves an interaction between thought and language. Efficient reading does not result from precise perception and identification of all elements, but from skill in selecting the fewest" (p. 260). In addition, Goodman and Burke (1973) argued that "reading is a psycholinguistic process by which the reader (a language user) reconstructs, as best he can, a message which has been encoded by a writer as a graphic display" (p. 22).

The goal of reading, according to K. Goodman (1972), was to understand the text (comprehend), a process that he believed began within the reader and not on the page. Four assumptions about the reading process underpin his thinking:

1. All readers bring an oral language system to the reading process.

2. All readers bring the sum total of their past experiences to the reading process.

3. Reading materials represent the language patterns and past experiences of the author.

4. Reading is an active language process which involves constant interaction between the reading and the text. (pp. 10–14)

He also identified three cueing systems readers used (graphophonic, syntactic, and semantic) and could identify the type of miscues made by the reader when a reader's oral reading strayed from the written text. Moreover, he believed that an analysis of qualitative and quantitative miscues could help determine the reading support a reader needs.

Goodman's miscue analysis was used in a study by Sims (1972), who charted the reading miscues of African American children to determine if the miscues could be attributable to Black English. She concluded that dialect differences accounted for very few miscues.

Her findings ran counter to K. Goodman's (1965) initial discussions of the relationship between Black English and miscues. Afterward, without admitting any misunderstandings, Y. Goodman and Burke (1973) declared, "The only special disadvantage which speakers of low-status dialects suffering learning to read is one imposed by teachers and schools. Rejection of their dialects and educators' confusion of linguistic differences with linguistic deficiencies interfere with the natural processes" (p.7). The work of Sims challenged and pushed them to reconsider their findings.

Another body of research that envisioned the intersection of language and text with prior knowledge and experiences of the reader is found in the work of Frank Smith. His 1971 publication of *Understanding Reading* was quickly followed by a second, *Psycholinguistics and Reading*. F. Smith (1971) defines reading comprehension as—*the extraction of meaning from text,* as "*the reduction of uncertainty*" (p. 185, italics in the original). He argued, in part, that comprehension/meaning, like knowledge, operates below the surface of letters and words at a deep structural level of language drawing on the cognitive and semantic levels. In a brief description of the structure of knowledge, he writes, "The perceiver brings a highly structured knowledge of the world into every perceptual situation" (p. 187). Smith resurrects the connection between one's oral reading ability/fluency and comprehension: "*the rate of reading aloud is also a reasonable indicator of the extent to which a reader can comprehend a passage*" (p. 195, italics in the original). His idea supports Goodman's work with oral reading miscues as indicators of the breakdown of comprehension. Drawing on transformational linguistics, Smith, in reference to a fluent reader, declares, "The identification of individual words is completely irrelevant to reading for meaning" (p. 200). He goes on to claim, "*Even if every word is articulated, there is still the problem of working out what it means; the meaning of language is no more given directly in its sound than it is available in the surface structure of writing*" (p. 200, italics in the original). To Smith, a reader must simultaneously employ both surface and deep structures to read for meaning or comprehension.

In his second book, F. Smith characterized psycholinguists as "theorists and researchers in the scientific study of the uniquely human skills of language learning and use" (p. v). As a psycholinguist he claimed the following:

1. Only a small part of the information necessary for reading comprehension comes from the printed page.

2. Comprehension must precede the identification of individual words.

3. Reading is not decoding to spoken language. (p. v)

Smith insightfully warned that as education gave way to technology and allowed large publishing houses to support and promote standardized reading testing as a way to improve instruction, educators would be forced to relinquish their hold on reading; gone would be the days of teacher insight of the process of teaching, understanding, and guiding children in reading comprehension. Detractors and critics began to label Smith and other researchers whose ideas were in opposition to traditional views, unpatriotic. This is a powerful moniker and a use of power and language that was meant to detract from the real issue of rethinking reading comprehension research and testing, or to envision reading comprehension more broadly. Dominant groups, whose work supported the status quo, who received federal funding, and whose books were sold to school districts, fought vigorously then, as now, to silence the oppositional viewpoints.

F. Smith's (1973) book is a compilation of reprinted articles and new thinking by reading researchers of various disciplines. For example, included are chapters by Carol Chomsky, Kenneth Goodman, George Miller, and Smith, among others. A premise held by Smith is "research into reading frequently fails to separate itself from matters of reading instruction, instructional theory, and social and educational bias" (p. 5). This is a powerful political statement about the state of reading research where he compared and contrasted how researchers in linguistics differed from those in cognitive psychology and education. Smith's notion of how one's external world knowledge influences the reader was not unlike ideas posited by social activists and critical and cultural studies theorists (e.g., Septima Clark, Stuart Hall, Myles Horton, Carter G. Woodson), who sought an emancipatory or liberatory education as well as more equitable literacy education. Their input is not included in his book, either because they lacked cachet within the academy or their ideas were silenced because of racial/ethnic prejudice or ignorance.

Teacher Expectations and Social Factors
that Affect Reading Comprehension

In 1973, 40 years after the Lemon Grove incident discussed in chapter 6, the U.S. Supreme Court ruled in *Lau v. Nichols* that the San
Francisco school system violated the 1964 Civil Rights Act when
they denied non-English-speaking students of Chinese ancestry the
opportunity to participate in public education. The decision brings
to mind the "separate but equal doctrine" imposed upon African
Americans, but here students of Chinese ancestry were given the
same educational facilities, curriculum, teachers, and so on. Irrespective of the similarities, English language was the language of
instruction, yet students were nonnative speakers of English who
needed to learn English in order to benefit equally from the education offered. Gramsci (1971) maintains:

> Each time that in one way or another, the question of language comes to
> the fore, that signifies that a series of other problems is about to emerge,
> the formation and the enlarging of the ruling class, the necessity to
> establish more "intimate" and sure relations between the ruling groups
> and the national popular masses, that is, the reorganization of cultural
> hegemony. (p. 16)

Gramsci's point is illustrated in the response to the work of
Labov (1970, 1972a) and Halliday (1973). These researchers demonstrated that language is acquired in social contexts and that
dialect can affect reading achievement. In addition, they maintained that the effects of race, class, and environment are important considerations in analyzing and understanding reading
comprehension. Labov (1972b) challenged educational psychologists who had very little contact with African American children
to defend their cultural deficit hypothesis of the children's home
and community environments. Significantly, he captures the
common sense notion—verbal deprivation—held by educational
psychologists regarding the lives of these children as well as their
linguistic prowess:

> Black children from the ghetto area are said to receive little verbal stimu-
> lation, to hear very little well-formed language, and as a result are impov-
> erished in their means of verbal expression. It is said that they cannot
> speak complete sentences, do not know the names of common objects,
> cannot form concepts or convey logical thoughts. ... The concept of ver-
> bal deprivation has no basis in social reality. (p. 377)

He strongly implies that educational psychologists brought dominant ideas to their research and held biases and stereotypes about the intellectual and linguistic abilities of African American children who lived in poverty that influenced their research findings and interpretations.

Other researchers (McDermott, 1974,1976; Piestrup, 1973; Rist, 1970; Taylor, 1973) revealed that with African American children, teacher expectations judged by dialect, grammar, and speech patterns greatly influenced student performance. Piestrup (1973) indicated that dialect affected teachers' expectations and interactions and student literacy performance among the more than 200 African American first-graders in her Oakland, California, study. In the case of Black English, the issue of language re-emerged in the 1990s (Rickford, 1999), as the Oakland School Board sought federal funds to support early literacy instruction in Ebonics for African American children, in part, by training their teachers to recognize Ebonics as a legitimate rule-governed language, not a bastardization of Standard English. Nonetheless, this body of research was criticized by Somervill (1975), among others, who counter-argued that dialect affects only oral reading, and not silent reading, comprehension.

Another way to understand the issue of dialect is to consider teacher knowledge. Does the teacher understand the student? Does she perceive when a student has understood the text regardless of the dialect he uses to convey meaning? Marjorie Johnson argued, "No instructional program can be any better than the teacher's knowledge of the children for whom it is planned. If they are known only superficially, the instructional program will be superficial at best, totally inappropriate at the worst" (quoted in Baumman, 1966, p. 19). Her findings appeared confirmed by the work of Rist (1970) whose longitudinal qualitative study "Student Social Class and Teacher Expectations: The Self-Fulfilling Prophecy in Ghetto Education" appeared in the *Harvard Educational Review*.

Rist (1970) documented African American middle-class teachers' expectations of African American children in Grades K–2 who attended an inner-city school. Specifically he examined "the relation of the teacher's expectations of potential academic performance to the social status of the student" (p. 413). Rist's research demonstrated that within the first eight days of school, children in the study were being placed in a caste system based on teachers' expectations. Perhaps more profound is that he noted that although the teachers and students were African Americans, the teachers' expectations were reflective of dominant ideology and racial distinctions. According to Rist, the teachers appeared to have embraced wholeheartedly the dominant or normative expectations and standards for what constitutes readiness for school (Rist did not member check; therefore, we cannot know exactly what the teachers thought or why they made the statements he recorded). His research illustrates that "the behavior, degree and type of verbalization, dress, mannerisms, physical appearance, and performance on the early tasks assigned during class" (p. 416) shaped the teachers' expectations of academic success and the performance of the students. Rist's findings appeared to confirm the notion of a self-fulfilling prophecy, in much the same way as Rosenthal and Jacobson (1968) found in *Pygmalion in the Classroom: Teacher Expectation and Pupil's Intellectual Development*. They observed the following:

> There are many determinants of a teacher's expectation of her pupils' intellectual ability. Even before a teacher has seen a pupil deal with academic tasks she is likely to have some expectation for his behavior. If she is to teach a "slow group," or children of darker skin color, or children whose mothers are "on welfare," she will have different expectations for her pupils' performance than if she is to teach a "fast group," or children from an upper-middle-class community. (p. viii)

Moreover, his research reveals how, in the day-to-day practice of teaching, the beliefs and values of the teacher are acted on and can (potentially) affect the educational opportunities of the students, especially those who least fit her expectations. Students whose appearance, speech, and behaviors mimicked the fictional norm (White, middle-class, speakers of Standard English) were more easily accepted and validated by the teacher. The behaviors and attitudes of the teacher, as described by Rist, were not novel. They are reminiscent of a similar idea expressed by Woodson (1933) years earlier:

> In this effort to imitate, however, those "educated people" are sincere. They hope to make the Negro conform quickly to the standard of the Whites and thus remove the pretext for barriers between the races. They do not realize, however, that if the Negroes do successfully imitate the Whites, nothing new has thereby been accomplished. You simply have a larger number of persons doing what others have been doing. The unusual gifts of the race have not thereby been developed. (p. 4)

Rist (1970) also suggests that the teachers in his study held views that reflected the larger (White, middle-class English dominant) mainstream society, more specifically, students that displayed

> ease of interaction among adults; high degree of verbalization in Standard American English; the ability to become a leader; a neat and clean appearance; coming from a family that is educated, employed, living together, and interested in the held; and the ability to participate as a member of a group. (p. 422)

Although these characteristics were highly prized, the ability to speak Standard English and behave as a member of the middle class set students apart in their interactions with and the level of expectations of, their teachers and eventually in the educational opportunities. Like other researchers had revealed before him, Rist found that students whose identity and reality best met those expected by teachers and reflected those in text, were the more successful academically.

Reading researchers Chall and Feldman (1966) and Weber (1971) also recognized the importance of the school principal's and classroom teacher's expectations on performance of inner-city children's performance. Other researchers pointed to the oral language of African American children, then called Black English, as well as to the characters and storylines in basals (readers) that did not reflect the lifestyles of many African American children, as possible causes for the reading achievement gap. Federal legislation through programs like Home Start, Head Start, Follow Through, and Upward Bound brought improved educational opportunities to the children of color, children who live in poverty, and children who did not speak English or Standard English. Instructional programs were implemented to improve the language and literacy of the children in these groups. Additionally, the National Assessment of Educational Progress (NAEP), established in the 1960s, began to publish data regarding reading achievement of students and included race, class, and gender demographic comparisons (later English proficiency and special needs designations were added). Furthermore, schoolbooks (readers) were developed to reflect the oral language of the children, or Black English with African American characters, though the pictures were often better labeled stereotypes of African American features.

Carroll (1977) challenged the reading research community to reconsider the understandings of the role of language in reading comprehension. He argued that definitions and discussions of reading comprehension were in fact actually definitions and discussions of language comprehension and, as such, could encompass all knowledge. His ideas are very similar to those expressed by Hall (1982) in his definition of an ideology. Here's how Carroll defines language comprehension: "To comprehend language, in whatever form is to comprehend the ideas, concepts, propositions, facts, questions, injunctions, arguments, inferences, qualifications, conditions, attitudes, emotions, and anything else that may be expressed in language materials that are spoken or written" (pp. 1–2). In addition, he explains that reading comprehension "entails cognitive processes of knowledge, reasoning, and inferencing that are supposed to be evoked by printed texts, oral discussions, and lectures" (p. 2). Moreover, he notes that reading comprehension includes the affective domain, anticipating the intent of the author, understanding literature and text of a discipline, and "appreciation of the ideas and ideologies of special interest groups" (p. 2). Finally, he writes, "In a practical way, all this suggests that we may be fooling ourselves or, at least, that we are sorely misguided, if we think we are teaching reading comprehension" (p. 3). He argued that language comprehension exists before reading comprehension and that reading "is only incidental to the development of language comprehension and cognitive ability" (p. 4).

Notions of language and reading comprehension informed the classroom research by Dolores Durkin (1978–1979). Her research revealed that very little instruction in public schools addresses reading comprehension, specifically, less than 1%. There was reading comprehension instruction, but it consisted of time spent on skill related worksheets or reading comprehension assessment. As a follow-up to the use of worksheets, Durkin (1981) conducted a study of five nationally popular basal reading series. She found little support of reading comprehension instruction but an abundance of skill worksheets, which led her to conclude, as she had earlier, that few reading researchers and educators differentiated between reading comprehension instruction and reading comprehension testing. Durkin's work begged the question: Can you honestly test a student's reading comprehension when he or she has not received such instruction? If reading comprehension tests were not testing reading comprehension achievement, what were they testing? Durkin's research spawned a series of other studies that examined the effect of teaching subskills (e.g., pre- and postquestioning, advanced organizers, underlining cues) on reading comprehension (e.g., Taylor, Pearson, Clark, & Walpole, 1999). While plentiful, the new investigations of reading comprehension did not change concepts or definitions of reading comprehension, reading comprehension tests, or interpretations of test results. They did, however, lead to a greater focus on applied research in reading comprehension instruction. Given their philosophical moorings, subskill testing supported greater testing of reading and reading comprehension.

Renewed Debates of Racial Bias in Standardized Testing

The national commitment to standardized testing as a measure of intelligence, achievement, and meritocracy, even when faced with disconfirming evidence, was stronger than a commitment to reconsidering the assumptions on which testing is based and by which the tests should be restructured in a democratic society. Standardized intelligence and reading comprehension tests continued to be an enslaving yoke for the students historically underserved by education in the United States. The ethnic bias within intelligence tests clearly was evident in the Stanford–Binet (1960 revision) described earlier in this book. This example marks the cultural boundary of reality used by the test developers and the ideological and cultural hegemony that supported the construction, use, and interpretation of this test. Black psychologists argued that standardized intelligence tests normed on White children consequently found White children's intelligence superior. They raised oppositional voices just as their predecessors in the 1930s had done. For instance, Boone and Adesso (1974) report the results of a *Black Intelligence Test* (BIT) where Black cultural references abound. The test was administered to Black and White children, and, not surprisingly, the Black children outperformed the Whites. The authors of the test declared that it validated concerns of cultural bias in standardized testing. Boozer (1978) detailed the concerns of the Association of Black Psychologists who opposed the use of standardized testing:

> Current standardized tests should not be used to test Black children because they have been used in labeling Black people as uneducable, placing Black children in special classes and schools, perpetuating inferior education for Blacks, assigning Black children to educational tracks, denying Black students higher educational opportunities, restricting positive growth and development of Black people, and destroying the delicate self image of many students. (p. 415)

The voices, research, and insights of these African American psychologists were dismissed within the academy. The Bay Area

Association of Black Psychologists virulently opposed the use of standardized testing and issued a Position Statement on Use of IQ and Ability Tests (1972) in which they called for a moratorium on the use of such tests for Black children (see Jones, 1972). Kent and Ruiz (1979) made similar findings for Chicano children.

In 1979, the U.S. District court found the use of standardized IQ tests in California public schools illegal. The decision in the case, *Larry P. v. Wilson Riles,* upheld the plaintiff's position that the tests discriminate against African American students. Children who performed poorly on standardized tests, including intelligence and reading comprehension, were labeled disadvantaged, culturally disadvantaged, culturally deprived, educationally deprived, and handicapped. Boozer (1978) argues that these labels are irresponsible: "To designate minority groups is value-laden. No one should be allowed to so label and degrade a culture or subgroup that does not conform to the value system of the majority group" (p. 414). Dominant groups promote these labels and images of intellectual inferiority as part of the common sense, whereas the counter discourse argues these labels feed into notions of victimology or "blaming the victim." Put another way, Apple (1996) articulates, "The word *disadvantaged* implies that one's problems are largely the result of bad luck. In essence, there are no agents of domination. To say 'oppressed' rather than disadvantaged implies something more powerful. It signifies that oppressive structures exist" (pp. 17–18, italics in the original).

In a similar way, standardized intelligence and reading comprehension tests have been used to represent a reality, one that test makers assume should be part of a larger "American" reality, although it is not. The poor performance of individuals or groups continues to be interpreted as an indication of inferior intellectual ability and inferior ability to comprehend text. The discourse surrounding the poor performance of the students of color suggests that inferior intellectual abilities are based on biological factors; "environmental" factors (i.e., communities, schools, homes, families); or individual factors (lack of motivation and unvalued education), but not on the dominant ideological structures that underpin tests. Moreover, as Boozer (1978) recalls, Black psychologists have argued that intelligence tests, and I add reading comprehension tests, do not appreciate, value, or attempt to measure the verbal dexterity of African American children.

The strengths of these children continued to be ignored as researchers accepted a new paradigm. Just as behaviorism overwhelmed research during the early part of the century, constructionism was a prevailing thought during the latter half.

Constructivism

In the latter half of the 20th century, *constructivism,* based on theories espoused by Piaget, re-emerged as an important approach to understanding reading comprehension research and testing. Constructivist theories emphasized a cognitive approach (the active independence of the learner) and a sociocultural approach (the importance of an individual's reality or lived experiences in shaping understandings). Both forms of constructivism presented new pathways for research in reading comprehension. The renewed interest in constructivism included the cognitive work of Bruner (early years) and Piaget, as well as the sociocultural constructivism of Russian psychologist Lev S. Vygotsky (1896–1934).

Adaptation of constructivist thinking in reading comprehension research is evinced in the research of Bransford and Johnson, as in their 1972 article "Contextual Prerequisites for Understanding: Some Investigations of Comprehension and Recall." In this article, they describe a series of experiments with high school age students and reveal their findings on appropriate contextual information given prior to hearing a story read. They found that following the reading of a passage, when assessed, students recalled the information given in "set idea units" much like Judd (1915) suggested. This led them to conclude that, given Standard English syntax, vocabulary, and grammar, contextual information, prior knowledge, and interest were important factors that improved listening comprehension. Drawing from the research of Ausubel (1968), Bartlett (1932), and Piaget (1950), among others, Bransford and Johnson argue that semantic context is critical and aids students' comprehension. In fact they claim, "The extent to which context availability becomes a problem will certainly vary with the circumstances" (p. 725). Their findings align with similar ideas expressed by scholars of color who found that the importance of contexts and interests affected levels of comprehension.

Another strong constructivist's influence or cognitive psychological perspective, on reading comprehension was research by Stein and

Trabasso (1982), although it is frequently overlooked. The authors list key components of reading comprehension commonly recognized by researchers and teachers:

1. Finding the main or the most important idea in a narrative;

2. Detecting or inferring cause and effect relationships among events;

3. Ordering narrative events in the correct temporal sequence;

4. Making inferences from the information given in a text and using this inferential information to make judgments about the text;

5. Paraphrasing or summarizing the events depicted in a narrative. (p. 213)

Furthermore, their ideas are presented as if universal. For example, drawing on the extant literature on schema (schemata) as applied to story or narrative comprehension, they outline key features of schema (schemata):

• Schemata are composed of generic or abstract knowledge.

• Schemata reflect prototypical properties of various experiences encountered by an individual.

• In the process of schema formation, an individual integrates over many instances.

• Schema may not be open to consciousness by the person using it and the formation may also proceed unconsciously.

• Although schemata are assumed to reflect an individual's experience, ... these structures are assumed to be general and shared across individuals.

• Once formed, schemata are thought to be relatively stable over time.

• Schemata are assumed to be acquired and altered or changed by induction from prior or ongoing experience. (pp. 215–216)

According to Stein and Trabasso (1982), schema function in specific ways in story comprehension:

1. Schema are thought to guide encoding, organization, and retrieval of information.

2. Schematic knowledge has been shown to have a significant effect on organization of ambiguous or disorganized stories.

3. In the process of encoding, representing, and retrieving narrative knowledge, schemata are assumed to guide the comprehender in constructing hypotheses about what types of information should occur in the text and what type of logical connections should link the various events in a narrative sequence. (pp. 216–217)

The authors reason that individuals use their narrative schemata to fill in missing information through inference. They make a very strong statement about epistemological difference in story comprehension:

> The use of schematic knowledge is so powerful that listeners have little control over the types of retrieval strategies used during recall of narrative information. Even when listeners are instructed to reproduce texts in a verbatim form, they *cannot* do so when the text contains certain types of omission or certain sequences of events. (Stein & Trabasso, 1982, p. 217, italics in the original)

They note that their thinking aligns with previous work by Bartlett in that ways of telling story, ways of understanding, are bound consciously or unconsciously by how an individual makes sense of the world. Their explanation of the process of reading comprehension (or, as they prefer, narrative understanding) and how it is accomplished and recognized, nonetheless, supports a dominant ideology and Western thought or Anglocentric thought.

One of the most significant advances in reading comprehension drew on the research on human memory, mental processing, and constructivism. Johnson-Laird (1983) and Rumlehart (1980) built on research by Bartlett (1932), Herbart (1902) and Henderson (1903) which investigated how humans represent knowledge in memory. Given the notion of schema theory, researchers moved farther away from behaviorist, mechanistic, and passive views of reading comprehension to views of reading comprehension as cognitive, purposeful, and active. The new research on schema theory changed how researchers conceptualized reading.

Working at the national Center for the Study of Reading at the University of Illinois, Anderson and Pearson (1984) applied constructivist views to reading comprehension research and testing. Along with their colleagues, these researchers helped to translate and apply the work in memory and human information processing to reading comprehension. Their application of schema theory to reading comprehension focused on cognitive processes, prior knowledge, and inference as readers constructed meaning from print. Every single act of reading began to be seen as an addition to a much larger and grander notion of schema for understanding texts and contexts. Anderson and Pearson (1984) define *schema* as "an abstract knowledge structure. ... in the sense that it summarizes what is known about a variety of cases that differ in many particulars" (p. 259). More important, they argue, "A schema is structured in the sense that it represents the relationships among its component parts. The theoretical issue is to specify the set of relationships needed for a general analysis of knowledge" (p. 259). Pearson and Stephens (1989) put it this way, "Comprehension of text occurs when we are able to find slots within particular schemata to place all the elements we encounter in a text" (p. 31). To that end, they focused on how prior knowledge informed readers' comprehension of text. Here's a classic example of a short passage used by constructivist theorists:

> John was hungry and decided to order a large meal. He was pleased that the waitress was attentive and prompt. After he finished the meal, he paid his bill and left an extra five dollars under his plate. (McNamara, Miller, & Bransford, 1991, p. 493)

Schema theorists contend that readers who have prior knowledge will fill in the "generic" slots of information and understand the text. Several reading researchers attempted to determine the role of cultural schema/ta in reading comprehension.

Research by Spiro, Coulson, Feltvoich, and Anderson (1988) encouraged reading researchers to broaden their notions of schema as pliable structures that can accommodate unknown and multiple perspectives of schemata. Several other reading researchers found that reading comprehension can be enhanced through direct instruction in reading comprehension, drawing inferences, and metacognitive awareness and monitoring. Reynolds, Taylor, Steffensen, Shirey, and Anderson (1981) wrote a short passage on sounding/cracking (African American verbal game) read by Black and White teenagers. In recalling the passage, White teenagers tended to emphasize the possibility of impending violence, whereas African American teenagers understood it as a form of joking. The researchers surmised that cultural schema/ta were helpful and could improve comprehension. The majority of research on cultural schema does not use intracultural group differences of U.S. citizens; instead, it tends to emphasize differences between internationals and the West (i.e., Pritchard, 1990).

Schema theories were extended by mental model theories to explain the reading comprehension process. McNamara, et al. (1991)

argue that schema/ta are inadequate for helping students understand the text. The theory of mental models improves on schema theory by considering perceptions of tasks and performance, especially in school settings and in the real world. Mental models offer a closer look at how individuals use knowledge and information to solve problems and follow procedures. The authors claim, "schema instantiation does not explain how or why readers understand texts about unfamiliar objects and events" (p. 493). Furthermore, they posit an alternative approach, mental models, that are more flexible and help to explain why readers make choices. Their definition of *mental models* notes, "Comprehension theories that involve the representation of situations described by the text have been termed mental models theories" (McNamara et al., 1991, p. 493). They suggest that readers construct mental models that are similar to those in the text. And, like other constructivists, they held that the essence of reading comprehension is the construction of meaning. However, they determined that meaning construction required, "the ability to construct appropriate mental models" (pp. 508–509). How does one determine appropriateness? When reading narrative text, McNamara et al. (1991) declare,

> readers seem to focus on information relevant to the main character in a narrative, recording and updating spatial relations between the protagonist and object with which he or she interacts. Readers also make perspective shifts from one character to another as the situation requires. While updating mental models, readers often must retrieve previously learned information. (p. 497)

According to McNamara et al. (1991), reading comprehension hinges on the selection of appropriate mental models. An alternative view of knowledge construction suggests that a mental frame "involves the claim of particular cultural practices to represent reality. Yet, it is not reality that is represented (and constructed); it is rather our relation into it, the ways we live and experience reality" (Grossberg, 2003, p. 159). Given the variance in realities among U.S. school children, the universality of the claim by McNamara et al. (1991) is inadequate unless it reflects a representative sample of U.S. school children, which it does not.

The basic forms of reading comprehension tests that emerged early in the last century, that is, written answers to questions and multiple choice testing, remain the most popular forms today. Then, as now, some educators have argued that an over-reliance on standardized tests of reading presents an artificial and incomplete understanding of a student's ability to comprehend. In addition, there are scholars who oppose the over-reliance on test performance. Madus wrote, "By mandating tests, policy makers create an illusion that educational quality is synonymous with performance on tests" (quoted in Farr & Carey, 1986, p. 19). Moreover, the underlying philosophical assumptions about the efficacy of tests to instantiate dominant ideas within each generation, the propaganda surrounding their use to improve education for all students, and the rhetoric that our nation needs intellectuals to sustain its world power, remain at the core of standardized test use.

Sociocultural Approach to Reading Comprehension Research

Although Bruner's early work reflects a cognitive approach to constructivism, his later work is more reflective of a sociocultural approach. For example, in his 1996 book *The Culture of Education*, Bruner advises educators:

> Education is not just about conventional school matters like curriculum or standards or testing. What we resolve to do in school only makes sense when considered in the broader context of what the society intends to accomplish through its educational investment in the young. How one conceives of education, we have finally come to recognize, is a function of how one conceives of culture and its aims, professed and otherwise. (pp. ix–x)

His thinking, while in line with literacy researchers who support critical and social constructivists' points of view, has largely been ignored. Most important he argues, "Culture shapes the mind. ... it provides us with the toolkit by which we construct not only our worlds, but our very conception of our selves and our powers" (Bruner, 1996, p. x). These more recent ideas are very similar to those supported by advocates of the importance of culture in knowledge production, language, and reading comprehension, but they are ignored because they are immeasurable variables. Bruner's new foci meld well with interest in the work of Vygotsky, who had a broad range of research interests including the sociocultural nature of learning.

  Bruner maintains that meaning making is a social process and that the construction of knowledge is shaped by the context in which it develops, an idea that is similar to that of Vygotsky. In fact, one of the most important elements of Vygotsky's theorizing is the notion of the zone of proximal development, the area between what the reader knows and what the teacher is trying to teach. To best accommodate the learner's levels, Vygotsky suggests scaffolding, where the teacher supports what the learner already knows as the learner is encouraged to move beyond that knowledge and acquire additional knowledge. His notion of social context includes culture and language, but also interaction with others, especially adults where he found they aided in the zone of proximal development by scaffolding. The strong emphasis on reading comprehension and its linkages to schema theory was not limited to studies of English but included several studies of the linkages with second language users (see Barnitz, 1986).

Bakhtin (1981) and Bleich (1978) acknowledge the importance of social contexts and their connections to reading comprehension. Applications of their perspectives have helped reading researchers to question the influence of a range of familial, community, linguistic, and experiential contexts on readers' comprehension. Reading comprehension, understood in this sense, is much more intimate, personal, and multifaceted in ways that are inadequately presented and assessed in current theories.

Research by Heath and Delpit exemplified this shift in focus. Heath (1983) conducted a 10-year ethnographic study in the Piedmont area of North Carolina, focusing on oral and written literacy in African American and White homes. Her work demonstrated that school literacy was more reflective of the types and purposes of literacy among middle-class Whites than among other groups. Her research added to the literature on the social and cultural significance of literacy acquisition that began in the 1960s. Unfortunately, her research has not been translated into how to best measure reading and comprehension abilities of children from non-White, non-Standard-English-speaking communities. Delpit's (1986, 1988) work pointed out how people of color view Whites' perception of their knowledge, differences in the home literacy practices of African Americans and Whites, and the differences in the perceived understandings of and expectations for teachers of African American students. Her work also explored the importance of acknowledging power relations in school literacy curricula, pedagogy, and instruction as well as the importance of using explicit instruction.

Theoretically, constructivism, in its varied forms, held the promise to correct the theories used in reading comprehension in the past, especially given its sociocultural foci, in part, because it appeared more flexible, less culturally bound (Western), and, in part, because it appeared more adequate to address multiple ways of knowing. Hall (1982), however, offers a biting critique:

> In the conventional or constructivist theory of language, reality came to be understood, instead as the result or effect of how things had been signified. It was because a statement generated a sort of "recognition effect" in the receiver that it was taken or "read" as a simple empirical statement. The work of formulation which produced it secured this closing of the pragmatic circle of knowledge. But this recognition effect was not a recognition of the reality behind the word, but a sort of confirmation of the obviousness, the taken-for-grantedness of the way the discourse was organized and of the underlying premises on which the statements in fact depended. (pp. 74 – 75)

In other words, even as some reading researchers began to move away from traditional philosophical assumptions that anchored the field to scientism and rigid quantitative methods, and as they began to adopt more qualitative methods of inquiry and use anthropological and ethnographic techniques, they did not stray far from the dominant groups' beliefs and values about non-White groups' intelligence. The promotion of constructivism, as used in reading comprehension research, supports the ideologies of dominant groups in its attempt to universalize consciousness and restrict sociocultural emphasis. The promotion of constructivism within education gave the appearance of consent, while simultaneously continuing to produce and reproduce the status quo (Hall, 1982). The idea of sociocultural differences (albeit unacknowledged) continues to be used by the majority of reading comprehension researchers to reflect differences primarily between Western and non-Western cultures, but not among Western cultural groups. In the minds and research of many researchers of color (Barrera, 1992; Gutiérrez, 1993; Gutiérrez & Rogoff, 2003; Henry, 1995; Moll, 1992) however, a very different vision of constructivism emerges: one in which consciousness is discussed in racial/ethnic terms and one that builds on sociocultural understandings and ways of knowing.

The deeply rooted ideological and cultural hegemony that had proven so successful in maintaining a sense of power among reading experts was not shaken by the upstart sociocultural approach.

Increasingly on university campuses across the nation, their ideas offered a new way of thinking about reading and reading comprehension research as advocates argued that previous approaches did not consider differences, whereas new approaches encouraged students to draw from their cultural/ethnicity and linguistic strengths as well as to think independently.

Reading Comprehension Research and Testing in the 1980s

Research of reading comprehension continued its torrid pace into the 1980s as part of the back-to-basics movement/backlash in education. Critics blamed public schools for what they believed was a decline in education and fueled fires of discord as they proposed that the United States was falling grossly behind other developed nations, namely Japan and West Germany, and losing global status and power. The report *A Nation at Risk,* issued by the National Commission on Excellence in Education (1983), declared the following:

> All, regardless of race or class or economic status, are entitled to a fair chance and to the tools for developing their individual powers of mind and spirit to the utmost. This promise means that all children by virtue of their own efforts, competently guided, can hope to attain the mature and informed judgement needed to secure gainful employment, and to manage their own lives, thereby serving not only their own interests but also the progress of society itself. (opening statement, italics in the original)

Next, the Committee described how we are at risk as a nation. They claimed, "The educational foundations of our society are presently being eroded by a rising tide of mediocrity that threatens our very future as a Nation and a people" (¶1). It is not clear on what basis these bold statements were made, but the political reaction to the report made concerns about educational reform a central part of each presidential campaign that followed the report.

> Under Recommendation B, the report strongly endorsed the use of standardized tests of achievement at regular intervals in schooling as "part of a nationwide (but not Federal) system of state and local standardized tests. This system should include other diagnostic procedures that assist teachers and students to evaluate student progress" (¶ 20). Further, this and subsequent reports failed to question the philosophical assumptions of standardized testing and therefore, perhaps unwittingly, supported the biases they contain.

Readence and Moore's (1983) review of selected standardized reading comprehension tests revealed that most reading comprehension tests continued to use a passage followed by several multiple choice items like those from the 1910s. They argued that the "one best answer" concept does not allow for the "opportunity to display important comprehension behaviors" (p. 307). In addition, they claimed, "tests may help us sort students and compare groups according to rough measures of general academic abilities, but those tests provide only limited information about students' specific comprehending abilities" (p. 313). Readence and Moore suggested that other comprehension skills can be exhibited by "retelling passages, dramatizing stories, producing miscues, discussing passages, following directions, and supplying words which are thought to be the ones purposely deleted (cloze)" (p. 307). Their ideas were very similar to suggestions made by Gates (1921b, 1921c) many years earlier. However, these authors also underscore the importance of examining the ideological assumptions that underlie theories in reading comprehension research and standardized reading comprehension testing and interpretation, and that help to maintain the "achievement gap" between U.S. White students and all others.

Federal interest in reading research in general and reading comprehension specifically began to mandate the evaluation of educational projects. In an effort to improve research in reading, the U.S. Department of Education funded The Reading Center at the University of Illinois at Urbana-Champaign (1976–1991). Then, as now, it was believed there was a crisis in reading education in the United States. The Reading Center was founded to help improve reading research and education. Among the many publications produced by scholars at the Reading Center, one of the most influential was *Becoming a Nation of Readers: The Report of the Commission on Reading* (1985) prepared by Anderson, Hiebert, Scott, and Wilkinson, among others. The authors declare from the outset, "Reading is a basic life skill. It is the cornerstone for a child's success in school, and, indeed, throughout life. Without the ability to read well, opportunities for personal fulfillment and job success inevitably will be lost" (p. 1). This sentence suggests a subtext that belies their ideological and cultural frames of reference and sounds very similar to ideas expressed by Thorndike. A conservative interpretation suggests that readers who are competent can expect to make greater economic gains than those who are less competent. And, in a slight bit of moralizing, the authors suggest that the lives of competent readers are more personally satisfying than nonreaders.

Anderson et al. (1985) also acknowledged the widespread use of standardized reading comprehension tests including norm-referenced tests, with accompanying reading comprehension subtests, and criterion-referenced tests that stated objectives. They maintain that "standardized tests of reading comprehension manifestly do not measure everything required to understand and appreciate a novel, learn from a science textbook, or find items in a catalogue" (pp. 97–98). In a more positive stance, they also argue, "The strength of a standard test is not that it can provide a deep assessment of reading proficiency, but rather that it can provide a fairly reliable, partial assessment cheaply and quickly" (p. 98). They also note, in line with their research and constructivist notions of reading comprehension, the importance of prior knowledge. For unknown reasons, in language that is almost archaic, they suggest that underserved children "may be" disadvantaged when reading comprehension is so dependent on prior knowledge:

> Some groups of children — for example, those who live in environments different from those assumed to be average—are at a disadvantage. They may be able to understand material about the world that is familiar to them, but they do not have a general knowledge needed to do well on standardized reading comprehension tests. (p. 98)

Without deconstructing what the authors could have possibly meant by "average" it appears that they have, perhaps more blatantly than in most texts, suggested that normalcy is equal to middle-class ways of life, with the implication being White, middle-to-upper-class, and English dominant. Not so clear, but perhaps implied, is that people with these characteristics are also more like the authors who perceive that their values, beliefs, and worldviews are superior to others. In another section, Anderson et al. (1985) clarify their frame of reference:

> It is difficult to imagine … kindergarteners could be called literate for their age if they did not know *Goldilocks and the Three Bears* or *Peter Rabbit*. For each age, there are fables, fairly tales, folk tales, classics and modern world of fiction and nonfiction that embody the core of our cultural heritage. A person of that age cannot be considered literate until he or she has read, understood, and appreciated these works. (p. 61)

Why is it so difficult to imagine? For whom is this imagined world difficult to conceive of? The authors' concept of cultural heritage and

worlds unlike their own reflect a taken-for-grantedness and com-
mon-sense making of the dominant class. The worldview and sense
of privilege held by the authors is unmistakable. Their concept of
literateness is obviously bounded by beliefs, values, and contexts that
may not exist for underserved students. Texts, especially those listed
by the authors, are not acultural because they reflect the views of
the authors. The authors presume that the texts listed are not only
familiar to children but are understood in much the same way by all
children. But, as we know, each reading by each child is individual
and contextually bound or, as Grossberg (2003) writes,

> Particular texts are consistently read with the same meanings, located
> within the same codes as if they were written there for all to see. Thus,
> every sign must be read and made to mean. There is not necessary corre-
> spondence between the sign and the meaning; every sign is multiaccent-
> tual. (p. 157)

Thus, in each reading there is the opportunity for alternative
readings, alternative ways of making sense of the text. There is no
one reading, no one true meaning of any text. However, and this is
perhaps the point the authors were trying to make, there is a clearly
traditional meaning attached to each of the texts they referred to, one
that is accepted as the "correct" way to comprehend the text. What
they do not say is that the "correct" reading reflects a particular view
of the world, not necessarily a view held by underserved children.

As noted throughout this book, the allusion of working for subaltern groups is a key strategy for power elites to win consent for
the leadership. This farce is most evident in federal legislation and
funding of reading comprehension research that allegedly is aimed
at improving the education and educational opportunities of the
underserved; however, seldom has the legislation or funding led to
sustained improvements.

In 1985, Madaus observed, "Policy makers have created the illusion that test performance is synonymous with the quality of education" (p. 610). In addition, Salganik (1985) warned,

> We can reasonably expect that increased reliance on technical evidence,
> decreased reliance on professional judgment, continued use of tests
> results to assess the quality of schools, and increased regulation of local
> school districts by states will continue and they will be absorbed into
> the set of norms that govern the assumptions of both educators and lay
> people about how the U.S. system of education should work. (p. 610)

Unfortunately, both warnings went unheeded and the standardized testing industry assumed an ever-increasing niche in American education. The public demanded accountability on the part of school districts, administrators, and classroom teachers. One way of "proving" accountability was to look to results of standardized tests as an indication of how well schools were educating students.

Reading: What Can Be Measured, Revisited

A second edition of the text *Reading: What Can Be Measured*, this time by Farr and Carey (1986), appears to confirm revisionist historians' observations for reading comprehension testing. In this volume, a few new chapters were added: accountability and reading assessment, a discussion of word recognition skills in reading, and a discussion of issues related to assessment of reading comprehension. The authors state their goal and purpose of writing the book were to answer the following question: "Do reading tests really measure reading?"

> At best, tests can provide some indication of how someone reads, but the relationship of such indications to actual reading behaviors must be inferred. ... Reading is not what reading tests test. ... Tests are activities to engage examinees in behaviors that are like what they do in everyday life. But tests are not reality. The testing conditions, the purposes of reading, the examinee's attitudes toward tests ... all influence test performance. (p. 16)

The authors identified two themes in their work. First, they argued, "Those who use reading tests often fail to consider why they are testing before they begin to ask what should be tested and how to test" (p. vi). Second, they declared,

> ... the need for improved selection and interpretation of reading tests. Test scores are too often relied on as the only measure of the quality of a child's reading or of a reading program. We believe that the misuse of tests, especially by policy makers, significantly diminish any value test results may have for improving education. (p. vi)

The authors raised several concerns about reading assessment: whether reading tests actually measure reading comprehension, if any single test could measure reading comprehension, if reading tests are helpful in educational decision making, and how are test results are used or misused.

Many of the concerns they raised have been raised before; for instance, they ask, "What is reading?" (p. 18). This query is much like comments teachers made to Gray in 1915 following the Cleveland study: "Reading tests can only indicate how well a child reads from a limited perspective, under a limited set of conditions, and with a limited set of responses" (Gray 1917c, p. 19). Farr and Carey's ideas also mimic those of Bond, Du Bois and others, as they wonder about the effect of reader background on tests results. They queried about "whether standardized instruments are fair to groups whose cultural experience is distinctively different from that reflected in the content of reading test passages" (Farr & Carey, 1986, p. 47). In terms of assessing reading achievement, the authors claim that standardized reading comprehension tests "indicate how a student performs in relation to other students at one point in time, but they rarely account for why the student performs as he does" (p. 80). From their review of the literature they surmised,

> If one seeks to get an accurate assessment of student achievement, it is advisable to use a wide variety of reading measures including informal inventories, standardized tests, teacher observations, and teacher assessment of performance in content areas. (p. 81)

The authors described several major criticisms of reading comprehension tests: They do not reflect the full range of student cultural backgrounds and thus they lead to decisions that are unfair to minority students; they have only limited value for holding teachers, schools, and school systems accountable for quality of education; tests exercise a limiting effect on classroom teaching; and tests are too narrow in scope to provide for fair evaluation of new approaches to teaching (p. 11). Moreover, Farr and Carey (1986) acknowledge, "Fundamental philosophical issues continue to be the major decision points in the development, selection, and administration of reading tests" (p. 211). In their conclusion they claim, "It must be stated that basic ways in which reading tests are used is consistent with the ways they were used fifty years ago" (p. 217). One is left to wonder if testing conditions and formats were changed, would we be better able to assess "what reading is" and how well a child understands what he or she read?

Valencia and Pearson (1987) added their voices to the calls for changes in how reading achievement was assessed in their oft cited article "Reading Assessment: A Time for Change!" in the *Reading*

Teacher. They observed an increase in testing, based in part on politically initiated school reform efforts, and questioned why new theories about reading comprehension remained "remarkably impervious
to advances in reading research" (p. 727). Their call to action seeks:

> One important focus for immediate research should be to develop and
> evaluate new assessment techniques that are both consistent with our
> understanding of reading and its instruction and amenable to large scale
> testing. Unless we can influence large-scale assessment, we may not be
> able to refocus assessment at all. (p. 730)

Valencia and Pearson suggested alternative formats for assessing
reading comprehension, including summary writing, metacognitive
judgments, question selection, multiple acceptable responses, and
prior knowledge.

Opponents of the use of standardized tests continued to point out
the cultural and linguistic differences among school children who
are required to take the same standardized tests, although they are
just as ignored by reading comprehension researchers as they are
by intelligence test designers. For instance, Hoover, Politzer, and
Taylor's (1987) review of the sociolinguistic biases in reading tests
revealed what they termed, a "self-fulfilling prophecy" in reading
comprehension tests. Specifically, they argued that reading tests
discriminate against bilingual/bidialectal speakers phonologically,
syntactically, and lexically. Using excerpts from selected reading
tests they analyzed how superstandard English phrases were used
in some tests. Complex phrasing such as "only the person to whom
you make it out" and "however, in and of itself" were used in the
test directions. These phrases can be misleading to any student, but
they particularly discriminate against working-class students (p.
87). Other examples include test items that represent unfamiliar pictures or words like "toboggan" and "chandelier." Hoover et al. (1987)
maintain, "Cultural or linguistically biased tests reinforce undesir-
able attitudes and give them the appearance of reflecting measurable
scientific objectivity" (p. 94). The authors do not have much hope
for the dismantling of standardized tests as measures of achievement. Therefore, they suggest rewriting the biased materials and
using directions that call for "following directions, true/false reading of short paragraphs, and paraphrasing of written materials" (p.
96). Not surprisingly, the results of their research have not been used
to promote change in reading comprehension research or testing.

Their research findings, in effect, have been silenced, marginalized, and ignored, in part because they challenge and call into question decades of research built on a different understanding of reality.

Farr (1992) summarized the world of reading comprehension assessment in the 1990s in his publication "Putting It All Together," after examining the many different audiences that used the results of reading comprehension testing in their decision making. He warned of the overuse and misuse of such tests and suggested that new constructivist definitions of reading warranted rethinking and consideration of reading assessments. In his opinion, traditional measures did not measure authentic reading behaviors. He also maintained that the best hope for change in assessment is authentic performance assessment: "Reading performance assessment must look at the reading act in process or judge comprehension of a text as it is applied in some realistic way" (p. 204). His ideas include observations, portfolios, and integrated assessments of reading, thinking, and writing as examples.

Tierney and Pearson (1992) also perceived that past theories of reading comprehension tended to view comprehension from the "point of view of the text" as a search for "author intentions" and as a test of recall.

> Implicitly, we valued … students' reproductions of someone else's text over a host of alternative indices of comprehension: a) their ability to integrate text with their existing knowledge, b) their disposition, in the face of conflict, to question their beliefs, assertions in the text, or both, c) their use of ideas from the text to do something, or d) their ability to transform ideas from the text into another medium of expression (art, music, and the like). (p. 517)

They went on to succinctly describe the heart of many current efforts in reading comprehension research. As hopeful as the authors' ideas are, they were short lived. They argued, in fact, that the thinking about reading research on comprehension of the early 1990s was different than in the past, and they implied that it was improved:

> We viewed assessment primarily as a means for teachers to gather information for making decisions about individuals and curriculum. Now we would view it more from its impact on students. Now we would ask whether our assessment techniques are helping students learn how to assess themselves and their own learning. (p. 517)

Indeed, sure and better promises are needed in reading comprehension research as well as testing. Hall mentioned as early as 1984 that it is important to understand that texts are "inscribed in the particular social relations which produce them" (Hall, 2003, p. 160). If so, how does this affect the comprehensibility of the text? Who is best served by reading a text that is written within or outside of their frame of reference? How are reading comprehension test questions then written to reflect multiple ways of understanding text? How do we write questions that are more informed and that generate responses that will better inform the researcher about the process of reading comprehension?

Rickford (2001) by way of example, uses ethnic folk tales and contemporary stories to interest, engage, and motivate African American, Asian Pacific Islanders, and Latino/a students to read. She queries students using higher order comprehension questions because she believes that a student's ability to read is not necessarily a mirror of one's ability to comprehend text. Furthermore, she surmises that teacher knowledge and instructional repertoire need to dramatically improve if students' reading comprehension is to improve. In another study, Bradford and Harris (2003) examined African American students' ethnocultural and mainstream knowledge in grades 4 and 6. Their study challenges the myth that African American children lack sufficient knowledge of the mainstream culture, resulting in poor or low reading comprehension test performance. They found that the students were bicultural, possessing knowledge of both the mainstream and African American cultures; however, their mainstream knowledge outpaced their ethnocultural knowledge.

Although the late 20th century is commonly identified as one of the most productive in the history of reading comprehension research and testing, one must wonder how the word *productive* is being used. If *productive* means increased numbers of funded research projects, federal support, and publications, indeed it was a productive period. However, change for underserved students continued to be marginalized and laced with deficit language. Despite the impact of psycho- and sociolinguisitics, notions of cultural and linguistic knowledge and how it impacts reading comprehension was ignored. Given the insightful and impressive work of Hall (1982), this thinking is just beginning to be applied to reading comprehension research. The discourse surrounding this period of reading comprehension research and testing belies the reasoning often used to support the research efforts: (a) Researchers conduct research in the best interest of all students. (b) Researchers conduct research to improve the performance of all students. (c) Cognitive and behavioral research is acultural and apolitical. The pursuit of research under any of these statements, wittingly or unwittingly, appeals to common sense or taken-for-grantedness, to universality, and to testaments of change and progress, all a part of the rhetoric of the ideological structure of the dominant class. What is more, these statements are meant to absolve historians and researchers from their responsibility to write a more thorough and accurate account of the history of reading comprehension research.

Furthermore, in some states there is legislation that seeks to ignore the centuries of discriminatory practices imposed on people of color, the poor, and women. Supporters of such legislation have called for an end to affirmative action; fortunately, efforts failed in 2003, but new charges are sure to surface.

The push to disavow the need for affirmative action policies suggests a shift in larger social and political forces to privilege the dominant class. The legal challenges to affirmative action were a type of litmus test by the dominant class to gauge how far it needs to go in winning popular support to re-inscribe forms of domination. Similar changes can be noted in reading comprehension research as past notions of scientism and psychologism resurface and challenge more innovative approaches to reading comprehension research.

Counter-Hegemonic Response to Literacy Education

The lives and work of Freire and Hall are presented here, separate from their historical chronology, in part because of their oppositional stance to the ideological and cultural hegemony. Similar to documented oppositional thoughts and activism of other Scholars of Color, the research of these two courageous men stands outside recognized research in reading comprehension, in part because their philosophical assumptions are built on critiques of positivism and in part because they offer a more adequate and appropriate means of understanding comprehension.

Reading the Word and the World

The life and work of Paulo Freire (1921–1997) is well known by most people in the field, and to summarize it in its entirety would result in a separate book of which several excellent works already exist (M. Freire & Macedo, 1998; P. Freire, 1996; Gadotti 1994). Therefore, my comments here are selective as they reflect his work in reference to reading comprehension research and testing, where appropriate. As documented in the lives of other philosophers and theorists explored throughout this book, Freire's early life had a profound effect on his view of the world and his understanding of society at large. He was born in Recife, Brazil into a middle-class family; however, as the world's economic crisis reached Brazil, his way of life changed dramatically. Freire (1995) recalls various moments in his life helped to shape his point of view, his philosophy, his pedagogy, and his lifework. Two of those moments stand out, the first of which is his life among the poor rural and urban workers, his hunger, and the economic and social conditions that caused the oppressed to fear (though *fear* is not a term he embraces). From this experience, he understood the evolution of what he calls a "culture of silence." That is, he became aware of how every second of the lives and bodies of the oppressed are dominated by political, military, social, and economic forces, seemingly beyond their control, that keep them dependent.

Second, his early teaching career influenced his ideas about the power of dialogic pedagogy. Although he had been a teacher since secondary school, it was during graduate school that he was exposed to the works of Althusser, Arendt, Dewey, Fanon, Fromm, Gramsci, Hegel, James, King, Mannheim, Marcuse, Marx, Mills, Piaget, Rousseau, Sartre, and Vygotsky. Many of their ideas seemed to meld with his thoughts about the connection between consciousness and learning. As he articulates the process, his awareness of social economic class differences began during graduate school and caused him to abandon developmental notions and embrace the dialogic process of meaning making *with*, not for or to people (Freire, 1995, p. 26).

Eventually Freire accepted an appointment as director of Education at the Industrial Social Service's (SESI) program to support the education of Brazil's rural labor force. It was during his tenure as director that ideas for his famous book, *Pedagogy of the Oppressed* (1993), began to crystallize. It also was during this time that he more clearly understood the gap between the education offered by the State and education needed to make informed, purposive, and proactive decisions. Importantly, he observed the power of the state to control the thinking of the masses through the instruction of a sterile curriculum. And, he understood that the educational system was a key component used by power elites to retain power and status.

Freire's literacy pedagogy calls for respect of the sociocultural ways of knowing and the life histories that learners bring with them to the classroom. He argues that teachers should be cognizant of their students' lives as well as their ways of knowing. He admonishes that "what is impermissible ... is disrespect for the knowledge of common sense. ... One has to respect the levels of understanding that those becoming educated have of their own reality" (quoted in Freire & Macedo, 1987, p. 41). He continues by suggesting that it also is impermissible to "conceal truths, deny information, impose principles, eviscerate the educands of their freedom, or punish them, no matter by what method, if, for various reasons, they fail to accept my discourse—reject my utopia" (p. 83). A commonly overlooked segment of his theory cautions that neither teachers nor students should allow their knowledge of life experiences to be their goal; such behavior, according to Freire (1995), supports an elitist ideology. Instead, Freire suggests that the life knowledge that teachers and learners bring to the classroom serve as a starting point for learning and as a point of dialogue for social transformation.

Among his more famous quotes in a book with his collaborator Macedo, Freire offers "reading the word and reading the world" (Freire and Macedo, 1987). His ideas are reminiscent of those expressed by Cooper, Du Bois, and Woodson (mentioned earlier). He calls for an education that draws on the life understandings of the learner and calls for the learner to make connections between their world and the text. In one of his last books, *Pedagogy of Hope: Reliving Pedagogy of the Oppressed*, Freire (1995) reviews his thinking and suggests "enabling the popular classes to develop their language: not the authoritarian, sectarian gobbledygook of 'educators', but their own language—which, emerging from and returning upon their reality, sketches out the conjectures, the designs, the anticipations of their new world" (p. 39). In order to accomplish this goal, Freire suggests learners need to develop a critical consciousness. Drawing on ideas that surfaced in his very first publication, he identifies three stages of critical consciousness: (a) semi-intransitive consciousness, (b) naïve transitivity, and (c) critical transitivity. In this stage-theory, an individual moves from a state of consciousness where one's reality centers on survival, to a state of nonconfrontation with reality, and finally to a state of critically assessing one's reality.

His specific methods call for the teachers and students to learn from one another, question, and participate in shared meaning making as well as to reflect on the process. As coworkers, they work for social transformation. His pedagogy is very similar to that used by Mrs. Robinson (mentioned earlier) in the education of African Americans seeking to exercise their right to vote in South Carolina, and calls for learners to examine the relationship between their world and words. He writes of his experience teaching reading among the rural poor. ... where the fundamental problem of the reading of the word, always preceded by a reading of the world (p. 42). Further, he observed, "The reading and writing of the word would always imply a more critical rereading of the world as a 'route' to the 'rewriting'— the transformation—of the world." (Freire, 1994, p. 42)

He also observed the importance of people becoming self-conscious, and seeing and believing in their self-worth, their humanness, and their humanity. Drawing on Fanon's theories of the effects of colonialism, Freire suggests that students pull away from the appearance of granting a casual consent to the ideas of the oppressor; they should "step back' from the oppressor, and localize the oppressor 'outside' themselves" (1995, p. 48). Freire believed that teaching reading and teaching students to understand (comprehend) what was read are a highly political act.

Although he does not use the term *reading comprehension*, much of Freire's literacy work centers on the process of comprehension. His writings help to clarify the ideological and cultural, as well as historical, basis for the alleged support of academic knowledge and linguistic supremacy foisted on the powerless:

> The dominant class, then, because it has the power to distinguish itself from the dominated class, first, rejects the differences between them, but, second, does not pretend to be equal to those who are different; third, it does not intend that those who are different shall be equal. What it wants is to maintain the differences and keep its distance and to recognize and emphasize in practice the inferiority of those who are dominated. (Freire, 1998, p. 71)

He claims that reading the word cannot be separated from reading the world. His thoughts on reading add to what we already know about reading comprehension:

> Reading does not consist merely of decoding the written word or language; rather, it is preceded by and intertwined with knowledge of the

world. Language and reality are dynamically interconnected. The understating attained by critical reading of a text implies perceiving the relations between text and context. (Freire & Macedo, 1987, p. 29)

Much like several other scholars, he observes,

Most of all, the reading of a text requires that one who does it be convinced that ideologies will not die. The practical application of this principle here means that the ideology with which the text is drenched —or the ideology it conceals—is not necessarily that of the one who is about to read it. (p. 76)

An example of his thinking is evinced by reading two separate texts that illustrate a similar lifestyle. For instance, Alex Kotlowitz's (1992) book, *There are No Children Here: The Story of Two Boys Growing Up in the Other America*, details the life of the lives of two African American brothers, Lafeyette and Pharoah Rivers, from Chicago's West Side. While a thoughtful and honest portrayal of their lives, their "story" is told through the eyes and understanding of the author, a middle-class White journalist. And, much like many slave narratives written by White transcribers of the plight of African Americans, it was really not the story of the two African American boys, as if it was his story of their lives, steeped in the knowledge, language, and images of someone whose life is more like the power elite than the young boys. By way of contrast, a much more authentic tale of the lives of two poverty-ridden lives is told with greater depth, understanding, and humor by Lealan Jones and Lloyd Newman (with David Isay) in *Our America: Life and Death on the Southside of Chicago* (1998). The authors were not tourists or journalists looking for a story; they were residents of the Ida B. Wells housing project. They understood the people in their families and neighborhood, the languages, and the context of their lives. Throughout their lives, they have learned to read their world and the word in order to survive. Without question, through their personal narratives the young authors detail a much more complex, insightful, and poignant understanding of their lives.

Freire questions the need to objectify reading that makes the process of comprehension appear devoid of personal input and whether in reading and testing the interests, desires, hopes, and dreams of students are considered. Freire and Macedo (1987) have observed:

Language also assures the power of envisagement: because we can name the world and thus hold it in mind, we can reflect on its meaning and imagine a changed world. Language is the means to a critical consciousness, which in turn, is the means of conceiving of change and making choices to bring about further transformations. (p. xv)

Recall how people of African descent living in the United States, reclaimed and renamed themselves in the 1920s, and again in the 1960s, in both eras, no longer willing to accept (allegedly accept, fabricate consent of, or offer imagined consent of) the histories, images, or names given to define their worth by the ideology of dominant class or cultural leaders, but fought and struggled for ideological and cultural recognition and autonomy.

Freire was not alone in his opposition to the ideological and cultural hegemony foisted on children who live in poverty. In England, the work of another cultural theorist began to impact our understanding of how text meaning was delimited by dominant groups.

Cultural Studies and Reading Comprehension Research

The needs and lives of the working classes was the focus of Hoggart's work at the University of Birmingham where he helped establish the Centre for Contemporary Cultural Studies (1963–1964), later known as the Centre for Contemporary Cultural Studies (CCCS) and the Birmingham School. Under Hall's leadership, scholars shifted their foci in the 1960s to the "interplay of representations and ideologies of class, gender, race, ethnicity, and nationality in cultural texts, including mass media culture" (Kellner, 1997, n.p.).

Hall's influence helped scholars to interrogate the struggle over meaning as expressed in the lives of oppressed groups (race/ethnicity, nationalities). He was interested in how racial/ethnic and national groups made meaning, most often in opposition to mainstream representations, and how these groups struggled to rename and represent themselves in opposition to popular images promoted by the power elites (through television, media, and text). Hall's writings and work are inspired by Gramsci, Marx, and Saussure, to name a few. As a cultural theorist, he observed that subordinate groups were much more active than presumed under early theories posited by Marx or those of the Frankfurt School and were much more aligned with the more radical and outspoken activism of Black Nationalists in the United States. Like other oppositional scholars, he did not support scientism, psychologism, racism, or mainstream notions of reality promoted by the dominant social class or cultural leaders. Hall's commitment to Marist and Gramscian theories encouraged him not to merely offer an intellectual discourse but to put action behind his thinking.

Among Hall's most influential work is his compelling essay, "Encoding and Decoding." The essay, originally published in 1973 and reprinted in 1980 and 1995, draws on Gramsci's notions of hegemony and ideology as Hall explicates how the media attempts to shape our thinking through the messages it encodes. He observes that there can be three distinctive readings; although his reference is to media, notions of encoding/decoding also are applicable to reading comprehension: (a) dominant (hegemonic) reading where the reader accepts the dominant or preferred meaning; (b) negotiated reading where the reader partially accepts the dominant or preferred meaning, or at least understands the benefits of doing so; and (c) oppositional (counter-hegemonic), where the reader rejects the dominant or preferred meaning, knowingly or unknowingly, and creates a new meaning that reflects the contexts of his or her life. As we have seen in other theories, words convey much more than definitions; even when there are agreed on definitions, they are bounded by the content and the context in which they are read. Text, in this context, is communicated and the listener/reader must be able to code/encode/decode the message. Hall (1980) argues that what is understood, or perceived, as naturalistic discourse is not all that natural: "It would be more appropriate to define the typical discourse ... not as naturalistic, but as *naturalized*: not grounded in nature but producing nature as a sort of guarantee of its truth" (p. 75, italics in the original). Put another way, some researchers are unwilling or unable to conceive of a reality beyond their own understanding. Later, he articulates links between ideology and discourse:

> The same concept is differently positioned within the logic of different ideological discourses. One of the ways in which ideological struggle takes place and ideologies are transformed is by articulating the elements differently, thereby producing different meaning: breaking the chain in which they are currently fixed ... and establishing a new articulation. This "breaking of the chain" is not, of course, confined to the head: it takes place through social practice and political struggle. (p. 19)

As discussed earlier, there are many ways to read the word and the world, and language is just one. In a recent republication of his key works, Hall (2003) writes, "The displacement of centered discourses ... entails putting into question its universalist character and its transcendental claims to speak for everyone, while being itself everywhere and no where" (p. 324). In the context of this discussion on reading comprehension, his thoughts suggest that what is needed are theories that adequately address individual and collective understandings of text, as well as theories that are both complex and practical enough to explain everyday lives and relationships.

New Literacies

An international group of literacy (predominantly White) researchers met at New London, New Hampshire, September 6–11, 1994 and began to rethink how concepts of literacy historically have been formed, distorted, and misappropriated. One outcome of the meeting, as well as subsequent meetings, was the New London Group's proposal to reconceptualize literacy. A statement to that effect is their article "A Pedagogy of Multiliteracies: Designing Social Futures," published in *Harvard Educational Review* (1996). While self-aggrandizing, the group's proposal has taken on a cult-like following among young reading researchers who have connected the core concepts to social theories. This latter group of researchers seeks to meld new concepts of literacy with the rapidly changing political, social, cultural, and technological world in which we live while simultaneously acknowledging the ideological and cultural hegemonic forces in the past that have created the present and that seek social transformative change for the future. Their research efforts are qualitative and emphasize popular culture while making references to, but not powerful deconstructions of, how culture is formed. Despite rhetoric to the contrary, most of the advocates are White, conduct research among participants of color, draw on the research of other White scholars, and ignore or marginalize the research conducted by scholars of color among their own racial/ethnic group. This trend delimits multicultural, multiracial, and multilinguistic issues and redefines them within a White-dominant framework. In many ways, their efforts are similar to those espoused by Cattell, Thorndike, and Gray, sans the notion of the inheritability of intellect. In short, the multiliteracies idea is an improvement on the past, but it also is an inadequate explanation for how to better understand reading comprehension in a multiraced, multilingual, complex and diverse society. Although Hall's theorizing was available to understand the role of ideological hegemony in framing and shaping our understanding of reading comprehension research and testing, it has largely been ignored. Other theories, like the New Literacies, took center stage by repackaging old ideas and labeling them anew. What is not new, but should be, is the deconstruction of race, class, and linguistic differences in reading comprehension research and testing. Meanwhile, some researchers of reading comprehension began extending their understanding of race/ethnicity, culture, and language, and powerful political and social conservative movements sought to reform education in general and reading comprehension research and testing in particular. The form of reading comprehension testing differed little: more opportunities for extended responses, as opposed to short answers, were added, but multiple-choice formats continued to dominate test questions. The sources of literature vary little, but there were efforts to include literature written by authors of color and not just about People of Color. In addition, there was greater emphasis at the primary grades to include literature that featured animals as opposed to people, in a feeble attempt to appear culturally neutral. Test results continue to be published as if all groups had equal access to educational opportunities, and the performance of White, middle-class, English-dominant students continued to be portrayed as superior to that of all other groups. Although, on most intelligence and reading comprehension tests, Asian Pacific Islanders out perform all students. This reporting came even when researchers knew that the Students of Color were from low-income neighborhoods or were bilingual, limited English proficient, or spoke varieties of English.

The concluding chapter documents the politics that coerced changes in how reading comprehension research and testing are understood, reverting to philosophical assumptions rooted in the past, complete with their racial, classist, and power undercurrents. The shift back to positivistic assumptions, although tied to the federally funded reading comprehension research, is a more powerful statement of how dominant ideologies work to sustain themselves. On the one hand, we see how reading comprehension research and testing has been used to discredit the intellect and morals of historically Underserved students and argue that most members of those groups are not capable of learning. On the other hand, we see how consent is manufactured as these same images of members of Underserved groups are used to promote the need for educational reform and change in reading research and testing.

8

Federal Involvement in Reading Comprehension Research and Testing

The last decade of the 20th century and early years of the 21st century are distinctive examples of how ideological hegemony is indeed a living process whereby, in this case, the amount of federal involvement and intervention in reading comprehension research and testing is immeasurable. Gramsci (1971) suggests the state can, and does, seize power:

> The apparatus of state coercive power which "legally" enforces discipline on those groups who do not "consent" either actively or passively. This apparatus is, however, constituted for the whole society in anticipation of moments of crisis of command and direction when spontaneous consent has failed. (p. 12)

The manner in which the federal government has seized power over how reading comprehension research is defined and which research methods receive federal support, thereby challenging all other forms of research as invalid, creates what Gramsci (1971) calls "a whole hierarchy of qualifications" (p. 13). Historically, reading comprehension tests have changed very little, and, as we have seen, reading comprehension tests are mechanisms of ideological and cultural hegemony used to inculate dominant ideologies. Moreover, standardized reading comprehension tests unashamedly have begun to shape curricula as federal funds are attached to test performance. This chapter illustrates how domination through the state, in cultural institutions like schools, occurs while promoting an alleged improvement in the education for the Underserved. The process by which the federal government has "legally" enforced its view about what constitutes reading comprehension and how it is best measured illustrates how consent is both manufactured and coerced by dominant groups. The following chronology outlines legislative actions that have led up to our current state of federally approved and supported reading comprehension research agenda.

The early struggles over the ideological and cultural terrain of reading comprehension research and testing has been reincarnated in the last few years in startling detail. Herein, I trace associations among a set of legislative actions that include A Nation at Risk (1983), the U.S. Department of Labor's SCANS Report (1991), Goals 2000 (1994), National Assessment of Educational Progress NAEP, (2003), National Institute of Child Health and Development (1998), National Reading Panel Report (2000), No Child Left Behind Act (2001), Rand Reading Study Group (2001–2002), and Reading Comprehension Research Grants (2002–2003). This brief discussion articulates how ideological and cultural hegemony work to sustain and promote the beliefs, values, and worldviews of dominant groups while simultaneously silencing counter-hegemonic groups and the voices of their allies. In addition, I question the interrelationship among a variety of federally sponsored committees, panels, and research agendas that support the eventual historic *No Child Left Behind Act* and an assemblage of reading research that has sought to outline the future reading research agenda for the next decade, identifying reading comprehension as the area in most need. Finally, in line with the presentation of a counter-hegemonic reading of events that have occurred, several federally funded research grant competitions are deconstructed.

It Is Political, It Is Always Political

In 1926, Eggen insightfully observed, "Legislators are often intimidated by scientific theories, whether they understand them or not" (p. 104). His insight continues today as legislators make laws, based on partial information and, in some cases, their own lack of understanding. Former President George Bush, the self-proclaimed "education president," with support of a growing conservative base, fought to establish national standards and national achievement tests in school subjects. His proclamation was informed by an earlier announcement of *A Nation at Risk* (National Commission on Excellence in Education, 1983) that implied there was a pending education crisis. It listed six national education goals (see Figure 8.1).

All children will start school ready to learn.

The high school graduation rate will increase to at least 90 percent.

American students will leave grades four, eight, and twelve having demonstrated competency in challenging subject mater including English, mathematics, science, history, and geography; and every school in America will ensure that all students use their minds well, so they may be prepared for responsible citizenship, further learning and productive employment in our modern economy.

U. S. citizens will be first in the world in science and mathematics achievement.

Every adult American will be literate and will possess the knowledge and skills necessary to compete in a global economy and exercise the rights and responsibilities of citizenship.

Every school in America will be free of drugs and violence and will offer a disciplined environment conducive to learning.

Figure 8.1 Goals 2000: Educate America Act, H. R. 1804.

In addition, the report was used to bolster the need to improve the nation's workforce as noted in the *U.S. Department of Labor's SCANS Report* (1991) where research by Carnevale, Gainer, and Meltzer (1988) was used to form ideas about what was needed to develop a skilled workforce. The report, sounding very much like Comte's vision of the role of education in society, listed a three-part intellectual foundation for all workers: 1. Basic Skills (reading, writing, arithmetic/mathematics, listening, speaking) 2. Thinking Skills (creative thinking, decision making, problem solving, visualizing, knowing how to learn, reasoning) 3. Personal Qualities (responsibility, self-esteem, sociability, self-management, integrity/honesty).

Despite the aforementioned differences among schools and students, President Bush presupposed that there was enough commonality among the nation's schools and school children to create tests that allow for massive testing. It almost goes without saying that the proposed tests would have reflected the dominant ideology and would have been supportive of the ideas, beliefs, and values of the dominant class, with little to no regard for the variance in schools and students. As demonstrated in previous chapters, the students most likely to be harmed by such testing are the underserved. His idea for national standards and testing can be evinced in *Goals 2000: Educate America Act*, signed on March 26, 1994. It emerged from a document crafted by governors without input from researchers or teachers. Given its authors, it greatly appealed to politicians and test makers. The bill's purpose was the following:

SEC. 302. PURPOSE.

(a) PURPOSE.—It is the purpose of this title to improve the quality of education for all students by improving student learning through a long-term, broad-based effort to promote coherent and coordinated improvements in the system of education throughout the Nation at the State and local levels.

(b) CONGRESSIONAL INTENT ... It is the intention of the Congress that no State or local educational agency will reduce its funding for education or for education reform on account of receiving any funds under this title. (¶ 1 & 2)

The legislative commissions, reports, and bills causes one to wonder, whose agenda is really driving education and reading research?

Federal Funding for Reading Comprehension
Research: A Drying Well

There is an African proverb that states, "When the water in the hole diminishes, the animals regard each other differently." The linkage between federal funding and the power to influence what is considered knowledge and how it is measured is obvious. By gaining access to funding, researchers can determine the types of research and research methods considered acceptable and supportive of social and political agendas. This viewpoint was most evident in the call for voluntary national tests in reading and math. On November 13, 1997, President Clinton signed P. L. 105–178, which reinstated *Elementary and Secondary Education Act* (ESEA) funding and attached the means for voluntary national testing under the guidance of National Assessment Governing Board (NAGB). One of the fears among some politicians, reading researchers, school administrators, teachers, and social activists was that voluntary national tests in reading would result in a return to very narrow definitions of reading. This has, in fact, become a reality. But, there were other concerns. First, there was a concern over the effects of an overuse of standardized reading tests in which the evaluation of reading performance would revictimize the very children that most politicians suggested they were aiming to help. Second was concern about the imposition of the federal government in determining the link between funding and involvement in the voluntary national tests. Whereas the federal government argued that there was no real link between the states and school districts that voluntarily became involved in the national testing movement, some politicians and researchers doubted this position. They argued that school funding would be affected by the results of national tests; their fears have been realized at all levels of funding. States and school districts that did not participate in voluntary national tests were concerned that the government would use "flex funds" (government funds that are used as the state deems fit) to create privileges and opportunities for the more able students, thus creating greater inequity between the "haves" and the "have-nots." Under the current administration of President George W. Bush, the voluntary national testing movement is mute as the *No Child Left Behind Act* (NCLBA) requires annual testing in reading, among other subjects and annual reports of test performance disaggregated by race, class, and gender.

Grassroots of Opposition

There is a growing discomfort among some reading researchers— Coles (2000), Cunningham (2001), McQuillan (1998), Willis and Harris (2000), among others—about what appears to be a return to a narrow definition of "reading" as bounded by experimental studies based on "biological" determinism, and inheritability of phonemic awareness genes, as measured by standardized intelligence and reading tests. The wars are more critical than may appear at face value. The debate on the surface level is a discussion of beginning reading instruction; however, the real debate is over who determines the definition of reading, how reading is measured, and the purpose of reading in schools. If the best that the federal government can do is to re-instantiate biases in research on reading while reclaiming the veracity of scientism, as a nation we have not come far over the last century.

The politicization of reading research at the close of the 20th century is unlike any time in its history. Reading comprehension research and testing have been spurred on by three separate, yet interconnected, interests: (a) the competition for government funding for reading research; (b) a return to positivistic, behaviorist, and mechanistic foundations of educational psychology; and (c) the revenue generated by the publication of school textbooks, tests, and consumable materials. In the United States researchers, as well as politicians and the general public, have been led to believe that "science" holds the answer to the alleged reading crisis. According to Popkewitz and Tabachnick (1992), this view of science "seeks to impose rigor by demanding that theoretical concepts be reducible to variables that can be statistically manipulated from which formal, logical statements can be derived" (p. 15).

Throughout this book, I have documented how, despite the changes in the theories of reading comprehension, the increased amount of research that offered insights into how reading comprehension occurred, and sophisticated statistical procedures, with few exceptions the field has remained virtually unchanged. Changes have not occurred because the philosophical assumptions that undergird most reading comprehension theories and tests are inadequate and cannot account for racial/ethnic epistemologies and linguistic variance that work together with reading the world and word, long before students arrive at school. Therefore, imprecise measures of reading comprehension continue to disappoint, especially for the Underserved.

As educational psychologists, reading researchers, and politicians create new legislation based on scientism, we are witnessing a resurgence of reading comprehension studies that support objective measures, yet fail to acknowledge that the measures have never been objective. They have always supported someone's idea or standard, in this case, White, middle-class, and English speaking. I submit that the debates are not really about beginning reading instruction, whole language versus phonics, or cognitive versus behavioral psychology. The debates are really over who will control the minds and the thinking of future generations of American school children as future workers. As Ladson-Billings (2000) warns, "We must be mindful of the ways 'the research' may render the researcher invisible" (p. 272). Why are the researchers still largely White middle-class folk who disregard the research of people of color (note the bibliographies and references they cite in their reports, articles, chapters)? It is little wonder why the research and reform efforts have done little to raise the reading scores of "at-risk" and poor children, as well as many Children of Color; they clearly are not the focus of the research, despite the claims to the contrary. Researchers who uphold biological, behaviorist, and mechanical notions of

reading and reading comprehension fail to acknowledge the philosophical as well as racist roots of their viewpoints.

As documented in previous chapters, there is research that suggests both standardized intelligence and standardized reading
comprehension tests are poor indicators of success for all students.
When taken to extremes this can be a very dangerous idea. In 2000,
for example, a small-town newspaper in Illinois informed the public that students failing to do well on statewide achievement tests
in reading and math were going to be held accountable. For what
will the students be held accountable, poor test construction? In
Illinois, for instance, test developers of statewide testing mistakenly
used White characters in their adaptation of a children's book about
African American children. This oversight drew criticism from the
author of the text, university researchers, test developers, and the
Superintendent of Education, who saw the change as a feeble and
misguided attempt to include literature about (although not by) children of color. Few teachers, parents, or students are impressed by
feeble attempts to be culturally sensitive to diversity by test developers who simply change the names of characters and their roles in
passages to sound more ethnically diverse. Whether consciously or
unconsciously, the test developers' use of works about people of color
does not compensate for their continued use of standardized tests
that employ the same methodology that was used nearly a century
ago. A more recent example is found on the New York Regents tests
that have altered literature selections so as not to offend students
and so as not to appear to be supportive of liberal thinking; it does
not seem to the testers that their support of conservative thinking is
tantamount to censorship. Our use of standardized reading tests as
a barometer of school success will continue until meaningful resistance among stakeholders is created.

National Assessment of Educational Progress

Since the 1960s, the U.S. government also has sought to understand
how well schools were educating the nation's children. Historically, the federal government has had interest in, and varying levels of oversight of, national education efforts. In 1963, for instance,
the U.S. Congress created the National Assessment of Educational
Progress (NAEP) to make "objective information about student per-

formance available to policymakers." Annual assessments began in 1969 in reading, mathematics, science, writing, U.S. history, civics, geography, and the arts; however beginning in 1980, assessments were conducted every two years.

The *Reading Framework for the National Assessment of Educational Progress: 1992– 2000* offered the following definition of reading comprehension: "Reading for meaning involves a dynamic, complex interaction among three elements: the reader, the text, and the context. The context of a reading situation includes the purposes for reading that the reader might use in building a meaning of the text" (p. 12). In line with these more constructivist understandings, changes also were made in the assessment of reading comprehension:

> • It examines students' abilities to construct, extend, and examine the meaning of what they read through the use of items that elicit a variety of responses to both multiple-choice and open-ended tasks.

> • It assesses student performance in different reading situations—reading for experience, reading to be informed, and reading to perform a task — by using authentic, "real-life" texts. Students in grades 8 and 12 are permitted to choose from among different short stories.

> • It includes special studies to examine other aspects of reading, including the reading fluency of students and their reading habits and practices. (NAEP, 2000, p. 1)

Similar to other educational reform efforts, changes in NAEP did not change at the philosophical level. The philosophical assumptions that drove NAEP at the onset continue, although there is now authentic narrative and expository texts drawn from students everyday experiences with text, in and out of school. In short, NAEP does not go far enough in reconceptualizing reading comprehension or reading assessment. Kincheloe and McLaren (2000) put it this way, "In this context power discourses undermine the multiple meanings of language, establishing one correct reading that implants a particular hegemonical/ideological message into the consciousness of the reader" (p. 284). Thus, NAEP, perhaps unwittingly, attempts to essentialize the "American experience" as if it were a singular experience for all U.S. school children.

Four different aspects of reading are being tested: forming a general understanding, developing an interpretation, making reader and text connections, and examining content and structure. Only the last aspect is new; the first three existed before but under slightly

> **Basic:** This level denotes partial mastery of prerequisite knowledge and skills that are fundamental for proficient work at each grade level.
>
> **Proficient:** This level represents solid academic performance for each grade assessed. Students reading this level have demonstrated competency over challenging subject matter, including subject-matter knowledge, application of such knowledge to real-world situations, and analytical skills appropriate to the subject matter.
>
> **Advanced:** This level signifies superior performance.

Figure 8.2   From National Assessment of Educational Progress, Achievement Levels.

different titles. Achievement levels also changed over time from five (rudimentary, basic, intermediate, adept, and advanced) to three (basic, proficient, and advanced). NAEP assessments now reflect one of the following achievement levels Accordingly, National Center for Educational Statistics (NCES) has agreed to temporarily use "the minimum scale scores for achievement levels as basic, proficient, and advanced … [as] provided by law" (p. 2). Figure 8.2 shows the NAEP recommended levels of proficiency in reading as a guideline for understanding reading performance.

Accommodations for students who are learning disabled or who have limited English proficiency are more clearly outlined than previously (beginning in 1998, prior to which no accommodations were made). Early versions of the NAEP used a traditional format to test reading comprehension, that is short and long reading passages followed by multiple choice questions ranging in difficulty from literal to inferential. Newer versions include space for constructed responses, written short or extended responses. The constructed response items are designed to offer students the opportunity to respond in their own words, which is a clear improvement over multiple choice (forced choice) responses. The written responses are evaluated based on "information from the reading passage" (NAEP, 2000, p. 16). This hardly seems to be drawn from constructivist notions, even those that suggest composing, mental, or propositional models, but instead is as text-bound as other earlier forms of comprehension measurement. In addition, students' written responses are evaluated by a rubric designed to guide evaluators (raters). Each rater evaluates the writing, both qualitatively and quantitatively. Implicit in this idea

---

Fourth Grade Reading Achievement

The following sample passage is from Charlotte's Web, by E. B. White, (1974). Similar to NAEP items, it helps illustrate the kinds of skills expected of students:

Having promised Wilbur that she would save his life, she was determined to keep her promise. Charlotte was naturally patient. She knew from experience that if she waited long enough, a fly would come to her web; and she felt sure that if she thought long enough about Wilbur's problem, an idea would come to her mind. Finally, one morning toward the middle of July, the idea came. "Why how perfectly simple!" she said to herself. "The way to save Wilbur's life is to play a trick on Zuckerman. If I can fool a bug," thought Charlotte, "I can surely fool a man. People are not as smart as bugs."

Students at the *basic* level are able to read the passage and tell what Charlotte promised Wilbur.

Students at the *proficient* level are also able to describe why Charlotte thought she could fool Zuckerman.

Students at the *advanced* level recognize that Charlotte compares waiting for ideas to entrapping a fly.

http://www.ed.gov/Speeches/04-1997/attach2.html

Figure 8.3   Attachment to Secretary Riley's April 29, 1997, Statement on voluntary national tests for reading and math.

is that raters are sufficiently knowledgeable of racial/ethnic and linguistis differences to make qualitative decisions that support a wide range of acceptable responses. (see Figure 8.3)

The evaluation of constructed responses is bounded by cultural understandings and common sense expectations, or what Hall (1982) might call a preferred reading much like responses on the multiple-choice items. Because of cultural beliefs, some children would find it difficult to reconcile animals that speak to one another.

Explanations for why students are performing poorly have reflected the reading comprehension theories popular when the data was released. The labels attached to students' low performance on standardized reading tests often are used to convey much more than academic progress. For example, from the racially and economically charged 1960s, educators have used phrases like "culturally disadvantaged" and "cultural deficit" to describe low performers. New labels that have replaced the old ones include "at-risk" and "struggling readers." The latter labels, like their predecessors, convey messages that reach beyond student academic achievement, especially when accompanied by NAEP aggregate group statistics. The labels provide encoded messages that suggest the failure of students (their family and racial ethnic group may also be implied) but not of the educational system or that a history of social and economic oppression is to blame for poor performance.

Historically, reading comprehension research has tried to distance itself from, and avoid the acknowledgment of, race/ethnic, and to some extent, linguistic differences among readers. Reading comprehension researchers have attempted to isolate their work "as if they operated in an unchanging world" (Jolly & White, 1995, p. 65). And, to re-emphasize the point, reading comprehension testing continues to highlight racial/ethnic differences by comparisons of the reading comprehension test performance of Whites, as superior, over all other groups. NAEP, for example, interprets and publishes "sub group" reports that detail race/ethnic, gender, and socioeconomic class differences, and more recently accommodations for limited English proficiency (LEP) and ableness (learning disabilities).

Theoretically, the NAEP tests are given to a nationwide representative sample of U.S. school-aged children. The NAEP reports, also known as *The Nation's Report Card*, makes special (and repeated) mention of the representativeness of their student populations, stating "the sampling design is rigorous and representative of the total U.S. population in terms of region, size, and type of community, gender, race, and ethnicity" (NAEP 1992, p. 15). The *2003 Report Card*, for instance, includes comparison of student reading scores nationally, by state, and by jurisdictions. The latter category consists of Department of Defense Domestic Dependent Elementary and Secondary Schools and Department of Defense's Dependent Schools (overseas). Unlike assessments in earlier years, where students self-identified their race/ethnicity, in 2003 school records were used. Importantly, there has been a racial/ethnic demographic shift in the nation. Therefore, a comparison of the 1992 and 2003 data reveals that of the 300,000 students in Grades 4 and 8 tested, the Latino/a population has risen (from 7% to 17% and from 8% to 15%, respectively); the White population has decreased (from 73% to 60% and from 72% to 63%, respectively) and the African American population has remained nearly constant (data were not supplied for Asian Pacific Islander and American Indian Alaskan Native students).

Aggregate group scores in the *2003 Report Card* for Grades 4 and 8 reveal the average reading scores by gender (female students scored higher than males); White and Asian Pacific Islander students scored higher than African American, Latino/a, and American Indian and Alaskan Native students (with Whites scoring highest); and students who received free or reduced lunch (as an indicator of economic status) improved over previous years and indicated little difference from those who did not receive free or reduced lunch. There is a cautionary note issued by NAEP (2003b) with regard to interpreting the data on reading group scores:

> ... it is important to keep in mind that there is no simple, cause and effect relationship between membership in a subgroup and achievement in NAEP. A complex mix of educational and socioeconomic factors may interact to affect student performance. (p. 11)

This statement is not new and adds little to what is already known, or at least what history elects to document. Even though supporters of NAEP acknowledge the shortcomings of their instrument, it does not absolve NAEP, or any other government agency, of their responsibility to create more socially just and equitable set of measures. By way of example, the performance measures presented make no accommodations for students from culturally and linguistically nonmainstream backgrounds. Equally disturbing in this set of guidelines is the notion that the literature used is free from cultural and linguistic bias; no such literature exists. As a way around such criticisms, NAEP has increased the number of expository passages as well as narratives that feature animals, with little regard to how students from some cultures do not engage in fantasies.

The literature used by NAEP, as well as on standardized intelligence and reading tests, is overly representative of thoughts, values, and beliefs of White male authors—even when they use protagonists of different cultural groups. The use of selective literature, in this case literature that reflects dominant groups interests more than the interests of other groups, suggests that those most familiar with the literature (either from personal reading or from assigned readings in school) will most likely perform better on the tests. The literature used in most standardized reading comprehension tests and the literature used by NAEP continue to reflect the worldviews, beliefs, values, and standards of dominant groups more than others. Although the more recent versions also include literature selections written by women and by People of Color, in a very real sense, they continue to empower those most like them. More importantly, test questions are written by members of dominant groups and tests are piloted on groups that are not representative of all U.S. public school children.

During fall 2003, NAEP released its latest findings on reading performance of U.S. school children (an unusual and perhaps political move since data were derived in 1998, 2000, and 2002). Over the past 30 years, one of the most consistent findings reveals that as a group, students of color (especially African American, Latino/a, and Native American) do not perform as well as their Euro-American peers on the reading comprehension subtest. Allegedly, the concern for the lagging performance of these students has become so great as to constitute (a) a national crisis in education; (b) a "new" research agenda that focuses on the improvement of reading comprehension research with federal grant support (but only research that is aligned with the official view of how reading comprehension is understood and best measured need apply); (c) identification of teacher qualities needed to improve reading comprehension instruction, albeit without any particular concern for context or power/authority issues within the classroom; and (d) improved reading tests, although most continue to repeat, in modified formats, tests constructed during the early 1900s.

Finally, despite concerns raised by Scholars of Color in the 1920s, NAEP results continued to be reported and published as if all groups were equal, that is, as if all groups had access to the education that would be most beneficial to meet their needs. In addition, the results of reading comprehension are disaggregated by race, class, and gender as well as English proficiency and ability (in the case of special needs students). McCombs, Kirby, Barney, Darilek, and Magee (2005) reveal in *Advancing Literacy,* a Carnegie Report, that despite modest improvement in reading achievement at the primary level, "many children are not moving beyond basic decoding skills to fluency and comprehension" (p. xi). As they note, Students of Color and students from economically depressed communities continue to lag behind.

National Institute of Child Health and Development

G. Reid Lyon (1997) of the National Institute of Child Health and Human Development (NICHD), Washington, D.C., is a psychologist who presents the ability to read as a public health issue and gave an overview of the reading research conducted by NICHD since 1965. NICHD is an extremely well-funded governmental agency (having garnered millions, if not billions, of dollars) that, according to Lyons, has conducted several theoretically driven longitudinal studies of reading involving thousands of children who reflect the entire population. Lyon outlined the three questions that have framed reading research by NICHD:

1. How do children learn to read?

2. Why do some people have difficulty learning to read?

3. For which children are which teaching approaches most beneficial at which stage of the development?

These questions represent a wonderful research agenda. I would certainly support research that seeks to answer them. But, what happens among the formation of research questions, research methods of inquiry, data collection, and interpretation that turns questions into boundaries? Is there more than one valid way of proposing answers to these questions?

I am struck by how similar these questions are to those posed nearly 70 years ago when two leading reading researchers, Gates and Bond (1936), published their review of studies of reading research conducted in New York City schools. The Director of Attendance and Welfare, George H. Chatfield, had expressed that "a large proportion of the cases of truancy, delinquency, and school maladjustments were the results of a frustration produced by inability to read well" (quoted in Gates & Bond, 1936, p. 466). Lyon's claims were not new. Historically, importance has been placed on the ability to read, especially its role in the future educational, economic, and social well-being of students. In addition, the failure to learn to read has been linked to students' lack of motivation, poverty, and defiant behavior. So, what has nearly 70 years and millions of dollars of NICHD reading research studies taught us about reading?

Lyon (1998), sounding a great deal like Herbert Spencer, queried, "Whose belief systems will drive research and practice?" Harding (1991) in her groundbreaking book *Whose Science? Whose Knowledge: Thinking From Women's Lives,* appeared to have answered this question over a decade ago:

> The norms themselves have been constructed primarily to produce answers to the kinds of questions an androcentric society has about nature and social life, and to prevent scrutiny of the way beliefs that are nearly or completely culturewide and in fact cannot be eliminated from the results of research by these norms. (p. 117)

Whose belief systems? Did Lyon mean to refer to the belief systems that have served as the foundation and shaped much of reading research—scientism, psychologisim, or racism—and the beliefs of the dominant class? Clearly, he stated the standards by which research would be accepted, only if it is perceived as "scientific" and interpreted as objective, replicable, unemotional, and free of individual belief systems, thus, revealing his own standards.

At the 1998 International Reading Association annual conference, I attended a session where Barbara Foorman of the Houston Research Center, former director of the Texas Interventions Project, and principal investigator of several reading studies funded by NICHD, gave a presentation offering some insight into how the questions (by Lyon listed earlier) can become re-envisionaged in the minds of researchers during the research process and following. Of particular import are her descriptions of the school district, schools, teachers, and students, which trace her associations to deeply held beliefs, values, and the philosophical assumptions of positivism, social Darwinism, and biological determinism as well as racism. These associations belie whatever she had to share regarding the theories or the statistics she used to support her claims.

First, she commented that the schools (in which the studies were conducted) were not the schools that the researchers would have liked; that is, they were populated by children of color, children who live in poverty, children who are recent immigrants, and children whose first language is not English or Standard English. Why would they have not chosen to conduct a study in these schools? Was it because the children were from inner-city, economically poor neighborhoods? Why was the school perceived as a "tough" school?

Second, she mentioned that the teachers were not pleased with the students' behaviors. Why did the teachers' perceptions of the children suggest that the children were emotionally and behaviorally troubled? Were the children in the study any tougher or more troubled than the children who attended the schools of West Paducah, Kentucky; Pearl, Mississippi; Jonesboro, Arkansas; Edinburgh, Pennsylvania; Stamps, Arkansas; Norwalk, California; Springfield, Oregon;

or Littleton, Colorado? In these latter communities, largely rural and White, were the children less troubled emotionally and behaviorally? I wondered, reconsidering Lyon's questions, what belief systems and values do the teachers and researchers hold that allow them to remain unaffected by their racial, class, and linguistic biases? What is most troubling about comments made by both Lyon and Foorman is that they represent an integral part of massive effort to win the consent of an unsuspecting public. Would people support research by researchers that viewed them as ignorant human beings?

Their descriptions of reading research returned full circle to where it began over a century ago. New reading comprehension research studies unapologetically claim that biological and genetic differences among children account for reading failures. Not surprisingly, the children who seemingly lack specific biological traits or specific genes, are those that look least like the researchers. More pointedly, the underserved consistently are represented as "allegedly" *genetically* and *intellectually* inferior to White, upper- to middle-class, native English speakers. The philosophical foundations of reading research as described by Lyon and Foorman are frighteningly similar to the earlier notions espoused by Comte, Spencer, Darwin, Peirce, James, and Dewey.

National Reading Panel Report

The National Reading Panel (NRP, 2000) was constituted in 1997, when the U.S. Congress mandated that a panel of experts be convened to review the extant research on reading. The Panel comprised 14 members, including physicians, educational psychologists, a nuclear scientist, an accountant, parents, teachers, and reading researchers. Reportedly, the panel's initial review of the literature in reading found an estimated 100,000 published research studies on reading since 1966 and an additional 15,000 prior to that date (actually, an electronic review was conducted using selective indicators or descriptors followed by a manual review). Due to the large volume of studies, the panel limited its review to those studies that met their concept of "scientific studies," which included experimental and quasi-experimental studies. And, because of the large volume and variety of research studies in reading, the panel elected to focus on the following key areas (many of which were identified in *Preventing Reading Dif-*

ficulties [PRD]): alphabetics; fluency; comprehension (vocabulary, text comprehension instruction, teacher preparation and comprehension strategies instruction); teacher education; and computer technology and reading instruction. Reminiscent of older chronicles and reviews of reading comprehension research, this federally supported project continues an Anglocentric tradition; that is, it reports all like-minded research conducted in countries where Anglo populations represent the majority. As Freire articulates, "Only those who have power can generalize and decree their group characteristics as representative of the national culture. With this decree, the dominant group necessarily depreciates all characteristics belonging to subordinate groups, characteristics that deviate from the decreed patterns" (Freire & Macedo, 1987, p. 52). What is interesting here is the absence of discussions of race, class, gender, and linguistic difference, given that the recommendations from this research are to be used in the reading instruction of all U.S. school children.

The National Reading Panel (NRP, 2000a, 2000b) *Executive Summary* on comprehension notes that comprehension:

> is critically important to the development of children's reading skills therefore to the ability to obtain an education. Indeed, reading comprehension has come to be … essential not only to academic learning in all subject areas but to lifelong learning as well. (p. 13)

The NRP identified three predominant themes in their review of the research on the development of reading comprehension:

> 1. Reading comprehension is a cognitive process that integrates complex skills and cannot be understood without examining the critical role of vocabulary learning and instruction and its development;
>
> 2. Active interactive strategic processes are critically necessary to the development of reading comprehension
>
> 3. The preparation of teachers to best equip them to facilitate these complex processes is critical and intimately tied to the development of reading comprehension. (p. 4-41)

This subgroup's report notes, "despite the critical and fundamental importance of reading comprehension, comprehension as a cognitive process began to receive scientific attention only in the past 30 years" (p. 4-11). The subgroup used Harris and Hodges's (1995) definition of comprehension: "The construction of the meaning of a written or spoken communication through a reciprocal holistic interchange of ideas between the interpreter and the message in a particular communicative context" (p. 39). The subgroup also notes that reading comprehension so defined is not new, citing Benjamin Franklin and Thorndike as proponents of similar ideas. However, the definition posed by Harris and Hodges also includes a further explanation that the subgroup also documents:

> The presumption here is that meaning resides in the intentional problem-solving, thinking processes of the interpreter during such an interchange, that the content of meaning is influenced by that person's prior knowledge and experience, and that the message so constructed by the receiver may or may not be congruent with the message sent. (National Reading Panel Report, 2000a, quoted on p. 4-41)

This addendum does not look significantly different from notions of comprehension suggested by Huey (1908).

The so-called scientific review used the descriptors "vocabulary" and "text comprehension" for studies published between 1979 and 2000. For studies to be included in the review they had to meet select criteria: (a) published in English in a referreed journal, (b) focused on children's reading development in the age/grade range from preschool to grade 12 and (c) used an experimental or quasi-experimental design with a control group or a multiple baseline method. In addition the comprehension subgroup required studies of text comprehension instruction to

> (a) be relevant to instruction of reading or comprehension among normal readers, (b) published in a scientific journal (they did make a few exceptions and used dissertations and conference proceedings), (c) have an experiment that involved at least one treatment and an appropriate control group or have one or more quasi-experimental variables with variations that served as comparisons between treatments, and (d) have the participants or classrooms randomly assigned to the treatment and control groups or matched on initial measures of reading comprehension. (National Reading Report Panel, 2000a, p. 4-41)

Using both sets of criteria of "scientific studies" as a guideline for comprehension instruction, the subgroup identified 47 vocabulary studies and 203 text comprehension studies. Many studies were eliminated because they failed one or more of the criteria (prompting the subgroup to note the lack of quality in the studies), or, as in the case of vocabulary, studies were eliminated from consideration if they dealt "exclusively with learning disabled or

other special populations, including second language learners"
(p. 4-16).

The subgroup identified 16 categories of instruction and 7 that
met their notion of "scientific" proof for use to improve comprehension with normal readers. The seven strategies are comprehension
monitoring, cooperative learning, graphic and semantic organizers, question answering, question generation, and summarization.
Further, the subgroup notes that in many of the studies, researchers
not the classroom teacher taught comprehension strategies during
experiments. The subgroup revealed that following instruction, there
was moderate improvement as determined by standardized reading
tests and greater improvement following more intensive instruction.
The use of multiple strategies appeared most effective, and the report
pointed out the need for improved teacher preparation in comprehension instruction.

The argument proposed by the subgroup on comprehension is
that there needs to be more rigorous "scientific" studies undertaken and that teachers need to be better prepared and encouraged
to teach comprehension strategies. Obviously, the notion of scientific studies is suspect, but more importantly the shift in perspective is that (a) reading researchers should conduct studies that are
"scientifically or evidenced based;" and that (b) teachers are to be
held accountable for knowing, implementing, and evaluating (to
some degree) comprehension. These ideas are interrelated to reading comprehension research as a struggle over ideology. What is
striking, though not surprising, given the scientism that underpins
this type of research and the rhetoric, if not outright stonewall-
ing on context issues, the subgroup that conducted the review of
research on reading comprehension avoids discussing race, class,
gender, and language (English proficiency) factors that affect reading comprehension processing and reading comprehension test
performance. The underserved, their ability to comprehend, as well
as a history of their marginalization in studies of reading comprehension is not mentioned.

Dissenting Points of View

Not every member of the original NRP supported the views expressed
in the report. In fact, Joanne Yatvin filed a minority view that is an
addendum to the Executive Summary. Yatvin (2000) begins by taking exception to the philosophical framework adopted by the panel:

> From the beginning, the Panel chose to conceptualize and review the field narrowly, in accordance with the philosophical orientation and the research interests of the majority of its members . ... The Panel quickly decided to examine research in three areas: alphabetics, comprehension, and fluency. (p. 1)

She goes on to suggest that the NRP needed to not only identify three models of reading instruction (word identification, word identification plus skills, and integration of language and thinking) but also to have examined the scientific basis of each model. I am struck by the lack of historical reference given to the identification of models for reading instruction, as this book has shown that from the early 1800s educators have identified reading as thinking.

Yatvin (2000) is convinced that the panel's hurried response has developed a set of criteria and procedures for evaluating reading studies because of the need to meet Congressional deadlines. However, she does concede, "The work of the NRP is not of poor quality; it is just unbalanced and, to some extent, irrelevant" (p. 3). Moreover, she did not believe it to be a sound guide for future reading research for the nation. She was correct in her assumption that the NRP's philosophical viewpoints, guidelines, and criteria for evaluating reading research are quickly becoming re-popularized and misunderstood by those in positions to offer federal and state funding and make policy decisions. She calls for greater attention to the diversity of the U.S. school population and the best way to meet the needs of all. Finally, Yatvin ends her response by calling on Congress "not to take actions that will promote one philosophical view of reading or constrain future research in the field on the basis of the panel's limited and narrow set of findings" (p. 3). While the NRP has encouraged and paid members to present at national conferences, Yatvin has used her own finances also to attend conferences to share her minority view.

Other researchers also have voiced dissenting views, while being labeled unpatriotic for the lack of support of the NRP. For example, in a recent essay review of the *Report of the National Reading Panel,* Cunningham (2001) suggests that it reflects a severely outdated form of positivism as espoused by Comte. Like Yatvin (2002), he is fearful, not so much of the use of this particular form of research, but of the "unapologetic appropriation of the term scientific to describe the result of their work" (p. 327) that has permeated facets of reading research for over a century. He wonders about the disinformation that accompanies the use of the term "scientific" and future implications of their framework and guidelines for "funding agencies, reviewers for journals and conference programs" (p. 327). He goes on to suggest that the report's framework may have a "chilling effect on the funding, publication, and influence of all of reading research that fails to follow the positivist methodological standards it prescribes for our field" (p. 329). Cunningham raises several serious questions regarding the definition of science used to inform the panel and several pragmatic questions regarding the Panel's application of their definition and guidelines in their research report.

Coles (2001) has added his dissenting opinion of the NRP *Report* by highlighting several important issues. First, he argues, "The Panel determined *a priori* what is central to successful reading instruction" (p. 3). Then, he suggests that the panel's recommendations mimic calls for direct instruction that surfaced in the mid-1990s. In reading comprehension, this means beginning reading that actually minimizes reading comprehension. Within a behaviorist framework, students would be instructed to learn a hierarchy of small decontextualized skills which, once mastered, would magically lead to comprehension. Finally, he articulates that family zip codes are good "predictors" of academic achievement. A student's zip code (an indication of family income and educational quality of schools in the area, a child's access to educational experiences) is strongly correlated with future school success.

The NRP was in a powerful and enviable position to create opportunities for change, but elected to take the road most often traveled, sustaining the status quo under the rhetoric of scientific research that was conducted for the common good. More troubling than the NRP report is the clear abuse of power used to encourage the adoption of "scientific research" as the only form of knowledge and theory building research worthy of support. By way of example, since the initial press release of the NRP report (April 2000), there has been an aggressive campaign to "get the message out," including free hard and electronic copies with an accompanying video. All these materials have been distributed to state-level educational administrators and administrators at colleges of education nationwide. The panel's overindulgent use and repetition of a "scientific" discourse with words that appear to be neutral and unbiased ("science," evidence-based, research-based, and rigorous research) whitewashes the philosophical and ideological foundations on which these concepts were constructed.

It would seem from the panel's report that race and gender are not important demographic characteristics of students. Given the data supplied in the studies, as well as in the report, the race, class, and gender of the classroom teachers, researchers, and training assistants appear unimportant and supportive of a universalist view in reading research. Such an approach attempts to sanitize research as acultural, neutral, and unbiased. Spina and Tai (1998) address this viewpoint, noting, "not seeing race is predicated on not seeing White as race and denying Whiteness as a focus of critique and analysis. Ignoring the racial construction of Whiteness reinscribes its centrality and reinforces its privilege and oppressive position as normative" (p. 37).

Race and gender are so obviously missing in the NRP, which raises the question "Does race matter?" or at least the question "Did race matter in the panel's review of studies and their final products?" Given the findings offered in the NRP, an uncritical reading would suggest that race does not matter. The Spina and Tai (1998) response centers on an analysis of how dominant White racial ideology works in U.S. society:

> It supports the assumptions that White youth are not all "at-risk" nor are they all "academic superstars." This position grants White youth the privilege to determine their own academic destiny. ... Whiteness remains the dominant racial ideology, not by promoting Whiteness as superior, but by promoting Whiteness as normative. (p. 36)

Not intending bias does not excuse the use of bias and it does not excuse biased stereotypical statements that exist in the original studies. A critical review and oppositional reading of the materials drawn from the NRP (albeit not produced by members of the panel yet seemingly published with their support) suggest a very different interpretation of the process undertaken by the researchers noted above.

There is one startling product, a video, that uses not only patriotic images, music, and text, but communicates a message, intended or not, that highlights the inherent biases of scientism, racism, and classicism that underpins the research. Unashamedly, the video seeks to convince the audience of the veracity of claims made by the research cited. The video clarifies one set of assumptions about race because in nearly every frame in which there are children of color they are being helped by White children. There also is one frame in particular that is deserving of special mention.

Picture this: In the video there are several urban young males of color who appear to be relaxing under a viaduct, in front of a trash bin while a subway car travels in the rear. The frame is accompanied by the following audio: "When children fail to learn to read this downward spiraling continues until children avoid reading and *develop a sense of failure* that affects all other aspects of their lives" (National Institute of Child Health and Human Development, 2000c, emphasis added). The voicing of an opinion held by dominant groups in a government-supported video is an inexcusable use of power that unfairly victimizes males of color. Why is this frame in a "research-based, scientifically rigorous, evidence-based video of early reading?" Where, in this allegedly racially and gender-free report, are the citations of longitudinal studies of young Males of Color who were participants in studies and their life outcomes as young adults?

The NRP's findings were accompanied by a deluge of materials (books, pamphlets, videos, and flyers of Children of Color), all freely distributed at the tax payers expense to academics, schools, and anyone with access to the Internet. I interpret the subtext of the materials filled with color pictures of Children of Color and discussions of (a) closing the achievement gap between low-achieving children and their counterparts (suggesting intellectually superior Whites) and (b) holding school administrators and teachers (and more subtly parents and care givers) accountable for improving reading performance as a means to win consent of the public. The use of these images suggest that the federal government has "played the race card"; that is, they have used race to support claims for educational/reading improvement and reform, while simultaneously ignoring the lack of discussion and acknowledgment of issues of race, specifically, but also issues of class, gender, and Standard American English in the research used to make their case.

The dissenting voices, as you might expect, have been trivialized in academic circles, silenced in political circles, and ignored in public forums. The articulation of how ideological and cultural hegemony becomes part of the terrain in reading comprehension research and testing however does not stop here. The next legislative actions include the historic *No Child Left Behind Act* of 2001 and subsequent support of various panels to mandate an ideology of scientism as educational research; wouldn't Edward L. Thorndike be proud. I suggest the legislation and the mandates that have followed amount to nothing less than coercion, that is legally mandating that the less powerful adopt a way of thinking about reading comprehension that is aligned with the worldviews, beliefs, and values of the power elites. The entire piece of legislation will not be reviewed here, but there are specific sections that pertain to reading comprehension that are worthy of mention.

No Child Left Behind Act of 2001

The "current reading crisis" and all others that came before this one are but a smoke screen for much larger weightier ideological and cultural struggles, that have little or nothing to do with reading and everything to do with who defines knowledge and who gains (or retains) the power to do so. Shortly after taking office, President George W. Bush promised to address the nation's "reading deficit" by ensuring that "no child would be left behind." He based many of his concerns on findings of the NRP, citing specifically their review of over 100,000 studies and their use of "scientifically based research." The President also noted that his legislation would provide funds for reading instruction, but only if it were "scientifically based." Furthermore, NICHD is the clearinghouse for information on reading and for creating standards for the "scientific" nature of reading research, and evaluating such research (Coles, 2001). Coles is correct in his concern for the future of reading research as we are aware many people in positions of power—from funding agencies, to tenuring committees, to publication outlets—strongly endorse scientism. The real danger is to be found in the decision-making based on these troublesome findings.

In accord with the reauthorization of the ESEA under NCLB, it calls for the use of "scientifically based research" as the foundation for many education programs and for classroom instruction. Central to the passage was the idea of helping to close the achievement gap between the academic achievement of White, middle- to upper-middle class, able, native English speakers and all others (available online at http://www.ed.gov/nclb/landing.jhtml). In fact, the NCLB Act states that its purpose is not only to close the achievement gap, but to do so "with accountability, flexibility, and choice, so that no child is left behind" (a term borrowed from M. Elderman's foundation and the cornerstone of the Republican 2000 educational plat-

The purposes of this subpart are as follows:

(1) To provide assistance to State educational agencies and local educational agencies in establishing reading programs for students in kindergarten through grade 3 that are based on scientifically based reading research, to ensure that every student can read at grade level or above not later than the end of grade 3.

(2) To provide assistance to State educational agencies and local educational agencies in preparing teachers, including special education teachers, through professional development and other support, so the teachers can identify specific reading barriers facing their students and so the teachers have the tools to effectively help their students learn to read.

(3) To provide assistance to State educational agencies and local educational agencies in selecting or administering screening, diagnostic, and classroom-based instructional reading assessments.

(4) To provide assistance to State educational agencies and local educational agencies in selecting or developing effective instructional materials (including classroom-based materials to assist teachers in implementing the essential components of reading instruction), programs, learning systems, and strategies to implement methods that have been proven to prevent or remediate reading failure within a State.

(5) To strengthen coordination among schools, early literacy programs, and family literacy programs to improve reading achievement for all children.

Figure 8.4   Part B—Student Reading Skills, Improvement Grants, Subpart 1—Reading First SEC. 1201. PURPOSES.

form). Figure 8.4 shows a detailed list of the student reading skills under this legislation (under Subpart 1—Reading First).

Among the definitions that accompany the *NCLB* is one for *reading*:

(5) READING—The term *reading* means a complex system of deriving meaning from print that requires all of the following:

(A) The skills and knowledge to understand how phonemes, or speech sounds, are connected to print.

(B) The ability to decode unfamiliar words.

(C) The ability to read fluently.

(D) Sufficient background information and vocabulary to foster reading comprehension.

(E) The development of appropriate active strategies to construct meaning from print.

(F) The development and maintenance of a motivation to read. (p. 126)

This definition clarifies what is now considered reading by the federal government. A casual reading of the list of components of reading merely summarizes and restates the research reviewed above, without explanation of its ideological and historical roots or an acknowledgement of shortcomings. Sallach's (1974) observations decades earlier appear to ring, "The suppression of ideological alternatives is an integral extension of the legal apparatus. In the absence of visible alternatives, no mass-based opposition emerges and the structure of control is able to continue unchallenged" (p. 41). Clearly, there is an unstated taken-for-grantedness that the definition is agreed on by all experts in the field. As Comte suggested (see chap. 2), a community of experts could determine the parameters of an idea. In this case, the definition of reading is written irrespective of the century-long journey to broaden reading beyond its cognitive scope. The latter idea suggests that the most adequate definitions of reading must include social, cultural, political, historical, mutivocal, gendered, and class bound understandings and accommodations. It is particularly distressing to learn of federal legislation that has formally established reading research guidelines under the guise of "objectivity" and science for the public health and national security, based on scientism and its inherent racism.

This perspective does not acknowledge the research in reading that has shown that there are multiple ways of interpreting text and that many of these ways represent the cultural and linguistic differences among U.S. school children. No amount of statistical finagling will replace the ideological and cultural hegemony that underlies this perspective.

Importantly, other definitions help to clarify what is considered research and why, again, without explanation of the ideological and historical roots that underlay the notion of scientifically based reading research. Here's the definition given:

(6) SCIENTIFICALLY BASED READING RESEARCH.—The term scientifically based reading research means research that—

(A) applies rigorous, systematic, and objective procedures to obtain valid knowledge relevant to reading development, reading instruction, and reading difficulties; and

(B) includes research that—

    (i) employs systematic, empirical methods that draw on observation or experiment;

    (ii) involves rigorous data analyses that are adequate to test the stated hypotheses and justify the general conclusions drawn;

    (iii) relies on measurements or observational methods that provide valid data across evaluators and observers and across multiple measurements and observations; and

    (iv) has been accepted by a peer-reviewed journal or approved by a panel of independent experts through a comparably rigorous, objective, and scientific review. (U.S. Department of Education, 2002, pp. 126–127)

The endorsement of scientifically based research in this piece of federal legislation articulates the relationship between ideology and practice and moves the notion of scientism from the academy into the schools, classrooms, and homes of the nation's students. Or, as Grossberg (2003) declares:

> It is the struggle to articulate certain codes into a position of dominance, to legitimate their claim, not only to define the meaning of cultural forms but to define the relation of that meaning (and hence the text) or reality as one of the representation, that defines the specificity of the ideological. That is, ideological practices entail a double articulation of the signifier, first as a web of connotation (signification) and second, to real social practices and subject-positions (representations). (pp. 158–159)

The ideas of criticalists notwithstanding, dominant groups have designated themselves as the leaders and intellectuals who will determine the criteria for evaluating all future education research, including renaming their federal office, the Institute of Education Sciences.

More importantly, under justification of the need for *NCLB*, the federal government's WebPages http://www.ed.gov/nclb/overview/importance/edlite-index.html and http://www.ed.gov/nclb/accountability/achieve/achievement_aa.html tie together data and ideas from several disparate sources.

The NCLB web site, for example, displays summarized information complete with colored graphs of the reading performance by racial/ethnic subgroups in comparison to Whites, along with a brief discussion of research findings drawn from NAEP. The composition of the Web Pages are intriguing, as the NRP findings used in support of NCLB did not attempt to disaggregate data based on race, class, or gender. In fact, members of the NRP were disinclined to discuss issues of race, class, or gender publicly. Supporters of NCLB have used the disaggregated NAEP data on racial/ethnic subgroup to emphasize the achievement gap between students of color and their White peers; implicitly this also points to the alleged racial superiority of Whites.

In contradistinction to the avoidance of race/ethnicity reading research, the NCLB Act requires that data on student progress be reported by states and school districts by race/ethnicity (class and gender). Supporters of NCLB reason that by requiring annual progress data by race (along with class and gender), it will make explicit which schools are showing progress and which fail to meet the needs of particular "subgroups." The obvious focus on race, class, and gender, in terms of reading research, is a change in foci. In addition, support of the bill was sought from popular, but conservative, African Americans. For example, conservative commentator Armstrong Williams admitted that he received $240,000 from the U.S. Department of Education to endorse the NCLB (Topper, 2005).

New reading comprehension research and testing initiatives (discussed next) must be aligned with the ideological and cultural hegemony of the dominant class. Furthermore, reading comprehension researchers are encouraged to consider research sites that reflect a diverse population. Given the assumptions on which the funded research is based under these conditions, such research efforts are illusionary; they will not add to what is already known about the performance of underserved children. Dissenters who have voiced similar concerns are portrayed as a threat to democracy because they resist the views of the dominant class.

"Fool's Gold"

The federal government moved swiftly to implement its ideas, especially the adoption of "scientifically based" reading research. In January 2001, at the Center for Advanced Study in the Behavioral Sciences in Stanford, California, there was a project underway: Scientific Principles in Educational Research: Exploration of Perspectives and Implications for OERI (CFEX-Q-00-02-A). Later, Towne,

Shavelson, and Feuer (2001) edited a paper "Science, Evidence and Inference in Education: Report of a Workshop," commissioned by the Committee on Scientific Principles in Education Research for the Center for Education, Division of Behavioral and Social Sciences and Education of the National Research Council. Their findings foreshadowed the text, *Scientific Research in Education* (2002), that Shavelson and Towne edited. In this book, the authors offer a historical perspective as well as an understanding of contemporary life in the pursuit of an education research agenda. The editors attempt to build bridges among all scientific research noting, what they call a "common set of principles" (p. 2). The six principles they identified are:

1. Pose significant questions that can be investigated empirically

2. Link research to relevant theory

3. Use methods that permit direct investigation of the question

4. Provide a coherent and explicit chain of reasoning

5. Replicate and generalize across studies

6. Disclose research to encourage professional scrutiny and critique. (pp. 3–5)

The editors also articulate a thoughtful consideration of the unique circumstances of education research. Their thoughts, supportive in part of arguments made for acknowledging and addressing difference and contexts, are worth quoting at length:

> Education is multilayered, constantly shifting, and occurs within an interaction among institutions … communities, and families. It is highly value laden and involves a diverse array of people and political forces that significantly shapes its character. These features require attention to the physical, social, cultural, economic, and historical environment in the research process because these contextual factors often influence results in significant ways. Because the U.S. education system is so heterogeneous and the nature of teaching and learning so complex, attention to context is especially critical for understanding the extent to which theories and findings may generalize to other times, places, and populations. (Shavelson and Towne, 2002, p. 5)

The intersection of their research and reading comprehension came to a head at the Working Group Conference on "The Use of Scientifically Based Research in Education," held at the Department of Education on February 6, 2002. The workshop strikingly illuminates the process by which the dominant ideology is resurrected as the common sense approach to conducting educational research in general and reading research specifically. The seminar brought to together a diverse group of education and science researchers to discuss "scientifically based research" and what this means for education (transcripts of the seminar are available online at http://www.ed./nclb). Several presentations focused on the meaning of scientifically based research made by Reyna, Feuer, Towne, and Raudenbush, to name a few. Of import here are their comments on what constitutes 'scientifically-based research' as well as Greer's (2002) articulation of the application of scientifically based research in reading.

Joseph C. Conaty (2002, August 8), the former acting deputy assistant secretary for the U.S. Department of Education's Office of Elementary and Secondary Education, seems confident that the new "gold standard" in education will lead to improved research. In short, the idea is to place education research on a hierarchical ladder, where the "gold standard" represents experimental research, the silver represents quasi-experimental research, and all others below these two. The research methods without precious metal distinctions represent ideologies and methods of inquiry that are in opposition to the gold and silver standards. The idea is that education research will follow a medical model. This appears as mythical as the notion of current 'scientific' research in education being a replication of science. Or, as Harding (1991) argues,

> Scientists and science theorists working in many different disciplinary and policy projects have objected to the conventional notion of a value-free, impartial, dispassionate objectivity that is supposed to guide scientific research and without which, according to conventional thought, one cannot separate justified belief from mere opinion, or real knowledge from mere claims to knowledge. (p. 138)

Besides Conaty, other power elites, for example, Grover Whitehurst, the assistant secretary for research, believe that companies that seek to produce educational products also will need to invest in clinical trials and evaluations (Olson & Viadero, 2002). Children, however, are not lab mice; it is difficult enough to have the attention of an entire elementary class at any given moment, much less assume that one will be able to conduct an experiment with little ones who are constantly changing. Oppositional views that challenge the veracity of using only experimental and quasi-experimental methods for educational research in reading have been criticized and trivialized by the power elites.

In terms of reading comprehension, Greer's comments were drawn from the *National Reading Panel Report*. She clarified several misconceptions about the alphabetics findings (where the misconceptions were generated is unclear), and reviewed the findings on reading comprehension. Greer also offered guidelines for future research directions: "We need to encourage research that focuses on finding out more about the reading achievement and instructional needs of more diverse student populations, including students with disabilities" (2002a, p. 60). Her recommendations, falling as they did within the boundaries of this conference on the importance of scientifically based and evidence-based research, are conservative restatements of traditional approaches that, nonetheless, have helped to frame a series of federal grant competitions for improved reading comprehension research and testing. Greer's recommendations appear legitimate, but they continue to beg the question, "what does reading comprehension testing test?" The cyclical thinking becomes a "mixture of prophecy and hope, with a brutal, hard-headed, behaviouristic positivism provided a heady conception which, for a long time, passed itself off as 'pure science'" (Hall, 2003, p. 59). I prefer the term *fool's gold*.

The Rand Reading Study Group

Following the National Academy of Science publication and at the onset of the work of the National Reading Panel, Rand Education and the Science and Technology Policy Institute (S & TPI), sponsored by the National Science Institute, began to focus on reading comprehension, although they had been working with the Department of Education's Office of Department Research and Improvement (OERI) since 1999 to improve education research. Specifically, Rand was asked to "examine ways in which OERI might improve the quality and relevance of the education research funded by the agency" (p. iii). The Rand Reading Study Group (RRSG) was commissioned to "summarize the state of research and research-based practice in the field of reading comprehension, in order to generate a well-motivated agenda for future research that will inform practice in this area" (RRSG, 2001, p. 2). RRSG represented a diverse group of researchers: racial/ethnic backgrounds, philosophical and theoretical viewpoints, research expertise and interests, methods of inquiry, and status in the field. They were brought together to work toward consensus and help shape an agenda for reading comprehension research. In response to the request, RRSG conducted several discussion groups with 14 reading experts (some who participated in the above initiatives supported by the federal government). RRSG posted a draft of its initial work on a public web site (www.rand.org/multi/achievementforall). The site also includes an open discussion board, list of panel members, presentations, outline of the process, responses to the draft (solicited from a group of external reviewers), e-mail updates, and the final report.

RRSG also identified a point of frustration among researchers and practioners: the demand for literacy skills is high and increasing, yet level of reading skills is remaining stagnant. Reading scores of high school students, as reported by NAEP, have not improved over the last 30 years (with States and Districts demonstrating no growth or very slow growth). RRSG (2001) observed that over the last decade reading comprehension instruction is often minimal or ineffective (with the achievement gaps between Whites and Blacks widening), high stakes tests are impacting reading comprehension instruction in unknown ways, the preparation of teachers does not adequately address children's needs for reading comprehension instruction, making good on the federal investment in education requires more knowledge about reading comprehension (pp. 3–6). The group worked over a year and a half and publicly shared the evolution of their thinking on RAND's web site. The culmination of their efforts has been two book-length publications *Reading for Understanding: Toward an R & D Program in Reading Ccomprehension* (RAND, 2002) and *Rethinking Reading Comprehension: Solving Problems in Literacy* (Sweet & Snow).

What has emerged is a reconceptualization of reading comprehension, a new definition of reading comprehension, request for improved reading comprehension assessments, and suggestions for a research and development agenda in reading comprehension. Their ideas, especially those that focus on the underserved, offer the most informed and uncorrupted insights to date; however, ironically their ideas on the latter issues have been virtually ignored. RRSG (2001) outlined what is known in the field and it is worthy of repeating at length:

that reading comprehension capacity builds on successful initial reading instruction, and that children who can read words accurately and
rapidly have a good foundation for progressing well in comprehension. *We know* that children with good oral language skills (large oral
vocabularies, good listening comprehension) and with well-developed
stores of world knowledge are likely to become good comprehenders.
We know that social interaction in homes and classrooms as well as the
larger sociocultural context influence motivation and participation in
literate communities and help construct students' identities as readers,
thus influencing their access to text. *We know* that children who have
had rich exposure to literacy experiences are more likely to succeed.
We know about several instructional practices that are related to good
reading outcomes, although such knowledge is much more extensive for
initial than for later reading. *Finally, we know* that instruction based on
an appropriate and well-articulated alignment between curriculum and
assessment can improve performance in reading as well as other areas.
We know that current approaches to teaching second language learners,
whether in ESL, bilingual, or all-English settings, often do not address
the particular challenges of reading comprehension. *We know* that the
enormous complexities of teaching and the brevity of teacher education
programs have the unfortunate consequence that the vast majority of
novice teachers are ill prepared to engage in practice that reflects the
existing knowledge base about reading. *We know* this situation is particularly critical for special education, ESL, and bilingual teachers who,
while requiring an even deeper understanding of reading, language, curricula and instructional practices than the mainstream teacher, in fact
have even fewer opportunities in their preparation programs to acquire
this expertise. *We know* that professional development in the domain of
early reading instruction is improving, increasingly incorporating information from research about the characteristics of good instruction, but
that such is not the case for reading comprehension instruction in the
later elementary grades. *We know* that a frequent consequence of failure
on high-stakes assessment, namely retention in grade, does not improve
long term reading achievement without specialized instruction. Finally,
while we have a fairly long list of instructional strategies that have been
shown to be effective in targeted interventions or experimental settings,
we need to know how to implement these teaching approaches on a large-
scale basis, into a coherent reading program that spans the elementary,
middle and high school grades. (p. 6, emphasis added)

Given the "knowns" it is surprising that the literature does not
reflect what is known and published about African American Vernacular English by African American scholars. Surely, the work of
Smitherman (1977) or Rickford and Rickford (1995), among others,
should have been read, interrogated, and cited among the "knowns,"
but was not. The failure to include scholarship critical of the mainstream as an alternative perspective is what helps to keep the dominant ideology intact. As Freire points out, "More often than not, U.S.
educators in general and literacy experts in particular fail to estab-

lish political and ideological linkages in their analyses that could illuminate the reproductive nature of schools in this society" (Freire & Macedo, 1987, p. 123). Such continues to be the case in the federal support of reading comprehension research in the United States.

Now that some reading comprehension researchers have admitted to the impact of contextual factors, what will change? Put another way, given this impressive list of what is known about the sociocultural and linguistic influences on reading comprehension by reading researchers, what is being done to adequately and more appropriately address these "knowns" in research and testing efforts? The answer to the question, then, is "very little." However, the rhetoric by the dominant class answers the same query differently. They argue that everything possible is being done to address the needs of the underserved, especially in their most current initiatives and reforms in reading comprehension research and testing. The reality is that the dominant ideology that is guiding federal funding of reading comprehension research and supporting annual testing in reading is likely to force the recognition of the "knowns" further away from academic research and public concern.

We can observe how the thinking of RRSG evolves to highlight that even informed reading comprehension researchers continue to support past ideologies and philosophical assumptions. It also illuminates how RRSG underestimates context and the discriminatory use of power/authority in the lives of underserved children. Ironically, RRSG believes they are speaking in support of the needs of these children. Their position suggests that despite their acknowledgments of the plight of these children, there is little regard for the humanity the children represent and is a sterling example of how the dominant group attempts to represent the interests and values of oppressed groups, yet whose needs are sacrificed by the "intellectual hegemony of the ruling class" (Gramsci, 1971, p. 161). The following statement by RRSG illuminates my point:

> The achievement gap between minority and mainstream children persists. Attention to reading comprehension is crucial in a society determined to minimize achievement gaps between mainstream children and those from ethnic and racial minority groups, between urban and suburban, as well as between middle and working class children. National Assessment of Educational Progress scores, for example, show that 17-year-old African-American students score at the level of 13-year-old European-American students—a gap that has decreased only minimally in the last 20 years. ... Some of the gap can be explained by cultural and social issues, reflected in

the increasing difficulty of making school-based literacy relevant to learners from some groups. Minority children, even middle class members of ethnic minority groups, are likely to have less access to excellent instruction than do White children. (RAND, 2002, p. 4)

The preceding draws attention to the shortcomings of test performance by African American children while offering a weak excuse of the "cultural and social issues" that have impeded progress as if they can explain away centuries of oppressive acts in a phrase, and offering no explanation for the lack of focused research and instructional change. Thus, their opportunity to make the links among these issues, that is, to articulate the relationship of sociohistorical and sociocultural concerns of the underserved to reading comprehension, remains unaddressed.

Redefinition of Reading Comprehension   Most importantly, the RRSG also offers a definition of their conception of reading comprehension. They write that reading comprehension is "as the process of constructing meaning through interaction and involvement with written language. The reading comprehension process includes three dimensions: the cognitive components involved, the outcomes, and reader differences" (p. 8). They claim that each is an important component of reading comprehension. Further, they have observed that these dimensions occur "within a larger sociocultural context which shapes and is shaped by the reader, and which comes into contact with each of the dimensions, influencing knowledge, processing, purposes, outcomes, and the nature of reader differences" (pp. 8–9). They go on to point out possible ways that the sociocultural context may affect student reading acquisition. RRSG notes that "the end of comprehension can be the acquisition of knowledge or the confirmation of knowledge" (p. 9). RRSG, having already acknowledged the sociocultural concerns listed earlier as "we know" statements, proceeds somewhat unwittingly to identify nine cognitive components of reading comprehension: vocabulary, word knowledge, motivation, purposes and goals, cognitive/metacognitive strategies, linguistic knowledge, discourse knowledge, fluency, and integrating nonprint information with text. Their list of these cognitive components of reading comprehension stand in stark opposition to the acknowledgement of sociohistorical concerns that are in conflict with the ideological and philosophical assumptions that are fundamental to the cognitive research in reading comprehension.

Undaunted by the incongruity between their pronouncements of sociocultural concerns and the use of cognitive components of reading comprehension, the RRSG outlines the need for further research in reading assessment. They recognize that "most currently used comprehension assessments reflect the purpose for which such assessments were originally developed—to sort children on a single dimension by using a single method" (RAND, 2002, pp. 111–112). Therefore, they list the following concerns raised by researchers and teachers over traditional forms of reading comprehension assessment:

- Inadequately represent the complexity of the target domain.

- Conflate comprehension with vocabulary, domain-specific knowledge, word-reading ability, and other reader capacities involved in reading comprehension.

- Do not reflect an understanding of reading comprehension as a developmental process or as a product of instruction.

- Do not examine the assumptions underlying the relationship of successful performance to the dominant group's interests and values.

- Are not useful to teachers.

- Tend to narrow the curriculum.

- Are one-dimensional and method-dependent, and often fail to address even minimal criteria for reliability and validity. (RAND, 2002, pp. 111–112)

RRSG suggests that reading comprehension research and testing improvements should include new requirements (while holding steady an empirical foci):

capacity to reflect authentic outcomes; congruence between assessments and the processes involved in reading comprehension; developmental sensitivity; capacity to identify individual children as poor readers; capacity to identify subtypes of poor comprehenders; instructional sensitivity; openness to intra-individual differences; utility for instructional decision-making; adaptability with respect to individual, social, linguistic, and cultural variations; and a basis in measurement theory and psychometrics. (pp. 113–115)

Although the recommendations by RRSG far outpace their predecessors in moving the field toward a more democratic and socially just research agenda, they falter as they compromise their position and side with conservativism and traditional cognitive approaches to reading comprehension research and testing. Given that the RRSG panel recognizes the importance of acknowledging (a) the underserved or racial/ethnic and linguistic difference (although not racial/ethnic epistemologies), (b) historical and contemporary context, and (c) the inadequacy of the philosophical assumptions on which reading comprehension research and testing have been historically based, their recommendations continue much the same research and testing processes. If, as indicated, so much is known about the shortcomings of reading comprehension research and testing, why not propose innovative research agendas that embrace racial/ethnic epistemologies and innovative research that offers culturally responsive assessment formats? For instance, as I have documented, current standardized reading comprehension tests reflect the interests and values of the dominant group, why not suggest tests that reflect the interests and values of children of color, children who live in poverty, children who are recent immigrants, and children whose first language is not English or Standard English? One would have hoped for a more progressive and proactive set of recommendations that acknowledge not only sociohistorical contexts but also the inadequacy of traditional assumptions. It is far more economical to produce reading comprehension tests or other forms of assessment that continue to support the interest and values of the dominant group (making them popular commodities), than to create reading comprehension tests or other forms of assessment that depict the dominant group as intellectually wanting, if not inferior.

Federal Funding of Reading Comprehension Research

A series of federal grant competitions have focused on reading comprehension beginning in 2002 (the awardees and a synopsis of their research projects also are available on the Internet). What is important to note here is that each grant draws from the research described earlier, especially the NRP and NAEP in its purposes, including closing the achievement gap, improving teaching practices, and helping diverse learners. The language used in the grants bespeaks limits in research methodology and racial/ethnic and linguistic groups.

The "background" matter of the Reading Comprehension Research Grant (CFDA 2001) that aims to improve reading comprehension among adolescents proves insightful for this discussion. Without documenting its sources, the grant repeats the negative stereotypes and ideas expressed in the NRP video mentioned earlier in this chapter. Specifically, the grant argues that students with poor reading comprehension skills experience academic failure, and "they suffer disproportionately from social ills such as delinquency and drug use. Their job prospects, and their ability to fully participate in a democracy in which voting requires basic levels of reading comprehension, are limited" (p. 2). These claims are made, without citing supportive research, as if the claims were part of the "common sense" knowledge that everyone believes.

One caveat is worth mentioning. This particular grant (CDFA 2001) states:

> Although earlier decoding problems and later comprehension problems are correlated (and decoding problems lead inevitably to comprehension problems), comprehension problems can occur even for children who are good decoders because of lack of background knowledge, vocabulary, and instruction on how to read for meaning. (p. 2)

In short, the grant merely summarizes and restates previous government supported research and closes rank around long held ideological and cultural hegemonic assumptions.

Likewise, a follow-up Reading Comprehension and Reading Scale-up Research Grant 84.305 (October 22, 2003) seeks to improve reading instruction for "struggling readers" (and by now we all know which students the NAEP data has identified as belonging to this group), and documents the effectiveness of interventions. The grants awarded thus far have gone to many researchers who have long been considered part of the power elite in reading research, some of whom were on the aforementioned federal panels, and to groups offering to use technology/computers to help improve reading comprehension. Although new technologies are provocative, they cannot overcome the use of the inadequate assumptions about reading comprehension. Paradoxically, new reading research funding highlights the importance of closing the achievement gap and addressing the achievement of students in low-income schools, schools that house children from culturally and linguistically diverse backgrounds, schools where children's first language may not be English or where the variant of English they speak is not standard English, but awards grants to many researchers (clearly, not all) whose knowledge of children from these communities as well as their own research among children from these communities is very limited.

Currently, there is a push within the federal government to fund research for a better understanding of reading comprehension. One such grant, NCER-03-2 or CFDA NUMBER: 84.305G seeks to

> (a) understand factors in reading comprehension that contribute to the achievement gap for students; (b) build on that understanding by developing targeted interventions and teaching practices designed to eliminate the achievement gap; and (c) develop assessments that are not only reliable and valid for diverse students of different ages, but that also efficiently identify weaknesses in comprehension that can be addressed through instruction. The Institute intends this program to establish a scientific foundation for educational practice by supporting high quality research on reading comprehension that is likely to produce substantial gains in academic achievement. (December 16, 2002)

One goal is to improve the reading comprehension achievement test performance of children of color, children whose first language is not English or Standard/Academic English, or children who are living in poverty, following a breakdown of performance on national tests (i.e., the National Assessment of Education Progress [NAEP] Report Cards for 2000 and 2002), but usually cloaked in language like "struggling reader," or "at-risk," or schools in high poverty neighborhoods, as if anyone was fooled. Although referencing only NAEP data, the background section of the federal grant offers some insightful language that demonstrates the ideological and cultural frames of reference used by the federal government in drafting the calls:

> Reading comprehension remains a challenge for many adolescents despite mastery of basic literacy skills. Unable to understand school texts, these students fall behind in achievement across the curriculum. Very few students with serious reading difficulties ever graduate from college. They suffer disproportionately from social ills such as delinquency and drug abuse. Their job prospects, and their ability to fully participate in a democracy in which voting requires basic levels of reading comprehension, are limited. (p. 2)

According to the NAEP data, Underserved children are performing poorly, they can trace trends in the NAEP data, but efforts to correct the achievement gap remain largely rhetorical. Nonetheless, insights gained from this type of research could be helpful if it were not restricted to inquiry methodologies that perpetuate racism, classism, and language preferences in their core. Although, issues of difference, especially racial/ethnic difference have always been important to those oppressed by the ideological and cultural hegemony that dictates the course of life in the Unites States, it has become extraordinarily important to take heed of the concerns of this group as the United States evolves into a more multiracial society.

Finally, reading comprehension research study after research study points to an "achievement gap" between White, native-English-speaking, upper- to middle-class students and all others on standardized reading tests (although rarely do these published reports point out that often times Asian American students outperform Whites). The innocuous term achievement gap is translated in reading comprehension research and testing into "at-risk" learner or "struggling reader." Collectively, they have become the 21st-century equivalent of a scarlet letter for children as school districts begin to address their academic needs, in part, to continue to receive federal funding, and, in part because the children have long been underserved academically.

What is troubling, as Baker and Linn (2000) point out is the use of linchpin metaphors, "closing the achievement gap" and "no child left behind." According to these researchers, the first is a metaphor for equity and suggests that "achievement test differences among groups of students differing in first language, socioeconomic status, or cultural background will be reduced by the educational efforts of the schools" (p. 1). The second, more often used metaphor, "no child left behind," "signals the intention of the educational system to address the specific needs of each student" (p. 1). Researchers seeking federal funding to conduct research among children who need to improve their academic reading comprehension performance on standardized reading tests will be attempting to adapt research that ideologically is at odds with the ways of knowing the knowing have developed, their (possible) oppositional reading of the world, and all while holding constant their personal biases and beliefs that the participants are intellectually inferior to White, middle-class, English-speaking children. Lewis (2000) argues that the current educational reform efforts are irresponsible. She characterizes them as attempts to "achieve in an environment that is not responsible for the delivery of universal access or the resources and capital they need to succeed" (p. 7). What new thing will researchers find? It is reminiscent of placing old wine in new bottles. The results are unlikely to change.

Reading researchers who are proponents of scientific and biological viewpoints will point to the inheritability of select genes, the cycle of poverty, and the lack of English proficiency and suggest that there is little to be done about the situation but to prepare laggards to become efficient and loyal workers. They also claim that the data that underpin their research is "scientifically based, evidence based" and ... above question. Further, they argue that it is aligned with medical research and poorly understood by most while ignoring the very paradoxical nature of their work—that is, the very philosophical and ideological basis on which their work was established and stands—clearly was an effort to create and maintain a socially stratified society with non-Whites and poor people on the bottom of the ladder by establishing White middle-class values, norms, beliefs, and language as normal and preferred. It is reckless to assign all social ills to the lack of reading ability, just as it is reckless to assign the inadequacies of reading research and testing to the same. By way of contrast, critical theorists argue that supporters of scientism (from positivism to behaviorism to constructivism) fail to acknowledge that "empirical data derived from any study cannot be treated as simple irrefutable facts. They represent hidden assumptions which the critical researcher must dig out and expose" (Kincheloe, 1998, p. 1198). Former Secretary of Education William J. Bennett claimed that "it is always worst for the underclass, the middle class drives everything. ... The problem is there is a blind unconsciousness in racism" (Range, 1995, p. 30). Later, he shared his observations about the unwillingness of those in power to change the status quo and noted that "if it was happening to White kids, they'd end the damn system" (p. 30).

What makes the current debate interesting is that the former U.S. Secretary of Education, Ralph Paige, is an African American male, who often stood shoulder to shoulder in press conferences, photo ops, and on the web site, with President Bush in support of the *NCLB* legislation. In fact, it was Paige's alleged success (although it has been challenged) as Houston's Superintendent of Schools when standardized tests scores improved dramatically that won him the President's appointment to Secretary of Education. Paige clearly illustrates that not all people of color, or African Americans, think alike. Three examples serve to illuminate this point and are supportive of Hall's (1982) discussion of the power and impact of language cited above. First among Paige's most oft quoted phrases are "soft bigotry of low expectations about who can learn and who can't" (Paige, 2003, March 12). This remark appears to be "tough talk" that swiftly denounces historical and contemporary racism, intolerance, and stereotypes as it proclaims that levels of expectations and attitudes will change. Freire's (1998) comments summarize the lack of logic in thinking:

> [E]ven if the ideological fog [produced by the dominant class] has not been deliberately constructed and programmed by the dominant class, its power to obfuscate reality undeniably serves the interests of the dominant class. The dominant ideology veils reality; it makes us myopic and prevents us from seeing reality clearly. The power of the dominant ideology is always domesticating, and when we are touched and deformed by it we become ambiguous and indecisive. (p. 6)

Although Paige acknowledges that the United States has endured a history of educational inequality—constructed within an ideology of scientism and sustained by the very instruments (standardizes tests) he has chosen to use to dismantle the system—he continues to support the idea that equality can arise from the use of standardized tests. He appears ignorant to the idea that *NCLB* also draws on the very same ideological and cultural hegemony he is supporting. If the philosophical foundations and the conceptual framework are inadequate, the results also will be inadequate. Nevertheless, Paige eschews these details in favor of a central preoccupation with getting the message out that all kids are learners in stalwart support of the *NCLB* legislation.

Second, Paige couples notions of low-income with students of African American and Latino/a descent stating, "I am particularly pleased to see that the achievement gap is starting to close as African American, Hispanic, and low income students account for some of the most significant improvement" (2003, November 13). His enthusiasm is not supported by the data; in fact, it is a zealous overstatement made to suggest the NCLB law is starting to take root and show progress. Continuing, Paige admits, "It is only one year since the last assessment (NAEP) in reading. So, we didn't expect to see much change this year" (2003, November 13). Significant change is unlikely unless the 2002 Trial Urban District Assessment (TUDA) in five large urban public school districts, Atlanta City, Chicago School District, Houston Independent School District, Los Angeles Unified, and New York City Public Schools, with heavily populated students of African American, Latino/a, and Asian Pacific Islander populations shows promise or the NAEP reading comprehension makes significant conceptual and content changes. Under current conditions, students of African American and Latino/a descent will perform significantly behind their White peers in reading achievement as measured on NAEP.

Finally, Paige remarked that the NCLB legislation is the "logical step after *Brown v. Board of Education*, and the *1964 Civil Rights Act* promised an equitable society. The Ancient Greeks used to say, education is freedom. Yes, it is. And *No Child Left Behind* is about freedom and equality and justice. It is about the way we learn about life; it is about life itself" (2004, January 7). Although *NCLB* is a sweeping piece of education legislation, it is hardly life itself. Paige's statement is an inaccurate historical synopsis and review of progress. He has taken two events and substituted them for the entire process of equitable education, a process that remains unfinished. It is significant that Paige, as an African American leader, is supportive of the legislation. And, it is noteworthy that Armstrong Wilson, an African American, Republican, conservative social commentator was paid to support the legislation. Both exemplify how dominant groups have become what Jackson (2005) calls "poverty pimps." That is, to support their claims of supporting oppressed classes, they swear to colorblindness as they elect a person of color from the oppressed class who grew up in poverty to support their causes, while simultaneously gutting social programs to the oppressed.

More Is Required than a Wink and a Nod

Reading comprehension research and testing is oddly positioned to be more proactive, democratic, and socially just. That is, to make real social change, not to pretend to "talk the talk" of equality of educational opportunity and the acknowledgment of difference, but to "walk the walk" for real improvement. First, reading researchers and those interested in reading can continue to trust in scientism to investigate reading performance, albeit a century of such research has only managed to bring us full circle. Second, reading researchers and those interested in reading can look to other philosophical views that are more socially just. The politicization of reading research should serve as a wake-up call for the field to more directly and expressly address the very issues they have denied existed for nearly a century:

the proclivity to disregard the philosophical foundations of reading research and standardized reading comprehension testing and to continue to ignore and marginalize the undercurrent of racism/classism and power that are inherent in past and current ruminations of reading comprehensions.

Under the most sweeping piece of educational legislation and funding to date, the *NCLB Act*, there are many states and districts struggling to meet standardized test score standards. School districts and schools are experiencing harsh federal oversight and crackdowns, if their reading scores remain low. In Illinois, thousands of scores were thrown out, as they did not appear to meet the attendance guidelines (December 2000). The result was that some schools are on the dreaded "watch list." As Gramsci (1971) foretold,

> The school as a positive educative function, and the courts as a repressive and negative educative function, are the most important State activities in this sense: but, in reality, a multitude of other so-called private initiatives and activities tend to the same end—initiatives and activities which form the apparatus of the political and cultural hegemony of the ruling classes. (p. 258)

As documented previously in this chapter, the federal government is not working alone, but has joined with business leaders, philanthropic groups, think tanks and other governmental agencies, and representatives to select expert panels and set agendas for funding educational research.

Supporters of what sounds like a promising, hopeful goal for all children often ignore the historical, cultural, social, linguistic, and economic barriers of reading that many children face. The field of reading research has been careening out of control in response to a rush for federal funding—at the expense of children of color, children who live in poverty, children who are recent immigrants, and children whose first language is not English or Standard English. The current government funding initiatives may well revictimize them. Power elites have been successful in diverting attention away from real social, political, and ethical concerns and solutions as they pinpoint the need to improve reading performance as a means of combating inequities. Political and educational pundits appear numb to the swiftly changing demographics of modern-day school populations and "fail to confront the complexity of the issue in a candid and critical manner" (Unger & West, 1998, p. 2). Ideas of education based solely on a European American middle-class model of upward mobility do not work well for children of color who face a very different set of circumstances in life. In the best-of-all-worlds scenario, educating all children equally would mean that they all had an opportunity to become proficient readers based on the instructional methods best suited for their learning style. Whereas the promises of helping all children "read by third grade" or reading on grade level sound hopeful, the tacit assumption is that all children will have the same opportunities to acquire the literacy skills they need. This "pie in the sky" view of the benefits of reading success suggests that those proposing such notions are insensitive to the challenges faced by the underserved and the nation's history that created and sustains their communities. The new guidelines for funding educational research, if followed, paint a very bleak future for the reading comprehension school experiences for children who have been historically underserved by traditional schooling, reading comprehension instruction, and reading comprehension testing. In the state of North Carolina, for example, end-of-grade reading comprehension tests (Grades 3, 5, and 8) consist of mutiple-choice items not unlike those constructed in 1915. To be promoted to the next grade, the student must successfully pass these reading comprehension tests (along with others in mathematics and writing). Collectively, the end-of-grade tests play a pivotal role in the high stakes standardized testing in North Carolina, prompting Judge Howard Manning to call the response to the achievement of children living in poverty and at risk of failure "academic genocide" (Boger, 2002). Reading comprehension research and testing is complicit in this academic genocide.

Postscript

"When I use a word," Humpty Dumpty said in a rather scornful tone, "it means just what I choose it to mean—neither more or less."

"The question is," said Alice, "whether you can make words mean so many different things."

"The question is," said Humpty Dumpty, "which is to be master—that's all."

(Carroll, 1947, p. 196)

Reading comprehension research and testing has been tossed about on the sea of change: historical, philosophical, and political. Interest in reading comprehension research and testing that began predominantly in educational (cognitive and developmental) psychology has, on occasion, ridden waves of interest from fields outside of education—anthropology, artificial intelligence, linguistics, neurology, and sociology, to name a few—only to become a ripple that fades to the shore. In each discipline, the concept of reading comprehension has been built on dominant ideologies and in support of ideological and cultural hegemony of dominant groups. Collectively the findings of these disciplines exhibit theories that are inadequate to address the complexity of reading comprehension.

In this book, reading comprehension has been portrayed as an idea, a social and political construct, and a mechanism used by dominant groups to help inculcate dominant group ideas, beliefs, values, and practices as *American* ways of knowing in schools and the minds of young children. Various subaltern groups, especially African American scholars, teachers, and activists, have resisted the dominant group's efforts.

In my analysis and interpretation of primary and secondary documents, I have examined and deconstructed associations among multiple sources to articulate how ideological hegemony encouraged dominant ideas to be reflected in reading comprehension research and testing. This account also reveals how deeply embedded ideologies of scientism, racism, and classism are within reading comprehension research and testing. Reading comprehension, so inspired, cannot account for an invisible, intimate, and individual process nor can it suggest how the process can be adequately measured.

As documented throughout this book, the history of reading comprehension research and testing has not followed an unknown, unknowable, or happenstance path. Its history mirrors that of education in the United States and its pathway has enabled dominant groups to use their idea of reading comprehension research and testing to oppress subaltern groups. This analysis of reading comprehension also has articulated relationships among histories and literacies of dominant and subaltern groups. The decision to do so was made very consciously and deliberately to better explain, what is central to understanding in reading comprehension research and testing. I have raised concerns about the insular manner in which reading comprehension research and testing presents the history of reading research, devoid of social and political events and dismissing its racist class based roots, as a celebratory march of scientific triumphs. I find these historical texts, and pretexts, particularly troubling as the nation proceeds to resurrect scientism, racism, and classism as the standard for conducting reading comprehension research and testing while ignoring the racial/ethnic, cultural, and linguistic demographic shifts in the U.S. school population, or because of the racial/ethnic, cultural, and linguistic demographic shifts in the U.S. school population as nearly one third of the U.S. population is now non-White (Berstein, 2007). It is hard to be certain, but my money is on the latter because in the midst of the resurrection of scientism is lip service about the importance of addressing racial/ethnic, cultural, and linguistic demographic shifts via scientific research methods. As we have discovered, this is an old tactic used by dominant groups—to appear to support the oppressed, or at least appear to be working in support of their needs—as they continue to support the status quo. If however, you desire that dominant groups continue the illusion of progress, with contemporary rhetoric that uses the master's tools in new ways, then, a two-tiered education system of haves and have nots will arise.

Reading comprehension is not limited to the definitions of dominant groups nor is it a mysterious act that only a few select people engage in well. At its core, reading comprehension remains an invisible, individual, and intimate process that researchers from various fields have tried to unravel, describe, capture, explain, and test. Most people acquire this skill with little conscious effort. Why, and how, individuals or groups understand the world and read the word in different ways is influenced by myriad of sources, including perceptions of society and their roles in society. Whether or not someone comprehends and how well a person comprehends cannot be measured. Reading comprehension tests were created, in part, to support the dominant ideologies and, in part, to test the theories of reading comprehension researchers.

Re-Envisaging Reading Comprehension

Reading comprehension researchers, historically, have sought to understand how a reader comprehends text, narrowly defined as the print on a page. This notion of text delimits the interpretations to those beliefs, ideas, values, and practices of the dominant class or groups from which the texts are drawn, and the test items created by members of dominant groups. Informed by their dominant ideologies, most reading researchers conceive of reading comprehension in response to the query: *How well* does the reader understand the text? which presupposes that there is a way to comprehend and a way *not* to comprehend the text. As we have seen, this concept of reading comprehension seeks to validate dominant ideologies and ideas by standardizing reading comprehension tests to measure how well theory(ies) match the task of reading and comprehending text.

Children learn to read their world long before they attend school, and like the little boy mentioned in the Introduction, they bring their understandings of the world to school with them as they interact and transact with text and context. When reading texts, especially those used in schools, students are faced with the task of determining which reading, is being called for: preferred, negotiated, or oppositional. For some students, like my son mentioned earlier, reading becomes a negotiation between what they think and believe and what they think the teacher or test wants them to think and believe. For other students, the task is easily negotiable; for still others, the cost of losing self—the freedom of uninhibited creative thought—is prohibitive. They struggle on the ideological and cultural terrain of schooling, and to survive they must negotiate among the racist and class-based landmines.

Inspired by Gardner's (1983) work, I envision reading comprehension research and testing as seeking answers to the question *why* the reader understands or makes meaning in the way that he or she does. Put another way, how is the reader comprehending—on what systems of knowing and meaning making is the reader drawing—and does the reader draw on these systems and sources efficiently (acknowledging that the systems and sources may not be those of dominant groups). This approach allows the reader to explain, share, and describe his or her understanding of text. I am not assuming that there is a correct or incorrect way to understand or that one way is more or less efficient, but I am asking the reader to make clear the sources that he or she uses in the process of understanding or making meaning of text, broadly defined.

What is a more adequate and equitable concept of reading comprehension research and testing? It would begin with an acknowledgment of, and respect for, the epistemologies that all learners use to make sense of their worlds, their experiences, and their realities. It would not be limited to worlds, contexts, and realities of the dominant group. The idea of double and multiple consciousness that informs our thinking and our readings of the world and the word would revolutionize the concept of reading comprehension, sever its ties from dominant ideologies, and permit more than one right answer or one best answer. Moreover, this vision of reading comprehension reflects multiple and multicontextual knowledges as well as multi-accentual and referential use of language as part of meaning making. The language(s) used by learners to express their understandings and their ability to communicate or articulate their understandings would be valued and accepted. Multiple literacies and multiple languages would be the norm, appreciated for their diversity and what they add to our understanding of the worlds in which we live and the words that we use to capture meaning. To comprehend in this sense is to articulate the connections, associations, and understandings between and among individuals and texts (broadly defined).

Reconceptualizing Reading Comprehension Testing

At the secondary level, I envision using excerpts from *The Woman Warrior: Memoirs of a Girlhood Among Ghosts* (Kingston, 1976), *The Joy Luck Club* (Tan, 1989), *The Color Purple* (Walker, 1982), *The*

Bluest Eye (Morrison, 1872), and *Beloved* (Morrison, 1987). I have selected these works because of the way the authors use language to convey more than words on a page. Their language use evokes a sense of place that is ethereal and reflective of the multiple consciousnesses that their protagonists use to read the world and the word, and to survive. Furthermore, each literary work offers a glimpse of our collective histories in the West and the lives we live, but they are so much more. They also offer multidimensional realities that represent very different readings of the world—the worlds we go home to—readings that intersect with the worlds of dominant groups, so often not reflected in reading comprehension theorizing or testing.

Paradoxically, whereas each celebrated author's work reflects her understandings, culture, and language as well as represents her realities, worldviews, beliefs, and values, these are the same systems of knowing that are ignored, maligned, and discouraged when Underserved children seek to make meaning from text. Although each author is a master of the use of Standard American English in the academy and is a recognized intellectual, when faced with ideas that they could not, or elected not to, translate into standard syntax, they drew from their cultural backgrounds as expressed in the language of their homes—their mother tongues—the languages they taste, feel, sing, and dream; the language of their hopes, desires, and heart—the untranslatable languages that carry cultural essence, nuance, knowledge; existing in their own right. Each author in intended and perhaps unintended ways, reconceptualizes, redefines, renames, her realities in stark opposition to the dominant group's portrayals of the model minority, immigrant woman, or single mother, respectively.

What happens when children go to school with a rich expressive language in which they are able to express themselves and their needs, only to be taught in school to disrespect and disvalue their language as inadequate, inappropriate, and ignorant? Their experiences are similar to those of Walker's (1982) protagonist, Celie, who remarks:

> Every time I say something that way I say it, she correct me until I say it some other way. Pretty soon it feel like I can't think. My mind run up on a thought, git confuse, run back and sort of lay down. … Look like to me only a fool would want you to talk in a way that feel peculiar to your mind. (pp. 222–223)

Isn't it ironic that students who look like the authors I have mentioned as members of racial/ethnic groups are repeatedly admonished in classrooms or in the press for their performance on standardized tests, including their results on reading comprehension tests as students who have difficulty comprehending. These children not only read the world well, but many have turned their understandings into word, literary and musical, that speak of the realities that define their world. What I am submitting to you is that the process of reading comprehension as traditionally defined, for many underserved students, may not be one of comprehending text in the traditional sense, but of understanding the context in the critical sense.

I find Hall's thinking about encoding and decoding appropriate for reconceptualizing reading comprehension. His thinking envisages knowledge as multiple and complex, not singular or simplistic. From this perspective, reading comprehension can be conceptualized as multicontextual, -accentual, and -referential. His ideas appreciate and account for, as no other theory or concept, the epistemological systems, culture, and languages of the sender and receiver as well as how each makes meaning possible. Hall (2003) argues convincingly:

> Language is the medium *par excellence* through which things are "represented" in thought and thus the medium in which ideology is generated and transformed. But, in language, the same social relation can be differently represented and construed. ... Because language is by its nature not fixed in a one-to-one relation to its referent ... it can construct different meanings around what is apparently the same social relation or phenomenon. (pp. 35–36, italics in the original)

Hall also suggests that language, in its varied forms, is alive, fluid, changing, and reinventing itself and its users.

Examples of the fluidity of language and its ability to transmit meanings abound. Recall how The Last Poets of the 1960s, early rap artists of the 1980s, and Spoken Word artists of the 1990s read their world, then stepped back from mainstream orthography, semantics, and syntax to re-present ideas through new words and images, creating the hip hop movement. To adopt and promote another view of reality and to communicate those understandings is revolutionary. Other examples reflective of a broader definition of comprehension, both in oral and written text as speakers, listeners, readers, and writers need to know multiple Englishes, hip hop slang, Ebonics, Spanglish, Spoken Word, and text messaging to write, rewrite, and read the word. Being able to understand and communicate what you hear and read, regardless of the medium in which it is sent, requires more than decoding, and more than reading the word, you must also be able to read the world in which it was generated. A final example comes from a reference I used much earlier in this book, from Lazarus's poem, "The New Colossus." This poem, now in light of homeland security concerns of a possible terrorist attack, prompted political cartoonist Scott Stantis (2004) of the *Birmingham News* to write:

> Give me your tired,
>   Your poor,
>   Your huddled masses
>   Your fingerprints,
>   Your DNA, and
>   Perhaps a
>   Urine sample.
>   (*Chicago Tribune*, 1/10/2004, Section 1, p. 11)

Language, and our ability to use it, even cynically, helps us to challenge ideas about life and reality. It is most important in today's context not to lose sight of how language is alive and changing, and what that means for how we conceive of reading comprehension. Hall's notion of communication, his understanding of language use and meaning making should inform reading comprehension research and testing.

Traditional histories of reading comprehension research and testing have supported the ideological and cultural hegemony of the dominant class in reading theories, reading comprehension research, reading comprehension tests, and readers. Unknowingly, educators, teachers, and students have given their consent or, on occasion, have been coerced into the adoption and reproduction of dominant beliefs, ideas, values, and practices. Given that the concepts of reading comprehension and reading comprehension tests are socially constructed and educationally inculcated, they can be dismantled. They must be dismantled if true change and improvement in educational access and opportunity are ever to be a reality in this country. Revolutionary change in reading comprehension calls for theories that are flexible enough to embrace multiple systems of knowing and determine why, under what conditions, and how reading comprehension occurs. It will radically shift educational reform efforts to center reading comprehension research on the very groups it historically has underserved.

References

A Nation at risk: An imperative for educational reform. (1983). http://www.ed.gov/pubs/NatAtRisk/index.html. Retrieved April 13, 2006.

Abell, A. (1894). Rapid reading: Advantage and methods. *Educational Review, #8*, 283–286.

Ackerman, H. (1957). *Leave it to Beaver*. [Television series]. Hollywood: CBS Broadcasting Inc.

Allen, J. (1979). *Taylor-made education: The influence of the efficiency movement on the testing of reading skills*. Washington, DC: U.S. Department of Education. (ERIC Document Reproduction Service No. ED239247) Alliance for Excellent Education: President's Letter sign-on: December 8. Retrieved June 4, 2004, from http://www.all4ed.org/whats_at_stake/PresidentLetter.html.

Allison, M. (1996). Children of the sun. In D. Johnson-Feelings (Ed.), *The best of the Brownies' Book* (p. 50). New York: Oxford University Press.

American Anthropological Association. (1998). *American Anthropological Association Statement on Race*. Retrieved June 14, 2004, from http://www.aaanet.org/stmts/racepp.htm

Anderson, J. (1988). *The education of Blacks in the South, 1860-1935*. Chapel Hill: University of North Carolina Press.

Anderson, J. (1995). Literacy and education in the African American experience. In V. L. Gadsden & D. A. Wagner (Eds.), *Literacy among African American youth* (pp. 19–37). Cresskill, NJ: Hampton Press.

Anderson, R. (1912). A preliminary study of the reading tastes of high school pupils. *Pedagogical Seminary, 19*, 438–460.

Anderson, R., Hiebert, E., Scott, J., & Wilkinson, I. (1985). *Becoming a nation of readers: The Report of the Commission on Reading*. Washington, DC: The National Institute of Education.

Anderson, R., & Pearson, P. (1984). A schema-theoretic view of basic processes in reading comprehension. In P. D. Pearson (Ed.), *Handbook of reading research* (pp. 255–292). New York: Longman.

Apple, M. (1986). *Teachers and texts: A political economy of class and gender relation in education*. New York: Routledge.

Apple, M. (1996). *Cultural politics and education*. New York: Teachers College Press.

Aptheker, H. (Ed.) (1968). *The autobiography of W. E. B. Du Bois: A soliloquy on viewing my life from the last decade of its first century.* New York: International Publishers.

Arlitt, A. (1921). On the need for caution in establishing race norms. *Journal of Applied Psychology, 5,* 179–183.

Arnold, S. (1897). *Stepping stones to literature.* Newark, DE: Silver, Burdett.

Arnold, S. (1899). *Reading: How to teach it.* Newark, DE: Silver, Burdett.

Arnold, S. (1984). *Waymarks for teachers.* New York: Silver, Burdett.

Ausubel, D. (1968). *Educational psychology. A cognitive view.* New York: Holt, Rinehart & Winston.

Ayers, A. (1977). *Language, truth, and logic.* London: Publisher. (Original work published 1936).

Ayers, L. (1918). History and present status of educational measurements. In G. Whipple (Ed.), *The Seventeenth Yearbook of the National Society for the Study of Education: Part 2. Measurement of educational products* (pp. 9–15). Bloomington, IL: Public School Publishing.

Baker, E., & Linn, R. (2000, Fall). Closing the gap. *The CRESST Line: Newsletter of the National Center for Research on evaluation, standards, and student testing,* 1–2, 8.

Baker, L., & Brown, A. (1984). Metacognitve skills and reading. In P. D. Pearson (Ed.), *Handbook of reading research, (Vol. I.,* pp. 353–394). New York: Longman.

Bakhtin, M. M. (1981). *The dialogic imagination.* Austin: University of Texas Press.

Bamman, H. A. (1970). Assessing progress in reading. In R. Farr (1969). *What can be evaluated in reading education,* (pp. 3–9). Newark, DE: International Reading Association.

Barlow, N. (Ed.). (1933). *The autobiography of Charles Darwin, 1809–1882.* New York: Norton.

Barnes, A. S. (1884). *New national fifth reader.* New York: Author.

Barnitz, J. (1986). Toward understanding the effects of cross-cultural schemata and discourse structure on second language reading comprehension. *Journal of Reading Behaviour,* 18 (2), 95–116.

Barrera, R. (1992). The cultural gap in literature-based literacy instruction. *Education and Urban Society, 24*(2), 227–243.

Bartlett, F. (1932). *Remembering: A study in experimental and social psychology.* Cambridge, UK: Cambridge University Press.

Baugh, J. (1999). *Out of the mouth of slaves: African American language and educational malpractice.* Austin: University of Texas Press.

Baugh, J., & Hymes, D. (2002). *Beyond Ebonics: Linguistic pride and racial prejudice.* Oxford, UK: Oxford University Press.

Bay Area Association of Black Psychologists. (1972). Position statement on use of IQ and ability tests, (pp. 92–94). In R. Jones (Ed.), *Black psychology*. New York: Harper Row.

Bell, Y., & Clark, T. (1998). Culturally relevant reading material as related to comprehension and recall in African American children. *The Journal of Black Psychology, 24*(4), 455–457.

Bellomy, D. (1987). Two generations: Modernists and progressives, 1870–1920. *Perspectives in American history* (pp. 269–306). Cambridge, UK: Cambridge University Press.

Bennett, W. (1995). *Modern Maturity.*

Bernier, N., & Williams, J. (1973). *Beyond belief: Ideological foundations of American education*. Englewood Cliffs, NJ: Prentice-Hall.

Bernstein, R. (2007). U.S. Census Bureau News: Minority population tops 100 million. (http://www.census.gov/PressRelease/www/releases/archives/population/010048. html). Retrieved, 6/2/07.

Best, S. (1995). *The politics of historical vision: Marx, Foucault, and Habermas*. New York: Guilford Press.

Best, S., & Kellner, D. (1991). *Postmodern theory*. New York: Guilford Press.

Best, S., & Kellner, D. (1997). *The postmodern turn*. New York: Guilford Press.

Binet, A., & Simon, T. (1905). Methodes nou velles pour le diagnostic du niveau intellectual des anormaux. *L' Année Psychologique, 11*, 191–336.

Binet, A., & Simon, T. (1916). *The development of intelligence in children (E. Kit, Trans.)*. Baltimore: Williams & Wilkins.

Bigelow, E. (1934). Improvement in reading as shown by standard tests. *Educational Method, 13*, 258–263.

Black, E. (2003). *War against the weak: Eugenics and America's campaign to create a master race*. New York: Four Walls Eight Windows.

Blanton, W., Farr, R., & Tuniman, J. (1974). *Measuring reading performance*. Newark, DE: International Reading Association.

Bleich, D. (1978). *Subjective criticism*. Baltimore: Johns Hopkins University Press.

Bloom, B. (1965). *Taxonomy of educational objectives: The classification of educational goals*. New York: David McKay.

Bloom, B., Engelhart, M., Furst, E., Hill, W., & Krathwohl, D. (Eds.). (1956). *Taxonomy of educational objectives. The classification of educational goals. Handbook I: Cognitive domain*. New York: David McKay.

Bobbitt, F. (1918). *The curriculum*. Boston: Houghton Mifflin.

Boger, J. C. (2002). Education's "Perfect Storm?" Racial Resegregation, "High Stakes" Testing, & School Inequities: The Case of North Carolina. Eric Doc. ED471935

Boggs, L. (1905). How children learn to read: An experimental study. *Pedagogical Seminary, 12,* 496–502.

Bond, H. (1924a). Intelligence tests and propaganda. *The Crisis, 28,* 63–64.

Bond, H. (1924b). What the Army "intelligence" tests measured. *Opportunity,* 197–202.

Bond, H. (1927). Some exceptional Negro children. *The Crisis,* 34, 257–259.

Bond, G. L., Clymer, T., and Hoyt, C. (1955). *Developmental Reading Tests.* Chicago: Lyons & Carnahan.

Boone, J., & Adesso, V. (1974). Racial differences on a Black intelligence test. *Journal of Negro Education, 43*(4), 429–436.

Boozer, B. (1978). An alternative to intelligence testing for minority children. *Journal of Negro Education,* 414–418.

Boring, E. (1950). *A history of experimental psychology.* New York: Appleton-Century Crofts.

Bormuth, J. (1963). Cloze as a measure of readability. In J. Figurel (Ed.), *Reading as an intellectual activity. Proceedings of the International Reading Association,* 8. New York: Scholastic Magazines.

Bormuth, J. (1965). Validities of grammatical and semantic classifications of cloze test scores. In J. A. Figurel (Ed.), *Reading and inquiry* (pp. 283–285). Newark, DE: International Reading Association.

Bormuth, J. (1967). Comparable cloze and multiple-choice comprehension tests scores. *Journal of Reading, 10,* 291–299.

Bormuth, J. (1969). Factor validity of cloze tests as measures of reading comprehension. *Reading Research Quarterly, 4,* 358–365.

Bowden, J. (1911). Learning to read. *Elementary School Journal, 12,* 21–23.

Bradford, A., & Harris, J. (2003). Cultural knowledge in African American children. *Language, Speech, and Hearing Services in Schools, 34*(1), 56–68.

Bransford, J., & Johnson, M. (1972). Contextual prerequisites for understanding: Some investigations of comprehension and recall. *Journal of Verbal Learning and Verbal Behavior, 11*(6), 717–726.

Bransford, V. (1906), Science and citizenship. *American Journal of Sociology, 11*(6), 722–762.

Bredo, E. (2002). The Darwinian center to the vision of William James. In J. Garrison, R. Podeschi, & E. Bredo (Eds.), *William James and education* (pp. 1–26). New York: Teachers College Press.

Brookfield, S. (2003). Racializing the discourse of adult education. *Harvard Educational Review, 73*(4), 497–523.

Brooks, F. (1926). *The applied psychology of reading with exercises and directions for improving silent and oral reading.* New York: Appleton-Century.

Brown, H. (1914). The measurement of efficiency in instruction in reading. *Elementary School Teacher, 14,* 477–490.

Brown, H. (1916). *The measurement of ability to read*. Concord, NH: State Department of Public Instruction.

Brown v. Board of Education of Topeka, Shawnee County, Kansas, 98 F. Supp. 797 (1951).

Brown v. Board of Education I, 347 U.S. 483 (1954).

Brown v. Board of Education II, 349 U.S. 294 (1955).

Bruner, J. (1960). *The process of education*. Cambridge, MA: Harvard University Press.

Bruner, J. (1996). *The culture of education*. Cambridge, MA: Harvard University Press.

Buchner, E. (1909). Review of E. B. Huey: The psychology and pedagogy of reading. *Psychology Bulletin, 6*, 147–150.

Buck, G. (1898). Herbartianism: Another phase of the new education. *The Forum*, 376–384.

Buros, (1965). *Sixth Mental Measurements Yearbook*. New Brunswick, NJ: Rutgers University Press.

Butchart, R. (1980). *Northern schools, southern blacks, and reconstruction: Freedmen's education, 1862–1875*. Westport, CT: Greenwood Press.

Cadenhead, K. & Robinson, R. (1987). Fisher's "Scale-Book": An Early Attempt at Educational Measurement. *Educational Measurement: Issues and Practice 6*(4), 15–18.

Caldwell, O., & Courtis, S. (1845,1923) *Then and now in education*. Yonkers-on-Hudson, New York: World Book Company.

Callahan, R. (1962). *Education and the cult of efficiency*. Chicago: University of Chicago Press.

Carlson, E. (2001). *The unfit: A history of a bad idea*. Cold Spring Harbor, NY: Cold Spring Harbor Laboratory Press.

Carnevale, A. R, Gainer, L. J. & Meltzer, A. S. (1988). *Workplace basics: The skills employers want*. Alexandria, VA: American Society for Training and Development.

Carroll, J. (1977). Developmental parameters of reading comprehension. In J. Guthrie (Ed.), *Cognition, Curriculum, and Comprehension* (pp. 1–15). Newark, DE: International Reading Association.

Carroll, J. (1987). The national assessments in reading: Are we misreading the findings? *Phi Delta Kappan, 68*, 424–430.

Carroll, L. (1947). *Through the looking glass*. New York: Doubleday.

Cattell, J. (1885). Ueber die Zeit der Erkennung und Benennung von Schriftzeichen, Bildern und Farben [On the time required for regonizing and naming letters and words, pictures and colors]. *Philosophische Studien, 2*, 635–650.

Cattell, J. (1886). The time it takes to see and name objects. *Mind, 11*, 63–65.

Cattell, J. (1888). The psychological laboratory at Leipsic. *Mind, 13*, 37–51.

Cattell, J. (1890). Mental tests and measurements. *Mind, 15*, 373–381.

Cattell, J. (1895). Measurements of the accuracy of recollection. *Science, 2*, 761–766.

Cattell, J. (1896a). Address of the president before the American Psychological Association, 1895. *The Psychological Review, 3*(2), 1–15.

Cattell, J. (1896b). Address of the president before the American Psychological Association, 1895. *Psychological Review, 3*, 134- 148.

Cattell, J. (1904). The conceptions and methods of psychology. *Popular Science Monthly, 31*, 176–186.

Cattell, J. (1913). Eugenics: With special reference to intellect and character. *Popular Science Monthly*, 1–128.

Cattell, J. (1914). Science, education and democracy. *Science, 39*(996), 154–164.

Cattell, J. (1928). Early psychological laboratories [1]. *Science, 67*, 543–548.

Cattell, J. (1929). Psychology in America. *Science, 70*, 335–347.

Cattell, J., & Farrand, L. (1896). Physical and mental measurements of the students at Columbia University. *Psychological Review, 3*(6), 618–648.

Chall, J., & Feldman, S. (1966). First-grade reading: An analysis of the interactions of professed methods, teacher implementations and child background. *Reading Teacher, 19*, 569–575.

Chall, J., & Stahl, S. (1982). Reading. In H. Mitzel, J. Best, & W. Rabinowitz (Eds.), *The encyclopedia of educational research* (pp. 1535–1559). New York: Macmillian.

Cherryholmes, C. (2002). James' story of the squirrel and the pragmatic method. In J. Garrison, R. Podeschi, & E. Bredo (Eds.), *William James and education* (pp 89–96). New York: Teachers College Press.

Chomsky, N. (1957). *Syntactic structures.* The Hague: Mouton.

Chomsky, N. (1965). *Aspects of the theory of syntax.* Cambridge, MA: MIT Press.

Chomsky, N. (1970). Phonology and reading. In H. Levin & J. Williams (Eds.), *Basic studies on reading* (pp. 3–18). New York: Basic Books.

Chomsky, N. (1971). The case against B. F. Skinner. *New York Review of Books, 30*, 18–24.

Cipolla, C. (1969). *Literacy and development in the West.* Harmondsworth, UK: Penguin.

Civil Rights Act of 1957, 71 Stat. 637.

Civil Rights Act of 1964, Public Law 88-352.

Clark, S. (1898). *How to teach reading in the public schools.* Chicago: Scott, Foresman.

Cole, W. (1870). *The institute reader and normal class-book, for the use of teachers' institutes and normal schools, and for self-training in the art of reading.* Cincinnati: Wilson, Hinkle.

Coleman, J., Campbell, E., Hobson, C., McPartland, J., Mood, A., Winfied, F., et al. (1966). *Equality of educational opportunity.* Washington, DC: U.S. Government Printing Office.

Coles, G. (2000). *Misreading reading: The bad science that hurts children.* Portsmouth, NH: Heinemann.

Coles, G. (2001). Reading taught to the tune of the "scientific" hickory stick. *Phi Delta Kappa, 83,* 205–212.

Comte, A. (1979). *The positive philosophy of Auguste Comte, II* (H. Martineau, Trans.). In C. Blanchard (Ed.), New York: AMS Press. (Original work published 1855).

Comte, A. (1971). *A general view of positivism.* (J. H. Bridges, Trans.). London, England: Trubner. (Original work published 1848).

Comte, A. (2000). *The positive philosophy of Auguste Comte.* London: George Bell & Sons. (Translated and Condensed, H. Martineau, Vol. 3). Batoche Books (2000, originally published 1830-1842).

Comte, A. (1968). *System of positive polity.* New York: B. Franklin. (Originally published, 1851–1854).

Conaty, J. (2000, August 8). Influencing policy. Speech delivered at the International Reading Association, Adolescent Literacy Workshop, Washington, DC.

Cooper, A. (1892). *A voice from the South, by a Black woman from the South.* New York: Negro Universities Press (Original work privately published, Xenia, OH: Aldine, 1892).

Courtis, S. (1914). Standard tests in English. *Elementary School Teacher, 14*(4), 374–392.

Courtis, S. (1915). Standards in rates of reading. In *The Fourteenth Yearbook of the National Society for the Study of Education: Part I. Minimum standards and current practices in the formal subjects* (pp. 44–58). Chicago: University of Chicago Press.

Courtis, S. (1917a). *Courtis standard research tests in silent reading.* (N. 2). Detroit, MI: Author.

Courtis, S. (1917b). The problem of measuring ability in silent reading. *American School Board Journal, 49,* 17–18, 81.

Cox, J., & Weber, E. (1989). Comprehension assessment: Can self-report techniques help? *Reading Improvement, 26*(4), 349–352.

Cross, D., & Paris, S. (1987). Assessment of reading comprehension: Matching test purposes and test properties. *Educational-psychologists, 22*(3&4), 313–332.

Cravens, H. Applied science and public policy: The Ohio bureau of juvenile research and the problem of juvenile delinquency, 1913–1930. In M. Sokol (Ed.), *Psychological testing and American society, 1890–1930* (pp. 158–194). New Brunswick, NJ: Rutgers University Press.

Cremin, L. (1964). *The transformation of the school: Progressivism in America Education 1876–1957.* New York: Vintage Press.

Cremin, L., Shannon, D., & Townsend, M. (1954). *A history of Teachers College, Columbia University.* New York: Columbia University Press.

Cunningham, J. (2001). The National Reading Panel Report. *Reading Research Quarterly, 36*(3), 326–335.

Cunningham, J., & Fitzgerald, J. (1996). Epistemology and reading. *Reading Research Quarterly, 31*(1), 36–60.

Currier, L., & Duguid, 0. (1916). Phonics or no phonics. *Journal of Educational Psychology 15,* 286–287.

Curti, M. (1935). *The social ideas of American educators.* Paterson, NJ: Pageant Books.

Curti, M. (1964). *The growth of American thought.* New York: Harper & Row.

Cyr, E. (1899–1901). *The Cyr Readers.* Boston: Ginn.

Darwin, C. (1839). *Journals of researches into geology and natural history of the various countries visited by J. M. S. Beagle under the command of Captain FitzRoy, R. N. from 1832–1836.* London: Henry Colburn.

Darwin, C. (1937). *The origin of species with introduction and notes (Vol 2).* In C. Eliot (Ed.), *The Harvard classics.* New York: Collier.

Darwin, C. (1952). *The origin of the species by natural selection, the descent of man and selection in relation to sex.* In R. Hutchins (Ed.), *Great books of the Western world.* Chicago: W. Benton: Encyclopedia Britannica. (Original work published 1871).

Darwin, C. (1979). *On the origin of the species: by means of natural selection: or The preservation of favoured races in the struggle for life* (Foreword, P. Horan). New York: Avenel Books. (Original work published 1859).

Darwin, C. (1958). The autobiography of Charles Darwin. In N. Barlow (Ed.), *The autobiography of Charles Darwin.* London: Collins. (Original work published in 1887).

Darwin, C. (1972). *The descent of man and selection in relation to sex.* New York: Heritage Press (originally published 1896).

Darwin, C. (1952). *The origin of the species by natural selection, The descent of man and selection in relation to sex.* In R. Hutchins (Ed.), *Great Books of the Western World.* Chicago: W. Benton : Encyclopaedia Britannica, Inc.

Davis, F. (1942). Two measures of reading ability. *Journal of Educational Psychology 33,* 365–372.

Davis, F. (1968). Research in comprehension of reading. *Reading Research Quarterly, 3*(4), 499–545.

Davis, F. (1972). Research in comprehension in reading. *Reading Research Quarterly, 7,* 628–678.

Davis, F. B., & Davis, C. C. (1956). *Davis Reading Test.* New York: Psychological Corporation.

Davis, F. B., Willis, M., Derrick, C., Neville, H. R., Bradford, J.M., Spaulding, G., & Davis, C. C. (1940–1953). *Cooperative English Tests: Reading Comprehension.* Princeton, NJ: Educational Testing Service.

DeGarmo, C. (1891). The Herbartian system of pedagogies. *Educational Review, 15,* 244–252.

DeGarmo, C. (1896). *Herbart and the Herbartians.* New York: Charles Scribner's.

DeGarmo, C. (1916). *Herbart and the Herbartians.* New York: Charles Scribner's. (Original work published 1895).

Delpit, L. (in press). Foreword. In R. Powell & L. Spears-Bunton (Eds.), *Language, literacy, and the African American experience: Defining moments.* Mahwah, NJ: Lawrence Erlbaum Associates.

Delpit, L. (1986). Skills and other dilemmas of a progressive black educator. *Harvard Educational Review, 56,* 379–385.

Delpit, L. (1988). The silenced dialogue: Power and pedagogy in teaching other people's children. *Harvard Educational Review, 58,* 280–287.

Denzin, N., & Lincoln, Y. (Eds.). (2000a). *Handbook of qualitative research,* (2nd ed.) Thousand Oaks, CA: Sage.

Denzin, N., & Lincoln, Y. (2000b). Introduction. In N. Denzin & Y. Lincoln (Eds.), *Handbook of qualitative research,* (2nd ed., pp. 1–28). Thousand Oaks, CA: Sage.

Deutsch, M. (1965). The role of social class in language development and cognition. *American Journal of Orthopsychiatry, 35,* 78–88.

Dewey, J. (1900). *The school and society.* Chicago: University of Chicago Press. (Original work published 1899).

Dewey, J. (1902). *The child and the curriculum.* Chicago: University of Chicago Press.

Dewey, J. (1910). *How we think.* Boston: Heath.

Dewey, J. (1916). *Essays in experimental logic.* Chicago: University of Chicago Press.

Dewey, J. (1922a). *Development of American pragmatism. Philosophy and Civilization,* Gloucester, MA: P. Smith 1968, p. 24–25 (originally published 1931).

Dewey, J. (1922b). *Human nature and conduct.* New York: The Modern Library.

Dewey, J. (1923). Progressive education and the science of education. *Progressive-Education,* 197-204.

Dewey, J. (1925). *Experience and nature.* La Salle, IL: Open Court.

Dewey, J. (1929a). *The quest for certainty: A study of the relation and knowledge and action.* New York: Minton.

Dewey, J. (1929b). *The sources of a science of education*. New York: Liveright.

Dewey, J. (1934). *A common faith*. New Haven, CT: Yale University Press.

Dewey, J. (1935). The acquisition of facts as measures of reading comprehension. *Elementary School Journal, 35*, 346–348.

Dewey, J. (1938a). *Experience and education*. New York: Collier.

Dewey, J. (1938b). *Logic: The theory of inquiry*. New York: Holt, Rinehart & Winston.

Dewey, J. (1939). Experience, knowledge and value: A rejoinder. In B. Schlipp (Ed.), *The philosophy of John Dewey* (pp. 515–608). New York: Tudor.

Dewey, J. (1944). *Democracy and education: An introduction to the philosophy of education*. New York: Macmillan. (Original work published 1916).

Dewey, J. (1946). The philosophy of William James. In J. Dewey (Ed.), *The problems of men* (pp. 379–395). New York: Philosophical Library.

Dewey, J. (1961). *Democracy and education*. New York: Macmillan.

Dewey, J. (1963). *Experience and education*. New York: Collier Macmillan. (Original work published, 1938).

Dolch, E. (1933). Testing reading. *Elementary School Journal, 34*, 36–43.

Douglass, F. (1881). *The color line*. Retrieved July 1, 2005, from http://etext.lib. virginia.edu/etcbin/toccer-new2?id=DouColo.sgm&images=images/ modeng&data=/texts/english/modeng/parsed&tag=publi c&part=1&division=div

Douglass, F. (1968). *Narrative in the life of Frederick Douglass, an American slave*. (Original work published 1845).

Du Bois, W.E. B. (1896). *The suppression of the African slave trade to the United States of America, 1638–1870*. New York: Schocken Books.

Du Bois, W. E. B. (1897). Strivings of the Negro people. *Atlantic Monthly, 80*, 194–198.

Du Bois, W. E. B. (1899). *The Philadelphia Negro*. New York: Lippincott.

Du Bois, W. E. B. (1903). *The souls of Black folks*. New York: Bantam.

Du Bois, W.E. B. (1940). *Dusk of dawn: An autobiography of the race concept*. Millwood, NY: Kraus–Thomson Organization.

Du Bois, W. E. B. (1968). *The autobiography of W. E. B. DuBois; a soliloquy on viewing my life from the last decade of its first century*. New York: International Publishers.

Dunkel, H. (1970). *Herbart and Herbartianism: An educational ghost story*. Chicago: University of Chicago Press.

Durkin, D. (1978-1979). What classroom observations reveal about reading comprehension instruction. *Reading Research Quarterly, 14*, 481–533.

Durkin, D. (1981). Reading comprehension instruction in five basal reading series. *Reading Research Quarterly, 16*, (4), 515–544.

Edwards, R. (1867). *Analytical fifth reader.* New York: Mason Brothers.

Eggen, J. (1926). The fallacy of eugen. *Social Forces, 5* (1), 104–109.

Elementary & Secondary Education, Part B — Student Reading Skills Improvement Grants. http://www.ed.gov/policy/elsec/leg/esea02/pg4.html, Retrieved January 24, 2004.

Elementary and Secondary School Act, Public Law 89–10 (April 11, 1965).

Ellison, R. (1952). *Invisible man.* New York: Signet.

Equiano, O. (1995). *The interesting narrative of the life of Olaudah Equiano, or Gustavus Vassa the African, written by himself.* Boston: Bedford Books (Original work published 1789).

Fanon, F. (1963). *Wretched of the earth.* New York: Grove.

Fanon, F. (1967). *Black skin, White masks* (C. Markmann, Trans.) New York: Grove. (Original work published 1952).

Farr, R. (1969). *Reading: What can be measured?* Newark, DE: International Reading Association.

Farr, R. (1992). Putting it all together: Solving the reading assessment puzzle. *Reading Teacher, 46*(1), 26–37.

Farr, R., & Carey, R. (1986) *Reading: What can be measured?* (*2nd ed.*). Newark, DE: International Reading Association.

Farr, R., Carrey, R., & Tone, B. (1986). Recent theory and research into the reading process: Implications for reading assessment. In J. Orasanu (Ed.), *Reading comprehension. From research to practice* (pp. 135–150). Hillsdale, NJ: Erlbaum.

Farr, R., & Tuinman, J. (1972). The dependent variable: Measurement issues in reading research. *Reading Research Quarterly, 7*(3), 413–423.

Federici, (1999). Eric Voegelin on scientism. Available: http://evans- experientialism.freewebspace.com/federici.htm

Ferguson, G. (1919). Intelligence of the Negroes at Camp Lee. *School and Society, 9,* 721–26.

Fisher, G. (1864). On the numerical mode of estimating and recording educational qualifications as pursued in the Greenwich Hospital Schools. *British Museum general catalogue of printed books* (1961). 73, 661. London: Trustees of the British Museum (printed by H. S. Richardson).

Fitzgerald, J. (Ed.). (1990). *Reading comprehension instruction, 1783–1987: A review of trends and research.* Newark, DE: International Reading Association.

Fonda, J. (1959). *Dennis the Menace.* [Television series]. Hollywood: CBS Broadcasting Inc.

Foorman, B., Francis, D., Beeler, T., Winikates, D, & Fletcher, J. (1997). Early interventions for children with reading problems: Study designs and preliminary findings. *Learning Disabilities 8,* 63–71.

Fordyce, C. (1916). *A scale for measuring the achievements in reading.* Chicago: University Publishing.

Forgacs, D. (Ed). (2000). *The Antonio Gramsci reader: Selected writings 1916–1935.* New York: New York University Press. (Original work published in 1988).

Foster, M. (1997). *Black teachers on teaching.* New York: The New Press.

Fouillee, A. (1896). The hegemony of science and philosophy. *International Journal of Ethics, 6*(2), 137–164.

Franklin, V. (1980). Black social scientists and the mental testing movement 1920–1940. In R. Jones (Ed.), *Black psychology,* (2nd ed., pp. 201–215). New York: Harper & Row.

Franklin, V. P. (1991). Black social scientists and the mental testing movement, 1920–1940. In R. L. Jones (Ed.), *Black Psychology* (3rd ed.), (pp. 207-224). Berkeley: Cobb and Henry.

Freeman, F. N. (1913). Educational News and Editorial Comment: "The new Courtis tests."*The Elementary School Teacher, 14*(4), 145–146).

Freire, M., & Macedo, D. (Eds.). (1998). *The Paulo Freire reader.* New York: Continuum.

Freire, P. (1993). *Pedagogy of the oppressed.* New York: Continuum. (Original work published 1970).

Freire, P. (1994). *Pedagogy of hope: Reliving pedagogy of the oppressed.* New York: Continuum.

Freire, P. (1995). *Pedagogy of hope: Reliving pedagogy of the oppressed.* New York: Continuum.

Freire, P. (1996). *Letters to Christina: Reflections on my life and work.* (D. Macedo, Trans.). New York: Routledge.

Freire, P. (1998). *Teachers as cultural workers: Letters to those who dare to teach.* Boulder, CO: Westview.

Friedan, B. (1963). *The feminine mystique.* New York: Norton.

Freire, P., & Macedo, D. (1987). *Literacy: Reading the word and the world.* South Hadley, MA: Bergin and Garvey.

Fries, C. (1963). *Linguistics and reading.* New York: Holt, Rinehart & Winston.

Frow, J., & Morris, M. (2000). Cultural studies. In N. Denzin & Y. Lincoln (Eds.), *Handbook of qualitative research, (2nd ed.,* pp. 315–346). Thousand Oaks, CA: Sage.

Fukuda, T. (1923). Some data on the intelligence of Japanese children. *American Journal Psychology, 34*(4) 599–605.

Gadotti, M. (1994). *Reading Paulo Freire. His life and work.* New York: SUNY Press.

Gallegos, B. (1992). *Literacy, education, and society in New Mexico, 1693–1821.* Albuquerque: University of New Mexico Press.

Galloway, F. (1994). Inferential sturdiness and the 1917 Army Alpha: A new look at the robustness of educational quality indices as determinants of interstate Black–White score differentials. *Journal of Negro Education, 63*(2), 251–266.

Galton, F. (1833). *Inquiries into human faculty and its development.* London: Macmillan.

Galton, F. (1904). Eugenics: Its definition, scope, and aims. *American Journal of Sociology, 10*(2), 1–25.

Garth, T. (1927). The intelligence of mixed blood Indians. *Journal of Educational Psychology, 11,* 268–275.

Gardner, H. (1983). *Frames of mind: The theory of multiple intelligences.* New York: Basic Books.

Gardner, H. (1993). *Multiple intelligences: The theory into practice.* New York: Basic Books.

Gardner, H. (1999). *Intelligence reframed: Multiple intelligences for the 21st century.* New York: Basic Books.

Garrison, J., Podesci, R., & Bredo, E. (Eds.). (2002). *William James and education.* New York: Teachers College Press.

Gates, A. (1921a). An experimental and statistical study of reading and reading tests. *Journal of Educational Psychology, 12,* 303–314.

Gates, A. (1921b). An experimental and statistical study of reading and reading tests. *Journal of Educational Psychology, 12,* 378–391.

Gates, A. (1921c). An experimental and statistical study of reading and reading tests. *Journal of Educational Psychology, 12,* 453–465.

Gates, A. (1921d). *Spelling difficulties in 3867 words.* New York: Teachers College Press.

Gates, A. (1930). *Interests and ability in reading.* New York: Macmillan.

Gates. A. (1937). *The measurement and evaluation of achievement in reading. Thirty-sixth Yearbook of the National Society for the Study of Education,* (Part 2, pp. 359–388). Bloomington, IL: Public School Publishing.

Gates, A., & Bond, G. (1936). Reading readiness: A study of factors determining success and failure in beginning reading. *Teachers College Record, 37,* 679–685.

Germane, C., & Germane, E. (1922). *Silent reading: A handbook for teachers.* New York: Harper & Row.

Giere, R. (1988). *Explaining science: A cognitive approach.* Chicago: University of Chicago Press.

Giere, R., & Richardson, A. (Ed.). (1996). *Origins of logical empiricism. Minnesota Studies in the Philosophy of Science* (Vol. 16). Minneapolis: U. of Minnesota Press.

Gilman, C. (1966). *Women and economics.* New York: Harper & Row. (Original work published 1898).

Gitlin, A. (Ed.). (1994). *Power and method: Political activism and educational research.* New York: Routledge.

Gitlin, T. (1980). *The whole world is watching.* Berkeley: University of California Press.

Glaser, R. (Ed.). (1962). *Training research and education.* Pittsburgh: University of Pittsburgh Press.

Goals 2000: Educate America Act. (1994). Retrieved July 19, 2005, from http://www.ed.gov/legislation/GOALS2000/TheAct/index.html

Goals 2000: Sec. 302. Purpose. (1994). Retrieved July 19, 2005, http://www.ed.gov/legislation/GOALS2000/TheAct/sec302.html

Goals 2000. Educate America. H. R. 1804. Retrieved January 24, 2004. http://www.ed.gov/legislation/GOALS2000/TheAct/index.html

Goddard, H. (1917). *Intelligence classification of immigrants of different nationalities.* New York: reading. *Harvard Educational Review, 43,* 217–333.

Goodman, K. (1965). A linguistic study of cues and miscues. *Elementary English, 42,* 639–643.

Goodman, K. (1967). Reading a psycholinguistic guessing game. *Journal of the Reading Specialist, 6,* 126–135.

Goodman, K. (1969). Analysis of oral reading miscues: Applied psycholinguistics. *Reading Research Quarterly, 5,* 9–30.

Goodman, K. (1973). Psycholinguistic universals in the reading process. In F. Smith (Ed.), *Psycholinguistics and reading* (pp. 21–27). New York: Holt, Rinehart& Winston.

Goodman, K. & Goodman, Y. (1977). Learning about psycholinguistic processes by analyzing oral reading. *Harvard Educational Review, 43,* 217–333.

Goodman, K., & Goodman, Y. (1979). Learning to read in natural. In L. Resnick & P. Weaver (Eds.), *Theory and practice of early reading* (Vol. 1, pp. 137–154). Hillsdale, NJ: Lawrence Erlbaum Associates.

Goodman, Y., & Burke, C. (1973). *Reading miscue inventory: Manual procedure for diagnosis and evaluation.* New York: Macmillan.

Gould, S. (1981). *The mismeasure of man.* New York: Norton.

Gould, S. (1996). *The mismeasure of man.* New York: Norton.

Graff, H. (1979). *The literacy myth: literacy and social structure in the nineteenth-century city.* New York: Academic Press.

Graff, H. (1987a). *The labyrinths of literacy: Reflections on literacy past and present.* Sussex, UK: Falmer Press.

Graff, H. (1995). *The labyrinths of literacy.* Pittsburgh: U. of Pittsburgh Press.

Graham, P. (1974). *Community and class in American education, 1865–1918.* New York: Wiley.

Gramsci, A. (1971). *Selections from the prison notebooks of Antonio Gramsci.* In Q. Hoare & G. Smith (Eds. & Trans.), New York: International Publishers.

Gray, C. (1922). *Deficiencies in reading ability: Their diagnosis and remedies.* Boston: Heath.

Gray, W. (1915a). *Standardized oral reading paragraphs*. Bloomington, IL: Public School Publishing.

Gray, W. (1915b). Selected bibliography upon practical tests of reading ability. In S. Parker (Ed.), *The Fourteenth Yearbook of the National Society for the Study of Education: Part 1. Minimum essentials in elementary-school subjects-standards and practice* (pp. 59–60). Chicago: University of Chicago Press.

Gray, W. (1916a). The co-operative study of reading in eleven cities of Northern Illinois. *The Elementary School Journal, 17*, 250–265.

Gray, W. (1916b). Descriptive list of standard tests. *Elementary School Journal, 17*, 24–34.

Gray, W. (1916c). Methods of testing reading I. *Elementary School Journal, 16*, 231–246.

Gray, W. (1916d). Methods of testing reading II. *Elementary School Journal, 16*, 281–298.

Gray, W. (1916e). A study of the emphasis on various phases of reading instruction in two cities. *Elementary School Journal, 17*, 178–186.

Gray, W. (1917a). Descriptive lists of standard tests. *Elementary School Journal, 17*, 56–61.

Gray, W. (1917b). The relation of silent reading to economy in education. In *The Sixteenth Yearbook of the National Society for the Study of Education. Part 1. Second report of the committee on minimum essentials in elementary-school subjects* (pp. 17–32). Chicago: University of Chicago Press.

Gray, W. (1917c). *Studies of elementary school reading through standardized tests* (Supplemental Educational Monograph, No. 1). Chicago: University of Chicago Press.

Gray, W. (1918). The use of tests in improving instruction. *The Elementary School Journal, 19*, 24–35.

Gray, W. (1919a). Principles of method in teaching reading, as derived from scientific investigation. In *The Eighteenth Yearbook of the National Society for the Study of Education: Part 2: Fourth report of the committee on economy of time in education* (pp. 26–51). Chicago: University of Chicago Press.

Gray, W. (1919b). Reading in the elementary schools of Indianapolis 1. *The Elementary School Journal, 19*, 336–353.

Gray, W. (1919c). Reading in the elementary schools of Indianapolis 2. *The Elementary School Journal, 19*, 419–444.

Gray, W. (1919d). Reading in the elementary schools of Indianapolis 3. *The Elementary School Journal, 19*, 506–531.

Gray, W. (1919e). Reading in the elementary schools of Indianapolis 4. *The Elementary School Journal, 19*, 608–627.

Gray, W. (1923). The importance of intelligent silent reading. *Elementary School Journal, 24*, 348–356.

Gray, W. (1925). *Summary of investigations relating to reading,* (Supplementary Educational Monographs No. 2A). Chicago: University of Chicago Press.

Gray, W. (1927). Summary of reading investigations. *The Elementary School Journal, 27,* 456–466, 495–510.

Gray, W. (1933). Curriculum investigations at the elementary and secondary school levels—Reading. *Review of Educational Research, 4,* 135–138.

Gray, W. (1937a). The nature and types of reading. *Thirty-sixth Yearbook of the National Society for the Study of Education,* (*Part 1* pp. 23–38). Bloomington, IL: Public School Publishing.

Gray, W. (1937b). The nature and organization of basic instruction in reading. *Thirty-sixth Yearbook of the National Society for the Study of Education,* (*Part 2* pp. 99–106). Bloomington, IL: Public School Publishing.

Gray, W. (1938). Contribution of research to special methods: Reading. In *Thirty-seventh Yearbook of the National Society for the Study of Education,* (Part 2 pp. 99–106). Bloomington, IL: Public School Publishing.

Gray, W. (1957). *The teaching of reading: An international view.* Cambridge, MA: Harvard University Press.

Gray, W. (1965). William S. Gray, Jr. In *National Cyclopeaedia of American Biography,* (Vol. 48, p. 106). New York: White.

Gray, C. (1917). *Types of reading ability as exhibited through tests and laboratory experiments, an investigation subsidized by the general education board.* Chicago: The University of Chicago Press.

Gray, W. (1914). A tentative scale for the measurement of oral reading achievements. Unpublished Masters Thesis. Columbia University, Teachers College.

Gray, W. (1931). Autobiographical Piece. (Personal communication, July 15, 1988, Associate Professor and Secretary, W. D. Patterson).

Gray, W. (1931). Summary of reading investigations. *Elementary School Journal, 32,* 510–520.

Gray, W. (1934). Reading through educational tests. *Review of Educational Research, 130,* 58–64.

Greenwood, D. J., & Levin, M. (2000). Reconstructing the relationships between universities and society through action research. In N. Denzin & Y. Lincoln (Eds.), *Handbook of qualitative research,* (*2nd ed.,* pp. 85–106), Thousand Oaks, CA: Sage.

Greer, E. (2002). Implications for Scientific Based Evidence Approach in Reading. A paper presented at the Working Group Conference on "The Use of Scientifically Based Research in Education," February, 6, 2002. Washington, DC.

Grossberg, L. (2003). History, politics, and postmodernism. In D. Morley & K. Chen (Eds.), *Stuart Hall: Critical dialogues in cultural studies* (pp. 151–173). London: Routledge.

Gurthrie, J. (Ed.). (1984). *Reading: William S. Gray: A research retrospective 1881–1941*. Newark, DE: International Reading Association.

Gutiérrez, K. (1993). How talk, context, and script shape contexts for learning to write: A cross case comparison of journal sharing. *Linguistics and Education, 5*(3 & 4), 335–365.

Gutiérrez, K., & Rogoff, B. (2003). Cultural ways of learning: Individual traits or repertoires of practice. *Educational Researcher, 32*(5), 19–25.

Habermas, J. (1971). *Toward a rational society*. Educational Books. London: Heinemann *(J. Shapiro, Trans)*.

Habermas, J. (1974). Rationalism divided in two. In A. Giddens (Ed.), *Positivism and sociology* (pp. 195–223). London: Heinemann.

Habermas, J. (1979). *Communication and the evolution of society* (T. McCarthy, Trans.). London: Heinemann.

Habermas, J. (1984). *The theory of communicative action: Vol. 1. Reason and the rationalization of society.* (T. McCarthy, Trans.). Boston: Beacon Press.

Habermas, J. (1987a). *Knowledge and human interests.* Cambridge, UK: Polity Press.

Habermas, J. (1987b). *The theory of communicative action: Vol. 2. The critique of functionalist reason* Boston: (T. McCarthy, Trans.). Beacon Press.

Habermas, J. (1971). *Knowledge and human interests.* Boston: Beacon Press. (Trans. J. Viertel).

Habermas, J. (1973). *Theory and practice.* Boston: Beacon Press.

Hall, S. (1980). Encoding and decoding. In S. Hall, D. Dobson, A. Lowe, & P. Willis (Eds.), *Culture, media, and language.* Working Papers in Cultured Studies, 1972–79, (PP. 128–138) London: Unwin Hyman. (Original work published 1973).

Hall. S. (1982). The rediscovery of "ideology": return of the repressed in media studies. In M. Gurevitch, T. Bennett, J. Curran, & J. Woollacott (Eds.), *Culture, society and the media* (pp. 56–89). London: Methuen.

Hall, S. (1984). Reconstruction work. *Ten–8,* 16, 2–9.

Hall, S. (1995). The Whites of their eyes—racist ideologies and the media. In G. Dines & J. Humez (Eds.), *Gender, race and class in media—A text reader,* (pp. 18–22). Thousand Oaks, CA: Sage.

Hall, S. (2003). The problem of ideology: Marxism without guarantees. In D. Morley & K. Chen (Eds.), *Stuart Hall: Critical dialogues in cultural studies* (pp. 25–47). London: Routledge.

Halliday, M. (1973). *Explorations in the functions of language.* London: Edward Arnold.

Hamilton, F. (1907). The perceptual factors in reading. *Archives of Psychology, 9*, 1–56.

Harding, S. (1991). *Whose science? Whose knowledge? Thinking from women.* Ithaca, New York: Cornell University Press.

Harre, R. (1972). *Philosophies of science.* Oxford, UK: Oxford University Press.

Harrington, M. (1962). *The other America.* New York: Scribner's.

Harris, C. (1948). Measurement of comprehension in literature. *School Research, 51*, 280–299, 332–342.

Harris, T. (1969). Reading. In R. Ebel, V. Noll, & R. Bauer (Eds.), *Encyclopedia of Educational Research,* (4ᵗʰ ed. pp. 1069–1104). New York: Macmillan.

Harris, T., & Hodges, R. (Eds.). (1995). *The literacy dictionary.* Newark, DE: International Reading Association.

Harris, W. (1894–1895). *Report of the U.S. Commissioner of Education, 1894–1995.* Washington, D.C.: U.S. Bureau of Education.

Hartshorne, C., Weiss, P., & Burks, A. (Eds.). (1933–1958). *Collected papers of Charles Sanders Peirce (Vols. 1–8).* Cambridge, MA: Harvard University Press.

Hayes, W. (1991). Radical Black behaviorism. In R. Jones (Ed.), *Black psychology* (pp. 65–78). Berkeley, CA: Cobb & Henry.

Haynes, E. (1921). *Unsung heroes.* New York: Du Bois & Dill.

Heaney, T. (1995). Issues in Freirean pedagogy. *Thresholds in Education,* "Freire Issues" section. Retrieved December 29, 2003, from http://nlu.nu.edu/ace/Resources/Documetns/FreireIssues.html

Heath, S. (1983). *Ways with words.* Cambridge, UK: Cambridge University Press.

Henderson, E. (1903). A study of memory for connected trains of thought. *Psychological Monographs, 5*(6), 1–94.

Hendricks, E. (1911). *A study in reading.* Newark, NJ: Silver, Burdett.

Henry, A. (1995). Growing up Black, female, and working class: A teacher's narrative. *Anthropology and Education Quarterly, 26*(3), 279–305.

Herbart, J. (1891). *A text book in psychology: An attempt to found the science of psychology on experience metaphysics and mathematics.* (M. K. Smith, Trans.). New York: Appleton.

Herbart, J. (1896). *Science of education and the aesthetic revelation of the world* (H. Felkin & S. Felkin, Trans.). Boston: Heath. (Original work published 1891).

Herbart, J. (1902). The science of education, its general principles deduced from its aim, and the aesthetic revelation of the world, by Johann Friedrich Herbart. Boston: D. C. Heath. (trans. H. M. Felkin and E. Felkin).

Hildreth, G. (1933). *A bibliography of mental tests and rating scales.* New York: Psychological Corporation.

Hillard, G. (1924). Probable types of difficulties underlying low scores in comprehension tests. In C. Robbins (Ed.), *University of Iowa Studies in Education, (Vol. 2*, pp. 1–60). Iowa City: University of Iowa.

Hinton, L. (1994). *Flutes of fire: The Indian languages of California.* Berkeley, CA: Heyday.

Hirsch, E. D., Kett, J., Tefil, J. (1988). *Cultural literacy: What every American needs to know.* New York: Vintage.

Hirsch, E., Kett, J. F., & Trefil, J. (2003). *The new dictionary of cultural literacy, (Rev., 3rd ed.)* Boston: Houghton Mifflin.

Hoare, Q., & Smith, G. (Eds. & Trans.). (1971). *Selections from the prison notebooks of Antonio Gramsci.* New York: International Publishers.

Hoffman, F. (1896). Race traits and tendencies of the American Negro. *Publications of the American Economic Association, 11*(1/3), 1–329.

Hofstader, R. (1959). *Social Darwinism in American thought.* New York: Braziller.

Holmes, H. (1915). Time distributions by subjects and grades in representative cities. In S. C. Parker (Ed.), *The minimum essentials in elementary-school subjects* (pp. 21–27). Chicago: University of Chicago Press.

Hoover, M., & Politzer, P. (1981). Bias in composition tests with suggestions for a culturally appropriate assessment technique. In M. F. Whiteman (Ed.), *Writing: The nature, development, and teaching of written communication: Vol. 1. Variation in writing: Functional and linguistic-cultural differences* (pp. 197–207). Hillsdale, NJ: Lawrence Erlbaum Associates.

Hoover, M., Politzer, P., & Taylor, O. (1987). Bias in reading tests for black language speakers. *The Negro Educational Review* 38(2–3), 81–98.

Horton, M. (1998). *The long haul: An autobiography.* New York: Teachers College Press. (with J, Kohl and H. Kohl).

Huey, E. (1898). Preliminary experiments in the physiology and psychology of reading. *America Journal of Psychology, 9,* 575–86.

Huey, E. (1900). On the psychology and physiology of reading. American Journal of Psychology, 11, 283–302.

Huey, E. (1901). On the physiology of reading. *American Journal of Psychology, 11,* 292-313.

Huey, E. (1908). *The psychology and pedagogy of reading; with a review of the history of reading and writing and of methods, texts, and hygiene in reading.* New York: Macmillan.

Hyatt, A. (1943). *The place of oral reading in -the school program: Its history and development 1880–1914.* New York: Teachers College. *1800–1941.* New York, NY: Teachers College.

Jackson, D. (2005, June 13). The GOP's poverty gambit. *Chicago Tribune,* p. A 13.

James, W. (1898). Philosophical conceptions and practical results: The annual public address before the union, August 26, 1898. Berkeley, CA: The University Press. James, W. (1899). *Talks to teachers on psychology and to students on some of life's ideals.* New York: Holt.

James, W. (1900). *Talks to teachers on psychology and to students on some of life's ideals.* New York: Holt.

James, W. (1902). *The varieties of religious experience.* New York: Longmans.

James, W. (1904). The pragmatic method. *Journal of Philosophy and Scientific Methods, 1,* 25, 673–687.

James, W. (1907a). Pragmatism's conception of truth, Lecture 6. In W. James (Ed.), *Pragmatism: A new name for some old ways of thinking (pp. 76–91).* New York: Longman.

James, W. (1907b). Pragmatism's conception of truth. *Journal of Philosophy, Psychology and Scientific Methods, 6*(4), 141–155.

James, W. (1909). *Pragmatism: A new name for some old ways of thinking.* New York: Longman.

James, W. (1923). *The principles of psychology.* (Original work published 1890). New York: Holt.

James, W. (1982). *Psychology,* briefer course. New York: Holt.

Janesick, V. (2000). The choreography of qualitative research design. In N. Denzin & Y. Lincoln (Eds.), *Handbook of qualitative research,* (2nd ed. pp. 379–399). Thousand Oaks, CA: Sage.

Jenkins, M. (1936a). A socio-psychological study of Negro children of superior intelligence. *Journal of Negro Education, 5*(2), 175–190.

Jenkins, M. (1936b). Case studies of Negro children of Binet IQ 160 and above. *Journal of Negro Education, 12*(2), 159–166.

Jenkins, M. (1939). The mental ability of the American Negro. *Journal of Negro Education, 8*(3), 511–520.

Jenkins, M. D. (1936c) A Socio-Psychological Study of Negro Children of Superior Intelligence. *Journal of Negro Education, 5*(2), 189–190.

Jenkins, M. D. (1950). Intellectually superior Negro youth: Problems and needs. *Journal of Negro Education 19*(3), 322–332.

Jensen, A. (1969). How much can we boost IQ and scholastic achievement? *Harvard Educational Review, 31,* 1–123.

Jiménez, R. (1990). *The history of reading and uses of literacy in colonial Mexico.* (Tech. Rep. No. 494). Champaign, IL: Center for the Study of Reading.

Joncich, G. (Ed.). (1962). *Psychology and the science of education: Selected writings of Edward L. Thorndike.* New York: Teachers College Press.

Joncich, G. (1968). *The sane positivist: A biography of Edward L. Thorndike.* Middletown, CT: Wesleyan University Press.

Johnson, C. (1923). Mental measurements of Negro groups. *Opportunity, 1,* 21–28.

Johnson, L. (1965). *Public papers of the Presidents of the United States: Lyndon B. Johnson (Continuing the public messages, speeches, and states of the President, 1963–1964). Book I.* Washington, DC: U.S. Printing Office.

Johnson, L. II, (2003). *Finding the good.* Nashville, TN: Rutledge Hill.

Johnson-Laird, P. (1983). *Mental models.* Cambridge, MA: Harvard University Press.

Johnston, P. (1984). Assessment in reading. In P. Pearson (Ed.), *Handbook of reading research,* (*Vol. I,* pp. 147–182). New York: Longman.

Johnston, P. (1987). Teachers as evaluation experts. *Reading Teacher, 40*(18), 744–748.

Jolly, C., & White, R. (1995). *Physical anthropology and archaeology.* (5th ed.). New York: McGraw-Hill.

Jones, L., & Newman, L. (with Isay, D.). (1998). *Our America: Life and death on the southside of Chicago.* New York: Pocket.

Jones, R. (Ed.). (1991). *Black psychology.* (3rd ed.). Berkeley, CA: Cobb & Henry.

Jones, E. (1991). Labeling children culturally deprived and culturally disadvantaged. In R. Jones (Ed.), *Black psychology,* (pp. 285–294). Berkeley, CA: Cobb & Henry.

Jones, L. V., & I. Olkin. (Eds.), (2004). *The nation's report card: Evolution and perspectives.* Bloomington, IN: Phi Delta Kappa Educational Foundation.

Jones, R. L. (Ed.), (1972). *Black psychology.* New York: Harper Row.

Jorgensen, C. (1995). The African American critique of White supremacist science. *Journal of Negro Education, 64*(3), 232–242.

Judd, C. (1913). Educational news and editorial comment. *The Elementary School Teacher, 15,*1–2.

Judd, C. (1914). Reading tests. *Elementary School Teacher, 14,* 365–373.

Judd, C. (1915). Educational writings, *Elementary School Journal, 16*(2), 71–73.

Judd, C. (1916a). Educational writings. *Elementary School Journal, 18,* 344–349.

Judd, C. (1916b). *Measuring the work of the public schools.* Cleveland, OH: Survey Committee of the Cleveland Foundation.

Judd, C. (1916c). Reading. In G. Whipple (Ed.). *The Fifteenth Yearbook of the National Society for the Study of Education. Part 1. Standards and tests for measurement of the efficiency of schools and school systems* (pp. 111–119). Chicago: University of Chicago Press.

Judd, C. (1917). Educational writings. *Elementary School Journal, 18,* 230–231.

Judd, C. (1932). Autobiography. In C. Murchison (Ed.) *History of biography* (Vol. 2, pp. 207–235). Worcester, MA: Clark University Press.

Judd, C., & Buswell, G. (1922). *Silent reading: A study of the various types* (Supplementary Educational Monographs No. 23). Chicago: University of Chicago Press.

Kaestle, C. (1983). *Pillars of the republic: Common schools and American society, 1780–1860.* New York: Hill & Wang.

Kaestle, C. (1983). Literacy and diversity: Themes form a social history of the American reading public. *History of Education Quarterly, 28*(4), 523–549.

Kaestle, C., Damon-Moore, H., Stedman, L., Tinsley, K., & Trollinger, W. (1991). *Literacy in the United States: Readers and reading since 1880.* New Haven: Yale University Press.

Kamil, M., Mosenthal, P., Pearson, P., & Barr, R. (Eds.). (2000). *Handbook of reading research* (Vol. 3). Mahwah, NJ: Lawrence Erlbaum Associates.

Kamil, M. L. (1984). Current Traditions of Reading Research. In R. Barr, M. L. Kamil, P. B. Mosenthal, P. D. Pearson, (Eds.), *Handbook of Reading Research*, (pp. 39–62). New York: Longman.

Karier, C. (1975). *Shaping the American educational state 1900 to the present.* New York: Free Press.

Karier, C. (1986). *The individual, society, and education: A history of American educational ideas* (2nd ed.). New York: Free Press. (Original work published 1967).

Karier, C., Violas, P., & Spring, J. (1973). *Roots of crisis: American education in the twentieth century.* Chicago: Rand McNally.

Katz, M. (1971). *Class, bureaucracy and schools: The illusion of educational change in America.* New York: Praeger.

Kelley, T. (1917). Thorndike's reading Scale Alpha 2 adapted to individual testing. *Teachers College Record, 28*, 253–260.

Kellner, D. (1984). *From 1984 to one-dimensional man: Critical reflections on Orwell and Marcuse.* January 24, 2004.

Kellner, D. (1989). *Critical theory, Marxism, and modernity.* Baltimore, MD: Johns Hopkins University Press.

Kellner, D. (1995). *Media culture: Cultural studies, identity and politics between the modern and the postmodern.* London: Routledge.

Kellner, D. (1999). Cultural studies and social theory: A critical intervention. Retrieved January 8, 2004, from http:www.gseis.ucla.edu/faculty/kellner/papers/CSST99.html

Kelly, F. (1915). *The Kansas silent reading tests.* Emporia, KS: Bureau of Educational Measurements and Standards 3.

Kelly, F. (1916). The Kansas silent reading tests. *Journal of Educational Psychology, 7*(2), 63–80.

Kelly, R. (1980). Ideology, effectiveness and public sector productivity. *Journal of Social Science, 4*, 76–95.

Kent, J., & Ruiz, R. (1979). IQ and reading scores among Anglo, Black, and Chicano third- and sixth-grade schoolchildren. *Hispanic Journal of Behavioral Sciences, 1*(3). 271–277.

Kincheloe, J. (1998). Critical research in science education. In B. Fraser & K. Tobin (Eds.), *International handbook of science education* (pp. 1191–1205). Boston: Kluwer Academic.

Kincheloe, J., & McLaren, P. (2000). Rethinking critical theory and qualitative research. In N. Denzin & Y. Lincoln (Eds.), *Handbook of qualitative research,* (2ⁿᵈ ed., pp. 279–313). Thousand Oaks, CA: Sage.

King, I. (1903). Pragmatism as a philosophic method. *The Philosophic Review, 12*(5), 511–524.

King, I. (1916). A comparison of slow and rapid readers. *School and Society, 4*(100), 830–834.

King, I. (1917). A comparison of the efficiency of slow and rapid readers. *School and Society, 7,* 203–204.

Kingston, M. (1976). *The woman warrior: Memoirs of a girlhood among ghosts.* New York: Knopf.

Kirk, M. (1899). *The Baldwin primer.* New York: American Book.

Kline, E., Moore, D., & Moore, S. (1987). Colonel Francis Parker and beginning reading instruction. *Reading Research and Instruction, 26*(3), 141–150.

Koch, S. (1959–1963). *Psychology: A study of a science (Vols. 1–6).* New York: McGraw Hill.

Kohler, (1968). Foreword. *The psychology and pedagogy of reading; with a review of this history of reading and writing and of methods, texts, and hygiene in reading* (pp. xiii–xxxix). New York: Macmillan.

Kotlowitz, A. (1992). *There are no children here: The story of two boys growing up in the other America.* New York: Anchor Books.

Kourany, J. (2003). A philosophy of science or the twenty-first century. *Philosophy of Science, 70,* 1–14.

Kuhn, T. (1996). *The structure of scientific revolutions.* (3ʳᵈ ed). Chicago: University of Chicago Press. (Original work published 1962).

Labov, W. (1970). *The study of nonstandard English.* Champaign, IL: National Council of Teachers of English.

Labov, W. (1972a). Academic ignorance and Black intelligence. *The Atlantic, 229*(6), 59–67.

Labov, W. (1972b). *Language in the inner city: Studies in Black English vernacular.* Washington, DC: Center for Applied Linguistics.

Laclau, E., & Mouffe, C. (1985). *Hegemony and socialist strategy: Towards a radical democratic politics.* London: Verso.

Ladson-Billings, G. (2000). Racialized discourses and ethnic epistemologies. In N. Denzin & Y. Lincoln (Eds.), *Handbook of qualitative research* (2ⁿᵈ ed., pp. 257–277). Thousand Oaks, CA: Sage.

Lagemann, E. (1997). Contested terrain: A history of educational research in the United States, 1980–1990. *Educational Researcher, 26*(9), 5–17.

Lagemann, E. (2000). *An elusive science: The troubling history of education research*. Chicago: University of Chicago Press.

Laing, M. (1909). *Reading a manual for teachers*. Boston: Heath.

Lamport, H. (1937). *A history of the teaching of beginning reading*. Unpublished doctoral dissertation, University of Chicago.

Landmark court cases: *Brown* v. *Board of Education I* (1954), Key Excerpts from the Majority Opinion, *Brown I:* Chief Justice Earl Warren delivered the opinion of the Court. Available: http://www.landmarkcases. org/brown/opinion1.html. Retrieved 3/29/06.

Lange, K. (1893). *Apperception* (The Herbart Club, Trans.). Boston: Heath.

Larry P v Wilson Riles U. S. District Court. (1979).

Lau v. Nichols, 414 U.S. 563, 94 Supreme Court. 786 (1974).

Lazarus, E. (1883). The new colossus. Available online from Jewish Women's Archive. Retrieved July 5, 2005, from http://www.jwa.org/exhibit/ wov/lazarus/el2.html

Lee, C. (1993). *Signifying as a scaffold for literacy interpretation*. Urbana, IL: National Council of Teachers of English.

Lennon, R. (1962). What can be measured? *The Reading Teacher, 15*(5), 326–337.

Lenzer, G. (Ed.). (1998). *The essential writings of Auguste Comte and positivism*. New Brunswick: Transaction Publications. (Reprint, original work published 1975).

Lewis, A. (2000). CRESST Conference proceedings. *The CRESST Line: Newsletter of the National Center for Research on evaluation, standards, and student testing* (pp. 3–7).

Lewontin, R. C., Rose, S. P., & Kamin, L. J. (1984). *Not in our genes: Biology, ideology, and human nature*. New York: Pantheon.

Lincoln, Y., & Denzin, N. (1994). The fifth moment. In N. Denzin & Y. Lincoln (Eds), *Handbook of qualitative research* (pp. 575–586). Thousand Oaks, CA: Sage.

Lippmann, W. (1922a, October 25). The mental age of Americans. *The New Republic*, 213–215.

Lippmann, W. (1922b, November 1). The mystery of the "A" men. *The New Republic*, 246–248.

Lippmann, W. (1922c, November 8). The reliability of intelligence tests. *The New Republic*, 275–277.

Lippmann, W. (1922d, November 15). The abuse of the tests. *The New Republic*, 297–298.

Lippmann, W. (1922e, November 22). Tests of hereditary intelligence. *The New Republic*, 328–330.

Lippmann, W. (1922f, November 29). A future for tests. *The New Republic*, 9–11.

Lippmann, W. (1923, January 3). The great confusion: A reply to Mr. Terman. *The New Republic*, 145–146.

Lockridge, K. (1974). *Literacy is colonial New England: An inquiry into the social context of literacy in the early modern west.* New York: Norton.

Lohnes, P. (1968). Review of the Gray oral reading tests. In O. Buros (Ed.), *Reading tests and reviews* (pp. 369–370). Highland Park, NJ: Gryphon Press.

Long, H. (1923). Race and mental tests. *Opportunity, 1*, 22–25.

Long, H. (1934). The intelligence of colored elementary pupils in Washington, DC. *Journal of Negro Education, 3*(2), 205–222.

Long, H. (1935a). Test results of third-grade Negro children selected on the basis of socio-economic status, I. *Journal of Negro Education, 4*(2), 192–212.

Long, H. (1935b). Test results of third-grade Negro children selected on the basis of socio-economic status, II. *Journal of Negro Education, 4*(4), 523–552.

Long, H. (1957). The relative learning capacities of Negroes and Whites. *Journal of Negro Education, 26*(2), 121–134.

Long, H. (1925). On mental tests and racial psychology: A critique. *Opportunity, 3*, 134–138.

Lynn, L. (with Vecsey, G.) (1976). *Cold miner's daughter.* Chicago: Contemporary Books.

Lyon, G. (1998). Why reading is not a natural process. *Educational Leadership, 55*(6). Retrieved December 30, 1998, from http://www.ascd.org/pubs/el/mar98/etlyon.htm

Lyon, G. R. (July 10, 1997). *Report on Learning Disabilities Research.* Testimony before the Committee on Education and the Workforce, U.S. House of Representatives. Available: http://www.ldonline.org/ld_indepth/reading/nih_report.html. Retrieved: March 28, 2006.

MacDermott, R. (1974). Achieving school failure: An anthropological approach to illiteracy. In H. Singer & R. Rudell, (eds.), *Theoretical models and processes of reading* (2nd ed.) Newark, DE: International Reading Association.

Madus, G. (1983, April). *Test scores: What do they really mean in educational policy?* Address presented to the National Consortium on Testing, Washington, DC.

Madaus, G. (1985). Test scores as administrative mechanisms in educational policy. *Phi Delta Kappan, 66*, 611–617.

Manicas, P., & Secord, P. (1983). Implications for psychology of the new philosophy of science. *American Psychologist*, 399–413.

Manguel, A. (1996). *A history of reading.* New York: Viking.

Malthus, F. (1798). *Essay on the principles of population as it affects the future of improvement of society with remarks on the speculations of Mr. Godwin, M. Condorcet, and other writers.* Retrieved January 13, 2004, from http://www.ac.wwu.edu/ Stephan/malthus.0.html

Mathews, M. (1966). *Teaching to read historically considered.* Chicago: University of Chicago Press Press.

Mavrogenes, N. (1985). *William Scott Gray; Leader of teachers and shaver of American reading instruction.* Unpublished doctoral dissertation, University of Chicago.

Mavrogenes, N. (1985). William S. Gray: The person. In J. Stevenson (Ed.), *William S. Gray: Teacher, scholar, leader* (pp. 1–23). Newark, DE: International Reading Association.

McCaul, R. (1971). Autobiography in American educational history. In R. Havighurst (Ed.), *The Seventieth Yearbook of the National Society for the Study of Education, Part 2: Leaders in American education* (pp. 500–504). Bloomington, Il.: Public School Publishing.

McCauley, S. (1987). *The object of my affection.* New York: Simon & Schuster.

McCombs, J. S., Kirby, S. N., Barney, H., Darilek, H., & Magee, S. (2005). *Achieving state and national literacy goals, a long uphill road: A report to Carnegie Corporation of New York.* Santa Monica, CA: RAND Corporation.

McDermott, R. (1974). Achieving School Failure: An Anthropological Approach to Illiteracy and Social Stratification. In G. Spindler (Ed.), *Education and Cultural Process,* (pp. 82–118). NY: Holt.

McDermott, R. P. (1976). Achieving school failure: An anthropological approach to illiteracy and social stratification. In H. Singer & R. B. Ruddell (Eds.), *Theoretical models and processes of reading,* (pp.). Newark, DE: International Reading Association.

McGuffey, W (1849). *McGuffey's newly revised eclectic fourth reader.* New York: Clark, Austin, & Smith.

McGuffey, W. (1857). *McGuffey's new fifth eclectic reader.* New York: Clark, Austin, & Smith.

McGuffey, W. (1866). *First eclectic reader.* New York: Clark, Austin, & Smith.

McMurry, C. (1899). *Conflicting principles in teaching and how to avoid them.* New York: Houghton Mifflin.

McMurry, C. A. (1903). *The Elements of General Method Based on the Principles of* Herbart. New York: Macmillan.

McNamara, T., Miller, D., & Bransford, J. (1991). Mental models and reading comprehension. In R. Barr, M. Kamil, P. Mosenthal, & P. Pearson (Eds.), *Handbook of reading research* (Vol. 2, pp. 490–511). New York: Longman.

McQuillan, J. (1998). *The literacy crisis: False claims, real solutions.* Portsmouth, NH: Heinemann.

Mead, C. (1917). Results in silent versus oral reading. *Journal of Educational Psychology, 7,* 367–368.

Mead, C. (1914). Silent versus oral reading with one hundred sixth-grade children. *Journal of Educational Psychology, 6,* 345–348.

Mead, M. (1926). The methodology of racial testing: Its significance for sociology. *American Journal of Sociology, 31*(5), 657–667.

Merrill, M. (1918). The ability of the special class children in the "Three R's." *Pedagogical Seminary, 25,* 88–96.

Miller, C. (Comp.). (1926). Teachers College in the news. Leaders of American science and their discoveries, Dr. Edward Lee Thorndike. *Teachers College Record,28,* 146–150.

Miller, G. (1965). Some preliminaries to psycholinguistics. *American Psycholinguist, 20,* 15–20.

Moll, L. (1992). Literacy research in community and classrooms: A sociocultural approach. In R. Beach, J. Green, M. Kamil, & T. Shanahan (Eds.), *Multidisciplinary perspectives on literacy research* (pp. 211–244). Urbana, IL: National Council of Teachers of English.

Monaghan, E. J. (1991). Family literacy in early 18th-century Boston: Cotton Mather and his children. *Reading Research Quarterly 26,* 342–370.

Monroe, W. (1916). *Monroe's standardized silent reading tests.* Bloomington, IL: Public School Publishing.

Monroe, W. (1917). A report on the use of the Kansas silent reading tests with over one hundred thousand children. *Journal of Educational Psychology, 8,* 600–608.

Monroe, W. (1918a). Existing tests and standards. In G. Whipple (Ed.), *The Seventeenth Yearbook of the National Society for the Study of Education: Part 2. The measurement of educational products* (pp. 71–104). Bloomington, IL: Public School Publishing.

Monroe, W. (1918b). *Monroe Standardized Silent Reading Test (Rev. ed.).* Bloomington, IL: Public School Publishing.

Monroe, W. (1918c). Monroe's standardized silent reading tests. *Journal of Educational Psychology, 9,* 303–312.

Monroe, W., De Voss, J., & Kelly, F. (1917). *A teacher's handbook on educational test and measurements.* Boston: Houghton Mifflin.

Monroe, W. S. (1924). *Educational tests and measurements.* Boston: Houghton Mifflin.

Monroe, W. S., DeVoss, J. C., Kelly, F. J. (1917). *A teacher's handbook on educational tests and measurements.* Boston: Houghton Mifflin.

Montagu, M. F. A. (1945). Intelligence in northern Negroes and southern Whites in the first world war. *American Journal of Psychology, 58,* 161–188.

Moore, D., Readence, J., & Rickelman, R. (1983). An historical exploration of content area reading instruction. *Journal of Reading, 26*(4), 307–313.

Moore, R. (1995). Racism in the English language. In P. Rothenberg (Ed.), *Race, class, and gender in the United States* (3rd ed., pp. 376–386). New York: St. Martin's Press.

Morely, D., & Chen, K. (Eds.). (2003). *Critical dialogues in cultural studies.* London: Routledge.

Morphett, M., & Washburne, C. (1931). When should children begin to read. *Elementary School Journal, 31,* 496–503.

Morrison, T. (1972). *The bluest eye.* New York: Washington Square Press.

Morris, R. (1981). *Reading, 'riting, and reconstruction: The Freedmen in the South, 1861–1870.* Chicago: University of Chicago Press.

Morris, C. (1970). *The pragmatic movement in American philosophy.* New York: George Brazeller Inc.

Morris, R. C. (1980). *Freedmen's schools and textbooks: An AMS Reprint Series,* Volume 4. New York: AMS Press, Inc.

Morrison, T. (1987). *Beloved.* New York: Random House.

Mosier, R. (1947). *Making the American mind: Social and moral ideas in the McGuffey Readers.* New York: King's Crown Press.

Murchison, C., Boring, E., Buhler, K., Langfeld, H., & Watson, J. (Eds.). (1932). *A history of psychology in autobiography.* Worcester, MA: Clark University Press.

Murray, L. (1826). *Introduction to the English reader.* Philadelphia: Scott.

NAEP 1992 Reading Report Card for the National and the States: Data from the *National and Trial State Assessments.* Washington, DC: U.S. Department of Education.

National Assessment of Educational Progress. (1994). *The 1994 National Assessment of Educational Progress in Reading.* Retrieved January, 1, 2003, from http://nces.ed.gov.nationsreportcard

National Assessment of Educational Progress. (2000). *Reading framework for the National Assessment of Educational Progress: 1992–2000.*

National Assessment of Educational Progress. (2003a). *Reading framework for 2003.* Retrieved January 15, 2003, from http://nces.ed.gov. nationsreportcard

National Assessment of Educational Progress. (2003b). *The nation's 2003 report card: Reading Highlights 2003.* Retrieved January 1, 2004, from http://www.nces.ed.gov.nationsreprotcard

National Commission on Excellence in Education. (1983). *A nation at risk: The imperative for educational reform.* Washington, DC: U.S. Government Printing Office. Retrieved July 19, 2005, from http://www. ed.gov/pubs/NatAtRisk/index.html

National Defense Education Act of 1958, Public Law 85-86.

National Intelligence Test. (1920). Yonkers: World Book.

National Institute of Child Health and Human Development. (2000a). *Report of the National Reading Panel: Teaching children to read: An evidence-based assessment of the scientific research literature on reading and its implications for reading instruction.* (NIH Publication No. 00-4769). Washington, DC: U.S. Government Printing Office.

National Institute of Child Health and Human Development. (2000b). *Teaching children to read—Summary report of the National Reading Panel.* Washington, DC: U.S. Government Printing Office.

National Institute of Child Health and Human Development. (2000c). *Report of the National Reading Panel: Teaching children to read: An evidence-based assessment of the scientific research literature on reading and its implications for reading instruction.* [Video]. (NIH Publication No. 00-4769). Washington, DC: U.S. Government Printing Office.

National Reading Panel. (2000). Available: http://www.nationalreading-panel.org. Retrieved, November, 2000.

Nelson, O. (Producer). (1952). *The Adventures of Ozzie & Harriet.* [Television series]. Hollywood: American Broadcasting Company.

New London Group. (1996). A pedagogy of multiliteracies: Designing social futures. *Harvard Educational Review, 66*(1), 60–92.

No Child Left Behind Act of 2001, Public Law 107–110, 115 Stat, 1425 (2002).

No Child Left Behind Act: Reauthorization of the Elementary and Secondary Act, Pub. L. No. 107-10, (2002).Retrieved 11/16/04.

Norris, F. (1901). *The octopus: A story of California.* New York: Penguin.

Norris, F. (1903). *The pit: A story of Chicago.* New York: Penguin.

Oberholzer, E. (1914). Testing the efficiency in reading in the grades. *The Elementary School Journal,* 313–322.

Olson, L., & Viadero, D. (2002, January 30). Law mandates scientific base for research. *Education Week, 21*(2), 1, 14.

Oppenheimer, J. (Producer). (1951). *I Love Lucy.* [Television Series}. Hollywood: CBS Broadcasting Inc.

Oransanu, J., & Penny, M. (1986). Introduction: Comprehension theory and how it grew. In J. Orasanu (Ed.), *Reading comprehension: From research to practice* (pp. 1–10). Newark, DE: International Reading Association.

Otis, A. (1917). The derivation of simpler forms of regression equations. *Journal of Educational Psychology, 8,* 619–622.

Otis, A., & Davidson, P. (1916). Considerations concerning the making of a scale for the measurement of reading ability. *Pedagogical Seminary, 23,* 528–549.

Otis, A. S. (1916). Considerations concerning the making of a scale for the measurement of reading ability, *Pedagogical Seminary, 23,* 528–549.

Paige, R. (2003, March 12). Paige blasts "soft bigotry of low expectations." [Press release]. Retrieved May 14, 2003, from http://www.ed.gov/news/pressreleases/2003/03/03122003.html

Paige, R. (2003, November 13). Results from Nation's Report Card show improvement in math; Narrowing the achievement gap. [Press release] Retrieved November 14, 2003, from http://www.ed.gov/news/pressreleases/2003/11/11122003

Paige, R. (2004, January 7). Prepared remarks of Secretary Paige before the American Enterprise Institute. [Speech]. Retrieved January 2, 2004, from http://www.ed.gov/news/speeches/2004/01/01072004.htm

Pak, Y. (2002). *Wherever I go, I will always be a loyal American: Seattle's Japanese American schoolchildren during World War II.* New York: Routledge Farmer.

Parker, F. (1883). *Notes of talks on teaching* (Reported by L. Patridge). New York: Kellogg.

Parker, R., & Watson, J. (1874). *The national reader.* New York: Barnes.

Parkhurst, H. (1922). *Education on the Dalton Plan.* New York: Dutton.

Pearson, P. (1981). A decade of research in reading comprehension. In V. Forese & S.B. Straw (Eds.), *Research in the language arts: Language and schooling* (pp. 255–264). Baltimore, MD: University Park Press.

Pearson, P. (1986). Twenty years of research in reading comprehension. In T. Raphael (Ed.), *The contexts of school-based literacy* (pp. 43–62). New York: Random House.

Pearson, P. (1992). Reading. In M. Alkin (Ed.), *Encyclopedia of educational research,* (6th ed,, Vol. 3, pp. 1075–1085). New York: Macmillan.

Pearson, P., & Hamm, D. (2001). *The assessment of reading comprehension: A review of practices—past, present, and future.* Retrieved January 30, 2001, from URL>. Prepared for the Rand Corporation.

Pearson, P., & Sarroub, L. (1998). Two steps forward, three steps back: The stormy history of reading comprehension assessment. *The Clearing House* 72(2), 97–105.

Pearson, P., & Stephens, D. (1989). Learning about literacy: A 30-year journey. In C. Gordon, G. Labercane & W. McEachern (Eds.), *Elementary reading instruction: Process and practice.* (pp. 22–42). Ginn Press.

Pelosi, P. (1977). The roots of reading diagnosis. In H. Robinson (Ed.), *Reading and writing instruction in the United States: Historical trends* (pp. 69–75). Newark, DE: International Reading Association.

Pendergast, C. (2002). The economy of literacy: How the Supreme Court stalled the civil rights movement. *Harvard Educational Review, 72*(2), 206–229.

Peirce, C. (1868a). Questions concerning certain faculties claimed for man. *Journal of Speculative Philosophy, 2,* 103–114.

Peirce, C. (1868b). Some consequences of four incapacities. *Journal of Speculative Philosophy, 2,* 140–157.

Peirce, C. (1877). The fixation of belief *Popular Science Monthly, 12,* 1–15.

Peirce, C. (1878a). Deduction, induction, and hypothesis. *Popular Science Monthly, 12,* 407–482.

Peirce, C. (1878b). How to make our ideas clear. *Popular Science Monthly, 12,* 286–302.

Peirce, C. (1878c). The order of nature. *Popular Science Monthly, 13,* 203–217.

Peirce, C. (1878d). The probability of induction. *Popular Science Monthly, 12,* 705–718.

Peirce, C. (1893a). Evolutionary love. *The Monist, 3,* 176–200.

Peirce, C. (1893b). Reply to The Necessitarian. In C. Hartshorne, P. Weiss, & A. Burks, (Eds.), *The collected papers of Charles Sanders Peirce* (Vols. 1–8, pp. 390–435). Cambridge, MA: Harvard University Press.

Peirce, C. (1901). The century's great men in science. *Annual report of the Board of Regents of the Smithsonian Institution.* (pp. 694–695). Washington, DC: Government Printing Office.

Peirce, C. (1905). What pragmatism is. *The Monist, 15*(2), 161–181.

Peirce, C. (1931). Science as a guide to conduct. Vol. 1. Principles of philosophy. In C. Hartshorne, P. Weiss, & A. Burks (Eds.), *Collected papers of Charles Sanders Peirce.* London: Thoemmes Continuum.

Peirce, C. S. (1931–1958). *The Collected Papers of Charles Sanders Peirce.* In C. Hartshorne, P. Weiss (Eds.), (Vols. 1–6) and A. Burks (Vols. 7–8). Cambridge MA: Harvard University Press.

Perry, T., & Delpit, L. (1998). *The real Ebonics debate: Power, language, and the education of African-American children.* Boston: Beacon Press.

Pestalozzi, J. H. (1894). *How Gertrude teaches her children* (L. Holland & F. Turner, Trans). London: Swan Sonnenschein.

Peterson, J. (1934). Basic considerations of methodology in race testing. *Journal of Negro Education, 3*(3), 403–410.

Piaget, J. (1936). *The origins of intelligence in children.* New York: Norton.

Piaget, J. (1955). *The language and thought of the child* (M. Gabain, Trans.). New York: Meridian Books.

Piaget, J. (1971). *Science of education and the psychology of the child.* New York: Grossman.

Piekarz, J. (1956). Getting meaning from reading. *Elementary School Journal, 56,* 303–309.

Pierpont, J. (1841). *The American first class book: or Exercises in reading and recitation.* Boston: Williams. (Original work published 1823).

Piestrup, A. (1973). *Black dialect interference and accommodation of reading instruction in first grade* (Language Behavior Research Laboratory Monograph No. 4). Berkeley: University of California.

Pihlbald, T. C. (1926). Mental tests and social problems. *Social Forces, 5*(1), 237–243.

Pinter, R. (1913a). Inner speech during silent reading. *Psychological Review, 20,* 129–153.

Pinter, R. (1913b). Oral and silent reading of fourth-grade pupils. *Journal of Educational Psychology, 4,* 333–337.

Pinter, R. (1917). The significance of intelligence testing in the elementary school. *Sixteenth yearbook of the National Society for the Study of Education. Part II: New materials of instruction complied by the National Society's committee on new materials of teaching. Chicago*: University of Chicago Press.

Pinter, R., & Gilliland, A. (1916). Oral and silent reading. *Journal of Educational Psychology, 7*, 201–212.

Pinter, R. (1923). Comparison of American and foreign children on intelligence test. *Journal of Educational Psychology, 14*(5), 292–295.

Plessy V Ferguson. (1898). 163 U.S. 537.

Popkewitz, T. (1984). *Paradigm and ideology in educational research: The social functions the intellectual.* Philadelphia: Falmer Press.

Popkewitz, T., & Tabachnick, B. (1981). Soviet and American pedagogical research: Differences and similarities in the two countries. In B. Tabachnick, T. Popkewitz, & B. Szekely (Eds.), *Studying teaching and learning trends in Soviet and American research.* (pp. 3–38). New York: Praeger.

Pratte, R. (1977). *Ideology and education.* New York: McKay.

Pratt, W. E., Young, R. V., Whitmer, C. A. (1941-1955). *American School Reading Readiness Tests.* Indianapolis, IN: Boobs-Merrill.

Prawatt, R. (2000). The two faces of Deweyan pragmatism: Inductionism versus social constructivism. *Teachers College Record, 102*(4), 805–840.

Pressey, S. (1922). *Introduction to the use of standard tests: A brief manual in the use of tests of both ability and achievement in the school subjects.* Yonkers-on-Hudson, NY: World Book.

Pressey, S., & Pressey, L. (1922). *Introduction to the use of standardized tests: A brief manual in the use of tests of both ability and achievement in the school subjects.* Yonkers-on-Hudson, NY: World Book.

Price, J. (1934). Negro–White differences in general intelligence. *Journal of Negro Education*, 424–452.

Pritchard, R. (1990). The effects of cultural schemata on reading strategies. *Reading Research Quarterly, 25*(4), 273–295.

Quantz, J. (1897). Problems in the psychology of reading. *Psychological Review Monograph Supplements, 2*(1). New York: Macmillan.

Raguse, F. (1930). Qualitative and quantitative achievements in first grade reading. *Teachers College Record, 32*, 424–436.

RAND. (2002). *Reading for understanding: Toward an R & D program in reading comprehension.* Santa Monica, CA: RAND.

RAND. (2000-2005). Achievement for all: Reading. Retrieved March 3, 2001, from www.rand.org/multi/achievementforall

Rand Reading Study Group. (2001). Reading for understanding: Toward a Research and Development Program in Reading Comprehension. MR-1465.0. Available, www.rand.org/pubs/monograph_reports/2005/MR1465.pdf.

Range, P. R. (1995, March). Interview with William J. Bennett. *Modern Maturity,* 38 (2), 26–30.

Rankin, J. (1911). The eight-grade vocabulary. *Elementary School Teacher,* 11, 465–68.

Raphael, C. (2003). *Theory of hegemony and ideology.* Retrieved June 27, 2005, from http:www.dangerouscitizen.com/Articles/244.aspx

Ratner, S. (1936). Evolution and the rise of the scientific spirit in America. *Philosophy of Science, 3*(1), 104–122.

Readence, J., & Moore, D. (1983). Why questions? A historical perspective on standardized reading comprehension tests. *Journal of Reading, 26*(4), 306–313.

Reading Comprehension Research Grant, CFDA. (2001). CFDA 34.305G. Retrieved February 4, 2001, from http://www.connsensebulletin.com/update1.html

Reading Comprehension and Reading Scale-up Research Grant (2003, October 22). CDFA Retrieved November 2, 2003, from http://www.ed.gov/programs/edreserach/applicant.html

Reading Comprehension Research Grants. (2002, December 16). CDFA. 84.305G. Retrieved January 22, 2003, from http://www.ed.gov/offices/IES/funding.html

Reading Framework for the National Assessment of Educational Progress: 1992–2000. NAEP Reading Consensus Project, National Assessment Governing Board, U.S. Department of Education. Washington, DC: U. S. Printing Office.

Reid, I. (1940). General characteristics of the Negro youth population. *Journal of Negro Education, 9*(3), 278–289.

Resnick, D. (1982). History of educational testing. In A. Wigdor & W. Garner (Eds.), *Ability testing; Uses, consequences, and controversies (Part 2,* pp. 173–194). Washington, DC: National Academy Press.

Resnick, D., & Resnick, L. (1977). The nature of literacy: An historical exploration. *Harvard Educational Review, 47,* 370–385.

Resnick, D., & Resnick, L. (1983). Improving educational standards in American schools. *Phi Delta Kappan, 65,* 178–180.

Resnick, D., & Resnick, L. (1985). Standards, curriculum and performance: A historical and comparative perspective. *Educational Researcher, 14*(4), 5–20.

Resnick, L. (1987). *Education and learning to think.* Washington, DC: National Academy Press.

Resnick, L. (1989). *Knowing, learning, and instruction.* Hillsdale, NJ: Lawrence Erlbaum Associates.

Resnick, L. (1995). From aptitude to effort: A new foundation for our schools. *Daedalus 124*(4), 55–62.

Reynolds, R., Taylor, M., Steffensen, M., Shirey, L., & Anderson, R. (1981). *Cultural schemata and reading comprehension* Center for the Study of Reading (Tech. Rep. No. 201). Urbana-Champaign: University of Illinois, Center for the Study of Reading.

Ribot, T. (1877). Philosophy in France. *Mind, 2*(7), 366–386.

Rice, J. (1893). *The public school system of the United States*. New York: Century.

Richards, A., & Davidson, P. (1916). Correlations of single measures of some representative reading tests. *School and Society, 4*, 375–77.

Richards, I. (1942). *How to read a page*. New York: Norton.

Richards, I. (1938). *Interpretation in teaching*. Boston: Harcourt.

Richards, I. (1929). *Practical criticism: A study of literary judgment*. New York: Harcourt, Brace.

Rickford, A. (2001). The effect of cultural congruence and higher order questioning on the reading enjoyment and comprehension of ethnic minority students. *Journal of Education of Students Place at Risk, 6*(4), 357–387.

Rickford, J. (1999). *African American Vernacular English*. Oxford, UK: Blackwell.

Rickford, J. (1997). The Ebonics controversy in my backyard: A sociolinguist's experiences and reflections. Retrieved December 30, 2003, from   http://www.stanford.edu~rickford/papers/EbonicsInMyBackyard.html

Rickford, J. (1998). *Using the vernacular to teach the standard*. Retrieved December 30, 2003, from http://www.Stanford.edu/~rickford/papers/VernacularToTeachStandard.html

Rickford, J., & Rickford, A. (1995). Dialects and education. *Linguistics and Education, 7*(2), 107–128.

Rickford, J., & Rickford, A. (2000). *Spoken soul: The story of Black English*. New York: Wiley.

Riis, J. (1890). *How the other half lives: Studies among the tenements of New York*. New York: Scribner's.

Riley, R. W. (1997). *Secretary Riley's April 29, 1997 Statement on Voluntary National Tests for Reading and Math*. Available: http://www.ed.gov/Speeches/04- 1997/970429.html

Rist, R. (1970). Student social class and teacher expectations. *Harvard Educational Review, 40*, 411–451.

Robinson, D. (Ed.), (1977). *Significant contributions to the history of psychology 1750-1920*. Washington, DC: University Publications of America.

Robinson, H. (Ed. & Comp.). (1966). Reading: Seventy-five years of progress. *Proceedings of the Annual Conference on Reading*. Chicago: The University of Chicago Press.

Robinson, H. (1967). *Why pupils fail in reading.* Chicago: University of Chicago Press. (Original work published 1946).

Robinson, H. (Ed.). (1977). *Reading and writing instruction in the United States: Historical trends.* Newark, DE: International Reading Association.

Robinson, H. (1985). William S. Gray: The scholar. In J. Stevenson (Ed.), *William S. Gray: Teacher, scholar, leader* (pp. 24–36). Newark, DE: International Reading Association.

Robinson, H., Faraone, V., Hittleman, D., & Unruh, E. (1990). *Reading comprehensi instruction, 1783–1987: A review of trends and research.* Newark, DE: International Reading Association.

Robinson, R. (1989). Reading teachers of the past—what they believed about reading. *Reading Improvement, 26*(3), 231–235.

Robinson, R. (Ed.). (2000). *Historical sources in U. S. reading education, 1900–1970: An annotated bibliography.* Newark, DE: International Reading Association.

Robinson, R., & Jennings, R. (1985). Reading education: A twenty-year perspective. *Reading Horizons, 26(1),* 25–32.

Roethlein, B. (1912). The relative legibility of different faces of printing types. *American Journal of Psychology, 23,* 1–36.

Romanes, G. (1884). *Animal intelligence.* New York: Appleton. (Original work published 1878).

Romanes, G. (1888). *Mental evolution in man: Origin of human faculty.* London: Kegan Paul.

Rosenblatt, L. (1978). *The reader, the text, the poem: The transactional theory of the literary work.* Carbondale: Southern Illinois University Press.

Rosenblatt, L. (1995). *Literature as exploration (5th rom ed.).* New York: Modern Language Association. (Original work published 1938).

Rosenthal, R., & Jacobson, L. (1968). *Pygmalion in the classroom: Teacher expectation and pupils' intellectual development.* New York: Rinehart & Winston.

Ruddell, R. (1964). A study of the cloze comprehension technique in relation to structurally controlled reading material. *Improvement of Reading Through Classroom Practice, 9,* 298–303.

Ruddell, R. (1965). Effect of the similarity of oral and written language structure on reading comprehension. *Elementary English, 42,* 403–410.

Ruffins, P. & Ruffins, F. D. (1997). Ten myths, half-truths and misunderstandings about Black history. *Black Issues in Higher Education, 13*(25), 23–25.

Rugg, H. (1917a). *Statistical methods applied to education: A textbook for students of education in the quantitative study of school problems.* Boston: Houghton Mifflin.

Rugg, H. (1917b). How I keep in touch with quantitative literature. *Elementary School Journal, 11,* 301–332.

Rugg, H. (1934). After three decades of scientific method in education. *Teachers College Record, 34,* 111–122.

Rugg, H. (1947). *Foundations for American education.* Yonkers-on-Hudson, NY: World Book.

Rumelhart, D. (1980). Schemata: The building blocks of cognition. In R. Spiro, B. Bruce, & W. Brewer (Eds.), *Theoretical issues in reading comprehension* (pp. 33–58). Hillsdale, NJ: Lawrence Erlbaum Associates.

Rury, J. (1988). Race, region, and education: An analysis of Black and White scores on the 1917 Army Alpha Intelligence Test. *Journal of Negro Education, 57*(1), 51–65.

Rury, J. (1985). American school enrollment in progressive era: An interpretive inquiry. *History of Education, 1,* 49–67.

Salganik, L. (1985). Why testing reforms are so popular and how they are changing education. *Phi Delta Kappan, 66,* 607–610.

Sallach, D. (1974). Class domination and ideological hegemony. *Sociological Quarterly, 15,* 38–50.

Samuels, J. (1976). Hierarchical subskills in reading acquisition process. In J. Gutherie (Ed.), *Aspects of reading acquisition* (pp. 162–179). Baltimore: Johns Hopkins University Press.

Samelson, F. (1987). Early mental testing. In M. Soko (Ed.) *Psychological testing and American society, 1890–1930* (pp. 113–127). New Brunswick, NJ: Rutgers University Press.

Samuelson, R. (2005, May 30). Sputnik time again. *Newsweek,* p. 43.

Sanders, C. (1867). *The school reader. Third book.* New York: Ivison, Phinney, Blakeman.

Saussure, F. (1960). *Course in general linguistics.* London: Owen.

Schmitt C. (1914). School subjects as material for tests of mental ability. *Elementary School Journal, 15,* 150–161.

Schwegler, R., & Winn, E. (1920). A comparative study of the intelligence of white and colored children. *Journal of Educational Psychology, 2,* 835–848.

Scientific principles in educational research: Exploration of Perspectives and implications. OERI (CFEX-Q-00-02-A), Retrieved March 31, 2002.

Secretary's Commission on Achieving Necessary Skills. (1991). *What work requires of schools* (ED 332 054). Washington, DC: SCANS, U.S. Department of Labor.

Seldon, S. (1999). *Inheriting shame: The story of eugenics in America.* New York: Teachers College Press.

Shannon, P. (1989). Paradigmatic diversity within the reading research community. *Journal of Reading Behavior, 21*(2), 97–105.

Shannon, P. (1985). Reading instruction and social class. *Language Arts,* *62*(6), 604–613.

Shavelson, R., & Towne, L. (Eds.). (2002). *Scientific research in education.* Washington, DC: National Academy Press.

Shepard, L. (2000). The role of assessment in a learning culture. *Educational Researcher, 29*(7), 4–14.

Shotly, M. (1912). A study of reading vocabulary of children. *Elementary School Teacher, 12,* 272–277.

Sims, R. (1972). *A psycholinguistic description of miscues generated by selected young readers during the oral reading of text material in black dialect and Standard English.* Unpublished doctoral dissertation, Wayne State University, Detroit, MI.

Sinclair, U. (1906). *The jungle.* New York: Doubleday.

Singer, H. (1987). A century of landmarks in reading research. In H. Singer & R. Ruddell (Eds.), *Theoretical models and processes of reading.* (3rd ed., pp. 8–20). Newark, DE: International Reading Association.

Singer, H., & Ruddell. R. (Eds.). (1987). *Theoretical models and processes of reading* (3rd ed.). Newark, DE: International Reading Association.

Skinner B. (1938). *The behavior of organisms: An experimental analysis.* New York: Appleton-Century.

Skinner, B. (1948). *Walden II.* New York: Macmillan.

Skinner, B. (1954). The science of learning and the art of teaching. *Harvard Educational Review, 24*(2), 86–97.

Skinner, B. (1950). Are theories of learning necessary? *Psychological Review, 57,* 193–216.

Skinner, B. (1953). *Science and human behavior.* New York: Macmillan.

Skinner, B. (1956). A case history in scientific method. *American Psychologist, 11,* 221–233.

Skinner, B. (1957). The experimental analysis of behavior. *American Scientist, 45,* 343–371.

Skinner, B. F. (1974). *About Behaviorism .* New York: Vintage.

Small, A. (1910). *The meaning of social science.* Chicago: University of Chicago Press.

Smith, F. (Ed.). (1973). *Psycholinguistics and reading.* New York: Holt, Rinehart & Winston.

Smith, F. (1971). *Understanding reading: A psycholinguistic analysis of reading and learning to read (2nd ed.).* New York: Holt, Rinehart & Winston.

Smith, N. (1986). *American reading instruction: Its development and its significance in gaining a perspective on current practices in reading.* New York: Silver, Burdett. (Originally published 1934).

Smith, L. (1999). *Decolonizing methodologies: Research and indigenous peoples.* London: Zed Books.

Smith, T. (1972). Native Blacks and foreign Whites: Varying responses to educational opportunity in America, 1880–1950. *Perspectives in American History, 6,* 309–335.

Smith, F. & Miller, G., (Eds.), (1966). The genesis of language; a psycholinguistic approach. Proceedings of a conference on language development in children. Cambridge, M.I.T. Press.

Smitherman, G. (2000). *Talkin that talk: Language, culture and education in African America.* New York: Routledge.

Smitherman, G. (1977). *Talkin and Testifyin: The Language of Black America.* Detroit: Wayne University Press.

Snow, C. (2000). *Reading for understanding.* Washington, DC: National Academy Press.

Sokol, M. (1971). The unpublished autobiography of James McKeen Cattell. *American Psychologist, 26,* 626–635.

Sokal, M. (Ed.). (1981). *An education in psychology: James McKeen Cattell's journal and letters from Germany and England, 1880–1888.* Cambridge, MA: MIT Press.

Sokol, M. (1987a). James McKeen Catell and mental anthropometry: Nineteenth-century science and reform and the origins of psychological testing. In M. Sokol (Ed.), *Psychological testing and American society, 1890–1930,* (pp. 21–45). New Brunswick, NJ: Rutgers University Press.

Sokol, M. (Ed.). (1987b). *Psychological testing and American society, 1890–1930.* New Brunswick, NJ: Rutgers University Press.

Soltow L. , & Stevens, E. (1981). *The rise of literacy and the common school in the United States.* Chicago: University of Chicago Press.

Somervill, M. (1975). Dialect and reading: A review of alternative solutions. *Review of Educational Research, 45,* 247–262.

Spearritt, D. (1972). Identification of subskills of reading comprehension by maximum likelihood factor analysis. *Reading Research Quarterly, 8,* 93–111.

Spencer, H. (1864). Reasons for dissenting from the philosophy of M. Comte. Retrieved June 24, 2003, from http://www.marxists.org/reference/subject/philosophy/works/en/spencer.htm

Spencer, H. (1892). *Social statics; Or the condition essential to human happiness specified, And the first of them developed.* New York: Appleton. (Original work published 1851).

Spencer, H. (1904). *An autobiography* (2 vols.). London: Watts.

Spencer, H. (1911). *Essays on education and kindred subjects.* London: Dent.

Spencer, H. (1949). *Essays on education.* London: Dent. (Original work published 1911).

Spencer, H. (1958). *First principles.* New York: Dewilt Revolving Fund.

Spencer, H. (1961). *The study of sociology*. Ann Arbor: University of Michigan Press.

Spencer, H. (1963). *The principles of psychology*. New York: D Appleton. (Original work published 1896).

Spencer, H. (1963). *Education: Intellectual, moral and physical*. Paterson, NJ: Littlefield, Adams. (Original work published 1861).

Spencer, H. (1862). *First principles*. London:

Spencer, H. (1852). A theory of population, deduced from the general law of animal fertility', *Westminster Review, 57*, 468-501. Available: http://www.victorianweb.org/philosophy/spencer/dagg2.html. Retrieved, March 24, 2006.

Spina, S., & Tai, R. (1998). The politics of racial identity. A pedagogy of invisibility. *Educational Researcher, 27*(1), 36–40, 48.

Spiro, R., Coulson, R., Feltvoich, P., & Anderson, D. (1988). Cognitive flexibility theory: Advanced knowledge acquisition in ill-structured domains. In *Proceedings of the Tenth Annual Conference of the Cognitive Science Society* (pp. 375–383). Hillsdale, NJ: Lawrence Erlbaum Associates.

Spring, J. (1972). Psychologists and the war: The meaning of intelligence in the Alpha and Beta tests. *History of Education Quarterly, 12*(1), 3–15.

Spring, J. (1986). *The American school 1642–1985 varieties of historical interpretation of the foundations and development of American education*. New York: Longman.

Spring, J. (1996). *The cultural transformation of a Native American family and its tribe 1763–1995: A basket of apples*. Mahwah, NJ: Lawrence Erlbaum Associates.

Stedman, L., & Kaestle, C. (1987). Literacy and reading performance in the United States, from 1880 to the present. *Reading Research Quarterly, 22*(1), 8-46.

Stanovich, K. (2000). *Progress in understanding reading*. New York: Guilford.

Starch, D. (1914). *The measurement of efficiency in reading, writing, spelling and English*. Madison, WI: The College Book Store. Retrieved January 3, 2004, from http://www.tc.columbia.edu/cice/vol5nr2/al152.htm

Starch, D. (1915). The measurement of efficiency in reading. *Journal of Educational Psychology, 6*, 1–24.

Starch, D. (1917). *Educational psychology*. New York: Macmillan.

Starch, D. (1918). The reliability of reading tests. *School and Society, 8*, 86–90.

Starch, D. (1927). *Educational psychology*. New York: Macmillan.

Stantis, S. (2004, January 10). Poem. *Chicago Tribune*, Section 1, p. 11.

Stedman, L., & Kaestle, C. (1987). Literacy and reading performance in the United States, from 1880 to the present. *Reading Research Quarterly, 22*(1), 8-46.

Stein, N., & Trabasso, T. (1982). What's in a story? An approach to comprehension. In R. Glaser (Ed.), *Advances in psychology of instruction.* (Vol.2, pp. 213–268). Hillsdale, NJ: Lawrence Erlbaum Associates.

Stepan, N., & Gilman, S. (1993). Appropriating the idioms of science: The rejection of scientific racism. In S. Harding (Ed.), *The "racial" economy of science* (pp. 170–193). Bloomington: Indiana University Press.

Stern, W. (1912). *The psychological methods of intelligence testing.* Baltimore: Warwick & York.

Stevenson, J. (1985). *William S. Gray: Teacher, scholar leader.* Newark, DE: International Reading Association.

Stillman, B. (1912). An experiment in teaching reading. *Atlantic Educational Journal, 6,* 168.

Stillo, M. (1999). Antonio Gramsci. Retrieved November 11, 2003, from http://www.theory.org.uk/ctr-gram.htm

Stoskopf, A. (1999). An untold story of resistance. *Rethinking Schools, 14*(1), 10–11, 20.

Stoskopf, A. (2000). The forgotten history of eugenics. In K. Swope & B. Miner (Eds.), *Failing our kids: Why the testing craze won't fix our schools* (pp. 76–80), Milwaukee, WI: Rethinking Schools.

Street, B. (2003). *What's "new" in new literacy studies? Critical approaches to literacy in theory and practice.* Retrieved January 12, 2004, from http://www.tc.columbia.edu/cice/articles/bs152.htm

Strang, R. (1938). *Explorations in reading patterns.* Chicago: University of Chicago Press.

Strinati, D. (1995). *An introduction to theories of popular culture.* London: Routledge.

Summer, W. (18883). *What social classes owe to each other.* New York: Harper & Bros.

Suppe, F. (1974). *The structure of scientific theories.* Urbana: University of Illinois Press.

Sweet, A. P., & Snow, C. E, and (Eds.), (2003). *Rethinking reading comprehension.* New York: Guilford Press.

Tabachnick, B., Popkewitz, T., & Szekely, B. (Eds.). (1981). *Studying teaching and learning trends in Soviet and American Research.* New York: Praeger.

Takaki, R. (1993). A different mirror: A history of multicultural America. Boston:Little, Brown & Co.

Tan, A. (1990). *The joy luck club.* New York: Ivy Books.

Tate, W. (1997). Critical race theory and education: History, theory, and implications. In M. Apple (Ed.), *Review of research in education* (Vol. 22, pp. 195–247). Washington, DC: American Educational Research Association.

Tatum, A. (2000). Breaking down barriers that disenfranchise African American adolescent readers in low-low tracks. *Journal of Adolescent and Adult Literacy, 44*(1) 52–64.

Taylor, W. (1953). Cloze procedure: A new tool for measuring readability. *Journalism Quarterly, 30,* 414–438.

Taylor, B., Pearson, P., Clark, K., & Walpole, S. (1999). *Schools that beat the odds* (CIERA Rep. 2-008). Ann Arbor: CIERA.

Taylor, O. (1973). Teachers' attitudes toward Black and nonstandard English as measured by the language attitude scale. In R. Shuy & R. Fasold (Eds.), *Language attitudes: Current trends and prospects* (pp. 174–201). Washington, DC: Georgetown University Press.

Terman, L. (1916a). *The measurement of intelligence: An explanation of and a complete guide for the use of the Stanford revision and extension of The Binet–Simon Intelligence Tests.* Boston: Houghton Mifflin.

Terman, L. (1916b). *Stanford Revision of the Binet-Simon Scale.* Boston: Houghton Mifflin. (Original work published 1906).

Terman, L. (1922a, December 27). The great conspiracy or the impulse imperious of intelligence testers, psychoanalyzed and exposed by Mr. Lippmann. *New Republic, 33,* 116–120.

Terman, L. (1922b). (includes page 655) qtd. in Gould (p. 265).

Terman, L., & Merrill, M. (1972). *Stanford–Binet Intelligence Scale (1972 norms ed.).* Boston: Houghton Mifflin.

Terman, L. M. & Merrill, M. A. (1960). *Stanford-Binet Intelligence Scale: Manual for the Third Revision Form L-M.* Boston: Houghton Mifflin.

Terman, L. M. & Merrill, M. A. (1972). *Stanford-Binet Intelligence Scale, 1972 norms edition.* Boston: Houghton Mifflin.

The Elementary and Secondary School Act. Public Law 89-10 (April 11, 1965).

The Immigration and Nationality Services Act of 1965, Pubic Law 89-236.

The Voting Rights Act of 1965, Public Law 89-10.

Thompson, C. (1934). The conclusions of scientists relative to racial differences. *Journal of Negro Education, 3*(3), 494–512.

Thompson, W. (1925). Eugenics and the social good. *Journal of Social Forces, 3*(3), 414-419.

Thorndike, E. (1898). Animal intelligence: An experimental study of the associative processes in animals. *Psychological Review Monograph Supplements, No. 8.*

Thorndike, E. (1901). *Notes on child study.* New York: Macmillan.

Thorndike, E. (1903). *Educational psychology.* New York: Teachers College.

Thorndike, E. (1904a). *An introduction to the theory of mental and social measurements.* New York: Science Press.

Thorndike, E. (1904b). *Theory of mental and social measurements.* New York: Science Press.

Thorndike, E. (1904c). *Heredity, correlation and sex differences in school abilities*. In E.

Thorndike, E. (Ed.), *Studies from the department of educational psychology at Teachers College, Columbia University*. New York: Columbia University.

Thorndike, E. (1906). *The principles of teaching based on psychology*. New York: Seiler.

Thorndike, E. (1911). *Individuality*. In G. Joncich (Ed.), *Psychology and the science of education: Selected writings of Edward L. Thorndike* (pp. 118–126). New York: Teachers College Press.

Thorndike, E. (1912). *Education: A first book*. New York. Macmillan.

Thorndike, E. (1913a). *The equality of equally often noted differences*. New York: Teachers College Press.

Thorndike, E. (1913b). Eugenics: With special reference to intellect and character. *Popular Science Monthly, 83*, 125–138.

Thorndike, E. (1913c). *Introduction to the theory of mental and social-measurement*. New York: Teachers College Press.

Thorndike, E. (1914a). The measurement of ability in reading. *Teachers College Record, 15*, 207–277.

Thorndike, E. (1914b). *Educational psychology: Briefer course*. New York: Teachers College Press.

Thorndike, E. (1915a). An improved scale for measuring ability in reading. *Teachers College Record, 16*, 445–467.

Thorndike, E. (1915b). An improved scale for measuring ability in reading. *Teachers College Record, 17*, 40–67.

Thorndike, E. (1916a). The measurement of achievement in reading: Word knowledge. *Teachers College, 17*, 430–54.

Thorndike, E. (1916b). *An introduction to the theory of mental and social measurements*. New York: Teachers College, Columbia University. (Original work published 1904).

Thorndike, E. (1917a). The psychology of thinking in the case of reading. *The Psychological Review, 24*, 220–234.

Thorndike, E. (1917b). Reading as reasoning: A study of mistakes in paragraph reading. *The Journal of Educational Psychology, 8*, 323–332.

Thorndike, E. (1917c). The understanding of sentences: A study of errors in reading. *The Elementary School Journal, 18*, 98–114.

Thorndike, E. (1918). The nature, purposes and general methods of measurements of educational products. In G. Whipple (Ed.), *The Seventeenth Yearbook of the National Society for the Study of Education. Part 2. The measurement of educational products* (pp. 16–24). Bloomington, IL: Public School Publishing.

Thorndike, E. (1920a, January). Intelligence and its uses. *Harper's 140*, 233.

Thorndike, E. (1920b). The psychology of the half-educated man. *Harper's*, 830, 664–670.

Thorndike, E. (1921). *The teacher's word book.* New York: Teachers College, Columbia University.

Thorndike, E. (1922). Intelligence tests and their use. *The twenty-first Yearbook of the National Society for the Study of Education: Part 1., The nature, history, and general principles of intelligence testing* (pp. 1–6). Bloomington, IL: Public School Publishing.

Thorndike, E. (1927). *Measurement of intelligence.* New York: Bureau of Publications, Teachers College, Columbia University.

Thorndike, E. (1931). *Human learning.* New York: Century.

Thorndike, E. (1932). Autobiography. In C. Murchison, *A history of psychology in autobiography.* (p. 3). Worcester, MA: Clark University Press.

Thorndike, E. (1934a). Improving the ability to read. *Teachers College Record, 36(1),*1–19.

Thorndike, E. (1934b). Improving the ability to read. *Teachers College Record, 36(2),* 123–144.

Thorndike, E. (1934c). Improving the ability to read. *Teachers College Record, 36(3),* 229–241.

Thorndike, E. (1962). *Education. A first book.* In G. Joncich (Ed), *Psychology and the science of education: Selected writings of Edward L. Thorndike* (pp. 70–82). New York: Teachers College Press. (Original work published 1912).

Thorndyke, P. (1977). Cognitive structures in comprehension and memory of narrative discourse. *Cognitive Psychology, 9,* 77–110.

Tiegs, E. W., and Clark, W. W. (1957). *California Reading Test.* Monterey, CA: California Test Bureau.

Tireman, L. (1929). Reading in the elementary schools of New Mexico. *Elementary School Journal, 30,* 621–626.

Tireman, L. (1949). *Mesaland series.* Albuquerque: University of New Mexico Press.

Tireman, L. (1951). *Teaching Spanish-speaking children.* Albuquerque: University of New Mexico Press.

Tierney, R., & Cunningham, J. (1984). Research on teaching reading comprehension. In P. D. Pearson (Ed.), *Handbook of reading research* (pp. 609–655). New York: Longman.

Tierney, R. J., & Pearson, P. D. (1992) Learning to learn from text: A framework for improving classroom practice. In E. K. Dishner, T. W. Bean, J. E. Readance, & D.W. Moore (Eds.), *Reading in the content areas: Improving classroom instruction* (3rd ed., pp. 87–103). Dubuque, IA: Kendall/Hunt.

Tierney, R., Readence, E., & Dishner, E. (1985). *Reading strategies and practices: A compendium.* (2nd ed.). Boston: Allyn & Bacon.

Toppo, G. (2005). "Education Dept. paid commentator to promote law", *USA Today,* 1/7/2005).

Towne, L., Shavelson, R., & Feuer, M. (2001). *Science, evidence and inference in education: Report of a workshop.* Washington, DC: National Academy Press.

Travers, R. (1983). *How research has changed American schools: A history from 1840 to the present.* Kalamazoo, MI: Mythos Press.

Trial Urban District Assessment. (2002). *2002 Trial Urban District. Assessment:* Retrieved January 14, 2003, from http://www.nces.ed.gov/nationsreportcard/reading/results2002/districtresults.asp

Trollinger, W. Jr. (1991). *Literacy in the United States: Readers and reading since 1880.* New Haven: Yale University Press.

Tse, L. (2001). *Why don't they learn English: Separating fact from fallacy in the U. S. language debate.* New York: Teachers College Press.

Tuinman, J. (1971). Thorndike revisited—some facts. *Reading Research Quarterly, 7*(1), 195–202.

Tyack, D. (1974). *The one best system: A history of American urban education.* Cambridge, MA: Harvard University Press.

Tyack, D., & Hansot, E. (1982). *Managers of virtue: Public school leadership in America,* 1820–1980. New York: Basic Books.

U.S. Department of Education (2002) The "No Child Left Behind Act of 2001," Executive Summary. Washington, D.C.: U.S. Government Printing Office.

U.S. Department of Labor's SCANS Report. (1991). What work requires of school.

Unger, R., & West, C. (1998). *The future of American progressivism: An initiative for political and economic reform.* Boston: Beacon Press.

Valencia, S., & Pearson, P. (1985). Reading assessment: Time for a change. *The Reading Teacher, 40*(18), 726–732.

Venezky, R. (1974). *Testing in reading assessment and instructional decision making.* Urbana, IL: ERIC Clearinghouse on Reading and Communication Skills and National Council of Teachers of English. (ERIC Document Reproduction Service No. EJ1614830).

Venezky, R. (1977). Research on reading progress: A historical perspective. *American Psychologist, 32,* 339–345.

Venezky, R. (1984). The history of reading research. In P. Pearson, R. Barr, M. Kamil, & P. Mosentthal (Eds.), *Handbook of reading research* (pp. 3–38). New York: Longman.

Venezky, R. (1987). A history of the American reading textbook. *Elementary School Journal, 87,* 247–265.

Venezky, R. (1986). Steps toward a modern history of reading instruction. In E. Rothkopf, (Ed.), *Review of research in education* (Vol. 13, pp. 129–167). Washington, DC: American Educational Association.

Venezky, R. (1990). *American primers: Guide to the microfiche collection; Introductory essay.* Frederick, MD: University Publications of America.

Venezky, R. (1991). The development of literacy in the industrialized nations of the west. In R Barr, M. Kamil, P. Mosenthal, & P. Pearson (Eds.), *Handbook of reading research:* (Vol. 2, pp. 46–67). White Plains, NY: Longman.

Venezky, R. (1986). Steps toward a modern history of American reading instruction. In E. Rothkopf (Ed.), *Review of Research in Education* (pp. 129–166). Washington, DC: American Educational Research Association.

von Mayrhauser, R. (1987). The manager, the medic, and the mediator: The clash of professional psychological styles and the wartime origins of group mental testing. In M. Sokol (Ed.), *Psychological testing and American society* (pp. 109–122). New Brunswick, NJ: Rutgers University Press.

Vostrosvky, C. (1899). A study of children's reading tastes. *Pedagogical Seminary, 6*, 523–535.

Vygotsky, L. (1978). *Mind in society: The development of higher psychological processes.* Cambridge, MA: Harvard University Press.

Waldo, K. (1915). Tests in reading in Sycamore schools. *Elementary School Journal, 15*, 251–268.

Walker, A. (1982). *The color purple.* New York: Simon & Schuster.

Walker, D. (1830). *Walker's Appeal, in Four articles; together with a Preamble, to the Coloured Citizens of the World, but in Particular, and Very Expressly, to Those of the United States of American, Written in Boston, State of Massachusetts, September 28, 1829.* Boston: Revised and Published by the David Walker.

Ward, L. (1883). *Dynamic sociology, or applied social science, as based upon statistical sociology and the less complex sciences.* New York: Appleton.

Ward, L. (1896). Contributions to social philosophy: IX. The purpose of sociology. *American Journal of Sociology, 2*(3), 446–460.

Watson, J. (1913). Psychology as the behaviorist views it. *Psychological Review, 20*, 158–177.

Watson, J. (1924). *Psychology from the standpoint of a behaviorist.* Philadelphia: Lippincott.

Watson, J. (1930). *Behaviorism* (2nd ed.). New York: Norton. (Original work published 1924).

Weber, G. (1971). *Inner-city children can be taught to read: Four successful schools* (Occasional Papers No. 18). Washington, DC: Council for Basic Education.

Weber, R. (1992). Even in the midst of work: Reading among turn-of-the-century farmers' wives. *Reading Research Quarterly, 28*, 293-302.

Webster, N. (1900). *Blue-back speller.* (Original work published 1783).

Wells, I. (1892). *Southern Horrors: Lynch law in all its phases.* New York: New York Age.

Werner, H., & Kaplan, B. (1952). The acquisition of word meanings: A developmental study. *Monographs of the Society for Research in Child Development, 15* (1, Serial No. 51). Evanston, IL: Child Development Publications of the Society for Research in Child Development, Northwestern University.

West, C. (1993). *Race matters.* Boston: Beacon Press.

West, C. (1989). *The American evasion of philosophy: A genealogy of pragmatism.* Madison, WI: University of Wisconsin Press.

Westbrook. A. (2002). *Hip hoptionary TM: The dictionary of hip hop terminology.* New York: Random House.

Wheatley, P. (1972). Poems on various subjects, religious and moral, by Phillis Wheatley, Negro servant to Mr. Wheatley of Boston. In R. Barksdale & K. Kinnamon (Eds.), *Black writers of America: A comprehensive anthology* (pp. 40–44). Englewood Cliffs, NJ: Prentice -Hall. (Original work published 1773).

Whiting, A. (1967a). *Negro art, music and rhyme, for young folks.* Washington, DC: Lois Jones. (Original work published 1938).

Whiting, A. (1967b). *Negro folk tales: For pupils in the primary grades.* Washington, DC: Lois Jones. (Original work published 1938).

Wiener, P. (Ed.). (1958). *Values in a universe of chance: Selected writings of Charles S. Peirce.* Stanford, CA: Stanford University Press.

Williams, R. (1977). *Marxism and literature.* Oxford, UK: Oxford University Press.

Willis, A. I. (1997). Historical considerations. *Language Arts, 74*(5), 387–397.

Willis, A. (2002). Literacy at Calhoun Colored School, 1892–1945. *Reading Research Quarterly, 37*(1), 8–45.

Willis, A., & Harris, V. (2000). Political acts: Literacy learning and teaching. *Reading Research Quarterly, 35*(1), 72–88.

Willis, A., & Harris, V. (1997). Expanding boundaries: A reaction to the first-grade studies. *Reading Research Quarterly, 32,* 439–445.

Wolfthal, M. (1981). Reading scores revisited. *Phi Delta Kappan, 62*(9), 662–663.

Woodson, C. (1933). *The mis-education of the Negro.* New York: First Africa World Press.

Woodworth, R. (1914). Professor Cattell's psychophysical contributions. *Archives of Psychology, 4*(30), 60–74.

Woodworth, R. (1944). James McKeen Cattell, 1840–1944. *Psychological Review, 51*(4), 201–209.

Woodworth, R. (1952). Edward Lee Thorndike, 1874–1949. *National Academy of Sciences Biographical Memoirs, 27*, 209–235.

Woody, C. (1923). Measurement of a new phase of reading. *Journal of Educational Researcher, 8*(4), 315–326.

Working Group Conference. (2002). *The use of scientifically based research in education. Conference at the United States Department of Education.* Retrieved April 3, 2003, from http://www.ed.gove/nclb/research

X, M., & Haley, A. (1965). *The autobiography of Malcolm X.* New York: Grove Press.

Yatvin, J. (2000). Minority report. In *Report of the National Reading Panel: Reports of the subgroups* (pp. 1–3). Washington, DC: National Institute of Child Health and Human Development.

Yatvin, J. (2002). Babes in the woods: The wanderings of the National Reading Panel. *Phi Delta Kappan, 83*, 364–369.

Yerkes, R., & Yoakum, C. (1920). Army mental tests. New York: Holt.

Yerkes, R. M. (Ed.), (1921). Psychological examining in the United States Army. *Memoires of the National Academy of Sciences*, 15, 1–890.

Yoakam, G. (1924). The effects of a single reading: A study of the retention of various types of material in the content subjects of the elementary school after a single reading. In C. Robins (Ed.), *University of Iowa Studies, 2*(7), (pp. 1–100). Iowa City: University of Iowa Press.

Youngquist, L., & Washburne, C. (1928). *Winnetka Primary Reading Materials.* Chicago: Rand McNally and Co.

Zenderland, L. (1998). *Measuring minds: Henry Herbert Goddard and the origins of American intelligence testing. Cambridge*, MA: Cambridge University Press.

Zeidler, R. (1916). Tests in silent reading in the rural schools of Santa Clara County, *Elementary School Journal*, California, 27, 55–62.

Zinn, H. (1980). *A people's history of the United States.* New York: Harper & Row.

Zirbes, L. (1918). Diagnostic measurement as a basis for procedure. *Elementary School Journal, 18*, 505–522.

Author Index

A

Abell, Adelaide, 96
Allison, Madeline G., 169–170
American Anthropological Association, 17–18
Anderson, Roxana, 96, 237, 238, 245
Apple, M., 234
Ausubel, D., 235

B

Baker, L., 300
Bakhtin, M.M., 241
Barnitz, J., 241
Barrera, R., 242
Bartlett, Sir Frederic S., 192, 235
Bernstein, R., 308
Best, S., xviii, xx, xxi, xxiii
Binet, Alfred, 151–152
Bleich, D., 241
Bloom, B., 199
Boger, J.C., 305
Bond, G.L., 200
Bond, Horace Mann, 167–168
Boone, J., 233
Boozer, B., 233, 234
Bormuth, J., 202–203
Bowden, Josephine, 96
Bradford, A., 251
Brookfield, S., 213
Brooks, F., 181–182
Brown, Harry A., 101–107
Bruner, J., 200, 235, 240–241
Buros, 216

C

Carnevale, A.R., 263
Carroll, J., 217, 231
Carroll, Lewis, 307
Cattell, James McKean, 90–94
Chall, J., 231
Chomsky, N., 203–204
Clark, S., 79–80
Cole, W., 78–79
Coles, G., 265, 281, 284
Comte, August, 3–7, 286
Conaty, Joseph C., 290
Cooper, Anna Julia, 42–44, 254
Courtis, Stuart, 101–103
Cunningham, J., 265, 281, 282

D

Darwin, Charles, 10–16
Davidson, Percy E., 159–162
Davis, F.B., 200, 217
Davis, Frederick, 198
Delpit, L., 241
Dewey, John, 32–36, 194, 200
Dolch, E., 194
Douglass, Frederick, 37–38
Du Bois, William Edward Burghardt, 44–49, 166, 169, 201, 213, 217, 254
Durkin, Dolores, 232

E

Edwards, Richard, 76–77

Eggen, J., 262
Eliot, George, 4
Elliott, Charles W., 78
Elllison, R., 206

F

Fanon, F., 206, 207, 208
Farr, R., 216, 218, 240, 247, 248, 250
Fauset, Jessie Redmon, 169
Federici, xxix
Finot, Jean, 16
Forgacs, D., xxvi
Foster, M., 210
Freire, Paolo, 252–257, 277, 294, 302
Friedan, B., 206

G

Galton, F., 155–156
Gardner, H., 310
Gates, A., 191, 193, 194, 244, 274
Germane, C., 181
Germane, E., 181
Giere, R., xxx
Gilman, Charlotte Perkins, 56
Gitlin, A., 219–220
Glaser, R., 199k
Goddard, Henry, 152–154
Goodman, Kenneth and Yetta, 225, 226
Gould, Stephen J., xxx
Gramsci, A., xxiv, xxv, xxvii, 219, 228, 261,
        294, 304
Gray, W., 175, 176, 180, 183, 191, 194–195,
        214, 248
Gray, William S., 109–119, 138–141
Greer, E., 290, 291
Grossberg, L., 205, 239, 246, 287
Gutierrez, K., 242

H

Habermas, J., xxix
Hall, S., xix, xxvi, xxvii, xxviii, xxxi, 197,
        204, 211, 212, 231, 242, 251, 258,
        270, 291, 301, 312
Halliday, M., 228

Hamilton, Francis, 96
Harding, S., xxix, 290
Harre, R., xxx
Harrington, M., 206
Harris, C., 195, 198, 214, 215, 216, 277–278
Haynes, Elizabeth R., 72
Heath, S., 241
Henry, A., 242
Herbart, Johann Friedrich, 62–66, 232
Hoover, M., 249
Horton, Myles, 209
Huey, Edmund Burke, 83–85, 278

I

Isay, David, 256

J

Jackson, D., 303
James, William, 28–32
Jenkins, Martin, 168
Jensen, Arthur, 212
Johnson, Charles, 167
Johnson, Lucas, 208
Johnson, Lyndon B., 205–206
Johnson-Laird, P., 237
Jolly, C., 271
Jones, Lealan, 256
Jones, R., 215
Judd, Charles, 97–99, 183, 235

K

Karier, C., 1
Kellner, D., xxvi, 257
Kelly, Frederick J., 141–146
Kelly, T.H., 166
Kent, J., 234
Kincheloe, I., xxvii, 268, 301
King, I., 146–147
Kingston, M., 310
Kirk, May, 75
Koch, S., xxx
Kotlowitz, Alex, 256
Kourany, J., xxx
Kuhn, Thomas, xxx, 200–201

L

Labov, W., 228
Laclau, E., xxvi
Ladson-Billings, G., 222, 266
Lagemann, E., xxx, 1
Laing, M., 80
Last Poets, 220
Lazarus, Emma, 60–61
Lennon, R., 217
Lewis, A., 300
Lewontin, R.C., xxx
Lippman, W., 170–173
Little, Malcolm, 211
Lohnes, P., 217
Long, H., 167
Lynn, Loretta, 206
Lyon, G. Reid, 273–276

M

Manguel, A., xxiii
Mathews, M., 214
McCauley, S., xxii
McCombs, J.S., 273
McDermott, R., 229
McNamara, T., 238, 239
McQuillan, J., 265
Mead, Cyrus, 103
Mead, Margaret, 165
Merrill, Maude, 96
Miller, C., 214, 224
Mills, John Stuart, 4
Moll, L., 242
Monroe, Walter S., 148–149
Morrison, Toni, 311
Murray, Lindley, 75

N

National Center for Educational Statistics, 269
National Commission on Excellence in Education, 243, 262
National Institute of Child Health and Human Development, 283
National Reading Panel, 276–279, 281, 283, 291
Newman, Lloyd, 256
Norris, Frank, 56

O

Olson, L., 290
Orasanu, J., 224
Otis, Arthur S., 159–162, 163

P

Page, R.P., xxx
Paige, R., 301–302, 303
Pak, Y., 197
Parker, Francis Wayland, 81–83
Parkhurst, H., 184
Pearson, P., 238
Peirce, Charles Sanders, 25–28
Pendergast, 210
Peterson, Joseph, 165
Piaget, J., 193, 235
Piekarz, J., 203
Piestrup, A., 229
Pihlblad, Terence C., 165
Pinter, R., 95–96
Popkewitz, T., 1
Pratt, W.E., 199
Pressey, S., 183
Price, Joseph St. Clair, 168, 169

R

Raguse, F, 190–191
Rand Reading Study Group, 291–297
Range, P.R., 301
Rankin, Jean, 96
Readence, J., 244
Richards, I., 195
Rickford, J., 229, 251, 293
Riis, Jacob, 56
Rist, R., 229, 230
Roethlein, Barbara, 96
Romanes, George J., 89–90
Rosenblatt, L., 195
Rosenthal, R., 230
Rugg, Harold, 189
Rumlehart, D., 237

S

Salganik, L., 246
Sallach, D., xxvii, 286

Samuels, J., 217
Samuelson, R., 205
Sanders, C., 76
Schmitt, Clara, 99–101
Shavelson, R., 289
Sheppard, L., xxx, 191–192
Shotly, Myrtle, 96
Simon, Theodore, 151
Sims, R., 225
Sinclair, Upton, 56–57
Skinner, B.F., 188–189, 199
Smith, F., 226, 227
Smitherman, G., 293
Somervill, M., 229
Spearritt, D., 217
Spencer, Herbert, 6–9, 274
Spina, S., 282
Stantis, Scott, 313
Starch, Daniel, 108–109, 138–141, 180
Stein, N., 235–236, 237
Stillman, Bessie, 96
Strinati, D., xxvi, 223

T

Tabachnick, B., xxix
Tan, Amy, 310
Taylor, Frederick Winslow, 66–67, 229
Terman, L., 154–155, 170–173
Thompson, Charles, 168
Thorndike, Edward L., 120–125, 125–126,
        126–135, 149–151, 155, 163, 164,
        175, 180, 190, 217
Tiegs,E.W., 200
Tierney, R., 250
Tireman, L., 185, 186, 214
Toppo, G., 288
Towne, L., 288–289, 289
Tuinman, J., 216

U

Unger, R., 304
U.S. Department of Labor, 262–263

V

Valencia, S., 248–249
Venezky, R, 193
Vostrovsky, Clara, 96
Vygotsky, Lev, 235, 241

W

Walker, Alice, 310, 311
Washburne, Carleton, 184
Watson, J., 188
Weber, R., 231
Werner, H., 202
White, E.B., 270
Williams, R., xxvi
Willis, A.I., 265
Woodson, C., 186–188, 230, 254
Woody, C., 183

X

X, Malcolm, 211

Y

Yatvin, Joanne, 279–280
Yerkes, Robert, 163
Yoakam, G., 182
Youngquist, Livia, 184

Z

Zeidler, R., 147–148

Subject Index

A

Abell, Adelaide, 96
Accountability, 267
Achievement gap, 300, 302
Affirmative action policies, disavowal of, 252
African American teachers
    displacement through busing, 210
    expectations of African American students, 229–230
African American Vernacular English, 293
African American viewpoints, ix, x, 38–39, 186
    African American scholars, 42–49
    Du Bois, 44–49
    historical background, 39–41
African Americans
    assimilation issues, 39
    ban on literacy, 40–41
    and Civil Rights movement, 208–211
    counter discourse on standardized intelligence testing, 166–170
    denial of voting rights, 40
    inappropriateness of standardized tests for, 234
    readers for, 71–73
    resistance to dominant ideologies, 206–208
    schoolbooks for, 53
    upsurge in literacy rates, 56
American way to live, 118
Apperception, Herbart on, 64–66
Aryan superior race, 158
Asian immigrants, 60–61
    denial of educational opportunities, 228
    World War II treatment of, 196–197
At-risk learners, 300

B

Barnes' Fifth Reader, 78
Behaviorism
    applications to reading comprehension research and testing, 189–192
    approach to reading comprehension research, 188–189
Bessie's Adventure, 103
Best answers, xxii
Binet, dismantling of intentions in U.S., 152
Biological determinism, 2–3, 10–16, 16, 29
Black Intelligence Test, 233
Black nationalism, 211
Blackness, discourse of, 221
Brownie's Book, 169–170

C

Cattell, James McKean, 90–94
    Thorndike and, 122
Child labor laws, 57
Children of the Sun, 169–170
Civil Rights movement, 208–211, 303
Class rank, 68
Classism, xxxi
    reinforcement of, 174
    Spencer and, 9
Cloze procedure, 202
Colonialism, 21, 51, 60
Colorblindness, 303
Comprehension
    and connected passages, 107
    independence from reading, 96–97
    and linguistic differences, 99
    in silent *vs.* oral reading, 103

Comte, August, 2, 3–6
Consensual theory of truth, 27
Constructivism, 235–240
Cooper, Anna Julia, 42
Counter discourses, x, 219–220
Courtis, Stuart, 101
    English Test No. 5, 103
Cultural deprivation, 201, 270
Cultural studies, and reading
        comprehension research,
        257–259

D

Darwin, Charles, 2, 10–16
Dawes Severalty Act of 1887, 22
Decoding, 217, 258, 313
Deferred memory, 147
Demographic shifts, lip service to
        addressing, 308
Descriptive statistics, Thorndike and, 123
Dewey, John, 32–36
Deweyian pragmatism/instrumentalism,
        32–36
Dialect, effects on oral reading, 229
Dick and Jane series, 117
Dispassionate observer myth, xviii,
        xxix–xxx
Dominant ideologies, vii, ix, xii, xxii, 21,
        152, 176, 179, 207, 242. See also
        Ideological hegemony
    continuing support by Rand study, 294
    counter discourses to, 219–220
    and counter-hegemonic response to
        literacy education, 252
    Du Bois' awareness of, 48
    in histories, xviii
    informing of NAEP by, 273
    lip service by, 308
    in reading comprehension research, 88
    reading comprehension research and
        testing role in maintaining,
        176–177
    and researcher networks, 134
    resistance by African Americans,
        206–208
    sustaining through reading
        comprehension research and
        testing, xxxi
Douglass, Frederick, 38
Du Bois, E.B., 28, 41, 44–49

E

Education
    Dewey on, 35
    efficiency and scientific management
        in, 66–68
    James' views on, 30–31
    and privilege, 29–30
Educational opportunities, lip service to,
        213
Educational progress, national assessment
        of, 267–273
Educational research
    as historical synonym for scientific
        study, 23
    racist history of, 89
Efficiency, 139
    in education, 66–68
Elementary and Secondary Education Act,
        264, 284
Empiricism, 23
Encoding, 258
End-of-grade tests, 305
English Reader, 75
Essay tests, replacement with objective
        tests, 67
Ethnic folk tales, motivational uses of, 251
Eugenics
    Cattell's support for, 92
    and intelligence testing, 155–159
    Thorndike and, 125–126
Evolution
    acceptance by educators, 24
    Darwin's ideas on, 10–16
    James on, 29
    Spencer's ideas on, 8–9

F

Fast reading rates, 146–147
Federal funding
    failures of, 303–305
    loss of, 264–265
    of reading comprehension research,
        297–303
Federal involvement
    adoption of "scientifically based"
        research, 288–291
    grassroots of opposition, 265–267
    loss of federal funding, 264–265

national assessment of educational
progress, 267–275
National Institute of Child Health and
Development, 273–276
National Reading Panel report, 273–279
No Child Left Behind Act of 2001,
284–288
politics and, 262–264
and Rand Reading Study group,
291–297
in reading comprehension research and
testing, 261–262
Fifteenth Amendment, 40
Fixation of belief, 25–26
Flex funds, effects on economic disparity,
265
Fourteenth Amendment, 39–40
Freedmen Series, 71, 72
Freedmen's Torchlight, 72
Freedom of thought, 211–212
Freire, Paolo, contributions to reading
comprehension research and
testing, 252–257

G

Gender differences
absence from NRP, 282
in reading ability, 116
Genetic theory of truth, 28
Germplasm, 153, 157
Goals 2000, 262, 263, 264
Gold standard, myth of scientific research
as, 290
Government, non-interference with nature,
8
Gray, W., as author of *Dick and Jane* series,
117
Gullah culture, 39

H

Hegemony, xxv–xxvii, 87. *See also*
Ideological hegemony
Herbart, Johann Friedrich, 62–66
Herbartianism, 62–66
History, as socially constructed narrative,
xvii
Huey, Edmund Burke, 83
Human suffering, as part of nature, 7

I

Ideological foundations
counter-hegemony of African American
scholars and activists, 38–49
Deweyian pragmatism/
instrumentalism, 32–36
early influences on U.S., 21–24
Jamesian pragmatism, 28–32
pragmaticism, 25–28
pragmatism, 24–25
of reading comprehension research and
testing, 19–21
scientism, psychologism, and racism in
U.S., 36–38
Ideological hegemony, vii, viii, ix, xi,
xviii, 51–53, 192, 307. *See also*
Dominant ideologies
and early synthesis of reading methods,
83–85
Freire's opposition to, 257
in historical schoolbooks, 70–71
measurement and, 66–67, 68–70
in professional books and teachers'
manuals, 78–80
Quincy method and, 81–83
in readers for African American
students, 71–73
in schoolbooks for white public/private
schools, 73–78
standardization and, 66–68
U.S. literacy education and, 53–66
Ideological struggle, 219
Ideology, xxvii–xxxii. *See also* Dominant
ideologies; Ideological
hegemony
Illinois State Normal School, 76–77
Immediate memory, 147
Imperialism, 51
and Treaty of Paris, 60
Indian Appropriations Act of 1871, 22
Individuality, as focus of education, 62
Inference, 198
Inheritance, 91
Darwin on, 12
of intelligence, 134, 152, 171
racist notions of, 118
Spencer's views on, 8
Institute Reader and Normal class-book, 79
Instrumentalism, 32–36
Intelligence testing
African American counter discourse on
standardized, 166–170
Cattell and development of, 93

ethnic bias in, 212
eugenics and, 155–159
generate basis of, 156
illegality of standardized, 234
increased support for national, 164
influence of reading comprehension
       testing on U.S. army, 159–166
Lippman-Terman debate, 170–173
race and standardization of, 212–213
role in predicting children's futures, 172
standardization of, 151–155
International Reading Association, 218

J

James, Henry, 28–32
    influence on Thorndike, 122
Jamesean pragmatism, 28–32
Jews, assumptions about intelligence, 173
Jim Crow segregation, 23
Judd, Charles, 97–101

K

Kelly, Frederick J., 141
    contributions to reading
        comprehension research,
        141–146
    Tests Grades 3, 4, 5, 144
King and Zeidler, contributions to reading
    comprehension research and
    testing, 146–148

L

Language
    devaluation of ethnic, 311
    fluidity of, 312
    and race in reading comprehension,
        181–188
    role in reading comprehension, 231–232
    rule governing of learning, 224
Law of association, in reading, 82
Law of Three Stages, 5
Learning
    approaches to, 199–201
    emphasis on vocabulary and linguistics,
        202–204

Liberalism, critique of scientism through,
    xxx
Linguistic differences, 100, 177, 298
    and comprehension, 99
    and differences in oral expression, 112
    emphasis on, 202–204
Lippman-Terman debate, on standardized
        intelligence testing, 170–173
Literacy
    and racism, 40–41
    U.S. rates, 52
Literacy education, counter-hegemonic
        response to, 252
Literacy tests, as condition of voting, 209
Literature, Herbart on merits of, 65
Long Slide, 106
Low expectations, soft bigotry of, 302
Lynchings, 46

M

Malcolm X, 211
Manifest Destiny, 21, 51
McGuffey's Readers, 73–74
Mechanics of reading, 161
Mental processing, in reading, 84
Metaphysical Club, 28
Metrics, xix–xxiv
    purported scientific methods of, 67
    in reading comprehension research and
        testing, 247–252
Mexican Americans, 186
    California legal fights, 185
    forced assimilation of, 59–60
Minorities, statistics on, xiii
Monroe, Walter S., contributions to reading
        comprehension research and
        testing, 148–149
Mulatto hypothesis, 166, 168
Multiple choice format, 174, 239

N

National assessment, of educational
        progress, 267–273
National Assessment of Educational
        Progress (NAEP), 262, 269
    supposed freedom from cultural bias,
        272

National Commission on Excellence in Education, 243, 262
National Defense Education Act (NDEA), 205
National Institute of Child Health and Development, 262, 271–273
National Intelligence Test, 169
National Reading Panel report, 262, 273–279, 291
    dissenting viewpoints, 279–284
National standards, early calls for, 94
National testing movement, 173
Nation's Report Card, 271
Native Americans, 58–59, 204
    code talkers, 197–198
    literacy texts for, 73
Natural selection, Darwin on, 12
New Colossus, 60–61
    alternative version, 313
New literacies, 259–260
New York Regents tests, neo-liberal changes to, 267
No Child Left Behind Act of 2001, vii, 265, 281–288, 283, 304
Non-whites, Cattell and deficit notions of, 93
Nonmainstream histories, marginalization of, 53

O

Objective tests, 143
    erroneous assumptions about, 146
    myths of, 266
    replacement of essay tests with, 67
    Thorndike's claims of, 127
Oral language
    of African American children, 231
    effects of dialect on, 229
    matches to comprehension test language, 216
Oral reading, 88, 93, 94
    errors in, 112
    standardized measure for, 110
    superiority of silent reading over, 84
Oral reading comprehension tests, 94–120
Orthography, 203–204
Otis Primary and Advanced Examinations, 169
Overpopulation, Darwin on, 12

P

Parker, Francis Wayland, 81
Peirce, Charles Sanders, 25–28
Peirce's consensual theory of truth, 27
Philosophical underpinnings, x
Phonemics, 203
Phonics practices, Dewey's opposition to, 36
Pinter comprehension tests, 95
Pluralism, 55–56
Politics, and federal involvement in reading comprehension research and testing, 262–264
Positivism, 1–6
    return to, 265
    and scientism, 6
Poverty
    assumptions about inferior intelligence in, 152–153
    beliefs about cycle of, 301
    equation with race, 206
Poverty pimps, 303
Power relations, in school curricula criteria, 241
Pragmaticism, 25–28
Pragmatism, 23, 24–25
    Du Bois and, 45
Prior knowledge theory, 100, 224
Professional books, ideological hegemony in, 78–80
Psycholinguistics, impact on reading comprehension, 223–227
Psychologism, in U.S. educational research, 36–38
Public education
    historical pressure to improve, 58
    surveys of reading in elite, 118

Q

Quantity/quality of reproduction, 105
Quincy method, 81–83

R

Race, 201
    absence from NRP, 282

and African American consciousness, 187

as ideology rooted in notion of inequality, 17

partial explanations for differences in intelligence, 166

and reading performance, 69–70

role in reading comprehension, 181–188

and standardized intelligence testing, 212–213

Terman on intersection of intelligence and, 154

Racism, xxviii, xxxi, 18

Cattell's support for, 92

Darwinian roots of, 14

in Gray's research, 113

Herbert Spencer and, 9

invasiveness of, 207

renewed debates regarding standardized testing, 233–235

scientific, 16–18

in Terman, 154–155

in U.S. army, 164

in U.S. educational research, 36–38

Rand Reading Study group, 291–297

Readers

for African American students, 71–73

(*See also* Schoolbooks)

efficiency in first grade reader, 109

Reading: A Manual for Teachers, 80

Reading: How to Teach It, 80

Reading comprehension

as complex mental process, 138–139, 150

connecting and redefining, 220–222

federal government definition under NCLB, 285–286

Freire on, 255–257

impact of psycholinguistics on, 223–227

James on, 31–32

measurables in, 247–252

methods of teaching beginning, 84

metrics of, xix–xxiv

re-envisaging, 309–310

as reading of world, xxiv

and reading rate, 180

role of race and language in, 181–188

social, economic, and linguistic barriers to, 304

social construction of, 313

as supposed measure of intelligence, 119

teacher education and, 179–181

teacher expectations and social factors impacting, 228–233

as thinking lesson, 80

Reading comprehension research

associated ideas influencing, 192–196

basis in white middle class, 215

behaviorist approach, 188–192

cultural studies and, 257–259

federal funding of, 297–303

normalization to support racist ideologies, 184

sociocultural approach to, 240–243

Reading comprehension research and testing

Cattell's influence on, 90–94

early historical phase, 87–89

expansion of, 119–120

federal involvement in, 261

Freire's contributions to, 252–257

genealogy of research, 89–94

ideological foundations of, 19–49

influence on U.S. Army intelligence testing, 159–166

King and Zeidler's contributions, 146–148

Monroe's influence, 148–149

oral and silent reading comprehension tests, 94–120

political and social construction of, xx

redefinition of, 223

reproducing, 179–181

reviews of, 214–219

role in maintaining dominant ideologies, 176–177

1980s era, 243–247

scientism, psychologism, and racism in, 36–38

Thorndike's contribution to, 126–135

Thorndike's second series of articles, 149–151

U.S. sociohistorical contexts, 51–85

Western European philosophical foundations, 1–18

wholly right/wholly wrong approach to, 141–146

World War I developments in, 137–177

World War II developments in, 196–199

Reading Comprehension Research Grants, 262, 297–298

Reading comprehension tests

disaggregation by race, class, gender, 273

as poor measures of real reading, 108

re-envisaging, 310–313

renewed debates on racial bias in, 233–235

standardizing, 97–101, 173–176
Reading performance, and race, 69–70
Reading rate, 105
    and intelligence, 180
Reading rules, 76
Reading the world, 254, 309, 310
Remembering, 192
Researcher networks, 131–133
Romanes, George, 89
Rural areas, testing in, 147–148

S

Schemata, 236, 237, 238–239
School Reader, Third Book, 76
School segregation, 58, 73
Schoolbooks
    for African American students, 71–73
    role in meritocracy, 49
    for white private and public school
        students, 73–78
Science
    appeal to early U.S. educators, 23
    Cooper's challenge to, 43
    false assumptions about, 266
    primacy of, 7
    vs. God, 44
Scientific management, in education, 66
Scientific method, 23
    Du Bois on, 45
    Peirce's support for, 25–26
Scientific racism, 16–18, 43–44
    Du Bois on, 45
Scientifically based research, 290
    federal adoption of, 288–291
    myth of, 288
Scientism, xxviii, xxix
    Cattell's commitment to, 91
    and Herbartianism, 64
    and positivism, 6
    replacement of religion with, 3
    resurrection of, 308
    in U.S. educational research, 36–38
Selective breeding, 157. See also Eugenics
Sentence reading, vs. word reading, 93
Separate but equal, 23
Signatures of wills, and literacy in colonial
        U.S., 54–55
Silent reading, 88, 149, 182, 183
    Gray's tests, 114
    Romanes on, 90
    standardized measure for, 110

superiority over oral, 84
Silent reading comprehension tests, 94–120
    early historical, 101–119
Skinner, B.F., 188–189
Slow reading rates, 146–147
Social constructivism, 200
Social contexts, importance of, 241
Social evolution, Darwin on, 13
Social factors, xi
    impact on reading comprehension,
        228–233
Sociocultural approach, to reading
        comprehension research,
        240–243
Soft bigotry, of low expectations, 302
Spanish-speaking children, difficulties in
        reading English, 185
Spencer, Herbert, 2, 6–10
    influence on American educational
        thinking, 9–10
Standard English, prizing of ability to
        speak, 231
Standardization, xii
    and African American's counter
        discourse on intelligence testing,
        166–170
    beliefs in equality arising from, 302
    and efficiency, 67–68
    of intelligence testing, 151–155,
        173–176, 212–213
    Judd on, 97–98
    and race, 212–213
    of reading comprehension tests, 97–101
    renewed debates on racial bias with,
        233–235
Standardized Oral Reading Paragraphs, 115
Stanford Achievement Test, 165
Stanford-Binet intelligence test, 153, 169
Starch and Gray, improvements to reading
        comprehension research by,
        138–141
Statement on Voluntary National Tests for
        Reading and Math, 270
Struggle for existence, 12
Summarizing, 198
Supra-reading, 160

T

Teacher education
    Quincy method, 81–82
    and reading comprehension, 181–184

Teacher expectations, impact on reading comprehension, 228–233
Teachers' manuals, 124
    ideological hegemony in, 78–80
Terman Group Test of Mental Ability, 169
Test performance, nonequivalence with education quality, 246
Testing, as measurement of school achievement, 95
Thirteenth Amendment, 39–40
Thorndike, Edward L.
    Derivation of Scale A, 131
    as eugenicist, 125–126
    role in reading comprehension research, 120–125
    role in U.S. army intelligence testing, 163
    Scale A, Visual Vocabulary, 128
    Scale Alpha 2 Extension, 133
    second series of articles, 149–151

U

Underserved children, vii, xxi, xxiii, 58–62, 213, 305
    growing population of, xii
    poor performance by, 299
    representations as genetically and intellectually inferior, 276
Urbanization, 57
U.S. Army, xi
    influence of reading comprehension research on intelligence testing, 159–166
    and lack of intellectual acuity among U.S. males, 137
U.S. Department of Labor SCANS Report, 262, 263
U.S. literacy rates, 52, 55

V

Verbal deprivation, 228
Vietnam War, 219
Vocabulary, emphasis on, 202–204
Voting rights, denial to African Americans, 40

W

War on Poverty, 205
Webster's Blue-back Speller, 73
Western European philosophical foundations
    biological determinism, 2–3, 10–16
    positivism, 1–6
    of reading comprehension research and testing, 1–2
    scientific racism, 16–18
    social Darwinism, 2–3, 6–10
White Americans
    educating, 56–58
    as followers of Spencer, 9
    native born vs. immigrant, 100, 111, 113
    notions of intellectual superiority, 118
    view of education as property, 210
    and Western European ancestry, 157
White race
    Darwin's presuppositions about, 14
    and eugenics, 156
    fear of African American uprising, 48–49
    racial superiority of, 158–159
    at top of hierarchy, 15
White supremacy, 37–38
    Thorndike's legitimization of, 130
Women, inferior intelligence of, 152
Women's rights, Cooper and, 43
Word reading, vs. sentence reading, 93
World War I, xi
    development of reading comprehension research and testing during, 137–138
    influence of reading comprehension testing on U.S. army intelligence testing, 159–166
    reading comprehension research and testing in early, 151
    Starch and Gray's improvements to reading comprehension research, 138–141
World War II
    postwar political, social, and cultural shifts, 204–205
    seeds of change following, 205–206
    U.S. policies and reading research and testing, 196–198